Business and Human Rights in Europe

Transnational business activities are important drivers of growth for developing and the least developed countries. However, they can also negatively impact the enjoyment of human rights. In some cases, multinational enterprises (MNEs) have even been accused of grave human rights abuses in the territory of the states where their subsidiaries operate. Since the parent companies of many MNEs are incorporated under the law of European states, those countries' domestic law and the European legal framework play a crucial role in establishing how their activities should be conducted – also throughout their supply chains – and which remedies will be available when corporate human rights violations occur. In recent years, the European Union, the Council of Europe and their Member States have been adopting policies and legislation to ensure respect for human rights by businesses and have developed a body of related case law. These legal instruments can be considered the European responses to the challenges posed at international-law level, and they constitute the focus of research of this book. Through its collected chapters – written by scholars and practitioners under the direction of the editor, Angelica Bonfanti – the book identifies the European solutions to the business and human rights international legal issues, provides an overall assessment of their effectiveness, and examines their potential evolution.

Angelica Bonfanti is Associate Professor in International Law in the Law Faculty of the University of Milan. Her research activity focuses chiefly on public and private international law, business and human rights, cyber law, and international trade and investment law.

Transnational Law and Governance

Series Editor: Paolo Davide Farah

West Virginia University, USA and gLAWcal – Global Law Initiatives for Sustainable Development, UK

In recent years the concepts of 'transnational law' and 'governance' have been explored by both scholars and practitioners with the terms taking on new meaning and significance, particularly in light of the ongoing economic crisis and a corresponding critical reappraisal of global institutional structures and governance. This multidisciplinary series aims to provide a home for research exploring these issues.

Transnational law covers a broad theoretical definition, which includes studies emerging from disciplines such as international law, comparative law, international economic law and administrative law undertaken by legal scholars but also features extensive research undertaken by scholars from other disciplines, including but not limited to, political sciences, international relations, public administration, sociology, history, philosophy and geography. Governance in particular is now seen as important when we refer to the general stability of the markets, to good faith and to other key principles that are fundamental to the notion of a fair market, one that is responsive to the needs of governments and citizens as well as businesses.

This series features cutting-edge works that critically analyse the relationship between governance, institutions and law from a variety of disciplinary perspectives.

Available titles in this series include:

Business and Human Rights in Europe
International Law Challenges
Angelica Bonfanti

Corporate Accountability under Socio-Economic Rights
Jernej Letnar Černič

A Radically Democratic Response to Global Governance
Dystopian Utopias
Margaret Stout and Jeannine M. Love

Sustainability and Peaceful Coexistence for the Anthropocene
Pasi Heikkurinen

Business and Human Rights in Europe

International Law Challenges

Edited by
Angelica Bonfanti

Routledge
Taylor & Francis Group
NEW YORK AND LONDON

First published 2019
by Routledge
52 Vanderbilt Avenue, New York, NY 10017, USA

and by Routledge
2 Park Square, Milton Park, Abingdon, Oxon, OX14 4RN

First issued in paperback 2020

Routledge is an imprint of the Taylor & Francis Group, an informa business

Library of Congress Cataloging-in-Publication Data
Names: Bonfanti, Angelica, editor.
Title: Business and human rights in Europe : international law challenges / edited by Angelica Bonfanti.
Description: Abingdon, Oxon ; New York, NY : Routledge, 2018. | Series: Transnational law and governance | Includes bibliographical references and index.
Identifiers: LCCN 2018021114 | ISBN 9781138484672 (hbk)
Subjects: LCSH: Social responsibility of business–Law and legislation–Europe. | Tort liability of corporations–Europe. | Liability for human rights violations–Europe.
Classification: LCC KJC2467 .B87 2018 | DDC 346.2407–dc23
LC record available at https://lccn.loc.gov/2018021114

ISBN 13: 978-0-367-58603-4 (pbk)
ISBN 13: 978-1-138-48467-2 (hbk)

Typeset in Galliard
by Wearset Ltd, Boldon, Tyne and Wear

Contents

Contributors

Editor

Angelica Bonfanti (PhD) is Associate Professor in International Law at the Faculty of Law, Department of Italian and Supranational Public Law, of the University of Milan (Università degli Studi di Milano), where she teaches *EU Law on Business and Human Rights* (Jean Monnet Module, co-funded by the Erasmus+ Programme of the European Union) and *Sustainable Development in Global Trade (WTO) Law*. She is the Head of Studies of the LL.M. in Sustainable Development at the University of Milan (scientific direction: Professor Nerina Boschiero, Dean of the Faculty of Law) and a member of the Coordinating Committee of the Interest Group of the European Society of International Law (ESIL) on International Business and Human Rights. Her research activity is mainly focused on public and private international law, business and human rights, international trade and investment law, and cyber law. She is the author of the book *Imprese multinazionali, diritti umani e ambiente. Profili di diritto internazionale pubblico e privato* (Milan: Giuffrè, 2012) and of many book chapters and articles published in collected volumes and peer reviewed law journals. She is also the co-editor (with F. Romanin Jacur and F. Seatzu) of the book *Natural Resources Grabbing: An International Law Perspective* (Leiden: Brill, 2015) and a member of the editorial committee of legal journals specialized in international law. She has often been invited to present the outcomes of her research at international and national conferences, has convened seminars, and recently organized the international conference *Business and Human Rights: International Law Challenges, European Responses* (University of Milan, May 2017). Professor Angelica Bonfanti has participated in research projects funded by the Italian government and the European Union, including the Jean Monnet Module on *EU Law on Business and Human Rights* she has been coordinating since 2015 and of which the current book is an outcome.

Authors

Daniel Augenstein is Associate Professor in the Department of European and International Public Law at Tilburg Law School. Dr Augenstein's research focuses on the legal and policy framework governing the relationship between global business operations and international human rights protection. He has published widely on issues relating to business and human rights and has conducted numerous policy studies on this topic for international organizations and national governments.

Tiphaine Beau de Loménie is Legal Advisor on Business and Human Rights at Sherpa. She holds a Master in Economic Law degree from Sciences Po Law School. At Sherpa, her work focuses mainly on the French Law on the Corporate Duty of Vigilance.

Marta Bordignon (PhD) is co-founder of Human Rights International Corner (HRIC); faculty member at Temple University in Rome; lecturer in International Law at the European University of Rome; member of the Working Group of the Research Project 'The implementation of the UN Guiding Principles on Business and Human Rights by the European Union and its Member States' at the International Law and International Relations Department, University of Seville (Spain); business advisor with particular reference to MENA countries and consultant in stakeholder assessment and engagement projects; and member of the Coordinating Committee of the ESIL Interest Group on International Business and Human Rights.

Leonardo Borlini is Assistant Professor of International Law in the Department of Legal Studies at Bocconi University and Fellow at the BAFFI CAREFIN (Centre for Applied Research on International Markets, Banking, Finance and Regulation). He received his PhD in International Law and Economics from Bocconi University in 2009 and his LL.M. from the University of Cambridge in 2007. He was technical assistance expert in the Legal Department of the International Monetary Fund between 2011 and 2012 and consulted different international organizations, including the European Union, the Inter-American Development Bank and the UNODC.

Claire Bright (PhD, European University Institute of Florence; LL.M., La Sorbonne Law School) is Senior Lecturer in Law at the London School of Business and Management. Dr Bright's research interests focus on Business and Human Rights. She is a Member of the BHRight Initiative for Interdisciplinary Research and Teaching on Business and Human Rights and of the Global Business and Human Rights Scholars Association. She has also worked as a Programme Associate on the Research Programme on Civil Justice Systems at the Centre for Socio-Legal Studies of the University of Oxford.

Paola Cavanna (PhD, Università Cattolica del Sacro Cuore, Milan) is Legal Advisor on human rights, migration and criminal law. Paola Cavanna holds a Master in Law from Università Cattolica del Sacro Cuore, where she obtained her PhD defending a thesis on the prevention of labour exploitation, specifically targeting the agri-food sector. She has also collaborated with one of the paramount law firms in Italy engaged in human rights protection against all forms of discrimination.

Ludovica Chiussi is Doctoral Research Fellow in Public International Law, University of Oslo and University of Bologna; former Visiting Scholar, Lauterpacht Centre for International Law, University of Cambridge (2017). Ludovica lectures on business and human rights and human rights law at the University of Oslo.

Sandra Cossart is Executive Director at Sherpa. As an international lawyer, she headed the Globalization and Human Rights Program within Sherpa for almost eight years, worked as a legal consultant in the UK and volunteered for the Business and Human Rights Resource Centre. Before that, she was an associate in a law firm in France and also worked within international organizations such as the European Parliament and the Council of Europe, as well as for the European Union in Russia. Sandra is also the author of many scholarly legal articles.

Adriana Espinosa González (PhD in International Law and Human Rights, University Carlos III, Madrid) has conducted research on the topic of transnational corporations and human rights for several years, and participated in international workshops and published on the topic. Her areas of expertise cover the regulation of transnational corporations under international law, the interactions between international investment and international human rights law, and the EU policies regarding Business and Human Rights.

Paolo Davide Farah (PhD, PhD, LL.M., JD) teaches at West Virginia University, John D. Rockefeller IV School of Policy and Politics, Department of Public Administration and College of Law; West Virginia University, Energy Institute and Center for Innovation in Gas Research and Utilization (CIGRU); and West Virginia University, Institute of Water Security and Science (IWSS), USA. He is Founder, President and Director of gLAWcal – Global Law Initiatives for Sustainable Development, UK (www.glawcal.org.uk) and Senior Fellow at the Institute of International Economic Law (IIEL), Georgetown University Law Center, Washington, DC, USA. He holds a dual PhD in International Law at Aix-Marseille University (France) and Università degli Studi di Milano (Italy); an LL.M. from the College of Europe, Bruges (Belgium); and a JD from the University of Paris Ouest La Defense Nanterre (France). He is Editor-in-Chief for the gLAWcal Book Series on 'Transnational Law and Governance' published by Routledge Publishing (London/New York).

Marco Fasciglione (PhD) is Researcher of International Law at IRISS-CNR (Naples, Italy), where he is Principal Investigator of the research 'Project Corporate human rights and environmental due diligence and the promotion of the Corporate Responsibility' (CO.RE). His scientific experience focuses on the international system of protection of human rights and, in particular, on the impact of business activities on human rights. Former legal officer at the European Court of Human Rights, he is member of the Interest Group on Business and Human Rights of the European Society of International Law and has developed extensive experience in evaluating scientific research by performing evaluation activities under national and international research programmes (REA-H2020, COST, DG Justice). He is Chief of the Editorial Committee of the journal *Diritti umani e diritto internazionale*.

Valentina Grado (PhD) is Associate Professor in International Law at the University of Naples L'Orientale, where she teaches International Law, International Organization and EU External Relations Law. Her research focuses on the governance of natural resources in conflict situations, certification schemes, business and human rights and labour rights.

Carmen Márquez Carrasco is Full Professor of Public International Law and International Relations at the University of Sevilla (Spain), where she teaches the general course of Public International Law, European Union Law, and International Human Rights Law. Her main areas of research are international law and conflict prevention, environmental law, governance and human rights, and business and human rights, including ongoing research activities on a new human rights approach to water management and extraterritorial human rights obligations of states. She has been the Chairperson of the European Master's Degree in Human Rights and Democratization at EIUC, Venice (2007–2012); and Vice-President and President ad interim of EIUC. She is a Member of the Academic Support Group of the ETOs Consortium and has been Member of the Academic Committee that supported the Human Rights Office of the Ministry of Foreign Affairs and Cooperation in the elaboration of the Spanish National Action Plan on Business and Human Rights.

Olga Martin-Ortega (PhD) is Reader in Public International Law at the University of Greenwich, where she leads the Business, Human Rights and Environment Research Group and undertakes research on multinational enterprises and human rights, post-conflict reconstruction and transitional justice. She has been Senior Research Fellow at the Centre on Human Rights in Conflict (CHRC) of the University of East London and lecturer in law at Napier University (Edinburgh). Olga has been Chair of the Board of the Interest Group on Business and Human Rights of the European Society of International Law and is a member of the London Transitional Justice Network.

Claire Methven O'Brien (MA (Cantab), LL.M., PhD) is Chief Adviser on Human Rights and Development at the Danish Institute for Human Rights, where her research and advisory practice focuses on business and human rights, the private sector role in sustainable development and public procurement. Claire is an Honorary Lecturer at the University of St. Andrews School of Management and a Visiting Research Fellow at the Department of International Law, University of Groningen. She holds a PhD in Law from the European University Institute (Florence) and has been called to the London Bar.

Paige Morrow is Executive Director of the EU Public Interest Clinic at New York University Paris and HEC Paris, and Lecturer of Law at the University of Kent. She has worked as a lawyer at McCarthy Tétrault LLP and held positions at the Centre for the Study of Human Rights of the London School of Economics and Political Science (LSE), the Kenya National Commission for Human Rights and the South African Legal Resources Centre. She has authored several articles and book chapters on governance and international law and received awards for academic excellence and pro bono service.

Lucas Roorda is Policy Advisor for the Dutch National Human Rights Institute, and PhD Candidate at the Institute of International, Social and Economic Public Law, Utrecht Centre for Accountability & Liability Law (UCALL), Faculty of Law, Economics & Governance, Utrecht University. Lucas Roorda holds an LL.M. from Utrecht University and is currently finishing a doctoral thesis on jurisdiction and the right of access to court in foreign direct liability cases in the European Union. He has published articles on private military and security companies, access to court in the EU and forum of necessity jurisdiction.

Deborah Russo (PhD) is Senior Researcher already qualified as Associate Professor of International Law at the Department of Legal Sciences of the University of Florence. In the same university, she teaches Advanced International Law and Public International Law and is member of the Doctorate Board on Legal Sciences. She has published the monograph *L'efficacia dei trattati sui diritti umani* (2012) and several articles on different topics of public international law and human rights law, such as the article 'Addressing the Relation Between Treaties by Means of "Saving Clauses"' in the *British Yearbook of International Law* (2015).

Marta Sosa Navarro (PhD in International Criminal Law and Human Rights Law) is a legal researcher and lawyer, and co-founder of Indago (a European initiative dedicated to training, consultancy services and research on Human Rights and Business). Her research work covers topics that range from pure international criminal law to mechanisms to guarantee accountability for serious human rights violations, especially when committed by corporations.

Florentine Vos (BA and MA, University of Cambridge; LL.M. and LL.B., Leiden University) is a lawyer at Allen & Overy LLP.

Cindy S. Woods (JD, Georgetown University Law Center; MPhil, University of Cambridge; BA, University of Oklahoma) currently works on immigration justice issues as a staff attorney with Texas RioGrande Legal Aid. Cindy's research has largely focused on corporate accountability at the intersection of indigenous rights and the extractive sector, with a focus on the Americas. Cindy previously served as a Legal and Policy Associate at the International Corporate Accountability Roundtable (ICAR), where she led their work on implementation of international norms, such as the UN Guiding Principles on Business and Human Rights through National Action Plans and ICAR's engagement in global governance processes.

Foreword

Paolo Davide Farah[1]

Business and Human Rights in Europe: International Law Challenges, edited by Angelica Bonfanti, represents a relevant collection of chapters about the interconnected areas of human rights and corporate activities, which mainly focus on profit maximization and securing various private interests on global markets. These issues have become particularly important in times of globalization of supply chains, which the world is currently witnessing, and perfectly fit into the broader discussions related to the necessary changes and improvements of the international legal norms and systems of governance towards the protection of Non-Trade Concerns (NTCs).[2] These topics are constitutive and pivotal of the gLAWcal book series on 'Global Law and Sustainable Development' and 'Transnational Law and Governance' both published by Routledge (New York/London).

Angelica Bonfanti (PhD) is an Associate Professor in International Law at the Law Faculty of the University of Milan, where she teaches *EU Law on Business*

1 Paolo Davide Farah, West Virginia University, John D. Rockefeller IV, School of Policy and Politics, Department of Public Administration and College of Law; West Virginia University, Energy Institute and Center for Innovation in Gas Research and Utilization (CIGRU); West Virginia University, Institute of Water Security and Science (IWSS). Founder, President, Director, Principal Investigator and Senior Research Fellow at gLAWcal – Global Law Initiatives for Sustainable Development. Senior Fellow at the IIEL – Institute of International Economic Law, Georgetown University Law Center. Editor-in-Chief for the gLAWcal Book Series 'Global Law and Sustainable Development' and for the gLAWcal Book Series 'Transnational Law and Governance' published by Routledge (New York/London). The research leading to this result has received funding from People Programme (Marie Curie Actions) of the European Union's Seventh Framework Programme under REA grant agreement no. 318908, Acronym of the Project: POREEN, entitled 'Partnering Opportunities between Europe and China in the Renewable Energies and Environmental Industries', within the results of the Research Team at gLAWcal – Global Law Initiatives for Sustainable Development (United Kingdom).

2 Paolo Davide Farah, Trade and Progress: The Case of China', 30 *Columbia Journal of Asian Law*, 2016, pp. 97–107; Paolo Davide Farah, Elena Cima (editors), *China's Influence on Non-Trade Concerns in International Economic Law*, Global Law and Sustainable Development Book Series. New York/London: Routledge, ISBN 978-1-4094-4848-8, September 2016, pp. 1–584. See also, Margaret Stout, Jeannine M. Love, *A Radically Democratic Response to Global Governance. Dystopian Utopias*, Transnational Law and Governance Series. New York/London: Routledge, Hardback, ISBN 9781138654051, 2016, pp. 1–242.

and Human Rights (Jean Monnet Module) and Sustainable Development in Global (WTO) Trade Law. She is the Head of Studies of the LL.M in Sustainable Development of the University of Milan and a member of the Coordinating Committee of the European Society of International Law (ESIL) on International Business and Human Rights.

I have had the pleasure of knowing Angelica Bonfanti for 15 years since she had decided to write her PhD dissertation, which became later a book (published in Italian) on multinational companies, human rights and environmental protection, from the perspective of Public and Private International Law.[3]

Similar to Angelica Bonfanti, I share the same concerns about the global expansion of free trade and liberalism that might permit multinational companies to operate without the necessary accountability measures (potentially affecting NTCs) that allow businesses to take advantage of the loopholes and the limits of the complex relations among global governance, international law and the domestic legal systems in different countries in the world. One can even notice the evident contradiction between the protection of individuals when it comes to their basic rights arising from the traditional notion of natural law, and the protection of modern commercial practices of corporations, often without a physical person embodying only a mere business model and being the joint quintessence of shareholders, management structures, employees and so on. These concerns are among the reasons that have convinced me of the need to establish a think-tank such as gLAWcal – Global Law Initiatives for Sustainable Development, of which I am Founder, President and Director. Through research, policy analysis and advocacy, gLAWcal attempts to shed new light on issues such as good governance, human rights, right to water, rights to food, social, economic and cultural rights, labour rights, access to knowledge, public health, social welfare, consumer interests, animal welfare, climate change, energy, environmental protection and sustainable development, product safety, food safety and security. All these values are directly affected by the global expansion of world trade and should be upheld to balance the excesses of globalization.

During the last 15 years, Angelica Bonfanti has been continuing to focus on different angles of these topics as demonstrated by another recent book collection on *Natural Resources Grabbing: An International Law Perspective.*[4] Her expertise has been recognized at national and international levels. In particular, among other awards, it is worth noting her Jean Monnet Module on *EU Law on Business and Human Rights*, funded in the framework of the European Union *Erasmus + Programme*, which she has been coordinating since 2015.

3 Angelica Bonfanti, *Imprese multinazionali, diritti umani e ambiente. Profili di diritto internazionale pubblico e privato*. Milan: Giuffrè, 2012.

4 Francesca Romanin Jacur, Angelica Bonfanti and Francesco Seatzu, *Natural Resources Grabbing: An International Law Perspective*. Leiden/Boston: Brill Nijhoff, ISBN 978-90-04-30566-3, 2015, pp. 1–462.

The present volume is an output of her Jean Monnet Module along with other initiatives, including the International Conference on Business and Human Rights: International Law Challenges, European Responses, held at Università degli Studi di Milano (Italy) on 29–30 May 2017, to which I was pleased to participate and present my paper.

Angelica Bonfanti and I have also collaborated through another initiative. She has been involved in the People Programme (Marie Curie Actions) of the European Union's Seventh Framework Programme (FP7/2007–2013) under REA grant agreement no. 318908, acronym of the project: POREEN (2013–2016), entitled 'Partnering Opportunities between Europe and China in the Renewable Energies and Environmental Industries'. The research leading to this book has received funding and was implemented in the framework of the POREEN project, within the results of the Research Team I lead as Principal Investigator at gLAWcal – Global Law Initiatives for Sustainable Development and in my capacities as POREEN Vice-Coordinator, and POREEN Legal Work-package Leader.

This book, through various differently oriented chapters, attempts to give an insight on how the European Union and its multilevel model of governance[5] must try to strike a balance between diverging interests and priorities. In particular, the EU and the European states (including the CoE's Members) should implement all possible actions to protect individuals' dignity, along with other important sustainable community priorities such as public health, sustainable development and the protection of the environment,[6] social values, and fundamental freedoms. At the same time the regulations and practices should be able to build-up an appropriate business environment that is sufficiently friendly to corporate activity to permit companies to produce growth and create new job opportunities, without affecting any of the individual substantial rights and liberties.

The book contains chapters providing an overview and comparison of different existing practices with constructive suggestions for future policymaking, as well as chapters dealing with more specific issues related to business and human rights.

My overview below does not replicate nor follow the chapter order of the table of contents, but focuses and elaborates the thematic areas covered by the different contributions included in the book.

5 Paolo Farah and Piercarlo Rossi, National Energy Policies and Energy Security in the Context of Climate Change and Global Environmental Risks: A Theoretical Framework for Reconciling Domestic and International Law through a Multiscalar and Multilevel Approach. 20 *Eur. Energy & Envtl. L. Rev.* 232, 232–44 (2011). See also Antonio Segura Serrano (editor), *The Reform of International Economic Governance*, Global Law and Sustainable Development Series. New York/London: Routledge. Hardback ISBN: 9781472471406, 2016, pp. 1–246.

6 Pasi Heikkurinen, *Sustainability and Peaceful Coexistence for the Anthropocene*, Transnational Law and Governance Series. New York/London: Routledge. Hardback, ISBN 978-1138634275, 2017, pp. 1–193.

After the general introduction from Angelica Bonfanti, the editor of this book, and the acknowledgements, the book starts with a chapter of mine (*Paolo Davide Farah*) which has the objective to give a broader view on the state of implementation of the Sustainable Development Goals (SDGs) in the European Union (EU) in the context of the EU's framework on governing business and human rights. This chapter follows a top-down approach: it explores the relevant EU legal and policy framework, takes into account the overarching European Commission's 2030 Agenda for Sustainable Development and the SDGs and related developments at the EU and broader international level, as well as the European Commission's strategy concerning corporate social responsibility (CSR)[7] and issues related therewith, aiming at examining their compatibility and, eventually, suggesting integrating proposals.

Daniel Augenstein is one of the authors analysing the global interdependence through law and governance, as well as focusing on the European approach to business and human rights. In particular, his chapter is arguing for a more proactive role of the EU towards supporting the implementation of the UN Guiding Principles (UNGPs), the domestic implementation of the UNGPs via national action plans (NAPs) and the fostering of international treaty initiatives on the domain of business and human rights. Additionally, this chapter suggests that particular consideration should be given to resolving collective action problems that derive from the state-centred conception of international law to the human rights impacts of global business operations.

Similarly, *Cindy Woods*' chapter focuses on various European approaches to promote responsible supply chains. In particular, the chapter analyses the regulations of some European states such as France, the Netherlands, Switzerland, the United Kingdom along with particular consideration of the EU Directive on the disclosure of non-financial information. This chapter advocates that the private sector can and should have an important role in the creation of a sustainable global economy. But what is necessary, and what is acknowledged by the author as an important development in the field, is a combination of due diligence requirements of corporate business (without any active State involvement or State nexus), along with the extraterritorial application of corporate obligations There is a large variety of binding and non-binding dõcuments dealing with the protection of human rights and introducing obligations to which companies must comply. Ultimately, this raises the question of appropriate means and their efficiency when it comes to implementation.

Marta Bordignon's chapter focuses on the issue of national action plans (an issue that is also by other chapters), which are meant to implement the UN Guiding Principles into national normative systems. The addition of this chapter in the framework of the book is the assessment of the suitability of such state-level action plans to influence national policymaking and eventually legislation

7 Jernej Letnar Černič, *Corporate Accountability under Socio-Economic Rights*, Transnational Law and Governance Series. New York/London: Routledge. Hardback, ISBN 9781138288782, 2018.

via clearly stating the priorities and state obligations, as well as setting up a framework to strengthen human rights protection. The chapter contribution analyses the Italian National Action Plan 2016–2021 as an example to evaluate the positive and negative features, regarding which the author takes an overall practical approach, considering these national action plans a step in the right direction.

Implementation efficiency is essential, but cannot realize its entire potential without the full enforcement of obligations posed on corporations by the State directly, or through international treaties setting up binding frameworks. The chapter by *Marco Fasciglione* suggests covering this gap and focuses more closely on enforcement of the States' obligation to protect under the aegis of the UN Guiding Principles. States should not omit to act, but should adopt precautionary measures and should cooperate to prevent violations of human rights, including when these infringements are perpetuated by multinational companies and other private entities that will try to avoid financial and legal responsibility by using the potential loopholes between international and domestic law. This chapter also addresses some of the judgments of the European Court of Human Rights with a critical analysis of possible means towards the protection of human rights and the environment. Despite the fact that this court cannot directly bind corporations, it can influence them via the State's responsibility either by posing positive or negative requirements when it comes to the way they do business.

According to the list of top issues to be tackled in the future, published in 2018 by the Institute of Human Rights and Business, one of the key challenges will be extensive action to promote and favour access to justice, the necessary removal of any barrier of access to judicial remedies and the creations of new schemes and mechanisms of litigation between right holders and companies. This book therefore also extensively addresses this topic. In particular, *Carmen Márquez Carrasco* tries to provide an assessment of the Fundamental Rights Agency's contribution to granting access to remedies when it comes to the victims of human rights violations by multinational companies. The work and analysis of this agency addresses the existing means and proposes solutions in an attempt to lower these barriers. Therefore, it is considered an additionally important tool to put further pressure on the EU Member States and the EU institutions to strengthen their proactive role in the development of the rules and regulations related to accountability of multinational corporations for their actions violating human rights. Such an extraterritorial jurisdiction regarding the activities of enterprises abroad can be questionable. Still, the EU's pillar principle of the creation of a common market and the gradually developed EU common foreign and security policy along with other instruments of foreign influence through trade grant the EU such transnational features and legal competences and powers to impose or favour harmonizing measures with the important objective of uniform protection and approach towards the victims of human rights violations.

Claire Methven O'Brien's Chapter 5 analyses whether the European home states of transnational corporations (TNCs) are accountable for their impacts abroad under the European Convention on Human Rights (ECHR). In the past, the authority for the 'state duty to protect' was drawn from UN treaty body commentaries, but later it was considered that a home state duty to regulate TNCs abroad is already in place as a matter of human rights law, with reference to decisions of the European Court of Human Rights (ECtHR). This chapter offers findings on the possible relevance of the exterritorial duty debate for the wider B&HR field. Transnational jurisdiction is also the centre of the analysis in *Lucas Roorda*'s chapter. It examines the issue of foreign direct liability within the parallel frameworks of the Brussels regime (Brussels I Regulation) and the domestic law of the EU Member States, where it identifies various shortcomings.

The challenges of access to justice and the use of specific judicial remedies influence and relate to both private and public law. This book analyses, through separate chapters, selected issues concerning all the legal areas (private, public, hybrid), offering a composite overview of the recent developments on the field of business and human rights.

From the private law perspective *Florentine Vos*'s chapter analyses various trends related to private and civil law remedies to address corporate human right abuses throughout Europe. This part of the book deals with the concept of an 'effective remedy', as well as with the evolution on the field of civil legal remedies, which are felt often insufficient, granting special attention to the distinction between their monetary and non-monetary instruments. Within the conclusions, this chapter expresses criticism because of the dominant monetary compensation trends, while non-monetary mechanisms are not frequently granted to the victims.

Claire Bright, in the chapter about civil liability of the parent company for acts and omissions of its subsidiary, provides a case study (Shell) through which multiple obstacles are identified related to the accountability of Europe-based companies for human rights violations abroad, often in least developed countries.

Deborah Russo focuses on public procurement, and the implications of the State's duty to protect. Additionally, the necessity of a mandatory human rights clause during the disposition and the consequent use of public resources is expressed and included in the analysis of this chapter. The State has an important incremental role to improve the life of its citizens and society as a whole. The prevention and the discretionary power of the State to lead to a better protection of social and environmental rights and justice well beyond the current national and international standards is also advocated in this chapter.

Tiphaine Beau de Loménie, *Sandra Cossart* and *Paige Morrow* in their chapter offer a comparison of the notions of due diligence and the duty of vigilance, taking France as a case study, extending it and applying it to the wider context of the EU. This contribution acknowledges that France has adopted a law on duty of vigilance that is of higher standards compared with other European countries. This might lead other individual EU Member States to follow this path in their own domestic legislations. At the same time it might also create a growing consensus at European level in view of adopting additional EU directives or regulations to introduce human rights due diligence related requirements applicable in the entire EU.

Regarding the more multidisciplinary areas, fundamental rights implications in communication and finances are also explored in two chapters. *Angelica Bonfanti* deals with information and communication technology from a human rights perspective, in particular regarding the right to privacy and the freedom of expression. The link between the IT sector and human rights puts a particularly large responsibility on companies to use and disclose data in compliance with human rights obligations. On the other hand, *Ludovica Chiussi*'s chapter contains a case study of the Norwegian Sovereign Wealth Fund, through which she analyses the relationship between corporate human rights compliance and disinvestment. It concludes that disinvestment can serve, under certain circumstances, as a leverage tool, forcing companies to more strictly enforce human rights requirements during their commercial activities.

The criminal law dimension is also analysed in this chapter, starting with a more general overview of its role when it comes to protecting individuals from unlawful corporate behaviour, as well as via a more particular study of judicial remedies available, especially in the Italian legal system. First, *Adriana Espinosa Gonzáles* and *Marta Sosa Navarro* focus on the corporate liability perspective of human rights, examining the role that criminal law might play in this field. They offer multiple case studies in order to emphasize legal and practical challenges, through which they argue for the wider role of criminal law remedies when dealing with human rights violations, without denying the importance of civil law litigation. However, in order to guarantee access to justice for a victim of corporate abuses, further policy and legal changes are needed both at national and international level. Second, *Paola Cavanna*'s chapter investigates how to combine human rights due diligence with criminal law, while examining the Italian approach. This chapter raises multiple questions related to the criminal liability of corporations for certain offences, as well as regarding the guarantees of access to judicial remedies for victims of human rights violations.

The book, besides trying to give a general insight into contemporary problems of business and human rights, also brings more specific examples. *Valentina Grado*, in her chapter, picks a widely discussed topic – the so-called 'conflict minerals'. These come from regions where their mining leads to various clashes, causing serious human rights violations. The author compares the EU regulation dealing with such minerals and the OECD Guidance, through which various shortcomings in the legislative framework are addressed. *Olga Martin-Ortega* deals with the United Kingdom's Modern Slavery Act, and its provisions related to transparency, reporting and due diligence of supply chains. An in-depth analysis of the reports' contents, compliance requirements and non-compliance consequences for corporations is offered throughout the chapter. Among the conclusions, several shortcomings of the Modern Slavery Act are pointed out – e.g. its narrow scope and multiplicity of similar obligations spread in various legal acts, as well as the overall progressive development towards greater transparency and efficiency of provisions protecting human rights.

Another very interesting and highly debated aspect of business and human rights is the promotion of human rights via preferential trade agreements (PTAs) between the EU and third countries, as analysed in *Leonardo Borlini*'s chapter. Such exportation of values can be perceived as controversial, since it can be considered as forcing European thinking on other countries with differences in culture and traditions. However, as argued in this book, human rights are common for all mankind, therefore there cannot be any limitations when it comes to fostering them and complying with them by all countries and all private entities.

Overall, this book attempts not only to summarize the outcomes of the most intensely debated challenges; it also tries to provide constructive criticism and valuable suggestions for the future for policymakers and legislators to move forward. Business and human rights hold many complex and intricate relations, as well as the interests of subjects who do not have an equal social and legal position. All these diverging values and opposing concerns require a very delicate and diplomatic approach in order to bring clarity and binding security for all the involved stakeholders. Nevertheless, the future outlook of the field looks promising, mainly due to the large amount of documents, frameworks, opinions, and bilateral agreements, but also thanks to the incessant and sometimes constructively obstinate activity of institutions, and national and international courts. This book has the potential to also be one of the sources for fostering incremental positive development in order to consolidate more human conditions and values in the global economy, free-trade and business, which should be primarily for humans. Not only for the privileged ones, but for all human beings.

Professor Paolo Davide Farah

Editor-in-Chief for the gLAWcal Book Series 'Transnational Law and Governance' published by Routledge (New York/London)

West Virginia University, USA and gLAWcal – Global Law Initiatives for Sustainable Development, UK

Acknowledgements

The publication of this book is co-funded by the Erasmus+ Programme of the European Union. This book is the outcome of the research developed by the Editor, as part of the activities implemented under the Jean Monnet Module on 'EU Law on Business and Human Rights' she has been coordinating from 2015 to 2018 at the Law Faculty of the University of Milan.

The European Commission support for the production of this publication does not constitute endorsement of the contents, which reflect the views only of the authors. The Commission cannot be held responsible for any use, which may be made of the information contained herein.

Abbreviations

AA	Association Agreement
ACP	African, Caribbean, Pacific
ATS	Alien Tort Statute
B&HR	Business and Human Rights
CAHRA	Conflict-Affected and High-Risk Area
CFSP	Common Security and Foreign Policy
CLS	Corporate Labour Standards
CoE	Council of Europe
CPA	Cotonou Partnership Agreement
CSDP	Common Security and Defence Policy
CSR	Corporate Social Responsibility
ECCJ	European Coalition for Corporate Justice
ECHR	European Convention on Human Rights and Fundamental Freedoms
ECJ	European Court of Justice
ECtHR	European Court of Human Rights
ENNHRI	European Network of National Human Rights Institutions
ENP	European Neighbourhood Policy
EPA	Economic Partnership Agreement
EU	European Union
FRA	Fundamental Rights Agency
FTA	Free Trade Agreement
HRDD	Human Rights Due Diligence
ICC	International Criminal Court
ICCPR	International Covenant on Civil and Politic Rights
ICESCR	International Covenant on Economic, Social and Cultural Rights
ICJ	International Court of Justice
ILC	International Law Commission
ILO	International Labour Organization
ILO Tripartite Decl.	ILO Tripartite Declaration of Principles Concerning Multinational Enterprises and Social Policy

IMF	International Monetary Fund
IO	International Organization
IPA	Instrument for Pre-accession Assistance
MEA	Multilateral Environmental Agreement
MNC	Multinational Corporation
MNE	Multinational Enterprise
NAP	National Action Plan
NGO	Non-Governmental Organization
NTC	Non-Trade Concern
OECD	Organization for Economic Cooperation and Development
OECD Guidelines	OECD Guidelines for Multinational Enterprises
OEIGWG	Open-Ended Intergovernmental Working Group on Transnational Corporations and Other Business Enterprises with Respect to Human Rights
OHCHR	Office of the High Commissioner for Human Rights
PTA	Preferential Trade Agreement
RTA	Regional Trade Agreement
SDG	Sustainable Development Goal
SRSGBHR	Special Representative of the Secretary-General on the Issue of Human Rights and Transnational Corporations and Other Business Enterprises
SWF	Sovereign Wealth Fund
TNC	Transnational Corporation
UDHR	Universal Declaration of Human Rights
UN	United Nations
UNCESCR	United Nations Committee on Social, Economic and Cultural Rights
UNCITRAL	United Nations Commission on International Trade Law
UNCTAD	United Nations Conference on Trade and Development
UNGPs	United Nations Guiding Principles on Business and Human Rights
UNHRC	United Nations Human Rights Council
UNWGB&HR	United Nations Working Group on the Issue of Human Rights and Transnational Corporations and Other Business Enterprises
WTO	World Trade Organization

1 Introduction

Angelica Bonfanti

Transnational business activities are important drivers of growth for developing and least-developed countries. However, business activities can also negatively impact the enjoyment of human rights. In some cases, multinational corporations (MNCs) have even been accused of grave human rights abuses in the territory of the states where their subsidiaries operate.

The relationship that exists between the development of business activities and the protection of human rights is ruled at international-law level. In addition to the customary and treaty-based human rights legal framework, some international soft-law instruments have blazed the trail in this field. Among them there are the ILO Tripartite Declaration of Principles Concerning Multinational Enterprises and Social Policy (hereinafter 'ILO Tripartite Declaration'),[1] the UN Global Compact,[2] the OECD Guidelines for Multinational Enterprises (hereinafter 'OECD Guidelines'),[3] and the UN Guiding Principles on Business and Human Rights (hereinafter 'UNGPs').[4] Their adoption has contributed to

1 ILO, *Tripartite Declaration of Principles Concerning Multinational Enterprises and Social Policy*, 5th Edition (2017), available at: www.ilo.org/empent/areas/mne-declaration/lang-en/index.htm, last accessed on February 20, 2018.

2 UN Global Compact, available at: www.unglobalcompact.org/ (last accessed 20 February 2018).

3 OECD, *Guidelines for Multinational Enterprises*, available at: www.oecd.org/corporate/mne/1922428.pdf (last accessed 20 February 2018).

4 OHCHR, *Guiding Principles on Business and Human Rights*, 16 June 2011, available at: www.ohchr.org/Documents/Publications/GuidingPrinciplesBusinessHR_EN.pdf (last accessed 20 February 2018). The literature about B&HR and the UNGPs is extensive. Among others, see: M. Addo, 'Reality of the United Nations Guiding Principles on Business and Human Rights', *Human Rights Law Review*, 2014, 14(1), 133: N. Bernaz, *Business and Human Rights. History, Law and Policy – Bridging the Accountability Gap*. London, New York: Routledge, 2017; A. Bonfanti, *Imprese multinazionali, diritti umani e ambiente: profili di diritto internazionale pubblico e privato*, Milan: Giuffrè, 2012; S. Deva, *Human Rights Obligations of Business: Beyond The Corporate Responsibility To Respect?* Cambridge: Cambridge University Press, 2013; N.M.C.P. Jägers, *Corporate Human Rights Obligations: In Search of Accountability*. Antwerpen: Intersentia, 2002; R. Mares, *The UN Guiding Principles on Business and Human Rights: Foundations and Implementation*. Leiden: Nijhoff, 2012; F. Marrella, 'Protection internationale des droits de l'homme et activités des sociétés transnationales'. In *Collected Courses of The Hague Academy of International Law*. Leiden: Martinus Nijhoff, 2016, 385, 33; F.J. Zamora Cabot, L. Heckendorn Urscheler, S. De Dycker (eds), *Implementing the U.N. Guiding Principles on Business and Human Rights: Private International Law Perspectives*. Genève: Schulthess Éditions Romandes, 2017.

the development of international law, through the identification of standards specifically tailored to business activities and the interpretation of international law in such a way as to adapt its rules to the specific actors involved and the abuses likely to occur within the development of economic activities.

Since the parent companies of many MNCs are incorporated under the law of European states, those countries' domestic legislation and the European legal framework should be given specific consideration. Indeed they play a crucial role in establishing how the business activities of European MNCs should be conducted and which remedies will be available when corporate human rights violations occur, thus providing specific responses to the challenges posed at international level. Against this backdrop, this book aims at identifying the solutions offered in Europe to the business and human rights (B&HR) international legal issues and at providing an overall assessment of their effectiveness.

To this extent, it should be premised that the EU has developed a specific root in the field of B&HR. The approach followed by the EU essentially focuses on the notion of Corporate Social Responsibility (hereinafter 'CSR'), originally conceived as 'a concept whereby companies decide voluntarily to contribute to a better society and a cleaner environment',[5] and thus 'integrate social and environmental concerns in their business operations and in their interaction with their stakeholders on a voluntary basis'.[6]

However, starting from 2011 the European Commission put forward a new definition of Corporate Social Responsibility (CSR): 'the responsibility of enterprises for their impacts on society',[7] which goes beyond the mere voluntary commitment to contribute to a better society or the compliance with applicable legislation, in order to encompass the adoption by corporations of processes

> to integrate social, environmental, ethical, human rights and consumer concerns into their business operations and core strategy in close collaboration with their stakeholders, with the aim of: maximizing the creation of shared value for their owners/shareholders and for their other stakeholders and society at large[8]

and 'identifying, preventing and mitigating their possible adverse impacts'.[9]

5 Commission of the European Communities, *Green Paper, Promoting a European Framework for Corporate Social Responsibility*, 18 July 2001, 6.

6 Ibid.

7 *Communication from the Commission to the European Parliament, the Council, the European Economic and Social Committee and the Committee of the Regions A renewed EU strategy 2011–14 for Corporate Social Responsibility*, COM/2011/0681 final, 6, available at http://eur-lex.europa.eu/legal-content/EN/TXT/HTML/?uri=CELEX:52011DC0681&from=EN (last accessed 20 February 2018).

8 Ibid.

9 Ibid.

The European Commission acknowledges that

> internationally recognized principles and guidelines, in particular the recently updated OECD Guidelines for Multinational Enterprises, the ten principles of the United Nations Global Compact, the ISO 26000 Guidance Standard on Social Responsibility, the ILO Tri-partite Declaration of Principles Concerning Multinational Enterprises and Social Policy, and the United Nations Guiding Principles on Business and Human Rights[10]

provide corporations, especially MNCs, with 'authoritative guidance'.[11] In light of this, in 2011, the EU committed to ensure the integration of internationally recognized principles and guidelines into its own CSR policies, promote respect for them, foster consistency between them, monitor their respect by the European enterprises, and encourage all large European corporations to make a commitment to comply with them. As regards specifically the UNGPs, the EU declared to expect 'all European enterprises to meet the corporate responsibility to respect human rights'[12] and invited all 'EU Member States to develop by the end of 2012 national plans',[13] the state of play of which, assessed later by the EU itself,[14] will be examined by this book.

Under the influence of the EU, several EU Member States have adopted National Action Plans (NAPs) and pertinent legislation.[15] The EU itself has proceeded to enact specific legislation directly or indirectly addressing B&HR. The example has also been followed by several non-EU members, and by the Council of Europe (CoE), whose Committee of Ministers' 2016 Recommendation on Human Rights and Business[16] provides useful indications as to the application of the European Convention on Human Rights and Fundamental Freedoms (ECHR) on this subject.[17]

This book comes from the position that the EU, the CoE, and their Member States in recent years have been adopting policies and legislation aimed at granting the respect of human rights by business activities, paying specific attention

10 Ibid., 6.

11 Ibid.

12 Ibid., 14.

13 Ibid.

14 European Commission, *Staff Working Document on Implementing the UN Guiding Principles on Business and Human Rights – State of Play*, Brussels, 14 July 2015, SWD(2015) 144 final; European Parliament, *Implementation of the UN Guiding Principles on Business and Human Rights*, EXPO/B/COMMITTEE/FWC/2013-08/Lot8/09 EN, February 2017.

15 M. Bordignon, 'State commitment in implementing the UNGPs and the emerging regime of national action plans: a comparative analysis'. *Human Rights & International Legal Discourse*, 2016, 10(1), 117.

16 CoE, *Committee of Ministers to Member States on human rights and business*, CM/Rec(2016)3, March 2016. See also CoE Committee of Ministers, *Declaration of the Committee of Ministers on the UN Guiding Principles on Business and Human Rights*, 16 April 2014.

17 Convention for the Protection of Human Rights and Fundamental Freedoms (ECHR) ETS 5, 213 UNTS 222, entered into force on 3 September 1953.

to the need (and corresponding duties) of transparency, disclosure of information, human rights due diligence, duty of care over the supply chain, and access to remedies.[18] These legislations and the related case law can be considered the European responses to the legal challenges posed at international-law level on B&HR and constitute the focus of the research developed by this book.

As a methodological remark, it is worth noting that the research developed herein follows the three-pillar structure of the UNGPs: the state duty to protect human rights, the corporate responsibility to respect human rights, and the victims' access to remedies.

The UNGPs were adopted in 2011 by the UN Special Representative of the Secretary General on Business and Human Rights (SRSGBHR), Professor John Ruggie, at the end of the mandate conferred in 2005[19] and renewed in 2008.[20] As concerns the first pillar, UNGP 1 establishes that 'States must protect against human rights abuse within their territory and/or jurisdiction by third parties, including business enterprises'.[21] The state duty to protect is a standard of conduct that implies an obligation of due diligence that leaves states the discretion to select the appropriate measures among the full range of permissible 'preventative and remedial measures, including policies, legislation, regulations and adjudication'.[22] States are not responsible for the human rights abuses committed by corporations, but breach their international human rights law obligations if such abuses can be attributed to them, or if they fail to take appropriate measures to prevent, investigate, punish, and redress them. More specifically, it is established that 'States should exercise adequate oversight in order to meet their international human rights obligations when they contract with, or

18 On the European approach to B&HR, among the others, see: D. Augenstein, M. Dawson, P. Thielbörger, 'The UNGPs in the European Union: the open coordination of business and human rights?'. *Business and Human Rights Journal*, 2018, 3(1), 1; J.L. Černič 'Towards a holistic approach to business and human rights in the European Union'. *Human Rights & International Legal Discourse*, 2016, 10(1), 160; M. Fasciglione, 'The enforcement of corporate human rights due diligence: from the UN guiding principles on business and human rights to the legal systems of EU countries'. *Human Rights & International Legal Discourse*, 2016, 10(1), 94; M. Requejo Isidro, 'Business and human rights abuses: claiming compensation under the Brussels I recast'. *Human Rights & International Legal Discourse*, 2016, 10(1), 72; C. Márquez Carrasco, I. Vivas Tesón (eds), *La implementación de los Principios Rectores de las Naciones Unidas sobre empresas y derechos humanos por la Unión Europea y sus Estados miembros*. Madrid: Thomson-Aranzadi, 2017.

19 OHCHR, *Human Rights and Transnational Corporations and other Business Enterprises*. Resolution 2005/69, 20 April 2005.

20 UNHRC, *Mandate of the Special Representative of the Secretary-General on the Issue of Human Rights and Transnational Corporations and other Business Enterprises*. Resolution 8/7, 8 June 2008.

21 See D. Augenstein and L. Dziedzic, 'State responsibilities to regulate and adjudicate corporate activities under the European Convention on Human Rights'. *EUI Working Papers*, 2017/15; H. Cantú Rivera, 'On the responsibility to protect and the business and human rights agenda'. In R. Barnes, V.P. Tzevelekos (eds), *Beyond Responsibility to Protect: Generating Change in International Law*. Cambridge: Intersentia, 2016, 203.

22 UNGP 1, Commentary.

legislate for, business enterprises to provide services that may impact upon the enjoyment of human rights',[23] including public procurement.

As far as extraterritorial protection of human rights is concerned, it is acknowledged – not without attracting a certain criticism[24] – that 'States should set out clearly the expectation that all business enterprises domiciled in their territory and/or jurisdiction respect human rights throughout their operations'.[25] This recommendation is based on the legal presumption that 'States are not generally required under international human rights law to regulate the extraterritorial activities of businesses domiciled in their territory and/or jurisdiction. Nor are they generally prohibited from doing so, provided there is a recognized jurisdictional basis'.[26]

The corporate responsibility to respect human rights is conceived as 'a global standard of expected conduct for all business enterprises wherever they operate'.[27] Pursuant thereto, companies 'should avoid infringing on the human rights of others and should address adverse human rights impacts with which

23 UNGP 5.

24 See: D. Augenstein and D. Kinley, 'When human rights "responsibilities" become "duties": the extraterritorial obligations of states that bind corporations'. In S. Deva and D. Bilchitz (eds), *Human Rights Obligations of Business*. Cambridge: Cambridge University Press, 2013, 275; N. Bernaz, 'State obligations with regard to the extraterritorial activities of companies domiciled on their territories'. In C.M. Buckley, A. Donald and P. Leach, *Towards Convergence in International Human Rights Law*. Leiden, Boston: Brill Nijhoff, 2017, 435.

25 UNGP 2. Among others, see: K. Buhmann 'Defying territorial limitations: regulating business conduct extraterritorially through establishing obligations in EU law and national law'. In J.L. Černič and T. Van Ho (eds), *Human Rights and Business: Direct Corporate Accountability for Human Rights*. Oisterwijk: Wolf Legal Publishers, 2015, 281; O. De Schutter, 'The accountability of multinationals for human rights violations in European law'. Center For Human Rights and Global Justice Working Paper No. 1, New York School of Law, 2004; C. Methven O'Brien, 'The home state duty to regulate the human rights impacts of TNCs abroad: a rebuttal'. *Business and Human Rights Journal*, 2018, 3(1), 47.

26 UNGP 2, Commentary.

27 UNGP 11, Commentary. Among the others, see: J. Bonnitcha and R. McCorquodale, 'The concept of "due diligence" in the UN guiding principles on business and human rights'. *European Journal of International Law*, 2017, 28(3), 899; J. Bonnitcha and R. McCorquodale, 'The concept of "due diligence" in the UN Guiding Principles on Business and Human Rights: a rejoinder to John Gerard Ruggie and John F. Sherman, III'. *European Journal of International Law*, 2017, 28(3), 929; J.L. Černič and T. Van Ho (eds), *Human Rights and Business: Direct Corporate Accountability for Human Rights*, op. cit.; M.E. Footer, 'Human rights due diligence and the responsible supply of minerals from conflict-affected areas: towards a normative framework?'. In J.L. Černič and T. Van Ho (eds), *Human Rights and Business: Direct Corporate Accountability for Human Rights*, op. cit., 179; C. Márquez Carrasco and K. Buhmann, 'Editorial introduction. The corporate responsibility to respect human rights: the emerging European Union regime'. *Human Rights & International Legal Discourse*, 2016, 10(2), 1; R. McCorquodale, L. Smit, S. Neely and R. Brooks, 'Human rights due diligence in law and practice: good practices and challenges for business enterprises'. *Business and Human Rights Journal*, 2017(2), 195; J.G. Ruggie, J.F Sherman III, 'The concept of "due diligence" in the UN Guiding Principles on Business and Human Rights: a reply to Jonathan Bonnitcha and Robert McCorquodale', *European Journal of International Law*, 2017, 28(3), 921.

they are involved'.[28] The corporate responsibility to respect human rights refers to the entire spectrum of international human rights, with specific attention to those at greater risk, depending on the sector and context of operation. Pursuant to UNGP 15, the tools to implement the corporate responsibility to protect human rights are: the policy commitment to meet the responsibility to respect human rights; the human rights due diligence process to identify, prevent the risks and mitigate their impacts on human rights; and the processes to enable the remediation of any adverse human rights impacts. Of specific relevance is the control over the supply chain and the adverse human rights impacts with which the corporations may be involved 'either through their own activities or as a result of their business relationships'.[29]

Finally, states 'must take appropriate steps to ensure, through judicial, administrative, legislative or other appropriate means, that when such abuses occur within their territory and/or jurisdiction those affected have access to effective remedy'.[30] Effective remedies include: state-based judicial mechanism (i.e. civil, criminal and administrative judicial means) and the provision for remedies such as 'apologies, restitution, rehabilitation, financial or non-financial compensation and punitive sanctions [...] as well as the prevention of harm through, for example, injunctions or guarantees of non-repetition';[31] state-based non-judicial grievance mechanisms (such as the instances filed within the OECD National Contact Points); and non-state-based grievance mechanisms, such as 'those administered by a business enterprise alone or with stakeholders, by an industry association or a multi-stakeholder group'.[32] It is explicitly acknowledged that in

28 UNGP 11.
29 UNGP 18.
30 UNGP 25.
31 UNGP 25, Commentary.
32 UNGP 28. On access to remedy, among the others, see: A. Bonfanti, 'No extraterritorial jurisdiction under the Alien Tort Statute. Which forum for disputes on overseas corporate human rights violations after Kiobel?'. *Diritti umani e diritto internazionale*, 2013, 379; N. Boschiero, 'Corporate responsibility in transnational human rights cases: the U.S. Supreme Court Decision in Kiobel v. Royal Dutch Petroleum'. *Rivista di diritto internazionale privato e processuale*, 2013, 49(2), 249; Ibid., 'The corporate responsibility to respect human rights and the question of universal civil jurisdiction in transnational human rights cases: the U.S. Supreme Court decision in Kiobel v. Royal Dutch Petroleum'. In B. Cortese (ed.), *Studi in onore di Laura Picchio Forlati*, Torino: Giappichelli, 2014, 3; L. Enneking, *Foreign Direct Liability and Beyond: Exploring the Role of Tort Law in Promoting International Corporate Social Responsibility and Accountability*. The Hague: Eleven International Publishing, 2012; S. Joseph, *Corporations and Transnational Human Rights Litigation*. Oxford: Hart Publishing, 2004; L. Roorda, C. Ryngaert, 'Business and human rights litigation in Europe and Canada: the promises of Forum of Necessity-based jurisdiction'. *Rabels Zeitschrift für ausländisches und internationales Privatrecht*, 2016, 783; J.J.Á. Rubio and K. Yiannibas (eds), *Human Rights in Business. Removal of Barriers to Access to Justice in the European Union*. London, New York, Routledge, 2017; J. Wouters and C. Ryngaert, 'Litigation for overseas corporate human rights abuses in the European Union: the challenge of jurisdiction'. *The George Washington International Law Review*, 2009, 40, 960.

terms of judicial remedies, states must remove 'legal, practical and other relevant barriers that could lead to a denial of access to remedy'.[33]

The methodological approach of this book to follow the three-pillar structure of the UNGPs is not ascribable only to the circumstance that they have been endorsed by the UNHRC, the EU, many inter-governmental and non-governmental organizations (IOs and NGOs) and enterprises, and are currently one of the main leading instruments in this field, but also to the fact that they have manifestly influenced the development of the international and European legal framework and the domestic legal systems on B&HR. For example, the 2011 revised edition of the OECD Guidelines (whose newly introduced Chapter IV is entitled 'Human rights'), the EU strategy 2011–2014 for Corporate Social Responsibility,[34] and the aforementioned CoE's recommendations were all adopted under the influence of the UNGPs, as it is for the current negotiation of an international treaty on B&HR by the Open-ended Intergovernmental Working Group on Transnational Corporations and Other Business Enterprises with Respect to Human Rights (OEIGWG).[35] This confirms the SRSGBHR's statement that 'Council endorsement of the Guiding Principles [...] [has marked] the end of the beginning: by establishing a common global platform for action, on which cumulative progress can be built, step-by-step, without foreclosing any other promising long-term development'.[36] Against this backdrop, the identification of the three pillars is key to the development of legal research on the corresponding embedded principles and their respective implementation at international, European, and domestic level. The three pillars in fact identify the three directions the international community should follow and the main challenges it must face through the adoption and the implementation of relevant legal instruments, in order to make the regulation of B&HR progressively more effective.

More precisely, after Chapter 2 by Paolo Farah, dealing with the implementation of the Sustainable Development Goals (SDGs) and their relationship with B&HR, and Chapter 3 by Daniel Augenstein, addressing overall issues

33 UNGP 26.

34 *Communication from the Commission to the European Parliament, the Council, the European Economic and Social Committee and the Committee of the Regions A Renewed EU strategy 2011–14 for Corporate Social Responsibility*, op. cit.

35 The preparatory works can be followed at: www.ohchr.org/EN/HRBodies/HRC/WGTransCorp/Pages/IGWGOnTNC.aspx (last accessed 20 March 2018). See also: L. Catá Backer 'Shaping a global law for business enterprises: framing principles and the promise of a comprehensive treaty on business and human rights'. *North Carolina Journal of International Law and Commercial Regulation*, 2016, 418; D. Bilchitz, 'The necessity for a Business and Human Rights Treaty'. *Business and Human Rights Journal*, 2016(1), 203; O. De Schutter, 'Towards a new treaty on business and human rights'. *Business and Human Rights Journal*, 2016(1), 41; S. Deva and D. Bilchitz (eds.), *Building a Treaty on Business and Human Rights*. Cambridge: Cambridge University Press, 2017; L. McConnell, 'Assessing the feasibility of a Business and Human Rights Treaty'. *The International and Comparative Law Quarterly*, 2017, 66(1), 143.

36 UNHRC, *Guiding Principles on Business and Human Rights: Implementing the United Nations' 'Protect, Respect and Remedy' Framework*, A/HRC/17/31, 21 March 2011, para 13.

concerning the European approach to B&HR and the implementation of the B&HR framework, the book is divided into three parts, respectively devoted to the European approach to the state duty to protect human rights (Part I), the corporate responsibility to respect human rights (Part II), and victims' access to remedy (Part III).

Part I includes Chapter 4 by Marco Fasciglione and Chapter 5 by Claire Methven O'Brien. These authors examine the state duty to protect in light of the ECHR, the CoE Recommendations, and the European Court of Human Rights (ECtHR) case law. More specifically, Chapter 4 focuses on the substantive and procedural standards developed in this area under the ECHR system, while Chapter 5 focuses on the extraterritorial application of the ECHR, seeking to assess whether it provides for the legal duty of the MNCs' home states to protect against human rights abuses occurring abroad. Part I also includes Chapter 6 by Deborah Russo, who examines a specific issue connected to the state duty to protect human rights: the respect of human rights in public procurement. The analysis is completed by Leonardo Borlini in Chapter 7, who focuses on the inclusion of human rights, CSR, and sustainable development obligations within the EU legal instruments governing international trade, and Marta Bordignon in Chapter 8, who examines the NAPs adopted at domestic level, especially by the EU Member States, with a specific focus on the Italian one.

Part II explores the corporate responsibility to respect human rights and the concept of mandatory human rights due diligence through the analysis of the EU and the European states' domestic approaches. Chapter 9 by Cindy Woods highlights the multiple ways followed in Europe to promote responsible supply chains. The topic is deepened through the insights on the domestic approaches developed in Chapter 10 by Olga Martin-Ortega, focusing on the 2015 UK Modern Slavery Act; Chapter 11 by Paola Cavanna, on the relevant Italian legislation; Chapter 12 by Tiphaine Beau de Loménie, Sandra Cossart and Paige Morrow, examining the recent French law that establishes a corporate duty of vigilance and the option to introduce a similar obligation at EU level; and Chapter 13 by Ludovica Chiussi on the Norwegian pension fund. The EU perspective is examined by Valentina Grado in Chapter 14 on the EU legislation on conflict minerals, and Angelica Bonfanti in Chapter 15 on the corporate responsibility of ICT companies to protect human rights.

Part III deals with access to remedy in Europe and includes Chapter 16 by Carmen Márquez Carrasco, about the recent Opinion of the EU Fundamental Rights Agency (FRA) on access to remedy, highlighting some of the shortcomings of the current domestic and EU legislations, and Chapters 17 and 18, respectively by Lucas Roorda and Claire Bright, exploring access to civil remedies in Europe. More specifically, Chapter 17 examines the European rules on the attribution of civil jurisdiction over B&HR cases, while Chapter 18 analyses parent company liability, with a specific focus on the cases brought against Shell before the English and Dutch courts for alleged human rights and environmental abuses in Nigeria. Access to criminal remedies is dealt with by Adriana

Espinosa González and Marta Sosa Navarro in Chapter 19, who assess whether and how the role of criminal judicial mechanisms to tackle human rights violations perpetrated by corporations should be enhanced. The analysis is completed by Florentine Vos in Chapter 20, who discusses the trends in the use of tort law remedies, other than the compensatory ones, in cases of human rights abuses by corporate entities.

The legal analysis developed throughout the book and the outcomes thereby reached are taken into consideration by the Editor in her concluding remarks, aimed at assessing whether the European approach to B&HR is effective, which are the fields where it proves to be more in line with the UNGPs' recommendations, which are the areas still to be improved (given also the weaknesses of the UNGPs in some regards), and whether the recent domestic and European reforms tackle the human rights concerns satisfactorily, or whether they present shortcomings and pitfalls worthy of being addressed by future action.

2 Sustainable Development Goals in Europe and Their Intersection with the Business and Human Rights Framework

Paolo Davide Farah[1]

Introduction

The state of implementation of the Sustainable Development Goals (SDGs) in the European Union (EU) in the context of the EU framework governing business and human rights (B&HR) is worthy of consideration. The nature of the SDGs and their impact on the different legal systems require acknowledgment of their inherent interconnectedness and the interdependence of economic, social cultural and environmental aspects; seen from the legal perspective, this would mean reinterpreting and articulating the existing norms in the light of social realities and implement the relevant changes.[2] This chapter will follow the top-down approach, exploring the relevant legal and policy framework, taking into account the overarching European Commission's 2030 Agenda for Sustainable Development and the SDGs and related developments at the EU and broader international level, as well as the European Commission's strategy concerning corporate social responsibility (CSR) and issues related therewith.

1 Paolo Davide Farah, West Virginia University, John D. Rockefeller IV, School of Policy and Politics, Department of Public Administration and College of Law; West Virginia University, Energy Institute and Center for Innovation in Gas Research and Utilization (CIGRU); West Virginia University, Institute of Water Security and Science (IWSS). Founder, President, Director and Principal Investigator at gLAWcal – Global Law Initiatives for Sustainable Development. Senior Fellow at the IIEL – Institute of International Economic Law, Georgetown University Law Center. Editor-in-Chief for the gLAWcal Book Series 'Global Law and Sustainable Development' and for the gLAWcal Book Series 'Transnational Law and Governance' published by Routledge (New York/London). Dual PhD in International Law at Aix-Marseille University (France) and Università degli Studi di Milano (Italy). LLM College of Europe, Bruges (Belgium), JD University of Paris Ouest La Defense Nanterre (France). The research leading to this result has received funding from People Programme (Marie Curie Actions) of the European Union's Seventh Framework Programme (FP7/2007–2013) under REA grant agreement no. 318908, acronym of the project: POREEN (2013–2016) entitled 'Partnering Opportunities between Europe and China in the Renewable Energies and Environmental Industries', within the results of the Research Team at gLAWcal – Global Law Initiatives for Sustainable Development (United Kingdom).

2 B. Mayer, 'Sustainable development law on environmental migration: the story of an obelisk, a bag of marbles, and a tapestry'. *Environmental Law Review*, 2012, 14, 111, 113.

This chapter will examine the compatibility of respective frameworks and, eventually, suggest integrating proposals. In general, the socially responsible approach to business is understood as a necessary prerequisite for the realization of the SDGs in practice. However, the EU steps in this regard have been criticized for not adequately addressing the negative social and environmental aspects of private sector activities.[3] The lack of concrete measures aimed at fostering the implementation of the SDGs in practice makes it also necessary to analyse the already existing regulatory frameworks at the EU and national levels relevant from the SDGs' perspective and evaluate their potential to contribute to the realization of the SDGs.[4]

The analysis will apply *inter alia* a human rights based approach incorporating international human rights standards in pursuing development as one of the underlying research methods. This approach fosters the need for monitoring and accountability, which are perceived as crucial for realization of the objectives in practice and the lack of which has been repeatedly criticized.[5] The investigation of the SDGs also presupposes an interdisciplinary approach to the research. Hence, the analysis of the relevant legal and policy frameworks will apply the elements of the New Legal Realism reasoning, which accentuates *inter alia* the necessity to take into account relevant empirical data.[6] In this regard statistical data, provided for instance by Eurostat, or selected case studies from EU Member States might be used as sources. Given the expected variety of specific issues related to the implementation of SDGs and matters related therewith at national level, the case studies will be used only as a non-probative sample in order to illustrate certain points, if relevant and applicable. At the same time, such an approach has the potential to reconnect the top-down implementation starting at the EU level with the realities at national levels in order to prevent occurrence of potential gaps in practice.

3 European Coalition for Corporate Justice, *EU Action Plan Overlooks Human Rights Risks of Corporate Activities*, 23 November 2016, https://business-humanrights.org/sites/default/files/documents/EU%20Action%20Plan%20on%20SDGs%20overlooks%20risks%20of%20corporate%20activity%20%28ECCJ%20Press%20Release%29.pdf (last accessed 25 March 2018).

4 SDG Watch Europe, *Statement on the European Commission's Communication on European Action for Sustainability*, 23 November 2016, www.sdgwatcheurope.org/single-post/2016/11/23/Statement-on-the-European-Commission%E2%80%99s-Communication-on-European-action-for-sustainability (last accessed 25 March 2018).

5 E. Bonnar, 'Exploring the human rights based approach principles and the value of their pragmatic application in being integrated with national performance frameworks as part of the Sustainable Development Goals implementation, monitoring, follow-up and review'. *Scottish Human Rights Journal*, 2016, 3.

6 A. Huneeus, 'Human rights between jurisprudence and social science'. *Leiden Journal of International Law*, 2015, 28, 255–256.

The Road from Millennium Development Goals to Sustainable Development Goals

The predecessor of the Sustainable Development Goals (SDGs) might be found in the Millennium Development Goals proclaimed in 2001. The incentive for their adoption might be seen in the necessity to respond to the process of globalization, which is heavily criticized because it is contested that its benefits are distributed rather unevenly, while the costs have to be borne by all.[7] In particular, without ever underestimating the advantages that globalization has brought to millions of people, it has to be considered how to better govern and regulate free-trade in view of reducing or eliminating the connected risks and damages occurring to non-trade concerns (NTCs) such as the protection of the environment and sustainable development, public health, human rights, social welfare, consumer interests, food and product safety. To a large extent, the results of the Millennium Development Goals can be regarded rather positively, especially the progress concerning the fight against poverty, hunger and disease.[8] The Millennium Development Goals were projected to last until 2015; however, the international community was already looking and planning for the timeframe going beyond this period.

The basis for the SDGs was set in 2012 by adopting the Rio+20 outcome document *The Future We Want*. This document stipulated that even though the SDGs were conceived as global in nature and universally accepted, they needed to take account of '[d]ifferent national realities, capacities and levels of development'.[9] Moreover, responding to the critique associated with the Millennium Development Goals, the SDGs were explicitly designed to integrate economic, social and environmental aspects in a holistic manner.[10] The process leading to the adoption of SDGs was also supported by the UN Global Compact framework – focusing mainly on the relationship between business and human rights – which highlighted the contribution of business in fostering the SDGs by the means of responsible business actions.[11] In 2015, the Agenda for Sustainable Development was adopted at the 70th UN General Assembly, introducing 17 SDGs and 169 associated targets, which entered into force in

7 J. Briant Carant, 'Unheard voices: a critical discourse analysis of the Millennium Development Goals' evolution into the Sustainable Development Goals'. *Third World Quarterly*, 2016, 38, 16.

8 J.D. Sachs, 'From Millennium Development Goals to Sustainable Development Goals'. *Lancet*, 2012, 379, 2206. See also P.D. Farah, 'Trade and progress: the case of China'. *Columbia Journal of Asian Law*, 2016, 30, pp. 97–107; P.D. Farah and E. Cima (eds), *China's Influence on Non-Trade Concerns in International Economic Law*. New York/London: Routledge, 2016.

9 U. Pisano *et al.*, 'The Sustainable Development Goals (SDGs) and their impact on the European SD governance framework'. *ESDN Quarterly Report*, 2015, no. 35, 6.

10 Ibid., 6.

11 UN Global Compact, *The Role of Business and Finance in Supporting the Post-2015 Agenda*, July 2014, www.unglobalcompact.org/docs/news_events/9.6/Post2015_WhitePaper_2July14.pdf (last accessed 25 March 2018); see also Pisano, op. cit., 12.

2016.[12] Different from the monitoring framework of the Millennium Development Goals, the SDGs' monitoring is based on a multi-level framework, including national, global, regional and thematic reporting.[13] Countries are encouraged to develop indicators at national and sub-national levels, which should complement global indicators.[14] Also, in contrast to the Millennium Development Goals, which concerned mainly developing countries, the SDGs address both developed and developing countries.[15]

In the context of the EU, sustainable development is a fundamental objective embedded in Article 3 of the Treaty on the European Union (hereinafter 'TEU').[16] The origins of the coherent sustainable development framework might be traced back to year 2006, when the EU introduced the EU Sustainable Development Strategy, setting seven key priorities and objectives until 2010.[17] This was followed by the Europe 2020 Strategy, advocating for smart, sustainable and inclusive growth, which was accompanied by five targets.[18] However, these initiatives, especially the Europe 2020 Strategy, have been criticized for including certain loopholes and inconsistencies resting, for

12 UN General Assembly, *Transforming Our World: the 2030 Agenda for Sustainable Development*, UN Resolution A/RES/70/1, 25 September 2015, available online: www.un.org/en/development/desa/population/migration/generalassembly/docs/globalcompact/A_RES_70_1_E.pdf (last accessed 25 March 2018); European Commission, *Communication to the European Parliament, the Council, the European Economic and Social Committee and the Committee of the Regions. Next Steps for A Sustainable Europe: European Action for Sustainability*, Document SWD(2016) 390 Final, Strasbourg, 22 November 2016, https://ec.europa.eu/europeaid/sites/devco/files/communication-next-steps-sustainable-europe-20161122_en.pdf (last accessed 25 March 2018).

13 Eurostat, *Sustainable Development in the European Union: 2015 Monitoring Report of the EU Sustainable Development Strategy*, 2015, 34, http://ec.europa.eu/eurostat/documents/3217494/6975281/KS-GT-15-001-EN-N.pdf (last accessed 25 March 2018).

14 J. Bequiraj, 'Future perfect: measuring access to justice in the post-2015 development framework'. *Public Law* 2016, 549.

15 Ibid.

16 A. Renda, 'How can sustainable development goals be "mainstreamed" in the EU's better regulation agenda?'. *Policy Insights*, 2017, 2.

17 Council of the European Union, *Renewed EU Sustainable Development Strategy*, Document 10917/06, Brussels, 5–16 June 2006. For the first time, the guiding principles behind sustainable development are included in a single framework from the perspective of the EU strategy towards sustainable development. These principles included climate change and clean energy; sustainable transport; sustainable consumption and production; conservation and management of natural resources; public health; social inclusion, demography and migration; global poverty and sustainable development challenges; and later also education and training; and research and development. See also U. Pisano, op. cit., 20.

18 European Commission, *EUROPE 2020 A Strategy for Smart, Sustainable and Inclusive Growth*, Document COM (2010) 2020 Final, Brussels, 3 March 2010. These targets include: 75 per cent of the population between 20–64 should be employed, 3 per cent of the EU's GDP should be invested in R&D; meeting the 20/20/20 climate and energy targets, including an increase to 30 per cent of emissions reductions; the share of early school leavers should be under 10 per cent and at least 40 per cent of the younger generation should have a tertiary degree; 20 million fewer people should be at risk of poverty. See U. Pisano op. cit., at 21–22.

instance, on the lack of cooperation – and incentives to cooperate – on the part of Member States, the lack of meaningful targets in fields such as research and development, and excessive top-down approach undermining political legitimacy.[19]

In 2016, the EU 2030 Agenda was presented, echoing the concept of SDGs as envisaged by the UN.[20] However, in this regard it needs to be mentioned that SDGs are formulated as global goals and there is a need – as well as a challenge – to tailor them to fit the EU's needs, let alone the specific needs and circumstances of its Member States.[21] The crux in this regard rests in the ability of the EU to accommodate its policy framework and find a compromise on sustainable development to reflect the interests and priorities of the EU in general, while leaving enough discretion and possibilities for the respective Member States to focus on and emphasize their own interests. One of the preferred options in this regard might be seen in the so-called decentralization of SDGs' targets and breaking them down into targets specifically tailored to each Member State, while it might be beneficial to introduce specific targets even at sub-national level, in order to reflect the specific needs of regions within respective Member States.[22]

Participatory and Inclusive SDGs' Governance Framework: The Challenge Ahead?

As has been already mentioned, the initiatives and plans preceding the adoption of SDGs have been to a large extent criticized for their underlying top-down approach, branded by some as the so-called 'cockpit-ism', '[t]he illusion that top-down steering by governments and intergovernmental organizations alone can address global problems'.[23] Even though the documents building the framework of SDGs make reference to '[a]ctive involvement of all relevant stakeholders',[24] they address business, civil society and cities only briefly.[25] The necessary precondition for the realization of SDGs is the inclusive governance framework, involving all important stakeholders, including not only

19 A. Renda, op. cit., 7.

20 Council of the European Union, *A Sustainable European Future: The EU Response to the 2030 Agenda for Sustainable Development, Council Conclusions*, Document 10370/17, Brussels, 20 June 2017.

21 A. Renda, op. cit., 8.

22 Ibid., 8.

23 M. Hajet *et al.*, 'Beyond cockpit-ism: four insights to enhance the transformative potential of the Sustainable Development Goals'. *Sustainability*, 2015, 1652.

24 See for instance, United Nations, Rio+20s UNDP, *The Future We Want, Outcome of the Conference*, A/CONF.216/L.1, Rio de Janeiro, Brazil, 20–22 June 2012.

25 Hajet *et al.*, op. cit., 1653.

governments, but also civil society and private sector.[26] This approach reflects the concept of the so-called 'energetic society', highlighting '[t]he transformative potential of the multiple initiatives for sustainable development taken by various agents of change within societies around the world'.[27]

In particular, the private sector, with its widespread reach, innovative technologies and ability to deliver solutions, should be intensively included into the sustainable development framework.[28] The business and finance sectors should be engaged as agents of change, which might be facilitated to accelerate the green economy. The narrative of sustainability has already penetrated the business logic. Examples at international level include, for instance, the Integrated Reporting Initiatives implemented by organizations such as International Integrated Reporting Council (IIRC), or the Global Reporting Initiative (GRI) for integrating sustainability and financial reporting,[29] Action 2020 proclaimed by the World Business Council for Sustainable Development and the initiative Risky Business,[30] evaluating the economic risk of climate change in the United States.[31] The guidelines and recommendations adopted under the auspices of the OECD are also quite influential at international, EU and national level.

26 As a demonstration of the need to involve all relevant stakeholders, in this particular case civil society, might be mentioned for instance the SDG 15, declaring to '[p]rotect, restore and promote sustainable use of terrestrial ecosystems, sustainably manage forests, combat desertification, and halt and reverse land degradation and halt biodiversity loss'. In the EU context, this SDG is materialized in the Birds and Habitats Directives and the network of protected areas under the Natura 2000 framework. One of the main objectives of these Directives is to halt the loss of biodiversity in the EU. According to art. 6 (3) and (4) of the Habitats Directive, development plans and projects are subjected to the so-called appropriate assessment. However, the practice of conducting the appropriate assessment process has been criticized on account of the fact that it often does not meet the high standards imposed on this process. This state-of-affairs is one of the factors that contributed to the continuing loss of biodiversity in the EU. According to the reports of environmental NGOs, a more intensive involvement of interested public, supervising the process and often being able to provide inputs specific to respective localities, might have a potential to remedy these deficiencies. The recent judgment of the ECJ, *Lesoochranárske združenie VLK vs. Obvodný úrad Trenčín,* C-243/15 even opens public participation possibilities in the appropriate assessment process under art. 6 (3) of the Habitats Directive. Examples like this demonstrate that the involvement of relevant stakeholders, such as civil society, in very concrete matters is crucial for the realization of the SDGs in the EU. See Justice and Environment, *Making Natura 2000 Impact Assessments Truly Appropriate: NGO Proposal for an Action Plan* (January 2017), available online: www.justiceandenvironment.org/fileadmin/user_upload/Publications/2016/NaturaActionPlanProposal_january2017.pdf (last accessed 25 March 2018).

27 Hajet *et al.*, op. cit., 1656.

28 J.D. Sachs, op. cit.

29 Available online: http://integratedreporting.org (last accessed 25 March 2018).

30 World Business Council for Sustainable Development works 'with member companies along and across value chains to deliver impactful business solutions to the most challenging sustainability issues with the objective of being a leading voice of business for sustainability', available online: www.wbcsd.org (last accessed 25 March 2018), and the Risky Business focuses 'on quantifying and publicizing the economic risks from the impacts of a changing climate' (available online: https://riskybusiness.org (last accessed 25 March 2018).

31 Hajet *et al.*, op. cit., 1657.

Valuable examples, which are also implemented at national level, include, for instance, the *OECD Guidelines on Multinational Enterprises and Responsible Business Conduct* (hereinafter 'OECD Guidelines')[32] or the recommendation *Common Approaches for Officially Supported Export Credits and Environmental and Social Due Diligence (the 'Common Approaches')*.[33] OECD guidelines also foster the adoption of code of conducts by business partners, suppliers or subcontractors, expanding in this way the number of businesses adhering to similar standards.

In the EU, the sustainable development framework needs to be seen in the context of corporate social responsibility (CSR) and efforts to implement the UNGPs. The role of the EU's CSR strategy in implementing the global principles on B&HR developed by the UN has also been mentioned in the 2011 *Communication of the European Commission on Corporate Social Responsibility*, pursuant to which a better implementation of the global principles on B&HR would equally contribute to the realization of the EU objectives.[34] This assumption has also been later reiterated in the European Commission's CSR Strategy in 2014. There has been a realization at the EU level that a wholly top-down approach from Brussels will not be a magic wand leading to the realization of these objectives in the whole of the EU: recognition of this might be seen for instance in the fact that the European Commission encouraged Member States to develop their own specific National Action Plans (NAPs) on implementation of the UNGPs.[35] Still, the involvement and effective activation of stakeholders other than the ones connected with the State-led governance framework in practice, such as civil society and private sector, remains questionable.

The European Strategy on CSR sets an agenda consisting of several steps, including *inter alia* the integration of CSR principles into education, training and research, emphasizing national and sub-national CSR policies and better alignment of European and global approaches to CSR.[36] This indicates the

32 OECD, *Guidelines for Multinational Enterprises*, 19, available online: www.oecd.org/daf/inv/mne/48004323.pdf (last accessed 20 March 2018).

33 OECD, Trade and Agriculture Directorate, Trade Committee, Working Party on Export Credits and Credit Guarantees, *Revised Text for the Recommendation of the Council on Common Approaches for Officially Supported Export Credits and Environmental and Social Due Diligence (the 'Common Approaches')*, Document TAD/ECG(2016)3, Paris, 6 April 2016, available online: www.oecd.org/officialdocuments/publicdisplaydocumentpdf/?cote=TAD/ECG%282016%293&doclanguage=en (last accessed 25 March 2018).

34 European Commission, *Communication to the European Parliament, the Council, the European Economic and Social Committee and the Committee of the Regions: A Renewed EU Strategy 2011–14 for Corporate Social Responsibility*, Document COM(2011) 681 Final, Brussels, 25 October 2011, available online www.europarl.europa.eu/meetdocs/2009_2014/documents/com/com_com(2011)0681_/com_com(2011)0681_en.pdf (last accessed 25 March 2018).

35 European Commission, *Commission Staff Working Document on Implementing the UN Guiding Principles on Business and Human Rights, State of Play*, Document SWD(2015) 144 Final, Brussels, 14 July 2015, https://ec.europa.eu/anti-trafficking/sites/antitrafficking/files/swd_2015_144_f1_staff_working_paper_en_v2_p1_818385.pdf (last accessed 25 March 2018).

36 Ibid., 7.

recognition of the necessity to apply a multi-level governance approach, activating and involving a potentially large group of various stakeholders. EU Member States at least officially subscribe to the need to introduce a multi-level governance approach: for instance, Lithuania's National Strategy for Sustainable Development sees CSR as the underlying priority of sustainable economic development, while the participation of enterprises and social partners is seen as a crucial precondition for its achievement.[37]

Compatibility of SDGs and B&HR Framework in the EU

Even though it has not been mentioned explicitly, the cooperation with the business sector at EU level might be relevant with respect to multiple SDGs. For instance, SDG 8 addresses the promotion of a '[s]ustained, inclusive and sustainable economic growth, full and productive employment and decent work for all'. The mobilization of the business sector might contribute to the achievement of the aim of 75 per cent employment of people aged 20–64 years. The involvement of the business sector in this regard is especially encouraged by the EU action on Corporate Social Responsibility and Responsible Business Conduct,[38] which fosters *inter alia* more sustainable and better working and environmental conditions.

The so-called Accounting Directives 2013/34/EU of the European Parliament and of the Council of 26 June 2013 and Directive 2014/95/EU of 22 October 2014[39] are examples of EU legislation paving the way for the implementation of these objectives in practice. They require *inter alia* the disclosure of a wide range of non-financial information, such as environmental, social and employee-related aspects.[40]

37 Permanent Mission of the Republic of Lithuania, *Lithuania's Action Plan on the Implementation of the United Nations Guiding Principles on Business and Human Rights*, February 2015, 7, www.ohchr.org/Documents/Issues/Business/NationalPlans/Lithuania_NationalPlanBHR.pdf (last accessed 25 March 2018).

38 European Commission, *Communication to the European Parliament, the Council, the European Economic and Social Committee and the Committee of the Regions: Next Steps for A Sustainable Europe: European Action for Sustainability*, op. cit., 5.

39 *Directive 2013/34/EU of the European Parliament and of the Council of 26 June 2013 on the annual financial statements, consolidated financial statements and related reports of certain types of undertakings, amending Directive 2006/43/EC of the European Parliament and of the Council and repealing Council Directives 78/660/EEC and 83/349/EEC; Directive 2014/95/EU of the European Parliament and of the Council of 22 October 2014 amending Directive 2013/34/EU as regards disclosure of non-financial and diversity information by certain large undertakings and groups.* See also European Commission, *Communication to the European Parliament, the Council, the European Economic and Social Committee and the Committee of the Regions: Next Steps for A Sustainable Europe: European Action for Sustainability*, op. cit., 10.

40 European Commission, *Commission Staff Working Document on Implementing the UN Guiding Principles on Business and Human Rights, State of Play*, op. cit., 10.

Similarly, with respect to SDG 9, declaring the ambition to '[b]uild resilient infrastructure, promote inclusive and sustainable industrialization and foster innovation', the business sector should represent a crucial partner for the EU and national governments. Taken together with the financial resources and objectives pursued by the European Structural and Investment Funds, the collaboration with the business sector might deliver fruits in a form of a strengthened position of the EU in the global innovation field.[41]

Similarly beneficial might be the role of the private sector with respect to SDGs 7 – aimed at ensuring access to affordable, reliable and sustainable energy – and SDG 13, aimed at tackling climate change.[42] One of the preconditions for this might be seen *inter alia* in addressing environmental matters.

The role of private sector is explicitly mentioned in SDG 17, aiming to '[s]trengthen means of implementation and revitalize the global partnership for sustainable development'. The European Commission, in close collaboration with Member States, shall implement policies boosting jobs, sustainable growth and investment in Europe and outside, by mobilizing *inter alia* the private sector.[43] Relevant legal basis in this regard might be seen in Article 207 (1) TFEU, stipulating that the common commercial policy shall be conducted in line with the principles and objectives of the EU's external action, and Article 208 (1) TFEU, stating the same about the EU's development policy, Article 212 TFEU on economic, financial and technical cooperation with third countries, and Article 214 TFEU for humanitarian aid.[44] An important policy document in this regard is the European Commission's Communication, *A Stronger Role of the Private Sector in Achieving Inclusive and Sustainable Growth in Developing Countries*,[45] which focuses on integration of the private sector into the EU development cooperation framework, while stipulating that the private sector needs to adhere *inter alia* to human rights standards.[46] The CSR standards shall also be promoted in developing countries by means of policy dialogue and development cooperation. A form of multi-level governance involving stakeholders from various fields might be found also in the Communication, *A Global*

41 European Commission, *Communication to the European Parliament, the Council, the European Economic and Social Committee and the Committee of the Regions: Next Steps for A Sustainable Europe: European Action for Sustainability*, op. cit., 6.

42 Ibid., 5.

43 Ibid., 7.

44 Ibid., 4–5.

45 European Commission, *Communication to the European Parliament, the Council, the European Economic and Social Committee and the Committee of the Regions. A Stronger Role of the Private Sector in Achieving Inclusive and Sustainable Growth in Developing Countries,* Document COM(2014) 263 Final, Brussels, 13 May 2014, available online: http://eur-lex.europa.eu/legal-content/EN/TXT/PDF/?uri=CELEX%3A52014DC0263&qid=1400681732387&from=EN (last accessed 25 March 2018).

46 European Commission, *Commission Staff Working Document on Implementing the UN Guiding Principles on Business and Human Rights, State of Play*, op. cit., 37–38.

Partnership for Poverty Eradication and Sustainable Development after 2015,[47] which promotes an inclusive form of global partnership involving the private sector as well as civil society. The activation and involvement of the private sector is expressly encouraged; for this reason, the Communication accentuates for instance the need for an effective legislative and regulatory framework. This might have the potential to create a form of the so-called Brussels effect,[48] which might bring the legislative and regulatory framework of the non-EU States closer to the EU standards of responsible business-making.

The Way Forward: Tracking of the Progress towards SDGs

The Eurostat statistics do not explicitly reflect the input of respective stakeholders on the SDGs' realization. For instance, with respect to SDG 8, the economic growth overall in the EU as well as its Member States is noticed;[49] however, the exact input and the role of the private sector in this context is not clear from statistical data. With respect to the overall employment rate the situation is similar: the employment rate of 70.1 per cent implies the positive role of the private sector in creating employment opportunities for the European population; however, more detailed data in this respect are not provided by Eurostat.[50]

The indicators concerning SDG 9 – aiming to build resilient infrastructure, promoting inclusive and sustainable industrialization and fostering innovation – seem to be more inclusive, as the pertinent SDG places a demand on industries to invest resources into development and innovation as well as environmental sound technologies and production processes.

For this sake, the so-called eco-Innovation Index works with several indicators grouped into five fields: eco-innovation inputs, eco-innovation activities,

47 European Commission, *Communication to the European Parliament, the Council, the European Economic and Social Committee and the Committee of the Regions. A Global Partnership For Poverty Eradication And Sustainable Development After 2015*, Document COM(2015) 44 Final, Brussels, 5 February 2015, available online: https://ec.europa.eu/europeaid/sites/devco/files/com-2015-44-final-5-2-2015_en.pdf (last accessed 25 March 2018).

48 In this case it would probably be a softer version of the Brussels effect, as it attempts mainly to introduce and strengthen certain minimum – not necessarily wholly hard-law – standards in other countries. In general, the Brussels effect describes a power of the EU to export its standards in the rest of the world through its legislation, without the need to use other institutions or other means of cooperation. The countries trading with the EU have then the tendency to adjust to the EU's standards. See A. Bradford, 'The Brussels Effect'. *Northwestern University Law Review*, 2012, 107, 2.

49 In the EU, a rather constant growth of GDP by 1 per cent has been noted. See Eurostat, *Sustainable Development in the European Union: A Statistical Glance from the Viewpoint of the UN Sustainable Development Goals*, 2016, 71, http://ec.europa.eu/eurostat/documents/3217494/7745644/KS-02-16-996-EN-N.pdf/eae6b7f9-d06c-4c83-b16f-c72b0779ad03 (last accessed 25 March 2018).

50 Ibid., 73.

eco-innovation outputs, resource efficiency and socio-economic outcomes. The eco-Innovation Index has a potential to identify countries with more progressive and environment-friendly industries.[51] The contribution towards the green economy at the EU level might be also seen in the mechanism of environmental management systems, which are codified *inter alia* by international standards, such as ISO 14001 and EMAS.

Further ambitions of SDG 9 might be seen in making industries more sustainable and increasing their share of employment, while combining these intentions and objectives with the application of progressive, environmentally sound technologies.[52] The review of data on research and development expenditure represents a specific instrument to determine and assess countries and regions with progressive industries. From this, it follows that the overall research and development intensity in the EU is ranked behind South Korea, Japan and the United States; however, it is still more progressive than in Russia, which might be perceived as a representative of the BRICS countries.[53] In the EU context, the highest intensity of investment in the research and development might be seen in the Nordic countries, such as Finland, Sweden and Denmark, followed by the Western and Central European Member States, such as Austria, Germany, Belgium and France. The other end of the scale belongs to the Southern and Eastern EU Member States, in which the investment into the research and development is half of the EU average or even less.[54] On the other hand, the largest share of investment in high and medium-high technology might be seen in the Central and Eastern EU Member States, such as the Czech Republic, Slovakia, Germany or Hungary.[55] The focus put on the type of business having the potential to employ a large number of people as well as the use and application of environmentally sound technologies demonstrate the holistic nature of SDGs, integrating social, economic and environmental aspects.

The impact of business on economic and social rights might be seen also in SDG 10, which advocates for reducing inequalities within and among countries. This should be translated into a sustained income growth, while promoting economic and social inclusion and reducing inequalities.[56] When conducting respective measurements, account is taken of the eventual irregularities concerning the measurement by the means of GDP per capita: some portion of the income

51 Eurostat, *Sustainable Development in the European Union: A Statistical Glance from the Viewpoint of the UN Sustainable Development Goals*, op. cit., 80.

52 Ibid., 78.

53 Brazil, Russia, India, China and South Africa. Eurostat, *Sustainable Development in the European Union: A Statistical Glance from the Viewpoint of the UN Sustainable Development Goals*, op. cit., 78.

54 However, there are also exceptions: countries, such as Slovenia, the Czech Republic, Estonia and Hungary invest in research and development a larger share of their GDP then their neighbours. See Eurostat, *Sustainable Development in the European Union: A Statistical Glance from the Viewpoint of the UN Sustainable Development Goals*, op. cit., at 79.

55 Ibid., 81.

56 Ibid., 85.

might be retained by corporations or governments and part of it might be transferred abroad, for instance, in case of multinational corporations.[57]

With respect to SDG 13 – combating climate change – it might be mentioned that the EU has reduced its greenhouse gas emissions by 23 per cent, in comparison with 1990, which is attributed mainly to reductions in the supply and use of energy across all sectors.[58] Even though this is not a sole result of the EU's CSR strategy, but mainly a result of deliberate efforts realized by the means of various instruments focused on tackling climate change, such as the EU emission trading scheme, the crucial role of the business sector cannot be understated in this regard. Voluntary commitments by companies concerning the evaluation of the environmental footprint in general and carbon footprint in particular also represent a valuable contribution, which supplements and reinforces the realization of binding commitments.[59]

As far as SDG 17 and its goal to implement and revitalize the global partnership for sustainable development are concerned, the role of the private sector is essential due to the fact that the pertinent SDG focuses on the process of implementation, rather than on the outcomes. For this reason, as a precondition, SDG 17 aims at building inclusive partnerships between all relevant stakeholders, involving governments, private sector and civil society.[60]

The Eurostat data works with two main data sets in this regard: one compares the spending on the Official Development Assistance, the target of which lies at 0.7 per cent of the Gross National Income (GNI). In reality, the EU's collective spending is at 0.47 percent of GNI, while some countries – Sweden, Luxembourg, Denmark and the Netherlands – exceed this target; however, the majority of Member States are below this target.[61] The other data set concerns EU imports from developing countries, which are continuously increasing. The reason for this lies mainly in the intensive trade relations with China, which has in the meantime become the largest exporter to the EU overall, but the imports from least developed countries also dynamically increase.

Further information on national measures contributing to the implementation of SDG 17 might be found in the National Action Plans (NAPs) on B&HR

57 For instance, the high GDP of Ireland and the Netherlands is to a large extent the result of the presence of a large number of foreign subsidiaries of multinational companies, which present a significant portion of the overall GDP. An example of this phenomenon in the context of national Member States might also represent the Bratislava region in Slovakia. It considers whether these practices, also involving in a larger context tax optimization schemes, should not be adequately addressed. See Eurostat, *Sustainable Development in the European Union: A Statistical Glance from the Viewpoint of the UN Sustainable Development Goals*, op. cit., 89.

58 Ibid., 109.

59 *Italian National Action Plan on Business and Human Rights 2016–2021*, available online: https://cidu.esteri.it/resource/2016/12/49117_f_NAPBHRENGFINALEDEC152017.pdf (last accessed 25 March 2018).

60 Ibid., Eurostat, *Sustainable Development in the European Union: A Statistical Glance from the Viewpoint of the UN Sustainable Development Goals*, op. cit., 135.

61 Ibid., 136.

in EU countries. In this regard it is worth noting that in 2013 the sector organizations of Dutch textile companies presented an action plan addressing abuses in the clothing industry, namely in the branch of clothing production, known for its unsatisfactory labour and social standards. The objective of the pertinent action plan rests on the global fostering of CSR standards.[62] The sustainable procurement policy implemented in the Netherlands, requiring suppliers to join either a reliable multi-stakeholder supply chain initiative, such as a quality mark or a certification institute, or by carrying out a risk analysis is another example of a concrete contribution to the realization of the SDG 17.[63] Given the international nature of global business, this might prevent the participation of companies not promoting sustainable development in the procurement processes.

Mechanisms such as this one acknowledge the fact that social and environmental standards need to be embedded in the rules and mechanisms governing global supply chains at international as well as national level. Due diligence mechanisms in the spirit of the OECD Guidelines and the UNGPs serve as a model for initiatives at national level in Italy, where information about conducting business with conflict-affected or high-risk areas as well as in textile sector are intensively distributed to SMEs.[64] Similar initiatives have been promoted in Denmark, the government of which elaborated the CSR Compass and the Global Compact Self-Assessment Tool,[65] including *inter alia* a guide for SMEs on how to conduct due diligence.[66]

Conclusion

There are clearly many initiatives aiming at implementation of SDGs at international, EU and national level, which acknowledge the necessity of an inclusive governance framework managing this process, including all relevant stakeholders at all levels. However, the complexity of such undertaking is reflected in its rather slow progress in translating the declared objectives from international and EU level to local level in a coordinated and deliberate manner. The number of NAPs on B&HR submitted to the European Commission by 2018 demonstrates that coherent and coordinated action towards explicit implementation of SDGs is probably not the priority of the day in many Member States. Still, the

62 Ministry of Foreign Affairs of the Netherlands, *National Action Plan on Business and Human Rights*, April 2014, 14, https://business-humanrights.org/sites/default/files/documents/netherlands-national-action-plan.pdf (last accessed 25 March 2018).

63 Ibid., 17.

64 *Italian National Action Plan on Business and Human Rights 2016–2021*, op. cit.

65 Available online: www.globalcompactselfassessment.org/aboutthistool (last accessed 25 March 2018).

66 The Danish Government, *Danish National Action Plan-Implementation of the UN Guiding Principles on Business and Human Rights*, March 2014, 14, www.ohchr.org/Documents/Issues/Business/NationalPlans/Denmark_NationalPlanBHR.pdf (last accessed 25 March 2018).

implementation of the ideas of an 'energetic society' into a governance framework, involving all relevant stakeholders, is highly encouraged.

With respect to the role of business and private sector, it needs to be mentioned that the consensus on the content of basic CSR principles seems to be shared by EU Member States, and standards, such as OECD Guidelines and the UNGPs, are becoming increasingly implemented at national level, which is a positive sign.

3 Managing Global Interdependencies through Law and Governance

The European Approach to Business and Human Rights

Daniel Augenstein

Introduction

Six years after the endorsement of the UNGPs by the UNHRC,[1] the B&HR debate has come to centre on two processes that were initially couched by many in oppositional terms: the domestic implementation of the UNGPs via national action plans (NAPs) and the development of an international treaty on B&HR. While proponents of the latter wish to corroborate the UNGPs' 'soft' law approach with a binding international legal framework, proponents of the former fear that the international treaty initiative (hereinafter, 'ITI') may prove too divisive to make real progress on the ground. The current chapter contributes to this debate by scrutinizing the European approach to B&HR at the intersection of international law and global governance. It is argued that the EU should assume a more proactive position in exploring complementarities between the UNGPs and the ITI given that both processes share a common goal.

This common goal is the resolution of collective action problems that result from the exposure of the state-centred conception of international law to the human rights impacts of global business operations. The ITI can play an important role in framing the UNGPs' global governance approach by providing much-needed legal guidance in areas of ongoing concern, such as extraterritorial human rights protection. However, the EU's early engagement with the international treaty process has been hardly constructive. At the same time, dismissing the UNGPs as too 'soft' or 'voluntary' an approach to corporate human rights accountability fails to acknowledge the crucial role that states' domestic law plays in their effective implementation. However, while the EU Member States have made an important early contribution to the development and implementation of NAPs on B&HR, their NAPs often do not live up to the requirements of the UNGPs.

1 UNHRC, *Guiding Principles on Business and Human Rights: Implementing the United Nations' 'Protect, Respect and Remedy' Framework*, A/HRC/17/31, 21 March 2011.

The UN Guiding Principles and the International Treaty Initiative

In June 2016, the Council of the European Union published its Conclusions on Business and Human Rights,[2] marking the fifth anniversary of the endorsement of the UNGPs by the UNHRC. The UNGPs are the first globally accepted framework on B&HR, developed by John Ruggie in his capacity as the United Nations Special Representative of the Secretary-General on the issue of human rights and TNCs and other business entities (SRSGBHR). They build on three pillars: (i) the state's duty to protect human rights against violations by third parties, including corporations; (ii) the corporate responsibility to respect human rights, meaning to act with due diligence to avoid infringing the rights of others; and (iii) greater access to effective remedies, both judicial and non-judicial, for victims of corporate human rights abuse. Following the end of the SRSGBHR's mandate, a UN working group was established to promote the 'effective and comprehensive dissemination and implementation' of the UNGPs.[3] The working group has *inter alia* encouraged states to develop NAPs on B&HR. A NAP is an 'evolving policy strategy developed by a state to protect against adverse human rights impacts by business enterprises in conformity with the UN Guiding Principles on Business and Human Rights'.[4]

The UNGPs represent an attempt to move beyond a purely voluntary approach to CSR, while also responding to the shortcomings of international law in addressing global B&HR challenges. An earlier attempt at legal reform – the 2003 UN Draft Norms that envisaged directly imposing human rights obligations on corporations in international law – had failed to garner the support of a majority of states and business entities.[5] Against this background, the SRSGBHR was not tasked to develop a new international legal instrument but merely to elaborate the implications of existing standards and practices. Embracing the importance of broader (non-legal) processes and dynamics in ensuring corporate respect for human rights, he embedded international human rights law in a global governance framework.[6]

> The root cause of the B&HR predicament today lies in the governance gaps created by globalization – between the scope and impact of economic forces and actors, and the capacity of societies to manage their adverse consequences.

2 Council of the European Union, *Council Conclusions on Business and Human Rights*, 10254/16, 20 June 2016.

3 UNHRC, *Human Rights and Transnational Corporations and Other Business Entities*, A/HRC/RES/17/4, 6 July 2011, para 6.

4 UNWGB&HR, *Guidance on National Action Plans on Business and Human Rights*, 3rd edition, November 2016, i.

5 UN Sub-Commission on the Promotion and Protection of Human Rights, *Norms on the Responsibilities of Transnational Corporations and Other Business Enterprises with Regard to Human Rights*, E/CN.4/Sub.2/2003/12, 26 August 2003.

6 For a restatement of the 'foundational logics' behind the UNGPs see J. Ruggie, 'Incorporating human rights: lessons learnt, and next steps'. In D. Baumann-Pauly and J. Nolan (eds), *Business and Human Rights: From Principles to Practice*. New York: Routledge, 2016, 64 ff.

> These governance gaps provide the permissive environment for wrongful acts by companies of all kinds without adequate sanctioning or reparation. How to narrow and ultimately bridge the gaps in relation to human rights is our fundamental challenge.[7]

The SRSGBHR's polycentric governance approach builds on the insight that corporate conduct at the global level is shaped by three different governance systems: a political governance system comprising the rules of domestic and international public law; a civil governance system in which stakeholders affected by business operations employ social and legal compliance mechanisms such as advocacy campaigns and strategic litigation; and a corporate governance system which internalizes pressures and expectations of the other two systems as constraints, risks and opportunities.[8] Intertwining these governance systems through creating mutual leverage and interdependencies should contribute to building a more effective global regime on B&HR. The three pillars of the UNGPs thus form a complementary whole: states are duty-bound to 'translate' international human rights norms into domestic laws and policies regulating corporate activities, while corporations respect human rights as globally recognized standards of expected conduct (their 'social licence to operate'), with both providing remediation for breaches of these overlapping governance systems within their respective jurisdictions.[9]

For proponents of the international treaty initiative, the UNGPs' global governance approach is insufficient to address widely acknowledged legal protection gaps in relation to corporate human rights abuse:

> We are mindful that soft law instruments such as the UNGPs [...] are only a partial answer to the pressing issues relating to human rights abuses by transnational corporations (TNCs). These principles and mechanisms fall short of addressing properly the problem of lack of accountability regarding TNCs worldwide and the absence of adequate legal remedies for victims.[10]

While the state duty to protect (first pillar) requires states to secure human rights against corporate-related violations, this duty is largely confined to violations committed on the state's territory, as its extraterritorial application remains

7 UNHRC, *Protect, Respect and Remedy: A Framework for Business and Human Rights*, A/HRC/8/5, 7 April 2008, para 3.

8 J. Ruggie, 'Regulating multinationals: the UN guiding principles, civil society, and international legalization'. *Regulatory Policy Program Working Paper RPP-2015-04*, 2015, 2.

9 L. Cata Backer, 'On the evolution of the United Nations' "Protect-Respect-Remedy" project: the state, the corporation and human rights in a global governance context'. *Santa Clara Journal of International Law*, 2011, 9, 37 ff.

10 Government of Ecuador, *Statement on Behalf of a Group of Countries at the 24th Session of the Human Rights Council: 'Transnational Corporations and Human Rights'*, September 2013, https://business-humanrights.org/en/binding-treaty (last accessed 8 February 2018).

'unsettled' in international law.[11] Relatedly, the corporate responsibility to respect (second pillar) lacks binding legal effect as 'respecting rights is not an obligation that current international human rights law generally imposes directly on companies'.[12] These legal protection gaps combine in impeding effective access to justice for victims of corporate-related human rights violations (third pillar).[13]

On 26 June 2014, the UNHRC adopted Resolution 26/9 that established an open-ended intergovernmental working group on TNCs and other business enterprises with respect to human rights (hereinafter 'OEIGWG') 'whose mandate shall be to elaborate an international legally binding instrument to regulate, in international human rights law, the activities of TNCs and other business enterprises'.[14] Resolution 26/9 was sponsored by Ecuador and South Africa and supported by states in the Global South and an alliance of international civil society organizations. Among the main goals of ITI are the adjustment of the imbalance between the rights and responsibilities of corporations in international law and the closing of legal (jurisdictional) protection gaps in relation to human rights violations committed in global supply and commodity chains.[15] In January 2017, the OEIGWG published an interim report,[16] followed by a discussion document of the Chairperson-Rapporteur that outlines possible 'elements' of the new international legal instrument.[17]

The initial reaction to the international treaty initiative by proponents of the UNGPs and many states in the Global North was defensive, if not openly hostile.[18] John Ruggie warned on several occasions that the treaty process

11 UNHRC, *Business and Human Rights: Towards Operationalising the 'Protect, Respect, and Remedy' Framework*, A/HRC/11/13, 22 April 2009, para 15.

12 UNHRC, *Business and Human Rights: Further Steps towards the Operationalisation of the "Protect, Respect, and Remedy" Framework*, A/HRC/14/27, 9 April 2010, para 55.

13 See further HRC, *Improving Accountability and Access to Remedy for Victims of Business-related Human Rights Abuse*, A/HRC/32/19, 10 May 2016.

14 UNHRC, *Elaboration of an International Legally Binding Instrument on Transnational Corporations and other Business Enterprises with Respect to Human Rights*, A/HRC/Res/26/9, 14 July 2014, 2.

15 Real News Network, *Urgent Need for Legally Binding Obligations On Transnational Corporations (2/2)*, Interview with the Chair of the Working Group, Maria Fernanda Espinosa, Permanent Representative of Ecuador to the UN-Geneva, January 32017, https://business-humanrights.org/en/videos-interviews-with-chair-of-un-intergovt-working-group-on-proposed-treaty-on-business-human-rights (last accessed 8 February 2018).

16 UNHRC, *Report on the Second Session of the Open-ended Intergovernmental Working Group on Transnational Corporations and other Business Enterprises with Respect to Human Rights*, A/HRC/34/47, 4 January 2017.

17 OEIGWG *Elements for the Draft Legally Binding Instrument on Transnational Corporations and Other Business Enterprises with Respect to Human Rights*, September 29, 2017, www.ohchr.org/EN/HRBodies/HRC/WGTransCorp/Pages/IGWGOnTNC.aspx (last accessed 8 February 2018).

18 See generally J. Martens and K. Seitz, *The Struggle for a UN Treaty: Towards Global Regulation on Business and Human Rights*. New York: Rosa Luxemburg Stiftung & Global Policy Forum, 2016.

might erode the consensus built around the UNGPs and undermine efforts directed at their further implementation.[19] For similar reasons, EU Member States in the UNHRC voted en bloc against Resolution 26/9. The EU delegation further complained that it was 'unclear how a possible treaty would relate to the policy framework already created by the UNGPs and what a legally binding instrument would involve, or how it would function in operational terms'.[20] Following a European Parliament Resolution that welcomed the work of ITI and called upon the EU and its Member States to 'constructively engage' in the negotiations,[21] the EU has expressed its (reserved) commitment to 'address outstanding issues as soon as possible'.[22] Nevertheless, the EU's contribution to the most recent (third) session of the OEIGWG was again rather stodgy and complacent.[23]

Meanwhile, old–new lines of conflict emerge behind the perceived dichotomy of hard international law and soft global governance. Representatives of business and civil society organizations have revived the debate as to whether human rights law does or should directly bind corporations *qua* non-state actors. This debate intersects with the diverging geo-political and geo-economic interests of developed and developing countries in their capacity as home and host states of corporate investment. Against this background, Europe's lopsided alignment with the UNGPs risks impeding progress on issues of common concern to both international processes, namely resolving collective action problems that result from the exposure of the state-centred conception of international law to the human rights impacts of global business operations. In a global market, the ability of states to enforce human rights in relation to businesses incorporated in their territorial jurisdiction increasingly depends on the human rights practices of other states. This enables large corporate groups to free-ride on inter-state competition and engenders the risk of a global 'race to the bottom' in regulatory and human rights standards.

19 J. Ruggie, *A UN Business and Human Rights Treaty?*, 28 January 2014; *A UN Business and Human Rights Treaty Update*, May 2014, www.business-humanrights.org/ (last accessed 8 February 2018).

20 EU, *Submission to the First Session of the Intergovernmental Working Group*, 6–10 July 2015, www.ohchr.org/EN/HRBodies/HRC/WGTransCorp/Session1/Pages/Session1.aspx (last accessed 8 February 2018).

21 European Parliament, *Resolution of 25 October 2016 on Corporate Liability for Serious Human Rights Abuses in Third Countries*, 2015/2315(INI), para 12.

22 EU, *Contribution in View of the Second Session of the Intergovernmental Working Group on Transnational Corporations and Other Enterprises with Respect to Human Rights – 29 August 2016*, www.ohchr.org/EN/HRBodies/HRC/WGTransCorp/Session2/Pages/Session2.aspx (last accessed 8 February 2018).

23 OEIGWG, *Draft Report on the Third Session of the Open-ended Intergovernmental Working Group on Transnational Corporations and Other Business Enterprises with Respect to Human Rights*, 23–27 October 2017, http://webtv.un.org/search/opening-of-session-3rd-session-of-open-ended-intergovernmental-working-group-on-transnational-corporations/5622067547001/?term=Session (last accessed 8 February 2018).

Responding to this challenge requires consistent international standards that ensure corporations comply with human rights wherever they operate. At the same time, these international standards must fit the requirements of diverse political and economic national contexts.[24]

The ITI can play an important role in framing the UNGPs' global governance approach by providing much-needed legal guidance in areas of ongoing concern such as extraterritorial human rights protection.[25] The UNGPs require states 'to protect against human rights abuse within their territory *and/or* jurisdiction',[26] which sidelines the contentious issue of extraterritorial human rights obligations.[27] Meanwhile, the UN Treaty Bodies have called upon some EU Member States to take appropriate legislative, judicial and administrative steps to prevent and redress corporate-related human rights violations committed outside their territories.[28] An international B&HR treaty could not only contribute to developing a consistent international approach to extraterritorial human rights protection. It would also mitigate concerns raised during the OEIGWG debate that (unilateral) assertions of extraterritorial jurisdiction may unduly interfere with time-honoured principles of sovereign equality and territorial integrity.[29] The OEIGWG discussion document places a strong emphasis on clarifying the scope and supporting the implementation of the state duty to protect human rights in complementarity with the UNGPs.[30] Given the very early stage of negotiations, it would be unwise to prejudge the political feasibility of reaching an international agreement – not least

24 See UNWGB&HR, *Guidance on National Action Plans on Business and Human Rights*, op. cit., para. 4.

25 O. de Schutter, 'Towards a new treaty on business and human rights'. *Business and Human Rights Journal*, 2015, 1, 41 ff.

26 UNHRC, *Guiding Principles on Business and Human Rights: Implementing the United Nations' 'Protect, Respect and Remedy' Framework*, op. cit., para. 1, emphasis added.

27 See further D. Augenstein and D. Kinley, 'Beyond the 100 Acre Wood: in which international human rights law finds new ways to tame global corporate power'. *The International Journal of Human Rights*, 2015, 19, 828–848.

28 Committee on the Elimination of Racial Discrimination, *Concluding Observations: United Kingdom of Great Britain and Northern Ireland*, CERD/C/GBR/CO/18-20, 14 September 2011; Human Rights Committee, *Concluding Observations on the Sixth Periodic Report of Germany, Adopted by the Committee at its 106th Session*, CCPR/C/DEU/CO/6, November 2012.

29 OEIGWG, *Draft Report on the Third Session of the Open-ended Intergovernmental Working Group on Transnational Corporations and Other Business Enterprises with Respect to Human Rights*, op. cit., paras. 25, 103–106. For examples from different regulatory domains on how international agreements can successfully mitigate concerns about extraterritorial jurisdiction see J. Zerk, 'Extraterritorial jurisdiction: lessons for the business and human rights sphere from six regulatory areas'. *Corporate Social Responsibility Initiative Working Paper No.* 59, Harvard University: Cambridge, MA, John F. Kennedy School of Government, 2010.

30 OEIGWG, *Elements for the Draft Legally Binding Instrument on Transnational Corporations and Other Business Enterprises with Respect to Human Rights*, op. cit.

because the present piecemeal approach to extraterritorial human rights protection also risks undermining an effective global implementation of the UNGPs.[31]

The European Implementation of the UNGPs via NAPs

While the SRSGBHR enshrined the idea that corporate respect for human rights is mandated by businesses' social licence to operate, this did not obviate concerns that his 'protect, respect and remedy' framework lacked binding legal effect. Accordingly, the UNGPs have frequently been criticized for their 'soft' and/or 'voluntary' nature, ultimately failing to require, and, where necessary, enforce, corporate respect for human rights.[32] However, equating the ITI with state compulsion and the UNGPs with corporate voluntarism tends to overlook that both processes deploy different regulatory techniques for *legally* binding corporations to international human rights standards. Whereas the ITI envisages international legal reform, the effectiveness of the UNGPs crucially depends on their diligent national implementation through states' domestic law. This, in turn, elucidates the critical role NAPs can play in mitigating ITI's concern that the UNGPs fail to ensure corporate legal accountability for human rights violations.

One important consequence of the UNGPs' polycentric governance approach is that states, as part of their duty to protect, have to assume a proactive role in ensuring corporate respect for human rights.[33] The concrete requirements this entails for the implementation of the UNGPs via NAPs are elaborated in international NAP guidance developed by the UN Working Group and the Danish Institute for Human Rights in collaboration with the International Corporate Accountability Roundtable (hereinafter 'ICAR').[34] States have to mainstream human rights into all business-related laws and policies. Their NAPs should address the full scope of the UNGPs and work towards an effective implementation of all three pillars of the 'protect, respect and remedy'

31 As it has become commonplace to compare the ITI with the dystopian experience of negotiating the 2003 UN Draft Norms, it should be noted that the latter, too, were arguably abandoned prematurely; see D. Kinley and R. Chambers, 'The UN human rights norms for corporations: the private implications of public international law" *Human Rights Law Review*, 2006, 3, 447 ff.

32 See, for example, C. Lopez, 'The "Ruggie process": from legal obligations to corporate social responsibility?'. In S. Deva and D. Bilchitz (eds), *Human Rights Obligations of Business*. Cambridge: Cambridge University Press, 2013, 58 ff.

33 This section draws on D. Augenstein, M. Dawson and P. Thielboerger, 'Implementing the UNGPs in the European Union: towards an open method of coordination for business and human rights'. *EUI Working Paper LAW 2017/01*, Fiesole: European University Institute, 2017.

34 UNWGB&HR, *Guidance on National Action Plans on Business and Human Rights*, op. cit.; DIHR & ICAR, *National Action Plans on Business and Human Rights: A Toolkit for the Development, Implementation, and Review of State Commitments to Business and Human Rights Frameworks*, June 2014.

framework.[35] To create the necessary leverage between the different governance systems, states should adopt a 'smart mix' of mandatory and voluntary measures in preventing and redressing corporate-related human rights violations.[36] Moreover, these measures should 'extend to all matters in the state's jurisdiction, including matters outside the state's territorial jurisdiction'.[37]

Affirming the EU's support of the UNGPs, the 2016 Council of the European Union's Conclusions welcomed the European Commission's intention to develop an Action Plan on Responsible Business Conduct that should outline an overall European policy framework on B&HR. They further noted that 'EU Member States have taken the lead internationally on developing and adopting NAPs to implement the UNGPs or integrating [them] into national Corporate Social Responsibility (CSR) Strategies'.[38] Already in 2011, the European Commission had published a new strategy on CSR in which it requested the EU Member States to develop NAPs to implement the UNGPs.[39] At present, 13 EU Member States have released NAPs on B&HR (Belgium, Denmark, Finland, France, Germany, Italy, Ireland, Lithuania, the Netherlands, Poland, Spain, Sweden, and the United Kingdom). The majority of member states have furthermore published NAPs on CSR that also refer to human rights.[40] In terms of quantity if not quality, this makes the EU a global leader in developing NAPs on B&HR.

However, the European NAPs have also been criticized for shortcomings in process and content. A 2014 assessment of the UK, Dutch, Danish and Finnish NAPs conducted by ICAR and the European Coalition for Corporate Justice (hereinafter, 'ECCJ') suggests that while states have made an explicit commitment to the UNGPs, their NAPs focus heavily on past actions and soft/voluntary measures at the expense of exploring forward-looking and regulatory options. Commitments to future action tend to remain vague and lack sufficient information about concrete steps to be taken and the agencies responsible for their implementation.[41] In a similar vein, the European Network of National Human Rights Institutions (hereinafter 'ENNHRI') has deplored that 'member states' published NAPs to date mostly describe historical actions, and lack

35 UNWGB&HR, *Guidance on National Action Plans on Business and Human Rights*, op. cit., para. 12.

36 Ibid., 13.

37 DIHR & ICAR, *National Action Plans on Business and Human Rights: A Toolkit for the Development, Implementation, and Review of State Commitments to Business and Human Rights Frameworks*, op. cit., para. 45.

38 Council of the European Union, *Council Conclusions on Business and Human Rights*, op. cit., paras 5–6.

39 European Commission, *A renewed EU strategy 2011–14 for Corporate Social Responsibility*, COM (2011) 681 final.

40 European Commission, 'Corporate Social Responsibility: National Public Policies in the European Union', June 2014.

41 ICAR & ECCJ, *Assessment of Existing National Action Plans on Business and Human Rights*, November 2014, paras. 3–5.

specific commitments capable of demonstrably improving UNGPs implementation at national level'.[42] These critical assessments are largely confirmed by more recent studies that draw on a broader sample of NAPs.[43]

A main weakness of existing EU Member States' NAPs is that they cover the three pillars of the UNGPs unevenly. Many NAPs focus on pillar two at the expense of exploring the full scope of the state duty to protect against corporate human rights abuse. One consequence is that, as with the Danish NAP, measures concerning pillar two appear reminiscent of the old 'voluntary' approach to CSR in that they heavily rely on corporate self-regulation and access to non-judicial remedies.[44] Relatedly, the vast majority of state actions listed under pillar one are confined to soft measures such as guidance, awareness raising and training. While important, such measures are not suitable to address well-documented protection gaps in the legal framework governing B&HR, particularly in the area of access to justice and effective remedies.[45] As the 2017 update of the ICAR & ECCJ assessment notes, 'one of the most significant weaknesses of the content of the assessed NAPs thus far is their failure to sufficiently explore regulatory options to ensure adequate human rights protection and access to remedy'.[46]

The failure to adopt a 'smart mix' of voluntary and mandatory instruments inhibits a proper alignment of the three pillars that would allow states to use their political and financial leverage in incentivizing or requiring corporations to respect human rights. The NAPs' approach to human rights due diligence – the heart of pillar two – is a good example. Human rights due diligence is not only relevant in relation to the corporate responsibility to respect in that it enables businesses to manage stakeholder-related risks. Requiring human rights due diligence is equally a means for states to comply with their duty to protect human rights.[47] The EU Member States' NAPs fail to sufficiently operationalize this mutually reinforcing relationship between pillars one and two. The Dutch government, for example, commits to taking a more proactive role in implementing the UNGPs and to analysing its current regulatory mix as applied to human rights due diligence. However, the Dutch NAP (currently under review) largely confines itself to listing supportive government actions and does not provide for legislative and enforcement measures. As

42 European Network of National Human Rights Institutions, *Recommendations for the next EU Strategy on CSR*, April 2015, para. 2.

43 Augenstein, Dawson and Thielboerger, op. cit.; European Parliament, *Implementation of the UN Guiding Principles on Business and Human Rights*, 2017, paras. 39–42.

44 Danish Government, *Danish National Action Plan: Implementation of the UN Guiding Principles on Business and Human Rights*, March 2014, paras. 17–18.

45 UNHRC, *Improving Accountability and Access to Remedy for Victims of Business-related Human Rights Abuse*, op. cit.

46 ICAR, European Coalition for Corporate Justice & Dejusticia, *Assessments of Existing National Action Plans (NAPs) on Business and Human Rights – August 2017 Update*, 2017.

47 Ruggie, 'Regulating Multinationals', op. cit., 4.

concerns the latter, the NAP concludes that consultations have 'failed to produce consensus on whether the obligations of Dutch companies in relation to CSR are adequately regulated by law'.[48]

To achieve the leverage required for operationalizing the UNGPs' polycentric governance framework, states' 'smart mix' of mandatory and voluntary measures should include extraterritorial instruments that reach out to corporate practice abroad. The UN working group guidance recommends, in line with the approach suggested by the SRSGBHR,[49] that 'measures outlined in the NAP take full advantage of the leverage home states have in order to effectively prevent, address and redress extraterritorial impacts of corporations domiciled within their territory and/or jurisdiction'.[50] In a similar vein, ENNHRI has urged the European Commission to develop NAP guidance emphasizing 'that NAPs extend in scope, like the UNGPs, to matters both inside and outside the state's territorial jurisdiction'.[51] There is some best practice in the EU Member States concerning the use of extraterritorial instruments in the B&HR domain, both legislative and court-driven.[52] Nevertheless, the relevant provisions in existing NAPs are very weak. Some NAPs confine themselves to expressing an expectation that corporations respect human rights when operating abroad or remain entirely silent on the issue. Other NAPs, including the Dutch and the Danish one, doubt the usefulness of extraterritorial instruments and envisage setting up working groups to discuss their need and feasibility.[53] This reluctance to endorse extraterritorial human rights protection sits uneasy with a basic premise that appears to inform all EU member state NAPs, namely that corporate human rights abuse is most likely to happen abroad.

48 Dutch Ministry of Foreign Affairs, *National Action Plan on Business and Human Rights*, April 2014, paras. 28, 41.

49 The SRSGBHR distinguished between 'direct extraterritorial jurisdiction' and 'domestic measures with extraterritorial implications'. While the former refers to 'jurisdiction exercised directly in relation to actors or activities overseas', the latter 'relies on territory as a jurisdictional basis even though it may have extraterritorial implications'; UNHRC, *Business and Human Rights: Further Steps towards the Operationalisation of the 'Protect, Respect, and Remedy'*, op. cit., para. 55.

50 UNWGB&HR, *Guidance on National Action Plans on Business and Human Rights*, op. cit., para. 18.

51 European Network of National Human Rights Institutions, *Recommendations for the Next EU Strategy on CSR*, op. cit., para. 2.

52 For an overview see European Parliament, *Implementation of the UN Guiding Principles on Business and Human Rights*, op. cit.

53 Dutch Ministry of Foreign Affairs, *National Action Plan on Business and Human Rights*, op. cit., para. 39; Danish Government, *Danish National Action Plan: Implementation of the UN Guiding Principles on Business and Human Rights*, op. cit., para. 16.

Conclusion

In his final report to the UNHRC, the SRSGBHR noted that

> Council endorsement of the Guiding Principles, by itself, will not bring B&HR challenges to an end. But it will mark the end of the beginning: by establishing a common global platform for action, on which cumulative progress can be built, step-by-step, without foreclosing any other promising long-term development.[54]

The UNGPs have been remarkably successful in forging a global consensus on B&HR. Nevertheless, it seems unlikely that they can dispense with the need for legal reform given the significant role the doctrinal constrictions of international (human rights) law play in today's B&HR predicament. The EU delegation noted in its contribution to the first session of the OEIGWG that 'the absence of an international legally binding treaty does not prevent the imposition of binding commitments for businesses at national level/regional level in accordance with existing international obligations'.[55] *A minori ad maius*, the success of the SRSGBHR's polycentric global governance approach crucially depends on states' diligent implementation of the UNGPs, including through binding instruments that reach out to corporate practice abroad. The shortcomings of EU member state NAPs in this regard not only condone double standards of human rights protection in home and host states of corporate investment but also incentivize globally operating business entities to free-ride on inter-state competition. Against this background, the current chapter argued that the EU should assume a more proactive position in exploring complementarities between the ITI and the UNGPs. On the one hand, the ITI offers a platform for reaching an international agreement on the appropriate scope of extraterritorial human rights protection in the B&HR domain. On the other hand, without reinforced state efforts at implementation, the consensus that crystallized around the UNGPs in 2011 could turn out to stifle further progress in building a more effective global regime on B&HR, at least from the perspective of the developing world that continues to bear the brunt of corporate-related human rights violations.

54 UNHRC, *Guiding Principles on Business and Human Rights: Implementing the United Nations' 'Protect, Respect and Remedy' Framework*, op. cit., para. 13.

55 EU, *Submission to the First Session of the Intergovernmental Working Group*, op. cit.

Part I

The State Duty to Protect Human Rights

The European Perspective

4 Enforcing the State Duty to Protect under the UN Guiding Principles on Business and Human Rights

Strasbourg Views

Marco Fasciglione

Introduction: The Rise of the Business and Human Rights Agenda within the Council of Europe

In recent years, highly publicized human rights violations that have occurred in the context of business operations have highlighted the need for accountability on the part of economic players and heightened the acknowledgment of the impact that businesses have on the enjoyment of human rights. Increasingly, the asymmetry between the operational capacities of MNCs and the regulatory capabilities of states have contributed to human rights abuse and have led to efforts to increase responsible business conduct by enhancing respect of human rights and to prevent and to remedy any negative impact on human rights. The adoption in 2011 of the UNGPs[1] has finally indicated a global standard to be applied by states and private actors in order to prevent business-related violations of human rights. The UNGPs have been internationally acknowledged and are being recognized by several major international organizations and institutions as a basis for the development of their own B&HR policies and standards.

As far as the CoE regional system is concerned, this system, unlike the EU, has long been absent from the international debate on human rights and business. The development within this organization of a policy framework on the impact of corporations' activities on human rights, dates back to 2009–2010 when the CoE Parliamentary Assembly adopted its Recommendation No. 1858 (2009) on Private military and security firms and the erosion of the state monopoly on the use of force, and Resolution 1757 (2010) (adopted on 27 September 2010) and Recommendation 1936 (2010) (of 6 October 2010), both on human rights and business. More recently, the Declaration on B&HR, of 16 April 2014, and the Recommendation CM/Rec(2016)3 on Human Rights and

1 UNHRC, *Guiding Principles on Business and Human Rights: Implementing the United Nations 'Protect, Respect and Remedy' Framework*, Report of the UNSRSG on the issue of human rights and transnational corporations and other business enterprises, John Ruggie, UN Doc. A/HRC/17/31, 21 March 2011.

Business, of 2 March 2016, have completed the formulation of a CoE policy framework in this area. As far as the state's duty to protect is concerned, the latter Recommendation recalls that both negative and positive obligations stem from the requirement that states 'secure' the rights and freedoms established by the ECHR (hereinafter also 'the Convention') to everyone within their jurisdiction (Article 1 ECHR) and that, specifically with regard to the positive obligations doctrine, the ECtHR (hereinafter also 'the Court') has found a way of monitoring, even though only indirectly, corporate compliance with human rights.[2] The following pages are intended to review substantive and procedural standards developed in this area under the ECHR system.

The State's Duty to Protect Human Rights in Business: General Remarks

It is generally acknowledged that by addressing the state's duty to protect against business impact on human rights, the first pillar of the UNGPs transposes a principle that is part of the international human rights regime's very foundation, i.e. the duty to protect human rights from violations of non-state actors. As observed by the UNSRSG, this duty is enshrined in the state's obligation 'to "ensure" (or some functionally equivalent verb) the enjoyment or realization of those rights by rights holders'.[3] Under the international human rights regime, accordingly, states bear a positive obligation to secure the human rights of everyone under their jurisdiction by taking all reasonable and appropriate steps in protecting individuals against violations perpetrated by non-state actors, including business enterprises. Also, 'guidance from international human rights bodies suggests that the state duty to protect applies to all recognized rights that private parties are capable of impairing and to all types of business enterprises'.[4] This duty extends to all organs of the state and requires that states take all measures that could reasonably be adopted to prevent the occurrence of a human rights violation.

General Comment No. 31 by the UNHRC provides a good overview on how this mechanism applies even with regard to corporations. It confirms that under the ICCPR (hereinafter also 'the Covenant')

> the positive obligations on States Parties to ensure Covenant rights will only be fully discharged if individuals are protected by the state, not just against violations of Covenant rights by its agents, but also against acts committed

2 See CoE Parliamentary Assembly, *Human Rights and business – Recommendation CM/Rec(2016)3 of the Committee of Ministers to Member States (2016)*, 2 March 2016, para. 15.

3 See UNHRC, *Business and Human Rights: Towards Operationalizing the 'Protect, Respect, Remedy' Framework*, Report of the UNSRSG on the issue of human rights and transnational corporations and other business enterprises, John Ruggie, UN Doc. A/HRC/11/13, 22 April 2009, para. 13.

4 Ibid.

> by private persons or entities that would impair the enjoyment of Covenant rights in so far as they are amenable to application between private persons or entities[5]

and further explains that states could breach Covenant obligations if they permit or fail 'to take appropriate measures or to exercise due diligence to prevent, punish, investigate or redress the harm caused by such acts by private persons or entities'.[6] The reference to due diligence clarifies that, whereas negative obligations involve duties of result, the duty to protect enshrined in a positive obligation incorporates a standard of conduct: in other words, states are not per se responsible for human rights abuse by private actors; they may, however, breach their international human rights law obligations when such abuse can be attributed to them given their failure to take appropriate steps to prevent, investigate, punish, and redress private actors' abuse.[7] Within these parameters, states have discretion as to how to fulfil their duty, with the main human rights treaties generally contemplating a variety of legislative, administrative and judicial measures.[8]

This scheme is applied by the most important regional human rights tribunals, including the ECtHR: according to the Strasbourg Court's case law, states bear two kinds of duties in relation to corporate negative impact on human rights: a positive obligation to protect human rights from corporate violations acting as third parties, and a negative obligation to respect human rights in relation to corporations acting as state agents.

The State's Duty to Protect, Positive Obligations, Corporate Human Rights Violations and the ECHR

It is well known that the 'structural gap' of the contemporary international system of human rights protection involves an 'imbalance in the scope of human rights protection between individual and businesses' and, as far as the ECHR system is concerned, this imbalance implies that

> while a company may bring a case before the Court claiming a violation by a state authority of its rights protected under the [ECHR], an individual alleging a violation of his or her rights by a private company cannot effectively raise his or her claims before this jurisdiction.[9]

5 UNHRC, *Nature of the General Legal Obligation Imposed on States Parties to the Covenant*, General Comment No. 31, UN Doc. ICCPR/C/21/Rev.1/Add.13, 26 May 2004, para. 8.

6 Ibid.

7 Report of the UNSRSG, *Business and human rights: Towards operationalizing*, op. cit., para. 14.

8 For a general analysis on the duty to protect human rights see E. Klein (ed.), *The Duty to Protect and Ensure Human Rights*. Berlin: Verlag, 2000.

9 See CoE Parliamentary Assembly, *Human Rights and Business*, Resolution 1757 (2010), 27 September 2010, para. 4.

Under Articles 33 and 34 of the ECHR, individual and inter-state applications may only be brought against High Contracting Parties and, according to Article 35 para. 3(a), any application brought against a private company is inadmissible as being incompatible *ratione personae* with the Convention provisions. Essentially, corporations are not entitled to passive *locus standi* within the ECHR system. Similarly, rights enshrined in the Convention do not contain any horizontal effect: the Court has in fact never recognized the principle of the third-party effect (the so-called *Drittwirkung*), applied in some domestic jurisdictions, according to which human rights may be considered as not only enforceable against the state but also directly against other natural or legal persons.[10]

Even if the ECHR does not directly impose obligations on non-state actors, it nevertheless requires Contracting Parties to protect human rights by the negative impact stemming from their conducts, including from the business operations of corporate entities. Accordingly, while private actors may not breach the Convention in a way that could give rise to a civil claim against them before the Court, the latter has accepted that corporations may exercise an 'interference' with, or even 'violate' the rights and freedoms guaranteed by the Convention.[11] Notably, in such circumstances, human rights violations by corporate operations are committed with the 'acquiescence' of Contracting Parties in the sense that they have failed to take all reasonable and appropriate measures to protect the individual against corporate negative impact. Therefore, in these cases, even though Contracting Parties may not be regarded as directly responsible for the interference of the enjoyment of human rights, they bear indirect responsibility for this interference on the grounds of violating their positive obligations and may be subject to a claim before the Strasbourg Court. The Court's own viewpoint is that the Convention creates obligations for states which may involve the adoption of measures 'even in the sphere of the relations of individuals between themselves'.[12] Such positive obligations extend to protective, preventive, and affirmative action, which may entail the adoption of measures (both legislative and policy measures, and deployment of resources, etc.) to ensure that rights can be freely exercised without interference from private individuals. The ECtHR has also read specific procedural obligations in most substantive articles

10 On this subject, A. Clapham, *Human Rights in the Private Sphere*. Oxford: Oxford University Press, 1993, 180.

11 The term 'interference' has been used in *Storck* case where the Court admitted that non-state actors may 'interfere' with the right to liberty (see ECtHR, *Storck v. Germany*, App. No. 61603/00, Judgment, 16 June 2005, para. 110). The term 'violate' has been used in 2001 in *Cyprus v. Turkey*, where the Court noted that 'that the acquiescence or connivance of the authorities of a Contracting State in the acts of private individuals which violate the Convention rights of other individuals within its jurisdiction may engage that State's responsibility under the Convention' (ECtHR, *Cyprus v. Turkey*, App. No. 25781/94, Judgment, 10 May, 2001, para. 81).

12 ECtHR, *X and Y v. the Netherlands*, App. No. 8978/80, Judgment, 26 March 1985, para. 23; ECtHR, *Case of Moldovan and Others v. Romania (No. 2)*, App. Nos. 41138/98, 64320/01, Judgment, 12 July 2005.

of the ECHR such as Articles 2 (right to life), 3 (prohibition of torture), 4 (prohibition of slavery and forced labour), and 8 (right to respect for private and family life), thereby admitting the existence of a procedural positive obligation to investigate situations of potential risk of human rights abuses when the matter comes to the attention of the authorities.

The case law of the Court in this field area is wide-ranging and involves several key situations. For instance, as to the environmental pollution engendered by corporate activities, the Court has recognized that positive obligations of Contracting States may be inferred by the necessity to protect the right to life enshrined in Article 2,[13] or the right to respect the private and family life set out in Article 8,[14] and that in these situations state responsibility stems from the 'failure to regulate private industry'.[15] In some of these cases the failure to provide the applicants an avenue for effectively reviewing the governmental policy, which has led to human rights interference by private actors, has been deemed by the Court to also amount to a violation of Article 13. A related area is represented by those situations in which the state's failure to control private-sector activities has resulted in acoustic pollution negatively impacting on the right to private and family life under Article 8.[16]

Another relevant area in which states bear positive obligations in respect of private entities' activities is the protection of individuals from treatments contrary to human dignity. Such treatments may fall within the prohibition of torture and inhuman and degrading treatment or punishment included in Article 3, or within the prohibition of slavery and forced labour set out in Article 4. As far as Article 3 is concerned, the Court has recognized that this provision requires states to take measures 'to ensure that individuals within their jurisdiction are not subjected to torture or inhuman or degrading treatment, including such ill-treatment administered by private individuals', which in principle should

13 ECtHR, *Öneryıldız v. Turkey*, App. No. 48939/99, Judgment, 30 November 2004, para. 71; ECtHR, *Kolyadenko and Others v. Russia*, App. Nos. 17423/05, 20534/05, 20678/05, 23263/05, 24283/05 and 35673/05, Judgment, 28 February 2012, especially para. 89 ff.

14 ECtHR, *López Ostra v. Spain*, App. No. 16798/90, Judgment, 9 December 1994, para. 51; ECtHR, Taşkin *and Others v. Turkey*, App. No. 46117/99, Judgment, 10 December 2004, para. 113; ECtHR, *Fadeyeva v. Russia*, App. No. 55723/00, Judgment, 9 June 2005, para. 89; ECtHR, *Tatar v. Romania*, App. No. 67021/01, Judgment, 27 January 2009, para. 88; ECtHR, *Budayeva and Others v. Russia*, App. Nos. 15339/02, 21166/02, 20058/02, 11673/02 and 15343/02), Judgment, 20 March 2008, paras. 129–132. The Court declared that states have the positive obligation to take all reasonable and adequate measures to protect the rights under art. 8 of the Convention, including a legislative and administrative system that effectively prevents environmental damages and protects the people on their territory, even where the activity is stemming from a private corporation.6

15 ECtHR, *Fadeyeva v. Russia*, op. cit., para. 89.

16 ECtHR, *Hatton and Others v United Kingdom* (Grand Chamber), App. No. 36022/97, Judgment, 7 August 2003, paras. 98, 119–120.

also include private companies.[17] As far as Article 4 is concerned, in this area the doctrine of the state's positive obligations has undergone significant development in recent decades, especially with regard to protection of domestic workers,[18] labour exploitation,[19] human trafficking, and migrant labour exploitation.[20] Again, also in such situations, state responsibility may be entailed by violations committed by corporate actors.

In the same vein, the case law of the ECtHR in the sector of labour-related disputes is very instructive. For instance, the Court has held the state's positive obligations to protect human rights, even when human rights violations occurred within corporate business activities, in regard to the freedom of assembly and association (Article 11) for detrimental corporate activities of the right to join trade unions.[21] Similarly, Article 8 has been invoked for the respect of safety standards in employment in situations where national authorities have been judged by the Court to have failed to ensure a legal framework of safety regulations to protect deep sea divers from negative impacts on their health.[22] Article 8 has also been invoked with regard to video surveillance in the workplace, performed by employers, when the employees have been unaware of such

17 ECtHR, *Z and Others v. the United Kingdom*, App. No. 29392/95, Judgment, 10 May 2001 (Grand Chamber), para. 73. According to the Court, these measures should provide effective protection, in particular, of children and other vulnerable persons and 'include reasonable steps to prevent ill-treatment of which the authorities had or ought to have had knowledge' (ibid.).

18 In ECtHR, *Siliadin v. France*, App. No. 73316/01, Judgment, 26 July 2005, para. 112, the Court has stated that 'Member States have a positive obligation under Article 4 of the Convention to penalise and effectively prosecute any act aimed at maintaining a person in such domestic servitude'.

19 In ECtHR, *C.N. and V. v. France*, App. No. 67724/09, Judgment, 11 October 2012, para. 104, and in ECtHR, *C.N. v. the United Kingdom*, App. No. 4239/08, Judgment, 13 November 2012, para. 65 ff., the Court has stressed that art. 4 of the Convention encompasses both the positive obligation to penalize and effectively prosecute actions in breach of art. 4 as well as a procedural obligation to investigate situations of potential exploitation when the matter comes to the attention of the authorities.

20 In ECtHR, *Rantsev v. Cyprus and Russia*, App. No. 25965/04, Judgment, 7 January 2010, para. 284, while admitting that human trafficking by itself falls within the scope of art. 4 ECHR, the Court has stressed that states have not only a positive obligation under this provision to put in place an appropriate legal and administrative framework to combat trafficking, but they have also to put in place 'adequate measures regulating *businesses often used as a cover for human trafficking*' (emphasis added). See also the recent decision in ECtHR, *Chowdury and Others v. Greece*, App. No. 21884/15, Judgment, 30 March 2017, paras. 103–105, in which Bangladeshi strawberry pickers were subjected to forced labour in a private farm.

21 ECtHR, *National Union of Belgian Police v. Belgium*, App. No. 4464/70, Judgment, 27 October 1975, para. 44; ECtHR, *Wilson, National Union of Journalists and Others v. the United Kingdom*, App. Nos. 30668/96, 30671/96 and 30678/96, Judgment, 2 July 2002, para. 41; ECtHR, *Redfearn v. the United Kingdom*, App. No. 47335/06, Judgment, 6 November 2012, para. 42 ff.

22 ECtHR, *Vilnes and Others v. Norway* [Grand Chamber], App. No. 52806/09 22703/10, Judgment, 5 December 2013, para. 244. The Court ruled that the national authorities had failed to take the necessary precautions ensuring that the companies employing divers observed full transparency about essential information.

surveillance. Here the Court observed that an employer's use of personal information (such as that relating to telephone, email, and internet use) may be disproportionate in the absence of a law regulating such monitoring.[23] Relationships among (corporate) employers and employees may be relevant to the positive obligations that states bear under the ECHR in terms of the prohibition of discrimination in the workplace when they have failed to ensure the enforcement of domestic court decisions. Such decisions include those finding discrimination on grounds of sex in favour of an employee asking for the reduction in working hours in order to look after their son,[24] or where the employer has not protected an employee from being dismissed for being HIV positive in response to pressure from other employees in the company,[25] and where the employer failed to provide clear and effective protection against the discrimination of an employee on the grounds of trade union membership.[26]

Finally, judgments where the Court reviews national court decisions in disputes between individuals and companies are another interesting source of corporate human rights standards that may be enforced through the state's duty to protect. This applies, for example, to defamation proceedings brought by MNCs against NGOs' campaigns criticizing a corporation's CSR policy, where legal aid had not been granted to the NGO. Here the Court has observed that the absence of legal aid amounted to a disproportionate interference with the applicants' rights of freedom of expression and violated the right to a fair trial (Article 6).[27] It goes without saying that the abovementioned list of states'

23 While ECtHR, *Copland v. the United Kingdom*, App. No. 62617/00, Judgment, 3 April 2007, concerned an employee of a statutory body administered by the state, the recent case ECtHR, *Bărbulescu v. Romania*, App. No. 61496/08, Judgment, 5 September 2017, paras. 135–141, involved an employee of a private enterprise. The Grand Chamber concluded that the domestic tribunals, in reviewing the decision of the applicant's employer to dismiss him after having monitored his electronic communications, failed to strike a fair balance between the interests at stake: namely Mr Bărbulescu's right to respect for his private life and correspondence, on the one hand, and his employer's right to take measures in order to ensure the smooth running of the company, on the other. However, it must be noted that where video surveillance operation has been carried out for limited periods, with limited scope and the information has only been handled by few persons for the purposes of court proceedings, they do not raise an issue under art. 8 (ECtHR, *Köpke v. Germany*, App. No. 420/07, Admissibility decision, 5 October 2010, para. 2).

24 ECtHR, *Garcia Mateos v. Spain*, App. No. 38285/09, Judgment, 9 February 2013, in which the Court found a violation of Art. 6 in conjunction with art. 14.

25 ECtHR, *I.B. v. Greece*, App. No. 552/10, Judgment, 3 October 2013, para. 71 (art. 8 in conjunction with art. 14), finding that such dismissal was discriminatory and could not be justified by the need to 'preserve the working environment in the company'.

26 ECtHR, *Danilenkov and Others v. Russia*, App. No. 67336/01, Judgment, 30 July 2009, paras. 130–136 (art. 11 in conjunction with art. 14).

27 ECtHR, *Steel and Morris v. the United Kingdom*, App. No. 68416/01, Judgment, 15 February 2005, para. 72. In this case, also known as 'McDonald's case', the lack of procedural fairness and equality found by the Court also gave rise to a breach of art. 10 in respect to the right to freedom of expression.

positive obligations when human rights violations occur within corporate operations is not exhaustive and is subject to further enlargement.[28]

Turning to the procedural positive obligations with regard to corporate negative impact on human rights, these encompass a series of measures that Contracting States are required to adopt in order to enable public participation, or to ensure an informed decision-making process grounded on investigations, scientific studies, and environmental impact assessments. According to the ECtHR, this requires consideration of 'all the procedural aspects, including the type of policy or decision involved'[29] as well as the quality of the decision-making process which 'must necessarily involve appropriate investigations and studies in order to allow [authorities] to strike a fair balance between the various conflicting interests at stake'.[30] State regulation 'must also provide for appropriate procedures, taking into account the technical aspects of the activity in question, for identifying shortcomings in the processes concerned and any errors committed by those responsible at different levels'.[31] Similarly, states are required to put in place 'a legislative and administrative framework designed to provide effective deterrence'[32] against threats to human rights including, in case of egregious violations, the duty to ensure an adequate response – judicial or otherwise – so that the legislative and administrative framework set up to protect rights is properly implemented, and any breaches of that right are repressed and punished. The judicial system, in particular,

> must make provision for an independent and impartial official investigation procedure that satisfies certain minimum standards as to effectiveness and is capable of ensuring that criminal penalties are applied where lives are lost as a result of a dangerous activity if and to the extent that this is justified by the findings of the investigation [...].[33]

For example, states are under a positive obligation to secure the right to life by putting in place effective criminal-law provisions to deter the commission of offences: these provisions must be backed up by law-enforcement machinery for the prevention, suppression, and sanctioning of breaches.

28 Other relevant areas include privacy and media freedom relationships, the right to manifest own religion (with the recent *Eweida and Others v. the United Kingdom*, App. Nos. 48420/10, 59842/10, 51671/10 and 36516/10, Judgment, 15 January 2013).

29 ECtHR, *Zammit Maempel v. Malta*, App. No. 24202/10, Judgment, 22 November 2011, para. 62; ECtHR, *Hatton and Others*, op. cit., para. 104; ECtHR, *Udovičić v. Croatia*, App. No. 27310/09, Judgment, 24 April 2014, para. 151.

30 ECtHR, *Zammit Maempel*, op. cit., para. 70.

31 ECtHR, *Öneryıldız v. Turkey*, op. cit., para. 90.

32 ECtHR, *Oneryildiz*, op. cit., para. 89. See, *mutatis mutandis*, ECtHR, *Perrin v. the United Kingdom*, App. No. 5446/03, Judgment, 18 October 2005; ECtHR, *Van Anraat v. the Netherlands*, App. No. 65389/09, Judgment, 6 July 2010.

33 ECtHR, *Oneryildiz*, op. cit., para., 94.

From this perspective, the state's duty to protect has both a preventative and a remedial function and its procedural positive obligations are consequently strictly intertwined with duties stemming from the right of access to justice (Article 6) as well as the right to an effective remedy (Article 13). Contracting States, accordingly, have the duty to take the necessary steps to prevent denial of justice and ensure the right to effective remedy and reparation. Addressing these challenges requires states to remove substantive, procedural, and practical barriers to remedies. In this area, the Court case law represents a useful source both for enhancing the remedies for victims of human rights violations committed by private companies, and for addressing a wide series of gaps which usually prevent victims of human rights violations, occurring as a result of corporate activities, from having access to remedial mechanisms before national courts.[34]

The State's Obligations to Respect Human Rights in Relation to Corporations' Activities Acting as State Agent

The second typology of duty that states bear with regard to corporate impacts on human rights encompasses the negative obligation to respect human rights in relation to corporations acting as state agents. In these cases, the secondary rule of state responsibility attribution applies and the ECtHR determines on a case-by-case basis whether corporate activities are directly attributable to the state. Criteria used by the Court include the corporation's legal status, the rights conferred upon the corporation by virtue of this status, its institutional independence from the state, its operational independence from the state, and the nature of the corporate activity (performance of 'public function' versus 'ordinary business', including the delegation of core state functions to private entities), and the context in which the corporate activity is carried out (for example, the relevance of the activity for the public good, and privatized state industries with a monopoly position in the market). The Court has applied these criteria when considering corporal punishment in private schools with regard to Article 3 of the Convention,[35] and nuisance from airports whose authority had been privatized in respect of Article 8 of the Convention.[36] Notably, the Court has highlighted that '[…] the State cannot absolve itself from responsibility by

34 On this issue see generally, EU Agency for Fundamental Rights, *Improving Access to Remedy in the Area of Business and Human Rights at the EU Level,* Opinion No. 1/2017, 10 April 2017. For a comment on the Opinion see M. Fasciglione, 'European Union Agency for Fundamental Rights [FRA] Opinion 1/2017', *OXIO – Oxford International Organizations* (online). Oxford: Oxford University Press, 2017, 296.

35 ECtHR, *Costello-Roberts v. the United Kingdom,* App. No. 13134/87, Judgment, 25 March 1993, paras. 25–28.

36 ECtHR, *Powell and Rayner v. the United Kingdom,* App. No. 9310/81, Judgment, 21 February 1990, paras. 37–46.

delegating its obligations to private bodies or individuals'[37] recognizing, therefore, that states' responsibility may also be triggered when state functions have been privatized. In situations where a strong state-business nexus exists, in order to fulfil their duty to protect, states may need to enact regulations or guarantee a certain degree of control to ensure that no violations of human rights occur and the very same corporations that are owned or controlled by the state, and/or that exercise state functions, are subject to the state's duty to protect.[38]

Conclusions

While the ECHR does not directly bind corporations, it imposes negative and positive obligations on states to protect human rights from negative corporate impact. The ECtHR case law in this area is built around three main typologies of state obligations: first, substantive obligations to regulate and control corporate activities including the licensing, setting up and control of dangerous activities and the provision of information about them to the general public; second, procedural obligations to ensure an informed decision-making process encompassing public participation, public investigations, scientific studies, and environmental impact assessments; and third, obligations related to law enforcement and the judicial process, including access to justice and the provision of effective remedies.[39] However, it is important to note that if the explicit demarcation between a state's duty to protect and the corporate responsibility to respect highlights the urgent need for the private sector to respect human rights, it also crystallizes the idea of the primary role that states still continue to play in this area. Such a role is echoed in the emphasis given to the first pillar by the

37 ECtHR, *Costello-Roberts*, cit., para. 27. The same approach may be found in *Storck* in which, with regard to psychiatric institutions run as a private entity, the Court found that Germany remained under a duty to exercise supervision and control over such institutions with regard to the right to liberty (art. 5) (ECtHR, *Storck*, op. cit., para. 103).

38 The UNSRSG has emphasized on various occasions that the expectation on states to protect human rights against corporate violations is particularly high where there exists a strong nexus between the state and the corporation. As the UNSRSG noted in his 2010 Report, 'where companies are owned by and/or act as mere State agents, the State itself may be held legally responsible for such entities' wrongful acts', see UNHRC, *Business and Human Rights: Further Steps toward the Operationalization of the 'Protect, Respect and Remedy' Framework,* Report of the UNSRSG on the issue of human rights and transnational corporations and other business enterprises, John Ruggie, UN Doc A/HRC/14/27, 9 April 2010, para. 27.

39 Less clarity exists as far as the extraterritorial dimension of the state duty to protect against corporate violations of human rights is concerned. In effect, while it seems that, provided there is the existence of a tangible jurisdictional link between states and individuals situated outside their borders, states may fall under the obligation to secure human rights against extraterritorial corporate abuse, it is less clear 'whether the necessary jurisdictional link with the victim can be established by virtue of (*de facto* or *de jure*) control that the State exercises over (constituent parts of) the corporate perpetrator of human rights violations domiciled within its territorial jurisdiction' (D. Augenstein and L. Dziedzic, 'State obligations to regulate and adjudicate corporate activities under the European Convention on Human Rights'. *EUI Working Papers. Law*, 2017, 15, 31).

majority of the National Action Plans adopted to date and in the marginal role of the duties enshrined in the other two pillars.[40]

It is our view that this emphasis on the first pillar's duty to protect simply 'restates' the contemporary level of evolution of the international human rights legal system in which, even if it is certainly admissible that private entities may also be granted the status of right-holders and, in some situations, also of duty-holders, states still remain the 'engine' of any legal mechanisms aimed at protecting human rights from corporate abuses.[41] In other words, when scrutinizing the modalities for enforcing human rights obligations of private economic actors, it must be acknowledged that, in the light of the evolution of international human rights law, this enforcement may still only be realized through the filter of national legal systems. The emphasis by the first pillar's state duty to protect human rights reflects *exactly* this conclusion.

40 In general, on NAPs see U. Cantú Rivera 'Planes de acción nacional sobre empresas y derechos humanos: sobre la instrumentalización del derecho internacional en el ámbito interno'. *Anuario Mexicano de derecho Internacional*, 2017, vol. XVII, 113–144.

41 Acknowledging this situation in our opinion does not *per se* involves the 'belief that the State-centric model in the field of human rights still is an insurmountable paradigm' (see Umberto Cantú Rivera, 'Blurred lines: from international to domestic and vice versa in the field of human rights and business', *ARACÊ – Direitos Humanos em Revista*, 2015, 3, 135–161, 136).

5 Are European Home States of Transnational Corporations Responsible for Their Impacts Abroad under the ECHR?

Claire Methven O'Brien

Introduction

Whether the European home states of TNCs are responsible for the impacts of their corporations abroad under the ECHR[1] is an important and topical question. Many companies domiciled in Europe are present in almost every country of the world via locally incorporated subsidiaries, investment or cross-ownership relations. Further, their impacts on human rights in 'host' states are well documented. This has led to calls for 'home' states of TNCs to control the activities of their foreign subsidiaries. The UNCESCR, for example, has indicated that state parties 'should take steps to prevent human rights contraventions abroad by corporations which have their main seat under their jurisdiction, without infringing the sovereignty or diminishing the obligations of the host States under the Covenant'.[2]

The first pillar of the UN Framework on B&HR comprises the 'state duty to protect' against business-related human rights abuses.[3] UNGP 2 maintains that, 'States should set out clearly the expectation that all business enterprises domiciled in their territory and/or jurisdiction respect human rights throughout their operations'.[4] To this, the Commentary adds:

> At present States are not generally required under international human rights law to regulate the extraterritorial activities of businesses domiciled in

1 Convention for the Protection of Human Rights and Fundamental Freedoms (ECHR) ETS 5, 213 UNTS 222, entered into force on September 3, 1953.

2 UNCESCR, *Statement on the Obligations of States Parties Regarding the Corporate Sector and Economic, Social and Cultural Rights*, E/C.12/2011/1, 20 May 2011, para. 5.

3 UN, *Report of the Special Representative of the Secretary-General, Protect, Respect and Remedy: A Framework for Business and Human Rights*, 7 April 2008, www.reports-and-materials.org/sites/default/files/reports-and-materials/Ruggie-report-7-Apr-2008.pdf (last accessed 11 February 2018).

4 UNHRC, *Human Rights and Transnational Corporations and Other Business Enterprises*, UN Doc. A/HRC/Res. 17/4, 16 June 2011, para. 1 endorsing UNHRC, *Guiding Principles on Business and Human Rights: Implementing the United Nations 'Protect, Respect and Remedy Framework*, UN Doc. A/HRC/17/31, 21 March 2011, Annex, para. 2.

their territory and/or jurisdiction. Nor are they generally prohibited from doing so, provided there is a recognized jurisdictional basis.[5]

Yet, amongst a broader literature on extraterritoriality in the context of globalization,[6] some scholars have concluded that a home state duty to regulate TNCs abroad already exists as a matter of human rights law.[7] Olivier de Schutter, for example, has suggested that there are 'extraterritorial human rights obligations of states including [...] the duty of states to control the corporations they are in a position to influence, wherever such corporations operate', so that the UNGPs 'set the bar clearly below the current state of international human rights law'.[8] Regional human rights bodies such as the ECtHR, according to De Schutter, have 'routinely affirmed that the responsibility of the state may be engaged as a result of its failure to appropriately regulate the conduct of private persons'.[9] Thus, an international instrument 'imposing [...] a duty to protect human rights by regulating the corporations over which the state may exercise influence [...]' would merely render explicit an existing duty and 'dispel any such confusion as might have been created' by the UNGPs.[10]

Augenstein and Kinley, similarly, have maintained that the 'problem of extraterritorial state obligations [...] was effectively sidestepped' by the UNGPs. They observe, first, that states are obliged to protect individuals from corporate violations within their territory, and, second, that businesses can be 'legally bound to

5 OHCHR, *Guiding Principles on Business and Human Rights. Implementing the United Nations 'Protect, Respect and Remedy' Framework*, 2011, www.ohchr.org/Documents/Publications/GuidingPrinciplesBusinessHR_EN.pdf (last accessed 11 February 2018), pp. 3–4.

6 See, for example, F. Coomans and M. T. Kamminga (eds), *Extraterritorial Application of Human Rights Treaties*. Antwerp: Intersentia, 2004; M. Langford *et al.*, *Global Justice, State Duties. The Extraterritorial Scope of Economic, Social and Cultural Rights in International Law*. Cambridge: Cambridge University Press, 2013. See also, ETO Consortium, *Maastricht Principles on Extraterritorial Obligations of States in the area of Economic, Social and Cultural Rights*, January 2013, www.etoconsortium.org/nc/en/main-navigation/library/maastricht-principles/?tx_drblob_pi1%5BdownloadUid%5D=23 (last accessed 18 February 2018).

7 For example, R. McCorquodale and P. Simons, 'Responsibility beyond borders: state responsibility for extraterritorial violations by corporations of international human rights law'. *Modern Law Review*, 2007, 70 (4), 598; F. Coomans, 'The extraterritorial scope of the international covenant on economic, social and cultural rights in the work of the United Nations Committee on Economic, Social and Cultural Rights'. *Human Rights Law Review*, 2011, 11(1), 1; N. Bernaz, 'Enhancing corporate accountability for human rights violations: is extraterritoriality the magic potion?'. *Journal of Business* Ethics, 2013, 117, 493, 506–508.

8 O. De Schutter, 'Towards a new treaty on business and human rights'. *Business and Human Rights Journal*, 2016, 1(1), 41–67.

9 Ibid., 44, footnote omitted.

10 Ibid., 46. A second, 'more radical' formulation of the state duty to regulate was at this point however rejected, specifically, the duty of states to 'control corporations over which they can exercise jurisdiction, including corporations established under the laws of another (host) state that are managed, controlled or owned, by legal or natural persons considered to have the "nationality" of the state concerned, because they are incorporated under the jurisdiction of that state, or have their principal place of business or central administration on the territory of that state' (pp. 46–47).

respect human rights in their global operations via the medium of state regulation and control'. From these premises they conclude that, 'In so far as states are under extra-territorial obligations to protect human rights, such obligations extend to the extraterritorial regulation and control of corporate actors'.[11]

Authority for Ruggie's 'state duty to protect' was drawn principally from UN treaty body commentaries.[12] But subsequent scholarly critiques frequently refer to decisions of the ECtHR. Accordingly, this chapter scrutinizes the case for a home state duty to regulate TNCs' extraterritorial human rights impacts with reference to the ECHR. It considers extraterritorial jurisdiction under the ECHR, then B&HR policy materials recently emanating from the COE in which the issue of extraterritoriality is addressed, and in closing it offers a few concluding reflections.

Extraterritorial Jurisdiction under the ECHR

Although 'jurisdiction' has a variety of meanings in human rights treaties, its most relevant in the present context is to refer to the scope of a state party's obligations.[13] Article 1 ECHR thus provides that 'The High Contracting Parties shall secure to everyone within their jurisdiction the rights and freedoms defined in Section I of this Convention'. Jurisdiction here functions as '[…] a threshold criterion, which must be satisfied in order for treaty obligations to arise in the first place […]'.[14]

Jurisdiction in human rights treaties is distinguishable from jurisdiction under public international law. The latter generally refers to a state's authority to regulate the conduct of persons, both natural and legal, via domestic law.[15] This right, limited by the equal rights and sovereignty of other states,[16] is primarily territorial.[17] One state may not exercise jurisdiction on the territory of another

11 D. Augenstein and D. Kinley, 'When human rights "responsibilities" become "duties": the extra-territorial obligations of states that bind corporations'. In S. Deva and D. Bilchitz (eds), *Human Rights Obligations of Business*. Cambridge: Cambridge University Press, 2013, 275.

12 UN, *Report of the UNSRSG on the Issue of Human Rights and Transnational Corporations and other Business Enterprises Addendum State Responsibilities to Regulate and Adjudicate Corporate Activities under the United Nations Core Human Rights Treaties: an Overview of Treaty Body Commentaries*. UN Doc. A/HRC/4/35/Add.1, 13 February 2007.

13 M. Milanovic, 'From compromise to principle: clarifying the concept of state jurisdiction in human rights treaties'. *Human Rights Law Review*, 2008, 8(3), 411; see generally M. Milanovic, *Extraterritorial Application of Human Rights Treaties. Law, Principles, Policy*, Oxford: Oxford University Press, 2011.

14 Milanovic, 'From Compromise to Principle', op. cit., 416.

15 Milanovic, op. cit., 411, with reference to M. Shaw, *International Law*, 5th edn. Cambridge: Cambridge University Press, 2003, 572; V. Lowe, 'Jurisdiction'. In Malcolm Evans (ed.), *International Law*, 2nd edn. Oxford: Oxford University Press, 2006, 335.

16 F. Mann, 'The doctrine of international jurisdiction revisited after twenty years'. *Recueil des Cours*, 1984, III: 186(9), 20.

17 See further R. Higgins, *Problems and Process*. Oxford: Clarendon Press, 1995, Chs. 4–5.

without consent, invitation or acquiescence, bar the circumstance of occupation. Any right to regulate the activity of corporations abroad is thus exceptional, a rule that applies across the three dimensions of public international law jurisdiction: legislative (or 'prescriptive'), executive (or 'enforcement') and judicial ('adjudicatory'). Accordingly, as reflected by UNGP 2, states may enact rules affecting the rights and duties of parties beyond their borders without consent from other states, only where there is some 'connecting factor' between the state and the target of its regulatory efforts. Such a link may arise, for example, by nationality, whereby a state is allowed to attempt to control the conduct of its nationals ('active personality') or to protect them ('passive personality'); by damage to the state's vital interests ('protective principle'); or by damage to the international community as a whole ('universality').[18]

However, human rights jurisdiction resembles public international law jurisdiction in that it is largely, if not entirely, co-extensive with a state's territory. This is because factual power over actors and events is generally a prerequisite to the fulfilment of a state's human rights obligations. This explains the fact that while the ECHR originally referred to all persons 'residing within the states parties' territories', ultimately its protection was broadened to encompass all persons 'within their jurisdiction', so as also to capture non-resident inhabitants.[19]

Yet, in the context of human rights treaties, the presumption of territoriality may, exceptionally, be overcome. Indeed, the ECtHR has extended jurisdiction beyond state borders in a range of situations that has gradually increased over time. Acts or omissions performed or producing effects outside a state's territory have been addressed either where a state exercises 'effective overall control' over foreign territory; or where it exercises authority and physical control over individuals outside its own territory. With reference to leading emblematic cases, rather than a comprehensive case law analysis, given space constraints, these two approaches are considered in greater depth in turn.

The first approach is sometimes referred to as the 'spatial' model of extraterritorial jurisdiction.[20] *Loizidou* arose from expropriation occurring after Turkey's military invasion of Northern Cyprus in 1974. According to the Court, 'Although Article 1 sets limits on the reach of the Convention, the concept of "jurisdiction" is not restricted to the national territory of the High Contracting Parties […]', but may also arise

> when as a consequence of military action – whether lawful or unlawful – it exercises effective control of an area outside its national territory.

18 C. Methven O'Brien, 'The home state duty to regulate TNCs abroad: a rebuttal'. *Business and Human Rights Journal*, 2018, 3(1), 47–73.

19 A.H. Robertson (ed.), *Collected Edition of the 'Travaux Preparatoires' of the European Convention on Human Rights* Vol. III. The Hague: Martinus Nijhoff, 1976, at 260, cited by Milanovic, op. cit., 433.

20 M. Milanovic, '*Al-Skeini* and *Al-Jedda* in Strasbourg'. *European Journal of International Law*, 2012, 23(1), 121, 122.

> The obligation to secure, in such an area, the rights and freedoms set out in the Convention, derives from the fact of such control whether it be exercised directly, though its armed forces, or through a subordinate local administration.[21]

Affirming this at the merits stage, the Court held that Turkey exercised 'effective overall control' of Northern Cyprus via large numbers of troops engaged in active duties. Consequently, the claimants were within Turkey's 'jurisdiction'.[22] Applying this line of reasoning, in *Cyprus v Turkey* the Court held that Turkish jurisdiction extended also to 'the acts of the local administration which survives by virtue of Turkish military and other support', with reference to the entire range of substantive ECHR rights. In reaching this conclusion, the Court had regard to its mission, under Article 19 ECHR, 'to ensure the observance of the engagements undertaken by the High Contracting Parties' and the Greek government's 'continuing inability to exercise their Convention obligations in northern Cyprus'. Consequently,

> any other finding would result in a regrettable vacuum in the system of human-rights protection in the territory in question by removing from individuals there the benefit of the Convention's fundamental safeguards and their right to call a High Contracting Party to account for violation of their rights in proceedings before the Court.[23]

The spatial approach was also applied in *Medvedyev and others v France*.[24] The applicants were the crew of a Cambodian-flagged ship captured by the French navy on the high seas during an anti-drug trafficking operation, who challenged their detention on board as breaching the right to liberty and security of persons. The claim fell within French jurisdiction because France, through its navy, had 'full and exclusive control [...] at least de facto' over the ship and crew.[25] *Al-Saadoon and Mufdhi v UK* (dec.) concerned Iraqi applicants detained by British forces who challenged their transfer to Iraqi authorities as a potential breach of Article 2 ECHR.[26] In determining the question of jurisdiction at the admissibility stage, the ECtHR observed that the UK was an occupying power; that it 'exercised control and authority over the individuals detained [...] solely as a result of the use or threat of military force'[27]; and that the UK had 'total and exclusive de facto, and subsequently also de jure, control [...] over the

21 ECtHR, *Loizidou v Turkey*, App. No. 15318/89, Preliminary Objections, 23 March 1995, para. 62.

22 ECtHR, *Loizidou v Turkey*, App. No. 15318/89, Judgment, 28 November 1996, para. 52.

23 ECtHR, *Cyprus v Turkey* [GC], App. No. 25781/94, Judgment, 26 June 1992, paras. 77, 78.

24 ECtHR, *Medvedyev and others v France* [GC], App. No. 3394/03, Judgment, 29 March 2010.

25 Cf. D. Gilfoyle, 'ECHR Rights at Sea: *Medvedyev and others v. France*', 19 April 2010, www.ejiltalk.org/echr-rights-at-sea-medvedyev-and-others-v-france/ (last accessed 15 August 2016).

26 ECtHR, *Al-Saadoon and Mufdhi v UK* (dec.), App. No. 61498/08, 30 June 2009.

27 Ibid., para. 8.

premises in question and individuals detained there' bringing the applicants within British jurisdiction.[28] Finally, albeit controversially, in *Bankovic*, the absence of effective overall control, indicated as generally requiring troops on the ground, precluded extraterritorial jurisdiction under Article 1 ECHR. Even the capacity to deploy lethal military power from the air was insufficient to establish jurisdiction, the ECtHR concluded, particularly since the regime of human rights provided for under the ECHR could not be 'divided and tailored': all rights would apply or none.[29]

Turning to the second or 'personal' model, this was applied in *Öcalan v Turkey*. The leader of the Kurdish Workers' Party was arrested by Turkish agents in an aircraft located in the international zone of Nairobi airport, flown to Turkey, detained, tried, convicted and the death penalty imposed. The applicant, the ECtHR found, was under Turkish jurisdiction, 'Directly after he had been handed over by Kenyan officials to Turkish officials [...] even though in this instance Turkey exercised its authority outside its territory'.[30]

Another case, *Al-Skeini & others v UK*,[31] concerned five persons allegedly killed by British troops on patrol, and one person who was arrested, detained, mistreated and killed at a UK detention facility in Iraq. In each case, the deceased's relatives claimed procedural requirements under Article 2 ECHR were breached. In judgment, the ECtHR distinguished state agent authority and control,[32] and effective control over an area,[33] as exceptional bases of extraterritorial jurisdiction. It then held that the UK had exercised authority and control over individuals killed in the course of its troops' security operations, 'establishing a jurisdictional link between the deceased and the [UK] for the purposes of Article 1 of the Convention'.[34] Notably, the decision affirms the exceptional character of extraterritorial jurisdiction: the required 'jurisdictional link' must go beyond an 'instantaneous act'. States' duties would still not be engaged, for example, in cases of military action without territorial control, such

28 Ibid., paras. 88–89, citing ECtHR, *Hess v. UK*, App. No. 6231/73, Commission decision, 28 May 1975, Decisions & Reports vol. 2, p. 72.

29 ECtHR, *Bankovic and Others v Belgium and Others* [GC] (dec.), App. No. 52207/99, Judgment, 12 December 2001, para. 75.

30 A point that was common ground between the parties: ECtHR *Öcalan v Turkey*, App. No. 46221/99, Judgment, 12 March 2003, para. 93. See further ECtHR, *Pad and others v Turkey* (dec.), App. No. 60167/00, Judgment, 28 June 2007; ECtHR, *Issa v Turkey*, App. No. 31821/96, Judgment, 30 March 2005.

31 ECtHR, *Al-Skeini and others v UK* [GC], App. No. 55721/07 7, Judgment, 7 July 2011.

32 Ibid., paras.133–137, citing inter alia *Öcalan*, *Al-Saadoon* and *Medvedyev*. *Al-Saadoon* however appears to have been wrongly cited as authority for the personal model. See further M. Milanovic, *Extraterritorial Application of Human Rights Treaties. Law, Principles, Policy*. Oxford: Oxford University Press, 2011, 132–133.

33 ECtHR, *Al-Skeini and others v UK*, op. cit., paras. 138–140, citing *inter alia Loizidou* and *Bankovic*, op. cit.

34 Ibid., para. 149.

as drone strikes. For the purposes of jurisdiction under human rights treaties, causation is neither a sufficient nor a necessary condition.[35]

To reiterate, then, scenarios in which extraterritorial human rights jurisdiction has been affirmed have related to: occupation; operational activities of military, police or security personnel or agents; abduction or rendition by state agents; and offshore detention. State activities in these contexts put individuals in situations of extreme vulnerability. On one hand, they are exposed to risks of torture, unlawful death, deprivation of liberty and excessive force. On the other, state conduct in such situations is usually subject to limited scrutiny. Under occupation, 'there may be a few if any third parties – journalists, civil society monitors, international organizations, and less-directly-interested States on the ground monitoring the treatment of individuals'.[36] Offshore detention and interrogation facilities may be selected specifically for their isolated character and exclusion from normal review regimes.[37] Accordingly there may be a far greater risk of human rights violations in such situations than domestically, and a 'compelling' case for overturning the presumption that state obligations under human rights treaties are territorially delimited.[38]

This strikes a marked contrast with the general extraterritorial scenario in the human rights and business context. Here, violations occur in no jurisdictional 'black hole' but in 'host' states, with laws, courts, regulators, civil society watchdogs and human rights obligations of their own, even if these are or appear to be imperfect from the point of view of advocates of extraterritoriality, or indeed victims. Curiously, however, this contextual difference is one whose potential significance advocates of a home state duty to regulate have not interrogated, even if considerations of context weigh heavily in ECtHR jurisprudence.

The responsibility of states that are parties to the ECHR as regards non-state actors is further circumscribed by rules on attribution and the doctrine of positive obligations. Responsibility attaches only to acts or omissions attributable to the state and in violation of an obligation binding on it.[39] States are thus responsible for acts of non-state actors where these are done under the state's instructions, or where it otherwise 'directs or controls' such actions.[40] Except

35 See further, P.V. Kessing, 'Transnational operations carried out from a State's own territory. Armed drones and the extraterritorial effect of international human rights conventions'. In T.G. Hansen, J. Vested-Hansen (eds), *Human Rights and the Dark Side of Globalisation*. Oxford: Routledge, 2016, 81–99.

36 R. Wilde, 'Legal "black hole"? Extraterritorial state action and international treaty law on civil and political rights'. *Michigan Journal of International Law*, 2005, 26, 739.

37 J. Steyn, 'Guantanamo Bay: the legal black hole, 27th F.A. Mann Lecture on the 27 November 2003'. *International and Comparative Law Quarterly*, 2004, 53(1), 14.

38 Ibid., 770.

39 ILC, *Draft Articles on Responsibility of States for Internationally Wrongful Acts*. Extract from the Report of the ILC on the work of its 53rd session, Supplement No. 10 (A/56/10), ch. IV.E.1, art. 2, November 2001, http://legal.un.org/ilc/texts/instruments/english/draft_articles/9_6_2001.pdf (last accessed 19 January 2017).

40 Ibid., art. 8.

for certain state-owned enterprises, in certain limited circumstances,[41] businesses cannot be assimilated to the status of de facto organs of the state, nor do they generally act under the instructions, direction or control of states. The only potential basis of state responsibility for acts of non-state actors beyond these two criteria, consequently, is an omission constituting a violation of a positive obligation to do the acts in question.

Yet there are no positive obligations in relation to extraterritorial acts by non-state actors. Positive obligations may require states to protect rights-holders against abuses by private entities or persons, for instance, through deterrent measures, such as legislation, or operational steps in the case of specific known threats.[42] The ECtHR has held that positive obligations require *inter alia* that states establish effective criminal and civil remedy mechanisms for abuses by non-state actors, including those caused by corporations.[43] It is also true that complicity or acquiescence with acts of individuals can, by virtue of positive obligations, engage state responsibility in certain circumstances.[44] But the fact that some positive obligations require states to prevent human rights abuses by non-state actors within their territorial jurisdiction does not entail an obligation to regulate the activities of TNCs abroad.

One reason for this is the 'sufficient nexus' requirement,[45] that is, the condition that the defaults of the state or specific public actors should have 'sufficiently direct repercussions'[46] on the human right in question. Given the intervention, between a home state and any offending TNC activities abroad, of the host state's laws and regulatory institutions, as well, in many cases, as a 'corporate veil' between home and host-country corporate entities, the satisfaction of this condition in the general case appears unlikely. Equally, positive obligations are circumscribed by reasonableness requirements: before extending the scope of their duties, the ECtHR takes account of states' need to balance rights and the potential resource implications of measures to protect them with

41 See further C. Methven O'Brien and O. Martin Ortega, 'Human rights and public procurement: Towards an holistic international law analysis', Paper for International Law Association Study Group on Business and Human Rights, March 2017 (on file with author), 7–8.

42 For example, ECtHR, *X and Y v Netherlands*, App. No. 8978/80, Judgment, 26 March 1985, para. 23; ECtHR, *Osman v. UK*, App. No. 23452/94, Judgment [GC], 28 October 1998, para. 116.

43 See, for example, ECtHR, *Lopez Ostra v. Spain*, 9 December 1994, http://hudoc.echr.coe.int/sites/eng/pages/search.aspx?i=001-57905 (last accessed 11 February 2018); ECtHR, *Taşkin and Others v. Turkey*, 10 November 2004. http://hudoc.echr.coe.int/sites/eng/pages/search.aspx?i=001-67401 (last accessed 11 February 2018); ECtHR, *Guerra and Others v. Italy*, 19 February 1998, http://hudoc.echr.coe.int/sites/eng/pages/search.aspx?i=001-58135 (last accessed 11 February 2018).

44 For example, ECtHR, *Ireland v. UK*, App. No. 5310/71, Judgment, 18 January 1978, para.159.

45 ECtHR, *Fadeyeva v. the Russian Federation*, App. No. 55273/00, Judgment, 30 November 2005, para. 92.

46 ECtHR, *Moldovan and Others v Romania*, App. Nos. 41138/98 and 64320/01, Judgment, 30 November 2005, para. 95, citing ECtHR, *Ilaşcu and others v Moldova and Russia* [GC] App. No. 48787/99, Judgment, 8 July 2004.

other public interests. Such factors should be expected to weigh heavily in any evaluation by the ECtHR of whether, by virtue of Article 1, states parties to the ECHR are potentially liable in Strasbourg for abuses in the world at large perpetrated by European-based TNCs.

There is little evidence to justify the claim that, 'The case law of the ECtHR in particular provides various examples of extraterritorial obligations to protect human rights against violations by non-state actors, akin to the UNSRSG's category of "direct extraterritorial jurisdiction"'.[47] To the contrary, it is suggested, there is no basis in the ECHR for a general state duty to control the conduct abroad of business enterprises incorporated under states parties' laws or having their headquarters in their territories, even when such conduct leads to human rights abuses, with one possible, and potentially significant caveat, for some acts of some types of transnationally-operating state-owned or controlled enterprises. Apart from this case, neither of the required standards, of 'effective control', applicable in the case of the spatial model, or a relationship of 'physical power and control', in the case of the personal model, are likely generally to apply as between a 'home' state and victims of abuses in which TNCs are implicated abroad.

Recent Policy Developments in the Council of Europe

This position is reinforced by the CoE's recently adopted Recommendation on human rights and business.[48] According to the preceding political Declaration on B&HR, the basis for CoE Member States' duties in this area is their 'obligation to secure to everyone within their jurisdiction the rights and freedoms defined in the European Convention on Human Rights (ETS No. 5) [...]'.[49] The Recommendation in turn provides that CoE Member States should apply such measures as may be necessary to require businesses operating within their territorial jurisdiction to respect human rights; and to apply such measures as may be necessary to require business enterprises domiciled within their jurisdiction to respect human rights throughout their operations abroad.[50] While this might appear to resonate with the opinions of other scholars cited above, rather than the analysis advanced here, according to the *Explanatory Memorandum* to the Recommendation, 'whenever [the Recommendation] refers to the term "jurisdiction", that term shall have the same meaning as in Article 1 [ECHR] as

47 Augenstein, Kinley, op. cit., 286.

48 CoE, *Committee of Ministers to Member States on human rights and business*, CM/Rec(2016)3, March 2016. See also Committee of Ministers, *Declaration of the Committee of Ministers on the UN Guiding Principles on Business and Human Rights*, 16 April 2014.

49 Ibid., Preamble, para. 3.

50 Ibid., Appendix, para. 13; see also Steering Committee for Human Rights, CM(2016)18-addfinal, *Explanatory Memorandum to Recommendation of the Committee of Ministers to Member States on Human Rights and Business*, CM/Rec(2016)3, 2 March 2016, https://search.coe.int/cm/Pages/result_details.aspx?Reference=CM/Rec(2016)3 (last accessed 11 February 2018), para. 28.

applied and interpreted by the European Court of Human Rights'.[51] While there is every reason, in terms of 'policy coherence', for states to adopt domestic measures to promote the prevention and remediation of human rights abuses in the context of business activities abroad, the Recommendation does not seek to depart from the position reflected in ECtHR case law that there is no legal obligation stemming from the ECHR to do so.

Conclusion

In closing, I offer three final thoughts. First, echoing some of the scholarly arguments discussed above, a recent UNCESCR General Comment refers to a home state duty to regulate TNCs abroad.[52] As noted, there are those who take the UNGPs' failure to recognize such a duty, amongst other deficiencies, as entailing the need for a B&HR treaty.[53] Yet, as demonstrated here, the ECHR does not mandate such a duty, nor have commentators so far been able to demonstrate convincing authority for such a duty from other sources.[54] It would therefore appear prudent for B&HR treaty proponents to rest the case for a new international legal instrument on the alternative grounds available to them.[55]

Second, human rights abuses inside Europe by companies domiciled, or whose parent companies are domiciled, outside the continent are now well documented.[56] Yet, European scholars have not attempted to play out the operation of a home state duty to regulate from this 'inverse' perspective. Does this provide support for the view that the extraterritoriality movement more broadly embodies an imperialist impulse? [57] Or imply that B&HR lawyers, like other

51 Steering Committee for Human Rights, *Explanatory Memorandum to Recommendation of the Committee of Ministers to member States on human rights and business*, op. cit., para. 8.

52 UNCESCR, *General Comment No. 24 on State Obligations under the International Covenant on Economic, Social and Cultural Rights in the Context of Business Activities*, E/C.12/GC/24, 10 August 2017, para. 30 et seq.

53 UNHRC, *Elaboration of an International Legally Binding Instrument on Transnational Corporations and other Business Enterprises with Respect to Human Rights*, A/HRC/RES/26/9, 14 July 2014, http://ap.ohchr.org/documents/dpage_e.aspx?si=A/HRC/RES/26/9 (last accessed 1 October 2017).

54 See further C. Methven O'Brien, 'The home state duty to regulate TNCs abroad: a rebuttal'. *Business and Human Rights Journal*, 2018, 3(1), 47–73.

55 J. Ford and C. Methven O'Brien, 'Empty rituals or workable models? Towards a business and human rights treaty'. *University of New South Wales Law Review, Special Issue on Business and Human Rights*, 2017, Issue 40(3), 1223.

56 See for example Business and Human Rights Resource Centre, *Briefing: Business and Human Rights Challenges in Eastern Europe and Central Asia*, 2016, https://business-humanrights.org/sites/default/files/eeca-regional-briefing-february-2016.pdf (last accessed 11 February 2018).

57 R. Wilde, 'Dilemmas in promoting global economic justice through human rights law'. In N. Buhta (ed.), *The Frontiers of Human Rights Extraterritoriality and its Challenges. Collected Courses of the Academy of European Law*. Oxford: Oxford University Press, 2016, 127–176.

international lawyers, are not as international as they think?[58] If not, what the reasons are for this approach might be worth exploring.

Finally, this chapter's analysis shows that the relationship between the flourishing but still emergent B&HR field and the broader domain of human rights is still developing. As B&HR scholars, I suggest, we need to exercise greater sensitivity to the multiple contexts – doctrinal, administrative and political – of general human rights materials when they are marshalled in argument. If cruder approaches may appear to deliver short-term, local normative advances, over time they may yet undermine the fabric of the whole.

58 A. Roberts, *Is International Law International?*, Oxford: Oxford University Press, 2017.

6 The Duty to Protect in Public Procurement

Toward a Mandatory Human Rights Clause?

Deborah Russo

Introduction

Public procurement is the procedure by which governments and public authorities purchase goods, works and services from the market. Both in developing and developed countries, states are increasingly contracting out public functions in different areas, such as social and health services, security and criminal justice, education, immigration, energy, water and others.[1] They also conclude contracts with private entities, which provide goods, works and services necessary to the exercise of public functions. Notwithstanding the relevant scale of this phenomenon and its possible impact on the protection of human rights, there has not been much elaboration on the international obligations of States as procuring operators.

Public procurement has been included in the global process toward market liberalization and free trade. In fact, states have concluded agreements aimed at boosting competition and assuring best value for money, such as the WTO Government Procurement Agreement (hereinafter 'GPA') and specific chapters of some regional trade agreements.[2] These agreements aim to prevent national legislation or practice from distorting competition and discriminating against multinational enterprises interested in entering the market.[3] They prohibit

1 C. Methven O'Brien, 'Essential services, public procurement and human rights in Europe'. *University of Groningen Faculty of Law Research Paper*, 22/2015, 24 January 2015, 16 p.

2 WTO, *Agreement on Government Procurement*, 1994, www.wto.org/english/docs_e/legal_e/gpr-94_e.pdf (last accessed 13 February 2018). For an overall analysis of the WTO agreement and its revision process see P. Pellentier, '2012 revision of the WTO Agreement on Government Procurement: coverage dimensions and context', www.econstor.eu/bitstream/10419/152257/1/87921872X.pdf (last accessed 13 February 2018); R.D. Anderson, S.L. Schooner and C.D., Swan, 'The WTO's revised government procurement agreement – an important milestone toward greater market access and transparency in global public procurement markets'. *GWU Legal Studies Research Paper*, No. 2012-7, https://scholarship.law.gwu.edu/faculty_publications/123/ (last accessed 13 February 2018).

3 D. Collins, 'Government procurement with strings attached: the uneven control of offsets by the World Trade Organisation and regional trade agreements' *Asian Journal of International Law*, 2016, 1 ff.

national measures that unduly give prevalence to domestic over foreign tenders. At the EU level, a similar goal is pursued by the directives on public procurement, which prohibit any measure of direct or indirect discrimination against European enterprises based on nationality.[4]

However, liberalizing the public procurement market might divert public authorities from other objectives of general concern, such as protecting human rights as a national public policy goal. This is also due to the uncertainty as to whether and to what extent social clauses may be interpreted as trade protectionism and obstacles to competition. For this reason, there are some attempts to 'humanize' public procurement at an international level, in order to direct its potential toward sustainable development and promotion of human rights. Before analysing this trend, in the section below we will briefly consider, from a theoretical standpoint, how the duty to protect affects public procurement. The final section will suggest a possible way forward in protecting human rights in public procurement.

The Scope of the Duty to Protect in Public Procurement

The new 2030 Agenda for Sustainable Development promoted by the UN calls on all States to implement action plans for 'sustainable public procurement'. This expression refers to the practices of integrating social and environmental considerations into the procedures for selecting private contractors. In particular, Target 12.6 is to 'encourage companies [...] to adopt sustainable practices and to integrate sustainability information into their reporting cycle'. Furthermore, Target 12.7 calls on states to 'promote public procurement practices that are sustainable, in accordance with national policies and priorities'.[5]

The UNGPs, adopted by the UNHRC in 2011, include public procurement within the framework of states' commitments to creating an environment conducive to business respect for human rights. The 2011 UNGPs assume that states do not relinquish their human rights obligations when externalizing services or trading with enterprises. Hence, the duty of states to protect human rights concerns the potential violations arising out of commercial transactions, public–private partnerships and public procurement.[6] In this regard, UNGP 5 affirms that 'States should exercise adequate oversight in order to meet their international human rights obligations when they contract with, or legislate for, business enterprises to provide services that may impact upon the enjoyment of

4 EU, *Directive 2014/24/EU on Public Procurement and Directive 2014/25/EU on Procurement by Entities Operating in the Water, Energy, Transport and Postal Services Sectors.*

5 These principles are included in UN General Assembly, Resolution A/RES/70/1, 25 September 2015, www.un.org/ga/search/view_doc.asp?symbol=A/RES/70/1&Lang=E (last accessed 13 February 2018).

6 The Guiding Principles implement the 'Protect, Respect and Remedy' Framework proposed by the Special Representative of the Secretary-General on the issue of human rights and transnational corporations and other business enterprises, A/HRC/17/3.

human rights'. As the commentary clarifies, privatizing does not relieve states of their international obligations. Accordingly, states are bound to specify the human rights obligations applying to future contractors in both their legislation and contractual documentation. Furthermore, the subsequent UNGP 6 calls on states to promote socially responsible business practices.[7]

UNGPs 5 and 6 reflect views already elaborated by the case law of the human rights treaty-based mechanisms – at least in the European system. In this regard, the ECtHR has affirmed that 'the State cannot completely absolve itself of its responsibility by delegating its obligations in this sphere to private bodies or individuals', and may be found responsible for violations of positive obligations deriving from the ECHR in case of wrongful acts committed by private entities.[8] It is also worth noting that the 'Draft Legally Binding Instrument on Transnational Corporations and Other Business Enterprises with Respect to Human Rights' includes the following provision:

> States shall take all necessary and appropriate measures to ensure that public procurement contracts are awarded to bidders that are committed to respecting human rights, without records of human rights violations or abuses, and that fully comply with all requirements as established in this instrument.[9]

The responsibility of states in the field of public procurement may be 'direct', when it arises from a breach to respect human rights, or 'indirect', when violations of due diligence are concerned. In the context of procurement law, direct responsibility may be ascribed when a state fails to insert social clauses into public contracts, in violation of specific obligations, such as those provided by the ILO Public Contracts Convention (whose content will be examined in the next section) or by virtue of a special relationship between the state and the enterprise, according to draft articles 5 and 8 of the ILC Draft Articles on Responsibility of States for Internationally Wrongful Acts.[10] As to their indirect responsibility, states may be held accountable for the failure to adopt appropriate preventive measures for violations caused by their private contractors or subcontractors in the performance of a contract.

However, when suppliers who are not located within a state's boundaries commit violations, the question arises of whether the state may be held

7 It says: 'States should promote respect for human rights by business enterprises with which they conduct commercial transactions'.

8 ECtHR, *Costello-Roberts v United Kingdom*, App. No. 22860/02, Judgment, 25 March 2003, para. 60; ECtHR, *Storck v. Germany*, App. No. 61603/00, Judgment, 16 June 2005, para 103.

9 UNHRC, *Draft Legally Binding Instrument on Transnational Corporations and other Business Enterprises with Respect to Human Rights*, UN doc. A/HRC/RES/26/9, 29 September 2017, p. 6.

10 ILC, *Draft Articles on Responsibility of States for Internationally Wrongful Acts*, 2001, http://legal.un.org/ilc/texts/instruments/english/commentaries/9_6_2001.pdf (last accessed 13 February 2018).

responsible for violations perpetrated abroad. International law is gradually evolving in this field toward a possible extension of the territorial scope of the human rights obligations assumed by states. In 2011, the UNHRC considered that the prohibition on states to allow the use of their territory in a way which causes damage within the territory of another state extends to human rights law.[11] The implications of this assumption are clarified in the 2017 General Comment on State obligations under the ICESCR in the Context of Business Activities. Here, the UNCESCR affirmed that States' Parties have to pay close attention to the adverse impact outside their territories of the activities of enterprises that are domiciled under their jurisdiction. In particular, this obligation extends to any business entities over which Parties may exercise influence by regulatory means.[12] According to this interpretation, state responsibility may be grounded on a factual criterion, which is based in turn on the effective influence of national regulation (or 'deregulation') on the conduct of enterprises abroad.[13]

More importantly, the UNCESCR affirmed that

> in discharging their duty to protect, States' Parties should also require corporations [...] domiciled in the territory and/or jurisdiction of States' Parties [...] to act with due diligence to identify, prevent and address abuses to Covenant rights by such subsidiaries and business partners, wherever they may be located.[14]

This passage contributes to enlarging the scope of the duty to protect with respect to business activities outside state borders. Furthermore, the duty to protect includes the obligation to put in place effective monitoring, investigation and accountability mechanisms to ensure access to remedies for victims. This implies that, in the context of public procurement, states

> could deny awarding of public contracts to companies that have not provided information on the social and environmental impacts of their

11 See UNHRC, *Resolution 21/11*, UN doc. A/HRC/21/39, 18 July 2012, para. 92: 'States have an obligation to respect and protect the enjoyment of human rights, which involves avoiding conduct that would create a foreseeable risk of impairing the enjoyment of human rights by persons living in poverty beyond their borders, and conducting assessments of the extraterritorial impacts of law, policies and practices'.

12 UN, *General Comment No. 24 (2017) on State obligations under the International Covenant on Economic, Social and Cultural Rights in the Context of Business Activities*, UN doc E/C.12/60/R.1, 10 August 2017, para. 35.

13 P. De Sena, 'Juridition étatique et imputation des violations extraterritoriales des droits de l'homme: quelques observations'. In D. Alland, O. De Frouville and J. Vinuales (eds), *Unité et diversité du droit international/Unity and Diversity of International Law Ecrits en l'honneur du Professeur Pierre-Marie Dupuy/Essays in Honour of Professor Pierre-Marie Dupuy*. Leiden, Boston: Brill, 2014, 785 ff.

14 Ibid., para. 38.

> activities or that have not put in place measures to ensure that they act with due diligence to avoid or mitigate any negative impacts on the rights under the Covenant.[15]

To comply with this principle, states should require tenderers to submit a due diligence report, including a human rights impact assessment of their activities.

Despite the increasing concern about human rights violations that may occur along government supply chains and the need to strengthen state accountability, compliance with the UNGPs is still limited. Particularly in the field of public procurement, the practice of states falls short of the mark.

As soft law seems insufficient to ensure human rights protection in business activities, the international community is moving toward negotiating a binding instrument on B&HR. The prospects of negotiation are still uncertain, as is its possible impact on public procurement law. In particular, the drafting of a provision requiring states (and IOs) to include human rights clauses when they contract with private enterprises has not been discussed yet. However, this option is highly desirable in order to ensure that states will properly fulfil their duty to protect. This point will be elaborated on further in the concluding remarks of this chapter, whereas the following section will briefly describe some international instruments concerning public procurement. A deeper insight into this practice might serve as a source of guidance and inspiration in the discussion about drafting a specific human rights clause.

A Brief Description of the Relevant International Practice

States and IOs have been promoting policies for the advancement of public procurement law. Within the WTO, public procurement is considered a relevant branch of the global market, which offers multiple business opportunities for all enterprises, irrespective of their nationality.

This is the prevailing objective of the WTO GPA (as well as of the procurement chapters of some other trade agreements), which is a plurilateral agreement adopted within the framework of the WTO with the goal of opening the public procurement market and promoting fair and transparent conditions of competition for all enterprises. The treaty is administered by the Committee on Government Procurement, which is composed of representatives of all the Parties and is entrusted with the function of settling disputes between the Parties and promoting the revision process of the agreement. Under the GPA, Parties are required to undertake further negotiations with a view to extending the coverage of the agreement. Negotiations to this end were successfully concluded in 2012 with the formal adoption of the Decision on the Outcomes of the

15 Ibid., para. 50.

Negotiations under Article XXIV:7.[16] This decision set out the future work programmes of the Committee, including 'a work programme on Sustainable Procurement'.[17] Accordingly, on 22 February 2017, the WTO Secretariat organized the first Symposium on Sustainable Procurement with the aim of defining the scope and objectives of 'sustainable procurement', analysing and comparing the key practices for incorporating social clauses at different stages of procurement procedures and discussing how to harmonize such practices with the free trade and 'best-value for money' principles.[18]

While this work is still in progress, there are currently limited obligations under the GPA concerning human rights standards. As far as the admissibility stage of a procedure is concerned, Article VIII does not mention human rights and only provides for the exclusion of suppliers who have been convicted for serious crimes or offences.

With respect to the awarding of contracts, paragraph 5 of Article XV provides that a public authority may use evaluation criteria based either on the most advantageous offer or the lowest price, provided that the relevant criteria are specified in the tender documentation. The criterion of the lowest price is problematic as it incentivizes offers based on economic considerations only, with a higher risk of reduced social protection.

Furthermore, Article X contains guidelines on the use of technical specifications, which are aimed at preventing the latter from creating an unnecessary obstacle to international trade. To this end, it requires that technical specifications be set out in terms of performance and functional requirements, rather than descriptive characteristics, and that they be based, where possible, on international, rather than national, standards. Tender documentation should always permit equivalent indications or certification of fulfilment of the relevant functional requirements. Public authorities are also allowed to introduce any technical specifications that may be necessary to promote the conservation of natural resources and protect the environment. However, the promotion of other social objectives, such as social protection of workers, is not permitted under the treaty, so that national measures for the protection of human rights might be found to conflict with the principles espoused by the GPA. For example, in a case brought before a WTO panel, *United States – Measure Affecting Government Procurement*, the European Community contended that an Act enacted by the Commonwealth of Massachusetts – prohibiting the procurement of goods and services from any person doing business with Myanmar, accused of serious human rights violations – breached the provisions on technical specifications

16 WTO, *Decision of the Committee on Government Procurement*, GPA 113, 2 April 2012. www.wto.org/english/tratop_e/gproc_e/negotiations_e.htm (last accessed 13 February 2018).

17 WTO, *The re-negotiation of the Agreement on Government Procurement (GPA)*, 2011. www.wto.org/english/tratop_e/gproc_e/negotiations_e.htm (last accessed 13 February 2018).

18 WTO, *Symposium on Sustainable Procurement*, February 2017. www.wto.org/english/tratop_e/gproc_e/gp_symp_22feb17_e.htm (last accessed 13 February 2018).

and exclusion from participation.[19] Although, the case was never judged by the panel, it provides evidence of how national discretion in protecting human rights might be called into question.

EU legislation is likewise premised on principles similar to those of the WTO, aimed at abolishing any obstacles to freedom of movement and competition law. According to EU law, Member States must remove from their public procurement regimes any barriers to the circulation of goods, workers and services, as well as any discrimination against EU companies. However, since the 1970s European legislation has largely evolved toward a progressive integration of human rights and social policy considerations into public procurement.[20]

The new directives on public procurement adopted in 2014 define the conditions under which Member States are allowed to include social and environmental clauses at different stages of the procurement process.[21] Article 67 of Directive 2014/23/EU includes, among the award criteria, a 'cost effectiveness approach, such as life-cycle costing', which allows public authorities to consider the environmental externalities of a product from its inception to its completion, delivery and disposal. It also considers the 'best price-quality ratio according to qualitative, environmental and/or social aspects', provided that these aspects are linked to the subject matter of the contract. The latter criterion enables public authorities to give preference to bids from tenderers who maximize social outputs, such as economic operators who employ a higher number of disadvantaged workers. However, this opportunity is restricted by the 'link to the subject matter' requirement, which Article 70 of the same directive has extended to contract performance requirements. As a consequence, clauses referring to the general policy of enterprises, or to social criteria, which are not related to the goods, works or services forming the subject matter of the future contract, are prohibited.

The interpretation given by the ECJ must also be taken into account.[22] In the *EVN* case, the ECJ made it clear that the inclusion of social criteria must not give public authorities an unrestricted freedom of choice: such criteria must be clearly specified together with the weighting of their importance for the

19 WTO, *United States – Measures Affecting Government Procurement*, Panel report, WT/DS88/4, 11 January 1999, www.wto.org/english/tratop_e/dispu_e/cases_e/ds88_e.htm (last accessed 13 February 2018).

20 O. Martin-Ortega, O. Outhwaite and W. Rooke, 'Buying power and human rights in the supply chain: legal options for socially responsible public procurement of electronic goods'. *The International Journal of Human Rights*, 2017, 19, 2015.

21 EU, *Directive 2014/23/EU of the European Parliament and the Council of 26 February 2014 on the Award of Concession Contracts*, OJ L94/1, 28 March 2014, http://eur-lex.europa.eu/legal-content/EN/TXT/PDF/?uri=CELEX:32014L0023&from=NL (last accessed 13 February 2018); EC, *Supporting Social Responsibility in the Economy through Public Procurement*, 9 February 2016, http://ec.europa.eu/growth/tools-databases/newsroom/cf/itemdetail.cfm?item_id=8667&lang=en&title=Supporting-social-responsibility-in-the-economy-through-public-procurement (last accessed 13 February 2018).

22 ECJ, *EVN AG and Wienstrom GmbH v Republik Österreich*, C-448/01, 4 December 2003, para. 33.

purpose of evaluating the tender. Moreover, in the case concerned, which regarded a contract for the supply of electricity, a criterion giving preference to electricity produced by renewable energy sources should have referred to a specific supply period 'in order to be linked to the subject matter of the contract'.[23] Analogously, in the *European Commission v. Kingdom of the Netherlands* case, the ECJ judged that a clause requiring that tenderers comply with the criteria of sustainable purchasing and socially responsible business was contrary to the obligation of transparency and insufficiently connected to the subject matter of the contract.[24] However, in the *Regio Post* case, the ECJ affirmed that a public authority may require tenderers and their subcontractors to undertake to pay staff – who are called upon to perform the services covered by the contract – a minimum wage provided for under the legislation of the State in which the contract will be executed. In order to be lawful, this requirement must be established through legislation or universally applicable collective agreements and relate to the subject matter of the contract only.

An interesting novelty in the new directives is the 'general social clause' pursuant to Article 18, paragraph 2, where it is provided that:

> Member States shall take appropriate measures to ensure that in the performance of public contracts economic operators comply with applicable obligations in the fields of environmental, social and labor law established by Union law, national law, collective agreements or by the international environmental, social and labor law provisions listed in Annex X.

This clause requires Member States to introduce the measures necessary to ensure that contractors will comply with the social and environmental standards established by national, EU and international treaties listed in Annex X in the performance of their contract. The relevant treaties include some ILO Conventions (Numbers 87, 98, 29, 105, 138, 111, 100, 182) and other environmental protection agreements. Such agreements become applicable even to contractors of states that have not ratified them and thus provide an interesting example of how international treaty law may be incorporated into EU law.

The above-mentioned clause leaves some questions open for interpretation, such as the possible relevance of other international treaties which are not mentioned in Annex X, but to which a state is party, and whether the clause may be applied to all subcontractors and suppliers along the supply chain.

Unfortunately, the wording of the clause is ambiguous. However, as to the first question, the scope of Article 18, paragraph 2, should embrace all treaties in the field of human rights and environmental law that have been ratified by

23 Ibid., paras. 66 ff.

24 ECJ, *European Commission v Kingdom of the Netherlands*, C-368/10, 10 May 2012, paras. 109 ff; ECJ, *RegioPost GmbH & Co. KG contro Stadt Landau in der Pfalz*, C-115/14, 17 November 2015, para. 88.

the procuring state. Such an interpretation would also comply with the national law requirement, given that the notion of 'national law' normally includes a state's international obligations.

Regarding the second question, it is worth considering that EU legislation requires transparency in the subcontracting chain. In fact, companies have to specify what part of the contract they intend to assign to a third party and identify the subcontractors for which a chain of responsibility may be drawn up. For this reason, the general social clause should be interpreted as covering not only the conduct of contractors, but also that of all subcontractors and suppliers involved in the performance of a contract. Moreover, in view of their duty to protect, as specified by the previously mentioned General Comment no. 24 of the UNCESCR, states should require all contractors and subcontractors to report their policies and procedures in the field of human rights protection and to provide effective means of accountability and redress for abuses.[25]

Another interesting provision is introduced by recital 101 of the preamble of the directive, which states that

> contracting authorities should further be given the possibility to exclude economic operators which have proven unreliable, for instance because of violations of environmental or social obligations, including rules on accessibility for disabled persons or other forms of grave professional misconduct, such as violations of competition rules or of intellectual property rights.

This rule provides for the possible exclusion, at different stages of procurement procedures, of enterprises that failed to comply with human rights law.

A weak aspect of EU policy seems its prevalent discretionary character. In fact, the actual implementation of social clauses is left up to the initiative of Member States. There is no obligation for them to use social clauses. The sole exception is represented by the new 'general social clause', which introduces the obligation to ensure compliance with human rights law in the performance of a contract. This clause follows the 'conditions of contract' model, but in a more flexible way, since it does not establish uniform general conditions within the EU. Therefore, it may be argued that the EU has inaugurated a combined strategy. This strategy includes a 'flexible hard law approach' – for the application, to states' contractors, of obligations that are binding on Member States or derive from an international core standard – and a prudent 'promotional approach', whereby standards higher that those imposed by the law may optionally be included in the procurement documents, according to the social policy objectives of each EU Member State.

The prevalent discretionary pattern may also be found in the instruments adopted by the UN, which draw the attention of its states to the importance of

25 UN, *General Comment No. 24 (2017) on State Obligations under the International Covenant on Economic, Social and Cultural Rights in the Context of Business Activities*, op. cit., para. 33.

wise public expenditure. The UNCITRAL Model Law on Public Procurement assists states in elaborating a modern procurement law and favours the harmonization of international standards, such as those provided by the GPA, the EU Directives on public procurement and the UN Convention against corruption.[26] It provides guidelines and procedures for achieving value for money and avoiding discrimination and corruption. Regrettably, it does not contain a human rights provision and leaves a wide margin of discretion to states with respect to the inclusion of social clauses.[27] In parallel, the UN is developing a strategy for promoting socially responsible procurement on the part of its Member States by investing in reports[28] documenting national policies, practices, drivers and opportunities for responsible public consumption and elaborating guidelines and recommendations for furthering the commitment of states in this field.[29]

While a soft law approach prevails in the UN system, an interesting instrument is the 1949 ILO Convention concerning Labour Clauses in Public Contracts, which establishes prescriptive requirements. This Convention obliges Contracting States to include clauses in their procurement procedures, which are designed to ensure conditions of contract for the workers concerned that are not less favourable than those established in the territory or area where the work is carried out. It also requires states to apply adequate sanctions for failure to insert those clauses in tender documentation. The content of this agreement is important even if it is limited to labour standards. Regrettably, it also omits any reference to conditions of contract applicable along the supply chain.

In conclusion, a common approach to socially responsible public procurement among the different international instruments is still lacking. A further harmonization in this area might be hampered by the fear that a uniform international standard would unduly restrict national discretion in accommodating the prevailing social needs of a local community or of a specific sector of services. As will be discussed in the next section, this concern is overestimated. The 'soft law approach' encourages states to develop their own national model in accordance with their respective social policies. However, this approach would not be sufficient to implement states' duty to protect in respect of possible

26 UNCITRAL, *Model Law on Public Procurement*, 2014, www.uncitral.org/pdf/english/texts/procurem/ml-procurement-2011/2011-Model-Law-on-Public-Procurement-e.pdf (last accessed 13 February 2018).

27 Article 9, paragraph 2b affirms that suppliers or contractors should respect ethical standards applicable in the territorial state but it is not easy to assume that the expression 'ethical standards' includes human rights and social standards binding on the state where the contract is to be performed.

28 See, for example, UN, *Sustainable Public Procurement: A Global Review (Final Report)*, 2013. www.globalecolabelling.net/assets/Documents/unep-spp-report.pdf (last accessed 13 February 2018).

29 See UN Environment Programme, *Buying for a Better World: A Guide on Sustainable Procurement for the UN System*, 2011, www2.senado.leg.br/bdsf/bitstream/handle/id/242706/Buying%20for%20a%20better%20world%20-%20sustainable%20procurement%20guide.pdf?sequence=3 (last accessed 13 February 2018).

human rights abuses perpetrated by contractors or subcontractors along the supply chain. For this reason, it is worth discussing in the section below a possible combined approach.

Concluding Remarks on a Possible Way Forward

As the survey on international practice has shown, obligations implied in the duty to protect are still mostly undefined.

The draft binding instrument on B&HR could fill the gap by requiring States to employ a model clause to enhance the different aspects covered by UNGPs 5 and 6: preventing human rights abuses and promoting social policy objectives.

The first aspect – namely the prevention of human rights abuses – entails extending the applicability of international human rights standards binding on the procuring state to both contractors and subcontractors. This objective is extremely relevant for states, since, as previously noted, it is a component of their duty to protect. As states must meet their international human rights obligations when they contract with enterprises, they have to specify in legislation and tender documentation that they expect contractors and subcontractors to respect human rights. Moreover, as was stressed earlier in the preliminary remarks, the scope of due diligence is progressively extending beyond their territorial border.[30] This means that a breach of due diligence could also derive from extraterritorial business activities, when it may be established that state regulation could have affected these activities. The evaluation should be based on the effective impact of the state regulation abroad. For this reason, the human rights clause should cover the activities of subcontractors along the supply chain.

The model clause could be shaped as a mandatory exclusion requirement or a contract performance condition. Hypothetically, it could provide for the exclusion of tenderers who have been already convicted for human rights violations and for those who do not provide a human rights impact assessment from their suppliers. In addition, it should establish the termination of the contract in the event of violations committed in the performance of a contract. Such violations could be ascertained in accordance with the national standards of the procuring states or, as it would be better, a common international human rights standard agreed in the future instrument.

The second aspect concerns the use of public procurement to further human rights protection and implies a promotional approach. For this purpose, the model clause (or its second paragraph) should encourage states to advance social and environmental protection above the threshold of law in accordance with their national social policy. In this perspective, public procurement might be

30 O. De Schutter and Z. Kedzia, *General Comment on State Obligations under the International Covenant on Economic, Social and Cultural Rights in the Context of Business Activities*, UN doc E/C.12/60/R.1, 17 October 2016, paras. 20 ff.

used as an instrument of national public policy for promoting the CSR of enterprises and pushing forward social goals. However, the challenge for states is to draft a clause that respects the criteria of objectivity, impartiality, efficiency and non-discrimination of procedures. In this regard, the establishment of a shared yardstick is not essential, given the importance of leaving each public authority a margin of discretion in defining its public policy objectives. At the same time, the development of an international system for measuring the 'added social value' of a tender – using conventional indicators that each public authority could combine according to its priorities – would be helpful for preventing the risk of bias.[31]

In conclusion, the drafting of a similar provision in a future binding instrument on B&HR would contribute to developing a comprehensive strategy for socially responsible procurement and could represent a starting point for future negotiations.

31 See V. Federico, D. Russo and E. Testi, 'Impresa sociale, concorrenza, valore aggiunto. Un approccio europeo', Padova: Cedam, 2012.

7 The EU's Promotion of Human Rights and Sustainable Development through PTAs as a Tool to Influence Business Regulation in Third Countries

Leonardo Borlini

Development and Progress: Markets as Social Constructions and the Two Souls of European Integration

> Progress is hence an ideal (social and political) notion, whereas development is a pragmatic and economic fact. Such dissociation requires a synchrony between 'development' and 'progress' as true progress is (apparently) not conceivable unless the economic premises needed to realize it are created.[1]

To begin an academic paper with a quotation, especially from one of the most controversial artists in the recent history of European literature and cinematic arts, is hazardous and, admittedly, somewhat pretentious. And yet still, this excerpt from Pasolini's '*Scritti corsari*' spectacularly catches some of the complexities the current chapter far more humbly attempts to deal with.

First, it hints at a multifaceted notion of 'market', not only as an actual or nominal place where forces of demand and supply operate, and where buyers and sellers interact (directly or through intermediaries) to trade goods, services, or contracts or instruments, for money or barter,[2] but also in its dynamic manifestation, as a place of experimentation and learning; as a composite and evolving institution in of itself.[3] Stated differently, the advocated synchrony between development and progress seems to posit that the very place where all business happens is a complex social construction: far from being jungles where the law of the strongest rules, markets are, in fact, a set of most sophisticated relations between producers and consumers, and between production factors, technical knowledge and organization in time and space. They are also a set of relations between economic actors and social, political, legal and civil institutions. From

1 P.P. Pasolini, *Scritti Corsari*. Milan: Garzanti, 1975, 175, loosely translated by the current author from the original text in Italian.

2 P. Krugman and R. Wells, *Microeconomics*, 3rd ed. London: Macmillan, 2013, 5.

3 See, *ex multis*, N. Irti, *L'ordine giuridico del mercato*, 3rd ed. Bari: Laterza, 2004, esp. 5–10, 73–79.

such a perspective, while, as widely known, a set of rules common to all economic actors and their enforcement are essential preconditions for the functioning of competitive markets, other kinds of rules are needed to ensure that business activities are carried out without unduly sacrificing non-economic interests. Among such rules, it is relatively simple, at least in advanced jurisdictions, to identify those aimed at protecting human rights against abuses by business enterprises.

Second, looking at the EU, the association of (economic) development and (social and political) progress depicts the tension between the two souls of European integration: the functionalist conception of integration, in which the EU is steered clear of political temptations, and the creeping evolution of the Union towards an entity that espouses universal principles internally and throughout the world.[4] Internally, this occurs also by accompanying its economic vision (the functioning and consolidation of a single competitive market) with political aspirations, reflecting the view that, since the eighth century, Europe has been seen as a place where there are multiple political communities with a shared way of life, involving both a questioning of the excesses of the market and, since the Second War World, the excesses of the nation-state.[5] Borrowing from Habermas and Derrida:

> [...] the triumph of capitalism was bound up with sharp class conflicts, and this fact has hindered an equally positive appraisal of free markets. That differing evaluation of politics and markets may explain Europeans' trust in the civilizing power of the state and their expectations for it to correct market failures.[6]

Externally the role, models and identity of the EU as an actor in international relations are steadily among the most investigated subjects by international law and international relations scholars.[7] The EU has, indeed, evolved into a

4 E. Cannizzaro, 'Human rights conditionality in the EU's international agreements by Lorand Bartels. Book Review'. *European Law Review*, 2007, 424.

5 J.-W. Müller, *Constitutional Patriotism*. Princeton, NJ: Princeton University Press, 2007, ch. 3.

6 J. Habermas and J. Derrida, 'February 15, or what binds Europeans together: plea for a common foreign policy in core Europe'. In D. Levy, M. Pensky and J. Torpe (eds), *Old Europe, New Europe, Core Europe: Transatlantic Relations after the Iraq War*. London: Verso, 2005, 5, 10–12, adding that: 'In Europe, [...] [i]n the context of the workers' movements and the Christian socialist traditions, the struggle for "more social justice", [...], asserted itself against the individualist ethos of market justice that accepts social inequalities as part of the bargain'.

7 See, for example, E. Cannizzaro (ed.), *The European Union as an Actor in International Relations*. Alphen aan den Rijn: Kluwer Law International, 2002; M. Cremona, 'The Union as a global actor: role, models, and identity'. *Common Market Law Review*, 2004, 41, 553; P. Eeckhout, *External Relations of the European Union: Legal and Constitutional Foundations*. Oxford: Oxford University Press, 2004; A. Dashwood and M. Maresceau (eds), *Law and Practice of EU External Relations*. Cambridge: Cambridge University Press, 2008; F. Jacobs, 'The state of international economic law: re-thinking sovereignty in Europe'. *Journal of International Economic Law*, 2008, 11 (1), 15.

major international actor as evidenced by its expanding membership (with the notable exception of 'Brexit'); the deep relations it has fostered with its neighbours and the extensive range of international treaties it has entered into with third States and other international organizations. Furthermore, it has become more visible as a single actor in a range of human rights related initiatives and fora.[8]

Against such a backdrop, it is unproblematic to define the key issues this chapter addresses. It proposes to appraise the evolving role of the EU in the promotion and protection of human rights by considering selected aspects of its external action which influence the regulation of markets and business activities. In doing so, the chapter questions whether the instruments the Union has at its disposal to foster its trade policy are, indeed, devised to 'export' its complex market model and, hence, to stimulate the adoption of human rights rules and/or policies in those jurisdictions, by contributing to shaping their markets.[9]

The EU as a 'Normative Power' and the Protection and Promotion of Human Rights

The EU is increasingly perceived as a 'normative power',[10] where human rights hold a primary position. Already before the Treaty of Lisbon there was no doubt that the EU has a human rights component, as a concern and field of action in its external projection. The Post-Lisbon evolution of formalizing protection within EU law has strengthened internal protection for and respect of human rights within Member States.[11] At the same time, with the Treaty of Lisbon, the EU has firmly anchored its external relations in an ambitious normative agenda.

8 See, for example, R. Burchill, 'Assessing the EU's position on human rights'. In J.E. Wetzel (ed.), *The EU as a 'Global Player' in Human Rights?* New York: Routledge, 2011, 17, 19–27.

9 On the 'exportation' of norms and institutions regulating the EU internal market beyond its borders, see generally M. Cremona, 'The single market as a global export brand: exporting the single market'. *European Business Law Review*, 2010, 4, 663.

10 I. Manners, 'Normative power Europe: a contradiction in terms?'. *Journal of Common Market Studies*, 2002, 40(2), 235; A. Williams, *EU Human Rights Policy. A Study in Irony*. Oxford: Oxford University Press, 2004; G. Majone, *Europe as a Would-be World Power: the EU at Fifty*. Cambridge: Cambridge University Press, 2009, 1. For a dated but informative overview of human rights' pervasiveness in the EU agenda see P. Alston (ed.), *The EU and Human Rights*. Oxford: Oxford University Press, 1999.

11 See A. Rosas, 'Is the EU a human rights organisation?' 2011, CLEER Working Paper No. 2011/1, www.asser.nl/media/1624/cleer-wp-2011-1-rosas.pdf (last accessed 22 November 2017).

In particular, Articles 3(5)[12] and 21[13] TEU have injected a normative approach into its external relations and established the promotion and the protection of human rights as a main directive of EU external actions,[14] be they trade, investment, development cooperation, Common Security and Foreign Policy (CFSP), Common Security and Defence Policy (CSDP), or migration.[15] The material scope and normative effects of Articles 3(5) and 21 TEU have recently been subject to lively debate.[16] To the limited scope of this writing, there is no need to follow retrospectively all the threads of such debate. However, since the two provisions contribute to drawing the legal perimeter of the specific instruments analysed in this chapter, we should provide some essential comments on their normative effects. An accurate interpretation of the same provisions leads us to conclude that, in spite of the broad set of objectives laid down, they do not confer new competences on the EU.[17] Assuming a defensive extraterritoriality paradigm as to the scope *ratione loci* of human rights obligations, it is contended 'in the EU domestic system, [...] the scope of human rights is further imposed by Articles 3(5) and 21 TEU, which establish the promotion, or even the protection, of human rights as a foreign policy *directive*'.[18] Due to the restraints flowing from the founding treaties, Articles 3(5) and 21 do not provide a sufficient legal basis for EU action designed to protect human rights overseas. By virtue of the afore-referred provisions, the EU is (only) 'under an

12 Article 3(5) TEU provides that: 'In its relations with the wider world, the Union shall uphold and promote its values [as defined in art. 2 TEU] and interests and contribute to the protection of its citizens. It shall contribute to peace, security, the sustainable development of the Earth, solidarity and mutual respect among peoples, free and fair trade, eradication of poverty and the protection of human rights, in particular the rights of the child, as well as to the strict observance and the development of international law, including respect for the principles of the United Nations Charter'.

13 Article 21 TEU features in some of the EU's more specific external policies. In particular, art. 21(1) TEU provides that: '[t]he Union's action on the international scene shall be guided by the principles which have inspired its own creation, development and enlargement, and which it seeks to advance in the wider world: democracy, the rule of law, the universality and indivisibility of human rights and fundamental freedoms, respect for human dignity, the principles of equality and solidarity, and respect for the principles of the United Nations Charter and international law'.

14 W. Weiß, 'Human rights in the EU: rethinking the role of the European Convention on Human Rights after Lisbon'. *European Constitutional Law Review*, 2011, 7, 64 argues that the Treaty of Lisbon challenges the substance and methodology of human rights protection in the EU.

15 See also G. De Búrca, 'The evolution of EU human rights law'. In P. Craig and G. De Búrca (eds), *The Evolution of EU Law*, 2nd edn. Oxford: Oxford University Press, 2011, 491–4.

16 See L. Bartels, 'The EU's human rights obligations to policies with extraterritorial effects'. *European Journal of International Law*, 2015, 25(4), 1071; E. Cannizzaro, 'The EU's human rights obligations to policies with extraterritorial effects: a reply to Lorand Bartels'. *European Journal of International Law,* 2015, 25(4), 1093; L. Bartels, 'The EU's human rights obligations to policies with extraterritorial effects: a rejoinder to Enzo Cannizzaro'. Available at: www.ejiltalk.org/rejoinder-to-enzo-cannizzaro/ (last accessed 4 March 2017) (hereinafter: 'Bartels – rejoinder').

17 See further Cannizzaro, 'The EU's human rights obligations to policies with extraterritorial effects: a reply to Lorand Bartels', op. cit., 1093.

18 Ibid., 1095, emphasis added.

obligation to ensure respect for human rights worldwide, in the sense that its action must *tend* to promote and protect human rights, without being restricted to a particular geographical functions or functional sphere'.[19] The legal import of these two provisions 'seems thus to confine the aspiration of the EU as a global champion of human rights to the narrows of the principle of conferral'.[20]

The above analysis is important because it evidences that (i) despite the pervasive character of human rights in EU law, the legal framework for their promotion and protection remains fragmentary and does not provide for a coherent legal system in both the internal and external sphere of EU action;[21] (ii) the principle of conferral remains absolutely central in defining the extent of the Union's external activities in the human rights field. In particular, whereas the CFSP can be used unconditionally for the promotion and protection of human rights, other instruments can be resorted to only to the extent that they fall within the scope of the substantive competences conferred to the EU to achieve the specific objectives assigned to them.[22] As a matter of fact, the EU has, over the past few years, developed a large range of potential foreign policy instruments that it can employ to promote human rights.[23] In line with the above considerations, we focus on selected instruments and practices with the capacity of influencing the regulation of markets and business activities in third jurisdictions.

Integrating Trade and Human Rights: Moving Towards Business Regulation

Human rights concerns feature prominently in EU external economic relations. The best-known application of human rights in the external context is related to the accession of new Member States. Respect for human rights, essentially meaning acceptance of the ECHR, has been a formal requisite for joining the Union since 1993,[24] and later codified in Article 49 TEU. In a more political sense it is also a commitment within the ENP.[25] The EU has indeed made the upholding of human rights an integral part of its external trade relations and required that all trade, cooperation, partnership and association agreements with

19 Ibid., 1097, emphasis added.

20 Ibid., 1099, adding that in order to entrust the EU with different and more engaging global human rights *powers* would require further Treaty amendments.

21 See Williams, op. cit., chapter 4.

22 But see *contra,* Bartels – rejoinder.

23 European Commission, *Furthering Human Rights and Democracy Across the Globe*. Luxembourg,: European Commission, 2007 and, more recently, Council of the European Union, *EU Action Plan on Human Rights and Democracy (2015–2019)*, Brussels: European Union, 2015.

24 EC Bulletin, 6/1993, 1.13.

25 See P. Leino and R. Petrov, 'Between "common values" and competing universals – the promotion of EU's common values through the European neighbourhood policy'. *European Law Journal*, 2009, 15(5), 654.

third countries,[26] including unilateral trade instruments, contain – with varying modalities and intensity – a commitment to respect human rights.[27] The use of 'conditionality' in the area of external trade, cooperation and association agreements has, thus, constituted the main source of 'legal export' in the area of human rights. The following analysis will illustrate its evolution and assesses how closely its different forms can influence business activities in the interested jurisdictions and whether, as a result of the adoption of the related agreements, the EU and its partners are left with sufficient domestic policy space to protect human rights, as recommended, *inter alia*, by UNGP 9.[28]

Since the mid-1990s, the Union has developed a sophisticated array of tools to promote human rights in its external trade policy such as human rights clauses in bilateral trade agreements and a set of human rights criteria in the Generalized System of Preferences (GSP). In 2010, the Communication on Trade, Growth and World Affairs emphasized the trade–human rights nexus by stating that the aim of the EU is to encourage the EU's partners to promote the respect of human rights, labour standards, the environment and good governance through trade.[29] In the new EU trade strategy, the shift in focus has been further expanded in order to include a parallel concern for the environment and human rights, including social rights.[30] An important catalyst of such development was the formal adoption in 1995 by the Council of the EU of a concrete policy of adopting operative human rights clauses in all future cooperation and trade agreements.[31] The EU has adhered to this policy ever

26 To date the EU has concluded and is in the process of negotiating an array of international trade agreements, which vary in nature and belong to very different contexts, namely from pure trade relationships to broader partnerships of which trade is only one component, such as, for example, trade and economic cooperation agreements (based on arts. 207, 211, 212, 218 TFEU); partnerships with southern or eastern neighbouring countries (based on art. 8 TEU); or ACP group countries or candidate countries (the legal basis varying), and association agreements (based on art. 217 TFEU), which, together with their Deep and Comprehensive Free Trade Areas (DCFTAs), represent the most comprehensive form of co-operation offered by the EU to its non-candidate neighbours.

27 See, among others, L. Bartels, *Human Rights Conditionality in the EU's International Agreement*. Oxford: Oxford University Press, 2005; Ibid., 'Human rights and sustainable development obligations in EU Free Trade Agreements'. University of Cambridge Legal Studies Research Paper Series, No. 24/2'12, U. Khaliq, *Ethical Dimensions of the Foreign Policy of the European Union: A Legal Appraisal*. Cambridge: Cambridge University Press, 2008.

28 According to the UNGP 9: 'States should maintain adequate domestic policy space to meet their human rights obligations when pursuing business-related policy objectives with other States or business enterprises, for instance through investment treaties or contracts.'

29 COM(2010) 612 final, 12. See also European Commission, *Communication on Trade, Growth and Development. Tailoring Trade and Investment Policy for Those Countries Most in Need*. COM(2012) 22, final.

30 European Commission, *Trade for All – Towards a More Responsible Trade and Investment Policy*. COM(2015) 497, final.

31 EU, Council Conclusions of 29 May 1995, EU Bulletin 1995-5, points 1.2.3.

since,[32] although in more recent cases it has done so by cross-referencing (sometimes by implication) human rights clauses in existing agreements between the parties.[33] In addition, the EU has expanded its external human rights conditionality policies to its autonomous instruments granting trade preferences and financial and technical cooperation, as well as to financing agreements with developing countries.[34]

Human rights clauses provide that the respect for human rights, democracy and the rule of law constitutes the basis for EU PTAs. They are normally composed of two main parts: an 'essential element clause' on which the reciprocal obligations of the parties are premised, so that human rights violations of a certain scale by one of them can amount to a material breach of the agreement and justify suspension or other counter-measures, according to the so-called 'non-execution clause' (the second main element of the clauses at issue).[35] In turn, the 'non-execution' clause states that in the event that one party fails to comply with its obligations, the other party is able to adopt 'appropriate measures'. According to the Commission, sanctions under the clause should be reserved only for the most extreme and flagrant violations of human rights.[36]

An overview of the human rights clauses in EU trade agreements currently in force shows that there are clear patterns in the drafting of the essential elements and, in particular, that these clauses have evolved over the years and can be grouped by country and/or regional blocks.[37] The core of all human rights clauses is an 'essential elements' clause, which is in relatively standard wording. The following, from the 2012 EU–Central America agreement, is a good example:

32 For a detailed reconstruction see E. Fierro, *The EU's Approach to Human Rights Conditionality in Practice*. The Hague: Martinus Nijhoff, 2003.

33 See Bartels, 'Human rights and sustainable development obligations', op. cit., pp. 3–9.

34 See, for example, M.E. Bartoloni, 'La cooperazione allo sviluppo dell'Unione Europea con Paesi Terzi: da politica contro la povertà a cooperazione globale?'. *Diritti umani e diritto internazionale*, 2014, 8, 693.

35 In line with Vienna Convention on the Law of Treaties (adopted on 22 May 1969, entered into force on 27 January 1980) 1155 UNTS 331, art. 60.

36 See T. King, 'The European Union as a human rights actor'. In M. O'Flaherty, Z. Kędzia, A. Müller and G. Ulrich (eds), *Human Rights Diplomacy*. The Hague: Martinus Nijhoff, 2011, 77, 91. This form of unilateral enforcement is well-illustrated by art. 8(3) of the 2012 *EU–Colombia and Peru Trade Agreement* (OJ, L 354, 21 December 2012; hereinafter 'EU-Colombia/Peru TA'), which provides that 'any Party may immediately adopt appropriate measures in accordance with international law in case of violation by another Party of the essential elements referred to in Articles 1 and 2 of this Agreement'.

37 L. Beke, D. D'Hollander, N. Hachez and B. Pérez de las Heras, *Report on the Integration of Human Rights in EU Development and Trade Policies*. FRAME Deliverable No 9.1, European Commission, 2014, Annex II, available at: www.fp7-frame.eu/wp-content/materiale/reports/07-Deliverable-9.1.pdf (last accessed 3 November 2017).

> Respect for democratic principles and fundamental human rights, as laid down in the Universal Declaration of Human Rights, and for the principle of the rule of law, underpins the internal and international policies of both Parties and constitutes an essential element of this Agreement.[38]

The link between human rights and trade concessions has been progressively strengthened through gradual refinement of the clause. The most sophisticated and common versions expressly affirm that the obligation relating to human rights assumes an essential character in the context of the agreement. One of the most important recent developments, now a standard feature of human rights clauses, is the inclusion of an 'implementation' clause, which states that '[t]he Parties shall adopt any general or specific measures required for them to fulfil their obligations under this Agreement'.[39] This clause derives from what is now Article 4(3) TEU, which has in the context of EU law been interpreted as imposing a variety of additional obligations on the EU Member States, including the obligation to take steps to ensure the effective application of EU law.[40] As noted by Bartels, '[t]his is not to say that an "implementation clause" in an international agreement should be read in exactly the same way as in EU law'.[41] However, such a clause must have some meaning beyond superfluously reiterating the principle *pacta sunt servanda*.[42] Quite what it could mean is hard to say outside of the context of a specific case, although it might 'have the effect of imposing on the parties not only a negative duty to ensure that human rights and democratic principles are *respected* but also a positive duty to ensure that these norms are *ensured* and *fulfilled*'.[43]

It is noteworthy that human rights clauses do not normally mention the individual rights with which compliance is sought. Frequently such rights are somewhat vaguely identified through reference to 'common accepted standards' or, in the most elaborated versions of the clause, a generic reference to political,

38 See *EU Association Agreement with Central America* (OJ, L. 346, 15 December 2012; hereinafter 'EUCAAA'). Examples of complex and refined human rights clauses are found in the new association agreements negotiated with Eastern countries such as, for example, the EU–Ukraine AA (OJ, L 161/3, 29 May 2014), art. 2; EU-Moldova AA (OJ, L 260/4, 30 August 2014), art. 2; and EU-Georgia AA (OJ L261/4, 30 August 2014), art. 2. See further, N. Ghazaryan, 'A new generation of human rights clauses? The case of association agreements in the Eastern neighbourhood'. *European Law Review*, 2015, 40, 391, and R. Petrov, 'EU values in integration agreements with Ukraine, Moldova and Georgia'. In S. Poli (ed.), *The European Neighbourhood Policy: Values and Principles*. New York: Routledge, 2016, 99, 103.

39 For example, EUCAAA., art. 355(1).

40 For an informed summary see C. Hillion and R. Wessel, 'Restraining external competences of EU member states under CFSP'. In M. Cremona and B. de Witte (eds), *EU Foreign Relations Law*. Oxford: Hart, 2008, 92, with further references.

41 Bartels 'Human rights and sustainable development obligations', op. cit., 5.

42 J. Klabbers, *An Introduction to International Institutional Law*. Cambridge: Cambridge University Press, 2002, 195.

43 Bartels, 'Human rights and sustainable development obligations', op. cit., 5, emphasis in original.

economic, social, economic and cultural rights, to the rule of law and to democratic principles. Such reference is nevertheless expressly meant to refer only to international obligations already in force between parties.[44] Most of the documents referred to by the clauses at issue have the nature of soft law and are deprived, as such, of binding force. Even when reference is made to treaties, such as the UN Covenants of 1996, they may not be in force between parties. Thus, it seems reasonable

> to assume that these documents are referred to as evidence of principles of customary rules of international law. Far from imposing new obligations, human rights clauses reveal commitment of the parties to the protection of such fundamental individual rights as are binding for all subjects of international law.[45]

As it clearly emerges from the above, human rights clauses do not have a direct bearing on the regulation of markets and business in the EU's trade partners, associate states or countries that benefit from the Union's financial/technical cooperation. Overall, they stimulate the promotion of human rights in the trade partners, normally in the context of complex agreements which anyway permit the parties to maintain adequate domestic policy space to meet their human rights obligations.

The impact on business regulation becomes far more evident in recently negotiated EU FTAs that incorporate dedicated chapters on social, labour and environmental protection issues (so-called 'sustainable development chapters') and, lately, also address corporate behaviours relating to these matters, also by incorporating corporate social responsibility (CSR) clauses.[46] With regard to labour provisions, the 2000 Cotonou Partnership Agreement (CPA)[47] is particularly worthy of mention as both the EU and the African, Caribbean and Pacific (ACP) countries have equally committed themselves to respect corporate labour standards (CLS) and to enhance cooperation in this area, for example, through the adoption and enforcement of ad hoc legislation and, at the same time, rejecting the use of labour standards for protectionist purposes, as provided in Article 50, the key labour clause of the agreement. While mainly

44 See E. Cannizzaro, 'The scope of the EU foreign power. Is the EC competent to conclude agreements with third states including human rights clauses?'. In E. Cannizzaro (ed.), *The European Union as an Actor in International Relations*, op. cit., 297, 301.

45 Ibid., 301–302, adding that by so doing, human rights clauses, rather than statically mirroring the present stage of evolution of international law, 'aim at advancing the evolutionary process and expanding the protection of human rights well beyond that stage'.

46 See F. Romanin Jacur, 'The reference to corporate social responsibility in bilateral and regional free trade agreement: an early assessment and possible ways forward'. Mimeo, 1.

47 *Agreement between the Members of the African, Caribbean and Pacific Group of States of the One Part, and the European Community and its Member States of the Other Part.* OJ L 317, 15.12.2000; OJ L 141, 7.6.2003.

programmatic in nature, the clause entrenches the CLS within the partnership as recommended by the World Commission on the Social Dimension of Globalization (WCSDG),[48] and implies that the objectives of the ILO can be best achieved with the cooperation of certain regional actors and through transposition into the CPA of those obligations stemming from the 1998 ILO's Declaration, which in turn are 'subject to the oversight of the parties and coordinated action under the EU-ILO strategic partnership'.[49] In addition, the CPA provides for the use of dispute settlement in relation to the interpretation and application of their human rights clauses,[50] including appropriate measures adopted under these clauses.[51]

The overarching legal commitment of the EU in the area of sustainable development has been given further weight with the adoption of so-called 'new generation' of FTAs[52] containing 'trade and sustainable development chapters' including provisions on cooperation and obligations to respect and 'strive' to improve multilateral and domestic labour and environmental standards. The same agreements often promote the effective implementation in law and practice of CLS.[53] In particular, a first set of obligations contains minimum obligations to implement certain multilateral obligations and other obligations which require the parties to the agreement not to reduce their levels of protection, encouraging them to raise their levels of protection, subject to a proviso that this is not done for protectionist purposes.[54] Examples of such agreements are the 2008 EU–CARIFORUM;[55] the 2010 EU–Korea FTA;[56] the 2012 EU–CAA;[57] the

48 Ibid., art. 50.

49 J. Kenner, 'Economic partnership agreement: enhancing the labour dimension of global governance?'. In B. Van Vooren, S. Blockmans and J. Wouters (eds), *The EU'S Role in Global Governance: The Legal Dimension*. Oxford: Oxford University Press, 2013, 316.

50 CPA, art. 78.

51 Ibid., art. 96.

52 This is the conventional label to indicate the agreements negotiated by the Union after announcing new trade policy strategies in 2006, with the Commission's *Communication Concerning Global Europe: Competing in the World. A Contribution to the EU' Growth and Jobs Strategy*. COM (2006) 567 final (4 October 2006).

53 For a comprehensive overview see L. Bartels, 'Social issues: labour, environment and human rights'. In S. Lester, B. Mercurio and L. Bartels (eds), *Bilateral and Regional Trade Agreements. Commentary and Analysis*, 2nd edn. Cambridge: Cambridge University Press, 2015, 364.

54 L. Bartels, 'Human rights and sustainable development obligations in EU Free Trade Agreements'. *Legal Issues of Economic Integration*, 2013, 40, 297, 306.

55 *Economic Partnership Agreement between the CARIFORUM States, of the One Part, and the European Community and its Member States, of the Other Part*. In OJ L 289, 30 October 2008, arts. 72–73.

56 *Free Trade Agreement between the European Union and its Member States, of the One Part, and the Republic of Korea, of the Other Part*, 2011 OJ (L 127/54, 24 May 2011), ch. 13.

57 EUCAAA, Part IV, Title VIII.

2012 EU–Colombia/Peru Agreement;[58] and the 2016 EU–Vietnam FTA[59] and the 2017 EU–Japan Economic Partnership Agreement (EPA) (both awaiting ratification).[60] The outcome of ongoing negotiations with MERCOSUR countries, Mexico, Chile, Australia and New Zealand will very likely incorporate similar chapters.

In general terms, while there is some variation between the provisions contained in the different agreements, there seems to be some level of commonality as to the substantive standards and the institutional set-up envisaged. Another common feature across EU FTAs of new generation is the reaffirmation of commitment to effectively implement international labour and environmental treaties to which states are Parties.[61] Moreover, in all the different formulations states adopt a 'mutually supportive approach' that endorses complementary and integration of economic provisions with rules focused on human rights and environmental protection.[62] Finally, as to the issue of domestic policy space, it is noteworthy that the FTAs of the new generation normally recognize the sovereign right of the Parties to establish their domestic policies and priorities on sustainable development, and their own levels of environmental and labour protection, consistent with the internationally recognized standards and agreements to which they refer.[63]

CSR clauses are one of the latest developments in the shift of trade and investment agreements towards a more sustainable economic globalization and the inclusion of non-trade and non-state actors consideration.[64]As rightly noted, however, the provisions of such agreements 'remain of an intergovernmental

58 See EU–Colombia and Peru TA, Title IX. The sustainable development chapter of the agreement contains obligations on the effective implementation of, and non-derogation from, domestic labour laws, recognition of the ILO recent work principles and their relevance for trade and labour. It also includes a provision on equality of treatment as regards working conditions with a focus on migrant workers legally employed in the Parties' respective territories (ibid., art. 276).

59 See *EU-Vietnam Free Trade Agreement: Agreed text as of January 2016*, available at: http://trade.ec.europa.eu/doclib/press/index.cfm?id=1437 (last accessed 4 December 2017), Ch. 15.

60 On 8 December 2017, the EU and Japan concluded negotiations on the EPA. Selected chapters of the agreement are available at: http://trade.ec.europa.eu/doclib/press/index.cfm?&id=1684&utm_campaign=a35cdb8be9-EMAIL_CAMPAIGN_2017_07_06&utm_medium=email&utm_source=POLITICO.EU&utm_term=0_10959edeb5-a35cdb8be9-189902969 (last accessed 15 February 2018).

61 See, for example, EU–Colombia/Peru TA, art. 270 (1) and (2). See further Romanin Jacur, op. cit., 5.

62 Ibid., 6. On the principle of mutual supportiveness see L. Boisson de Chazournes and M. Mbengue, 'A propos du principe du soutien mutuel – Les relations entre le protocole de Cartagena et les accords de l'OMC'. *Revue Générale de Droit International Public*, 2007, 829; R. Pavoni, 'Mutual supportiveness as a principle of interpretation and law-making: a watershed for the "WTO-and-competing-regimes" debate?'. *European Journal of International Law*, 2010, 649.

63 See, for example, EU–Colombia/Peru TA, art 268.

64 J. Hepburn and V. Kuuya, 'Corporate social responsibility and investment treaties'. In M-C. Cordonier Segger, M.W. Gehring and A. Newcombe (eds), *Sustainable Development in World Investment Law*. Alphen aan den Rijn: Kluwer Law International, 2011, 589.

nature and do not provide for direct obligations for business operators'.[65] Despite the lack of vertical effects and the consequent limited implications on enterprises, the incorporation of CSR clauses is evidence 'of the role that these actors play as potential promoters, on the one hand, but also of potential infringers, on the other hand, of human and labour rights and of environmental protection' standards.[66] The first EU agreement to include references to CSR is the 2008 EU–CARIFORUM Economic Partnership Agreement. States' obligations addressing CSR fall in three broad categories that operate at different level: first, the obligations to cooperate at the international level bilaterally and within the competent institutions and their regulatory processes;[67] second, the commitments to adopt domestic measures addressing corporate behaviour and to encourage enterprises operating on their territory or under their jurisdiction to adopt CSR instruments;[68] third, states' commitments to provide a sort of preferential treatment for goods produced through sustainable supply chains which take into consideration CSR schemes.[69]

To conclude, while the promotional features of the 'new generation' of FTAs contribute to injecting a social dimension into the EU's trade policy, it remains to be seen whether they entail an effective improvement of the implementation-capacity of developing countries and other partners to respect and protect the labour and environmental standards they promote. Factors that may contribute to the effectiveness of such provisions vary with the different agreements. An example is the combination of AAs with dedicated technical assistance deployed by the EU in the context of the ENP[70] and the pre-accession phase.[71] Even more so, the credibility of the membership prospects with the approach of accession may significantly incentivize the implementation of the rules at issue.

Concluding Remarks

The practice of making the effect of economic and trade agreements mainly dependent upon the respect for human rights, democratic principles and, more recently, sustainable development standards is clearly the standard *modus operandi* of the EU. In such a context, human rights clauses, development chapters

65 Romanin Jacur, op. cit., 6.

66 Ibid., 6.

67 See, for example, EU–Georgia AA, art. 231, let.(c); and EU–CARIFORUM, art. 196.

68 See, for example, *Comprehensive Economic and Trade Agreement (CETA) between Canada, of the One Part, and the European Union and its Member States, of the Other Part* (OJ L 11, 14 January 2017), Preamble.

69 See, for example, EU–Georgia AA, art. 231, let (d); EU–Korea FTA, art. 13.6(2).

70 See Burchill, op. cit., 27–28.

71 This kind of technical cooperation is currently delivered under the Instrument for Pre-Accession Assistance II– IPA II. See *Regulation (EU) No 231/2014 of the European Parliament and of the Council of 11 March 2014, establishing an Instrument for Pre-Accession Assistance (IPA II)*. OJ L 77/11. See A. Albi, 'Ironies in human rights protection in the EU: pre-accession conditionality and post-accession conundrums' *European Law Journal*, 2009, 15(1), 46.

and CSR norms serve precisely to bind the functionalist conception of the Union and its rising political and social aspirations, by leveraging its economic might as a tool to promote compliance with human rights standards, the principles of democracy and sustainable development. Put differently, they serve to promote a synchrony between 'development' and 'progress' in third countries (trade partners, associate states, potential and actual candidates to accession) being embedded in international agreements which, considered in their entirety, leave the parties with adequate domestic policy space to meet their human rights obligations when pursuing business-related policy objectives. In incorporating such rules, EU FTAs seem to adhere to the directive provided by Articles 3(5) and 21 TEU for the Union's external relation. In particular, the inclusion of refined sustainable development chapters and CSR clauses mark a definitive shift towards the promotion of business regulation in third jurisdictions. A political assessment of such practices goes beyond the purpose of the current chapter. However, it should be noted that opposite appraisals often arise in this respect: some contend that projecting the EU model to the wider world is about the Union's representing a unique historical experience that can bring sustainable global development to the international system;[72] others, like Koskenniemi, contend that it reflects the European tendency to universalize the regional,[73] with the EU seeking to exert some degree of political and economic influence over third countries because the failure to export its (internal) standards to other outside its territory would penalise European firms.

72 See, for example, R. Prodi, *Shaping the New Europe*. Speech given at the European Parliament Strasbourg, 15 February 2000, SPEECH/00/41.

73 M. Koskenniemi, 'International law in Europe between tradition and renewal'. *European Journal of International Law*, 2005, 16, 113.

8 National Action Plans

A Pathway to Effective Implementation of the United Nations Guiding Principles?

Marta Bordignon

Introduction[1]

Since the endorsement of the UNGPs in 2011 by the UNHRC, the objectives of diffusion and implementation of the B&HR framework have gained attention among international institutions, states, enterprises and other involved stakeholders. The first action was taken by the UN Working Group on the issue of human rights and transnational corporations and other business enterprises (UNWGB&HR), followed by the EU which – through the adoption in 2011 of the Communication *A Renewed EU Strategy 2011–14 for Corporate Social Responsibility*[2] – tried to apply a regional approach to the UNGPs' implementation. Pursuant to the 2011 Communication, National Action Plans (NAPs) should be the turning points for the policy-making processes of national implementation of the UNGPs and should facilitate a convergent approach among States. Furthermore, in the wording of the UNWGB&HR, NAPs are the 'key tool[s] for effective implementation of the Guiding Principles'[3] and contribute to the 'evolving policy strategies developed by States to prevent and protect against human rights abuses by business enterprises in conformity with the Guiding Principles on Business and Human Rights'.[4]

1 This research work is the result of the analysis carried out by the co-founders of the Human Rights International Corner (hereinafter 'HRIC') – namely Marta Bordignon, Giacomo Maria Cremonesi and Maria Francesca Cucchiara – on the Italian NAP published on the HRIC website in May 2017. The research was also conducted in the frame of the University of Seville (Spain) Research Project DER2013-41956-P, entitled *La implementación de los Principios Rectores de las Naciones Unidas sobre empresas y derechos humanos por la Unión Europea y sus Estados Miembros* (The implementation of the United Nations Guiding Principles on Business and Human Rights by the European Union and Member States), granted by the Spanish Ministry of Economy and Competitiveness.

2 European Commission, *A Renewed EU strategy 2011–14 for Corporate Social Responsibility*, 25 October 2011, www.europarl.europa.eu/meetdocs/2009_2014/documents/com/com_com(2011)0681_/com_com(2011)0681_en.pdf (last accessed 20 November 2017).

3 UNHRC, *Report of the Working Group on the Issue of Human Rights and Transnational Corporations and other Business Enterprises*, UN Doc. A/HRC/26/25, 5 May 2014, 11.

4 Ibid., 6.

The aforementioned initiatives were followed by other initiatives carried out at EU level and within the CoE framework. Currently, the EU institutions are even considering the adoption of an international treaty on B&HR and have joined the international negotiation process of it at the UN.

The proposed adoption of NAPs has, to date, attracted high levels of participation, both inside and outside the EU. Since 2013, 21 states at global level have released a NAP on B&HR, namely: Belgium, Chile, Colombia, Czech Republic, Denmark, Finland, France, Georgia, Germany, Indonesia, Ireland, Italy, Lithuania, Norway, Poland, Spain, Sweden, Switzerland, the Netherlands, the UK, and the US. Fourteen are EU Member States.

Against this background, following a global overview of the NAPs already adopted at global level, this chapter will analyse a specific case study: the NAP released by the Italian Government and officially presented by the Interministerial Committee for Human Rights (hereinafter 'CIDU') in December 2016.[5]

The Domestic Implementation of the UNGPs: Why through National Action Plans?

According to Surya Deva, a NAP 'allows the government to assess the current legal-cum-policy framework so as to identify what is working and what is not in terms of ensuring that companies respect human rights'.[6] Likewise, the study published by the EU Directorate General for External Policies in February 2017 (hereinafter: 'the EU Directorate Study')[7] emphasizes the broader consensus on these government-led instruments, highlighting that, together with the UNGPs, they are helping states to comply with their duty to protect human rights, specifically against the adverse impact of business activities.

In general terms, NAPs are policy tools that outline governments' commitments, planned measures and initiatives regarding a specific area. In particular, NAPs on B&HR are instruments whereby states express their commitments and priorities for the implementation of their internationally recognized obligations to protect and respect human rights, as set out in the first pillar of the UNGPs.

5 CIDU, Piano di azione nazionale impresa e diritti umani 2016–2021, December 2016, http://cidu.esteri.it/resource/2016/12/49118_f_PANBHRITAFINALE15122016.pdf (last accessed 15 March 2018); Italian National Action Plan on Business and Human Rights 2016–2021, December 2016, https://cidu.esteri.it/resource/2016/12/49117_f_NAPBHRENGFINALEDEC152017.pdf (last accessed 15 March 2018) (hereinafter 'Italian NAP').

6 S. Deva, *Background Paper for India's National Framework on Business and Human Rights*, The Ethical Trading Initiative, March 2016, http://s3-eu-west-1.amazonaws.com/www.ethicaltrade.org.files/shared_resources/india_national_framework_bhr_background.pdf?FeQtVeqQG8lntPXXHzNOIGnH3hUOPIlc (last accessed 20 November 2017).

7 EU Directorate General for External Policies (Policy Department), *Implementation of the UN Guiding Principles on Business and Human Rights*, February 2017, www.europarl.europa.eu/RegData/etudes/STUD/2017/578031/EXPO_STU(2017)578031_EN.pdf (last accessed 20 November 2017).

The aforementioned EU Directorate Study identifies the benefits arising from the application of a NAP as a main vehicle for the UNGPs' implementation. They are (i) a greater coordination and coherence within government on the range of public policy areas; (ii) an inclusive process to identify national priorities and concrete policy measures/actions; (iii) a process of continuous monitoring, measuring and evaluation of implementation; (iv) a platform for ongoing multi-stakeholder dialogue; (v) a format that facilitates international cooperation, good practices exchange, and coordination; and (vi) transparency and predictability for interested domestic and international stakeholders.[8]

At European level, the adoption of NAPs for implementing the UNGPs is strongly recommended. For instance, the 2011 EU Communication on a Renewed Corporate Social Responsibility Strategy[9] was followed by a Declaration issued by the CoE in April 2014, reaffirming that an effective implementation of the UNGPs by both states and enterprises is essential to ensure the respect for human rights in the business context. In March 2016, the Committee of Ministers of the CoE adopted Recommendation CM/Rec (2016)3,[10] providing a more specific guidance for the establishment of preventing and monitoring mechanisms, especially in relation to the third pillar of the UNGPs,[11] along with the invitation to conduct a review of the existing national legislation and practice in the field of B&HR. Furthermore, the Recommendation calls for more transparency about the drafting and consultation phases of NAPs, and also suggests sharing some very specific information about the process through a dedicated co-sharing platform to be established by the CoE. It also provides detailed suggestions in the field of access to remedy and advises a mid-term review of NAPs in 2021.

In order to understand what a NAP on B&HR should contain and thus impartially evaluate its content, it is possible to refer to the existing assessment tools drafted by international civil society organizations (hereinafter 'CSOs') committed in the field of B&HR. The first example is the European Group of National Human Rights Institutions (hereinafter 'EGNHRIs'),[12] which in 2012 published a Discussion Paper setting out recommendations on NAPs. In the Discussion Paper, the EGNHRIs pointed out some essential requirements of a

8 Ibid., 22.

9 European Commission, *A Renewed EU strategy 2011–14 for Corporate Social Responsibility*, op. cit.

10 Committee of Ministers of the CoE, *Recommendation to Member States on Human Rights and Business*, CM/Rec (2016)3, 2 March 2016, para 1.

11 In this regard it is worth mentioning the Opinion of the European Union Agency for Fundamental Rights, *Improving Access to Remedy in the Area of Business and Human Rights at the EU Level*, released on 10 April 2017.

12 European Group on National Human Rights Institution, *Implementing the UN Guiding Principles on Business and Human Rights: Discussion Paper on National Implementation Plans for EU Member States*, June 2012, https://business-humanrights.org/sites/default/files/media/eu-nhris-paper-on-national-implementation-plans-for-ungps-210612-short.pdf (last accessed 20 November 2017).

NAP and called for the adoption of a human-rights based approach focused on inclusion, transparency, participation, and accountability. A year later, the Danish Institute for Human Rights (hereinafter 'DIHR') and the International Corporate Accountability Roundtable (hereinafter 'ICAR') launched a project to create a step-by-step guidance on NAPs with the objective of ensuring that both the process and its outcomes comply with a human-rights based approach.[13] The project led to the adoption of the report *Assessment of the Existing National Action Plans on Business and Human Rights*, released by ICAR, European Coalition for Corporate Justice (hereinafter 'ECCJ') and the Centre for the Study of Law, Justice, and Society (Dejusticia) in August 2017.[14] At the UN level, the UNWGB&HR published a first draft guidance on NAPs in December 2014, followed by updated versions in November 2015 and November 2016.[15] Also relevant is the article authored by Damiano de Felice and Andreas Graf published in 2015, introducing eight criteria for the NAP's development process and content.[16]

All these tools identify the essential features of NAPs. The latter should aim at achieving a multiplicity of benefits, by: (i) following principles such as transparency, inclusion, participation, and non-discrimination; (ii) empowering rights-holders by providing them with a common communication platform; and (iii) creating a starting point for dialogue between stakeholders. Moreover, the assessment tools also identify some so-called milestones, such as: (i) establishing a clear NAP's governance and budget; (ii) organizing a consultation process with all relevant stakeholders; (iii) publishing a National Baseline Assessment (hereinafter 'NBA'); (iv) giving an exhaustive definition of scope, content, and priorities; and, finally, (v) following transparency and accountability principles, and establishing follow-up mechanisms.

13 Danish Institute for Human Rights, International Corporate Accountability Roundtable, *National Action Plans on Business and Human Rights – A Toolkit for the Development, Implementation, and Review of State Commitments to Business and Human Rights Frameworks*, June 2014, http://accountabilityroundtable.org/analysis/napsreport/ (last accessed 20 November 2017). UNWGB&HR, *Guidance on National Action Plans on Business and Human Rights*, November 2016, www.ohchr.org/Documents/Issues/Business/UNWG_NAPGuidance.pdf (last accessed 20 November 2017).

14 ICAR, ECCJ, Dejusticia, *Assessment of the Existing National Action Plans on Business and Human Rights*, August 2017 www.icar.ngo/publications/2017/8/23/assessments-of-existing-national-action-plans-naps-on-business-and-human-rights-august-2017 (last accessed 20 November 2017).

15 UNWGB&HR, Guidance on National Action Plans on Business and Human Rights, November 2016 www.ohchr.org/Documents/Issues/Business/UNWG_NAPGuidance.pdf (last accessed 20 November 2017).

16 D. de Felice and A. Graf, 'The potential of National Action Plans to implement human rights norms: an early assessment with respect to the UN guiding principles on business and human rights'. *Journal of Human Rights Practice*, 2015, 7(1), 40–71.

A Snapshot of the Existing National Action Plans

As stated above, the 21 states that have already adopted and published a NAP on B&HR come from three different continents (America, Asia and Europe), although most of them are EU Member States (Belgium, Denmark, Finland, France, Germany, Ireland, Italy, Lithuania, the Netherlands, Poland, Spain, Sweden and the UK). Five NAPs are available only in the country's home language (Belgium, Chile, Colombia, France and Spain), while the others have been translated at least into English. Apart from the first two published in 2013 (the UK, updated in 2015, and the Dutch one), in 2014 only two NAPS were published (Danish and Finnish), followed by an increasing trend of publication in 2015 (Colombian, Lithuanian, Norwegian, Swedish), in 2016 (German, Italian, Swiss and the US) and up until the time of writing (Belgian, Chilean, Czech, French, Georgian, Indonesian, Irish, Polish and Spanish).

In order to analyse the content of the NAPs and conduct a cross-assessment, this chapter will apply the criteria proposed by the most updated related assessment tool – namely the third edition of the *Assessment of the Existing National Action Plans on Business and Human Rights* released by ICAR, European Coalition for Corporate Justice (hereinafter 'ECCJ') and the Centre for the Study of Law, Justice, and Society (Dejusticia) in August 2017.[17] This study was conducted using the so-defined NAPs Checklist developed by ICAR and the DIHR and already published in Annex 5 of the aforementioned joint 2014 ICAR-DIHR NAPs report.[18] The Checklist sets out 25 criteria concerning both the content of NAPs and the drafting process for developing them.

In relation to the content of the existing NAPs, on the one hand some positive trends can be found in the expressed commitment to the UNGPs, in the clear reference to international and regional organizations and standards, and in the inclusion of some thematic and sector-specific human rights topics. Regarding the first point, the Italian, Colombian, and Norwegian NAPs lay out commitments to future actions. However, in most of the NAPs the planned actions are extremely vague and do not provide information about concrete steps that the state will take, making it difficult for stakeholders to monitor the NAP's implementation. NAPs often refer to the most vulnerable or excluded groups, such as children, women, indigenous peoples, peoples with disabilities, human rights defenders, and lesbian, gay, bisexual, transgender, and intersex persons (e.g. Finnish, Italian and Colombian NAPs, while other ones – such as

17 ICAR, ECCJ, Dejusticia, *Assessment of the Existing National Action Plans on Business and Human Rights*, August 2017, www.icar.ngo/publications/2017/8/23/assessments-of-existing-national-action-plans-naps-on-business-and-human-rights-august-2017 (last accessed 20 November 2017).

18 Danish Institute for Human Rights, International Corporate Accountability Roundtable, *National Action Plans on Business and Human Rights – A Toolkit for the Development, Implementation, and Review of State Commitments to Business and Human Rights Frameworks*, op. cit., Annex 5.

the British, the US, and Swiss – mention vulnerable or excluded groups to a lesser extent).

As regards the weaknesses of NAPs, they persist especially in relation to the failure to sufficiently explore regulatory options to ensure adequate human rights protection and access to justice. The majority of future and planned actions mainly focus on measures involving awareness raising, training, research and other voluntary initiatives, with very limited attention to supporting the adoption and development of regulatory and legal actions that could more easily address existing governmental gaps. At the same time, while there have been some improvements in the general discussion on the third pillar of the UNGPs, NAPs usually mention only very briefly access to remedy: the ones that address it mostly lack specific state commitments to improve access to remedy. Moreover, NAPs even fail to address existing domestic barriers to access to judicial remedy for corporate-related human rights abuses which occur at home or abroad – with the exception of the Italian, UK, Swedish and Danish NAPs – and focus instead on regional or international bodies and non-State-based non-judicial mechanisms.[19] Lastly, only a few NAPs fully refer to the scope of state territorial jurisdiction.

The following sections will analyse the Italian experience, starting with a brief recap of the initial drafting and consultation phases and then providing an in-depth analysis of the Italian NAP.

The Way Forward for the Italian NAP 2016–2021

Given the joint publication in September 2013 of the Italian Action Plan on Corporate Social Responsibility by the Ministry of Labour and Social Policies and the Ministry of Economic Development, the CIDU was established as the leading authority for the elaboration of the Italian Action Plan on B&HR. Among the activities carried out by this institution – mandated to grant the implementation by Italy of its international commitments in the field of human rights protection – it is worth mentioning the support to the adoption of new instruments aimed at achieving full compliance with international and European instruments legislations, such as the Communication of the EU Commission on a Renewed Strategy on CSR 2011–2014.

In order to promote the adoption of the NAP, the Italian OECD National Contact Point financed the drafting of a mapping study on the state-of-art of the Italian B&HR legislation. The study was conducted by the Scuola Superiore Sant'Anna (Pisa, Italy) and presented at the Italian Chamber of Deputies in

19 In this regard, the Norwegian NAP solely commits to participate in international or regional initiatives, while the UK's NAP engages the State to continue supporting remedy procedures in other countries. Similarly, the Italian and US NAPs focus on non-judicial remedies, such as the OECD National Contact Point (NCP), or grievance mechanisms under the International Code of Conduct for Private Security Service Providers.

November 2013.[20] The study focused on 13 main issues connected to the UNGPs and their relevance within the Italian legal and political system. This document can be considered as the National Baseline Assessment (hereinafter 'NBA') of the Italian system in terms of B&HR – namely, the gap analysis recommended by the European Group of National Human Rights Institutions, as well as by the other assessment tools published afterwards.

The NBA was followed by a first draft version of the Italian Plan on B&HR, entitled *The Foundations of the Italian Action Plan on the United Nations Guiding Principles on Business and Human Rights*, published in English in March 2014. This document focused on the first and the third pillars of the UNGPs, without recommending any actions or planned measures to be implemented in future. In light of the aforementioned toolkits and guides on NAPs (i) it contains references to the relevant international and regional standards and to the most impacted human rights; (ii) the planned measures and actions for the implementation of the NAP are missing, as well as the involvement of the most vulnerable groups of stakeholders during the drafting phase; (iii) it is completely focused on the first and the third pillars, lacking any provisions about corporate accountability (second pillar); (iv) and there is no information about the definition of an appropriate funding, it lacks the organization of the drafting and consultation processes, and no precise timeline is provided.

The next section analyses the content of the final version of the Italian NAP, as well as the drafting and consultation processes that led to its publication, according to the research work conducted by Human Rights International Corner (HRIC), of which the author is a co-founder.

The Italian Action Plan: Weaknesses and Strengths

The current version of the Italian NAP – launched by the CIDU in December 2016 – is the result of a consultation and drafting process that lasted more than a year and a half (from January 2015 to July 2016). The Italian Action Plan was finalized with the assistance of an institutional Working Group (composed of all the Ministries involved) and a non-institutional one (composed of representatives of academia, enterprises, trade unions, business associations, CSOs and legal experts). Both Working Groups worked in parallel from the outset, and then shared their outputs during joint meetings. The first draft was released in July 2016 and was available for an open consultation. It received a large number

20 Scuola Superiore Sant'Anna, *Imprese e Diritti Umani: il caso Italia. Analisi del Quadro Normativo e delle Politiche di Salvaguardia*, November 2013, www.sviluppoeconomico.gov.it/images/stories/documenti/Imprese_e_diritti_umani_Il%20caso_Italia_FINALE_NOV_2013.pdf (last accessed 20 November 2017). Available only in Italian.

of contributions and inputs from CSOs and NGOs, as well as business associations, trade unions and companies.[21]

In March 2017, the first Implementation Workshop of the NAP was held in Rome. It was coordinated by the CIDU in collaboration with the Italian Alliance for Sustainable Development. However, the event did not clarify either the timeline for the implementation of the measures recommended by the NAP or the roles played by the Working Group on Business and Human Rights (in Italian, GLIDU, Gruppo di Lavoro Impresa e Diritti Umani) – which covers a monitoring role pursuant to the NAP – and the non-institutional Working Group. A successful participation of all the relevant stakeholders, especially those representing the most affected and engaged groups, was still lacking. The first official multi-stakeholder meeting between the GLIDU and the representatives of businesses, trade unions, civil society, academia, and experts took place in Rome only in November 2017.

As far as state commitment is concerned, the implementation of the measures proposed by the NAP reveals a multidisciplinary approach by the Italian Government, in line with the Sustainable Development Goals (SDGs) and the UN Agenda 2030.[22] This conclusion can be referred also to the National Strategy on Sustainable Development, recently adopted by the Ministry of Environment.[23] Among the National Strategic Objectives, the latter document recalls the promotion of CSR and of a sustainable management of natural resources. Moreover, the multi-stakeholder approach aforementioned – both in terms of state commitment and monitoring mechanism – is in line with the international best practices suggested by the assessment tools.

The clear reference in the Italian NAP[24] to the introduction of Human Rights Due Diligence (hereinafter 'HRDD') processes must be favourably welcomed, especially in the light of the recent adoption of the corresponding French law providing for a mandatory HRDD (*devoir de vigilance*) for multinational corporations.[25] However, different from the French law, the Italian NAP recommends a mere 'promotion' of HRDD, without providing for the

21 HRIC, ECCJ, MANI TESE and FIDH, *Contribution to the Italian National Action Plan on Business and Human Rights 2016–2021*, 15 September 2016. https://docs.wixstatic.com/ugd/6c779a_4d8e7673ff454e359133a4616d225ce0.pdf (last accessed 20 November 2017).

22 Italian NAP, Part I, 5.

23 Italian Ministry of Environment, *National Sustainable Development Strategy 2017/2030 (NSDS)*, July 2017. www.minambiente.it/sites/default/files/archivio/allegati/sviluppo_sostenibile/snsvs_bozza_2_0_13032017.pdf (last accessed 20 November 2017).

24 Italian NAP, Part II, 7.

25 See HRIC, *Remarks on the Italian Action Plan on Business and Human Rights 2016–2021*, May 2017 https://docs.wixstatic.com/ugd/6c779a_7f3f54bdedab4632b8a79d7b6ad887d9.pdf. Conseil Constitutionnel, *Decision no. 2017-750 DC 23 Loi relative au devoir de vigilance des sociétés mères et des entreprises donneuses d'ordre*, March 2017, www.conseil-constitutionnel.fr/conseil-constitutionnel/root/bank/download/2017750DC2017750dc.pdf (last accessed 11 December 2017).

adoption of a legal instrument establishing an obligation for enterprises to annually publish a 'plan de vigilance'.[26]

At the same time, it is worth mentioning the inclusion in the NAP of measures to tackle *caporalato* (i.e. practices of treatment of agricultural workers in disregard of core labour standards) and any form of exploitation, forced labour, child labour, slavery and irregular work, with a particular reference to migrants and modern slaves. These measures are in line with the recently adopted Italian Law 199 of 29 October 2016,[27] and are suitable to restate a renewed commitment of the Italian Government in this field. The planned measures are mainly aimed at prevention, rather than at protecting victims, in particular irregular migrants.[28]

In terms of equal opportunities, it is interesting to note that the NAP extends the concept of diversity management to corporations, based on Law 76/2016.[29] As regards environmental sustainability, the clear reference among the national priorities to the promotion of environmental protection and sustainability could be read in the framework of the implementation of the Paris Agreement on Climate Change (COP21), ratified by Italy in October 2016 and entered into force in November 2016, which provides effective instruments for environmental protection and the promotion of legislative initiatives (such as concerning environmental crimes).

Moreover, the NAP recalls the transposition by the Italian Government of the EU Directive on Non-Financial Reporting, through Decree 254/2016 (entered into force in January 2017) which obliges enterprises (with more than 500 employees, or a turnover of more than €20 million or net revenues of more than €40 million) to annually publish a Non-Financial Report.[30]

In addition to the promotion of HRDD for small and medium enterprises (which represent the majority of Italian enterprises), the NAP also highlights the need for companies operating in 'weak governance zones' to apply HRDD throughout their supply chains, in compliance with the EU Regulation on conflict minerals approved in May 2017.[31]

Moreover, the NAP recommends the development of a 'comprehensive study' of Decree No. 231/2001 on corporate administrative liability for offences

26 The law adopted by the French Parliament does not provide criminal penalties in case of non-compliance, according to the decision of the French Constitutional Council.

27 Law 199 of October 29, 2016 amended Article 603 bis Criminal Code by widening the scope of application to the crimes of illegal intermediation and labour exploitation.

28 Italian NAP, Part IV B, 15–16.

29 Law 76/2016, *Regolamentazione delle unioni civili tra persone dello stesso sesso e disciplina delle convivenze* (16G00082), published in the *Italian Official Journal* on 21 May 2016.

30 Italian NAP, Part III, 9.

31 EU, *Regulation 2017/821 of the European Parliament and of the Council of 17 May 2017 Laying Down Supply Chain Due Diligence Obligations for Union Importers of Tin, Tantalum and Tungsten, their Ores, and Gold Originating from Conflict-affected and High-risk Areas*, OJ L 130, 19 May 2017, 1. See Italian NAP, Part IV B, 23.

committed by legal entities, in order to assess the scope of its implications in relation to the UNGPs.[32] The Decree provides for the adoption of models of organization, management and control and has the effect of raising awareness among companies on how to prevent offences, in accordance with the objectives of HRDD. By providing such corporate administrative liability – to be ascertained within criminal proceedings – the Decree guarantees access to judicial remedies for victims of the alleged offences listed in Article 24 et seq. The list of the offences has been extended over time and currently includes specific human rights violations, such as the practice of mutilation of female genitalia, child prostitution and pornography, human trafficking, and slavery. In 2015, environmental crimes were included (environmental disaster, environmental pollution and failure to decontaminate). In order to avoid liability, the company must demonstrate that it has efficiently adopted a 'model of organization, management and control' which is suitable to prevent the commission of offences, and that it has established an internal body entrusted with monitoring and supervising compliance with the model. If it fails to do so, it may be fined and sanctioned through the interruption of business activity.

As for the measures related to the right to access to an effective judicial remedy provided by the NAP, they represent a step forward toward greater access to justice for victims. The NAP provides the following planned measures: (i) the activation of training courses on B&HR for judges and lawyers (also through the collaboration with the *Ordine Forense*); (ii) the maintenance of an adequate level of legal aid funding in order to ensure access to legal assistance for non-national and non-resident claimants, in particular irregular migrants. The provision of legal aid for non-national claimants is an important and ambitious objective, which could facilitate access to justice for economically disadvantaged people who are often victims of crimes. Other measures should address the excessive length of civil proceedings and the possibility to introduce new legal remedies such as class action.

The identification of 'eventual gaps and/or existing barriers jeopardizing access to judicial remedy for victims of business-related human rights abuses especially with regard to extraterritorial violations', also based on the relation between parent company and subsidiaries, and the related introduction of 'relevant additional legislative measures to strengthen access to effective remedy both in civil, criminal and administrative law' are important for guaranteeing effective access to justice for victims of corporate-related human rights violations.[33] An analysis of the existing legal and practical barriers that impede access to judicial remedies could certainly lead to the introduction of legislative measures aimed at ensuring victims' rights, although the NAP does not explicitly provide for them.

32 Decreto legislativo 231 dell'8 giugno 2001. See Italian NAP, Part IV B, 15.
33 Italian NAP, Part IV B, 26.

Finally, it is worth mentioning the reference to corporate extraterritorial violations of human rights.[34] This issue is crucial in order to undertake research on the excessive burden of proof on victims in civil cases and to establish new rules granting greater access to the evidence in the possession of corporations and in terms of information disclosure.

The GLIDU will be in charge of the implementation and supervision of the aforementioned measures planned in the NAP.

Concluding Remarks

Some conclusions about the Italian NAP can be drawn.

First, the Italian NAP establishes a clear and specific overview of the actions already implemented by the Italian Government in the field of B&HR, without identifying an effective timeline for the implementation of the identified measures and without monitoring the objectives achieved. Furthermore, during the consultation and drafting phases, the process of selection of the stakeholders involved, as well as the timeline and the organization of the two Working Groups, have never been disclosed.

As a positive remark, it is worth mentioning the government's commitment (even if not well-defined) to implement HRDD processes, through the adoption of legislation in this field.

Finally, in terms of the update, monitoring, and dissemination of the NAP, the establishment of the GLIDU represents a useful tool, although its function and role are not well defined. The planned mid-term review – scheduled by the end of 2018 – is fundamental for filling the existing legal gaps and for informing all the involved stakeholders about the results achieved. In order to conduct an effective mid-term review and facilitate an ongoing dialogue with the CIDU and the involved institutions, the author suggests the CIDU to provide relevant information concerning the list of the institutions accountable for implementing the single planned measures, and to disclose all the implementation data. The establishment of small Working Groups tasked with assisting and helping the GLIDU in its monitoring and implementation activities would certainly be useful.

34 Ibid.

Part II

The Corporate Responsibility to Respect Human Rights

European Approaches

9 European Approaches to Promoting Responsible Supply Chains

Cindy S. Woods

Introduction

Increasingly, the international community has recognized the responsibilities of MNCs to ensure respect for human rights, including labour rights, throughout their supply chains. This respect is most often conceived of as voluntary human rights due diligence. Due diligence is the process of identifying possible human rights harms and impacts, taking steps to prevent or mitigate such harms, and accounting for and reporting on how any adverse human rights impacts are addressed. While a number of frameworks and guidance documents exist to help orient and facilitate voluntary due diligence, these measures are inherently limited in their ability to stimulate increased and meaningful due diligence processes and reporting of high quality and comparability. As the need for more responsible business practices in the global economy continues to draw into focus, some states have begun taking steps to require full due diligence or reporting for certain sectors or companies as part of their own international law obligation to protect human rights.

In particular, the EU and individual European states have spearheaded a number of mandatory initiatives that seek to ensure that businesses respect human rights throughout their supply chains. This chapter will describe and analyse a number of regulations that the EU and European countries are installing to promote responsible supply chains and uphold international legal requirements and expectations in this regard, and provide preliminary insights in the normative impacts and efficacy of such developments.

European Regulatory Approaches to Promoting Responsible Supply Chains

Recent years have seen the proliferation of numerous voluntary initiatives and guidance on due diligence and reporting, motivated by a growing recognition that business entities have a responsibility to respect human rights in their global operations.

While an increasing number of businesses subscribe to voluntary due diligence and reporting initiatives,[1] their efficacy and meaningfulness has been called into question given a lack of quality control and slow uptake. Increased focus at the European level on the state obligation to ensure that corporations which fall within their jurisdiction or regulatory control respect human rights in their supply chains has led to the nascent growth of both mandatory (1) due diligence and (2) non-financial reporting regulations.

Mandatory Due Diligence

At the individual state level, a handful of countries have passed or are considering regulatory action to mandate general or issue specific due diligence, inspiring increased conversation at the EU level in relation to requiring due diligence activities.

French Duty of Vigilance Law

In 2017, France passed the 'duty of vigilance' law, which creates a legally binding obligation on certain large companies headquartered in the country to establish and implement a *plan de vigilance* to 'identify and prevent adverse human rights and environmental impacts resulting from their own activities, from activities of companies they control, and from activities of their subcontractors and suppliers, with whom they have an established commercial relationship'.[2] More specifically, the vigilance plan must include: (a) a mapping that identifies, analyses and ranks risks; (b) procedures to regularly access, in accordance with the risk mapping, the situation of subsidiaries, subcontractors, or suppliers with whom the company maintains an established commercial relationship; (c) appropriate action to mitigate or prevent serious violations; (d) an alert mechanism that collects reporting or actual risks, developed in working partnership with the trade union organization representatives of the company concerned; and (e) a monitoring scheme to follow up on the measures implemented and assess their efficacy.[3] The bill is the first of its kind to recognize the

1 In relation to guidance on voluntary human rights due diligence initiatives, see the OECD Guidelines for Multinational Enterprises, sector specific guidance from the OECD on agricultural supply chains, supply chains of minerals from conflict-affected and high-risk areas, and supply chains in the garment and footwear sector. In relation to voluntary reporting, guidance frameworks include Global Reporting Initiative (hereinafter 'GRI'), the Sustainability Accounting Standards Board (hereinafter 'SASB'), and the UNGPs Reporting Framework.

2 ECCJ, *French Corporate Duty of Vigilance Law, Frequently Asked Questions*, 24 March 2017, http://corporatejustice.org/documents/publications/french-corporate-duty-of-vigilance-law-faq.pdf (last accessed 15 May 2017).

3 European Coalition for Corporate Justice (ECCJ), *French Duty of Vigilance Law – English Translation,* Business and Human Rights Resource Centre, 14 December 2016, https://business-humanrights.org/en/french-duty-of-vigilance-bill-english-translation (last accessed 15 May 2017).

legal responsibilities of parent companies in relation to the acts of their subsidiaries, suppliers and contractors operating at home or abroad.

The law is applicable only to companies who, at the end of two consecutive fiscal years, employ either 5000 employees and are headquartered in France or employ 10,000 employees and are headquartered in France or abroad.[4] It is estimated to impact around 150 companies.[5] Vigilance plans must be published annually, and companies can be held liable for harms occurring in the absence of or failure to implement one, and anyone with legal standing before a French court can refer a case of non-compliance to the court. If the company does not fulfil its obligations within three months of receiving formal notice to comply, the court may require compliance through financial compulsion if appropriate, and sentence the company to up to €10 million in civil fines.[6] The first vigilance plans required under this new law will be published in 2018.

Dutch Child Labour Law

The Dutch government has also adopted legislation to mandate human rights due diligence, in specific relation to issues of child labour. In February 2017, the lower house of Parliament adopted the *Child Labour Due Diligence Law*, which as of November 2017 is currently awaiting approval by the Senate. The exact contours of the law are still to be determined; following Senate approval, the Executive will issue a General Administrative Order (hereinafter 'GAO'), which will outline in more detail the implementation of the regulation. Generally, the law requires covered companies to submit to Dutch authorities a statement that they have conducted due diligence in relation to child labour throughout their full supply chain; this includes assessing whether there is a 'reasonable presumption that the goods and services to be supplied have been produced with child labour' and if so, 'draw[ing] up an action plan in line with international guidelines (UNGPs or the OECD Guidelines for Multinational Enterprises) to prevent this impact'.[7]

The law also has extraterritorial application, and would apply not only to companies registered in the Netherlands, but also to any company that delivers products or services to Dutch markets at least twice a year – although the GAO is likely to exempt certain sectors or company sizes where the risk of child labour is low.[8] While the exact specifications of the child labour statement are yet to be defined, statements must be provided to the government only once (not on an annual basis). While this one-off requirement undermines the efficacy of the law,

4 Ibid.

5 ECCJ, *French Corporate Duty of Vigilance Law, Frequently Asked Questions*, op. cit., para. 12.

6 ECCJ, *French Duty of Vigilance Law,* op. cit., art. 1.

7 MVO Platform, Frequently Asked Questions about the New Dutch Child Labour Due Diligence *Law,* 14 April 2017, www.mvoplatform.nl/news-en/frequently-asked-questions-about-the-new-dutch-child-labour-due-diligence-law (last accessed 3 December 2017).

8 Ibid., para. 10.

according to Dutch civil society, 'it has been clear during the entire political debate that this law is not about reporting requirements but about compulsory due diligence'.[9]

The Child Labour Due Diligence Law will enter into force pending Senate approval in January 2020, after which time companies have six months to submit their statement of due diligence compliance.[10] Companies that fail to publish a statement will be fined a nominal fee, which can be raised in the case of continued non-compliance; however, state authorities will not actively monitor compliance with the law.[11] Third parties with evidence of child labour in a company's products or services must first lodge a complaint with the company in question, and may only file a complaint with regulators following an 'inadequate' response from the company.[12] If the regulators find the company non-compliant, they can issue legally binding instructions and a time frame for implementation; the company can incur fines for failure to comply with such legal instructions.[13] If a company is fined twice in a five-year period, the third violation could lead to imprisonment of the responsible director, and/or fines of up to €750,000 or 10 per cent of the company's annual sales.[14]

Swiss Responsible Business Initiative

In 2016, the Swiss Responsible Business Initiative, a coalition of over 70 Swiss NGOs gathered the requisite signatures to launch a federal popular initiative seeking to require companies registered in – or whose principle place of business is in – Switzerland to conduct human rights and environmental due diligence throughout their supply chains.[15] According to the Initiative, companies would also be liable for damage caused by enterprises under their control where they have violated internationally recognized human rights or international environmental standards through the course of their business activities, unless they can prove they 'took all due care per [due diligence processes] to avoid the loss or damage, or that the damage would have occurred even if all due care had been taken'.[16] As part of the popular initiative process, both the Federal Council and Parliament have an opportunity to review the proposal and can submit a

9 Ibid., para. 5.

10 Ibid., para. 6.

11 Ibid., paras. 13–14.

12 Ibid., para. 13.

13 Ibid., para. 15.

14 Ibid., para. 14.

15 Swiss Coalition for Corporate Justice, *Over 140,000 signatures for the Swiss Responsible Business Initiative*, 15 April 2016. http://konzern-initiative.ch/over-140000-signatures-for-the-swiss-responsible-business-initiative/?lang=en (last accessed 15 May 2017).

16 Ibid.

counter-proposal to the initiative.[17] The Federal Council first reviewed the initiative and issued a pre-decision dismissal in January 2017, releasing a detailed reasoning in September 2017 which highlighted the government's interest in pursuing voluntary due diligence measures.[18] The initiative passed to Parliament for review, and in November 2017 the Legal Affairs Committee of the Council of States proposed a counter-proposal that included mandatory due diligence for certain large companies and other companies active in risk sectors.[19] A popular vote is expected in 2018.[20]

Other Potential Mandatory Due Diligence Initiatives

Other European states, including Germany, Italy and the UK, are also considering mandatory due diligence legislation. The governments of Germany and Italy had both highlighted the possibility in their NAPs on B&HR. The German NAP establishes that, by 2020, 50 per cent of all German companies with more than 500 employees should have human rights due diligence processes in place.[21] Progress will be reviewed every year after 2018 with random samplings of companies falling under this criterion.[22] If the target goal is not achieved in that time, the German government will consider mandatory human rights due diligence regulations.[23] Similarly, in the Italian NAP, the government commits to conducting a review of commercial and civil law to 'assess and evaluate legislative reform introducing provisions such as the "duty of care" or due diligence

17 Schwizerische Eidgenossenschaft, *What is a Federal Popular Initiative?*, www.ch.ch/en/demokratie/political-rights/popular-initiative/what-is-a-federal-popular-initiative/ (last accessed 3 December 2017); Schwizerische Eidgenossenschaft, *What is a Direct Counter-proposal or an Indirect Counter-proposal to a Popular Initiative?*, www.ch.ch/en/demokratie/political-rights/popular-initiative/what-is-a-direct-counter-proposal-or-an-indirect-counter-pro (last accessed 3 December 2017).

18 Confédération Suisse, Message relatif à l'initiative populaire, *Entreprises responsables-pour protéger l'être humain et l'environnent*, 15 September 2017. www.admin.ch/opc/fr/federal-gazette/2017/5999.pdf (last accessed 3 December 2017).

19 Business and Human Rights Resource Centre, *Swiss Parliament Decides to Issue Counter-proposal to Referendum Initiative on Responsible Business Conduct*, 14 November 2017, https://business-humanrights.org/en/switzerland-ngo-coalition-launches-responsible-business-initiative#c165045 (last accessed 3 December 2017).

20 The public is entitled to vote on a popular initiative within 18 months of its launch. *What is a Federal Popular Initiative?* Schwizerische Eidgenossenschaft, op. cit., para. 4.

21 Netzwerk für Unternehmensverantwortung, Forum Menschenrechte, Verband Entwicklungspolitik und Humanitäre Hilfe, *et al.*, *No Courage to Commit: Comments of German Non-Governmental Organisations on the German Government's National Action Plan on Business and Human Rights*, 6 February 2017, https://germanwatch.org/en/download/17767.pdf (last accessed 3 December 2017).

22 Ibid., 6.

23 Ibid., 2.

for companies'.[24] The UK has also expressed interest in initiatives of this sort. In its 2017 enquiry on human rights and business, the UK Joint Committee on Human Rights called on the government to 'bring forward legislative proposals to make reporting on due diligence for all [...] relevant human rights compulsory for large businesses'.[25]

In addition, a number of European States have also sought to bring the issue forward at the regional level. In May 2016, eight national parliaments launched a 'green card' initiative at the EU Commission to jointly support enhanced political dialogue around the creation of mandatory due diligence procedures at the EU level.[26] Similarly, in October 2016, in its *Report on Corporate Liability for Serious Human Rights Abuses in Third Countries*, the European Parliament called on EU and Member States to establish clear rules requiring that companies within their territory or jurisdiction 'must respect human rights throughout their operations, in every country and context in which they operate, and in relation to their business relationships, including outside the EU' through mandatory due diligence.[27]

Mandatory Non-financial Reporting

The due diligence component of reporting on impacts is sometimes promoted separately from full due diligence requirements. The EU and European states have also taken global leadership in relation to requiring mandatory reporting on human rights impacts.

EU Directive on the Disclosure of Non-financial Information

In November 2014, the EU Directive on the disclosure of non-financial information by certain large companies entered into force, requiring public interest entities with more than 500 employees to report annually on their 'principal risks' relating to 'environmental, social and employee matters, respect

24 Italian Inter-Ministerial Committee for Human Rights (CIDU), *Italian National Action Plan on Business and Human Rights 2016–2021*, 1 December 2016, www.cidu.esteri.it/resource/2016/12/49117_f_NAPBHRENGFINALEDEC152017.pdf (last accessed 3 December 2017).

25 UK Parliament, *Human Rights and Business 2017: Promoting Responsibility and Ensuring Accountability: Conclusions and Recommendations*, 4 April 2017, https://publications.parliament.uk/pa/jt201617/jtselect/jtrights/443/44311.htm (last accessed 3 December 2017).

26 CIDSE, *NGOs Welcome Support of European Parliamentarians for Duty of Care Legislation of EU Corporations towards People Affected by their Activities*, 16 May 2016. www.cidse.org/newsroom/media-alert-ngos-welcome-support-of-european-parliamentarians-for-duty-of-care-legislation-of-eu-corporations-towards-people-affected-by-their-activities.html (last accessed 3 December 2017).

27 Ignazio Corrao, *Report on Corporate Liability for Serious Human Rights Abuses in Third Countries*, European Parliament, 2015/2315(INI), 19 July 2016, 17–18.

for human rights, anti-corruption, and bribery matters'.[28] More specifically, the report must include: (a) a brief description of the undertaking's business model; (b) a description of the policies pursued by the undertaking in relation to those matters, including due diligence processes implemented; (c) the outcome of those policies; (d) the principal risks to those matters linked to the undertaking's operations including, where relevant and proportionate, its business relationships, products or services, which are likely to cause adverse impacts in those areas, and how the undertaking manages those risks; (e) non-financial key performance indicators relevant to the particular business.[29]

According to the European Commission, the Directive would increase the number of companies in the EU producing an annual non-financial report by more than 86 per cent, from 2500 to 18,000 required companies.[30] While reporting is mandatory, reporting companies are not obligated to identify environmental, social and employment risks in their operations and supply chains per se, or seek to mitigate that risk. Instead, companies may 'comply or explain'; if a company does not pursue due diligence policies in relation to the identified issues, the non-financial statement need only 'provide a clear and reasoned explanation for not doing so'.[31] The failure to make human rights due diligence mandatory is one major shortcoming of the Directive. Similarly, limiting language can serve to restrict the extent to which companies must report on risks from their supply chains and business relationships – companies must only report on their 'principal risks' and only on risks in their supply chains if this information is 'relevant and proportionate' to their business operation – terminology open for broad interpretation.[32]

The transposition deadline for the non-financial reporting act was December 2016. As of November 2018, 27 Member States have fully transposed the directive, while only one Member State has not reported any transposition measures to the European Commission.[33] The first reports are expected in 2018 over the information relevant for fiscal year 2017.

28 EU, *Directive 2014/95/EU of the European Parliament and of the Council of 22 October 2014 amending Directive 2013/34/EU as regards Disclosure of Non-financial and Diversity Information by Certain Large Undertakings and Groups*, 2014/95/EU 2014 O.J. (L 330), 15 November 2014, art. 1.

29 Ibid.

30 European Commission, *Commission Staff Working Document: Impact Assessment Accompanying the Document: Proposal for a Directive of the European Parliament and of the Council amending Council Directives 78/660/EEC and 83/349/EEC as regards Disclosure of Non-financial and Diversity Information by Certain Large Companies and Groups*, 16 April 2013). http://eur-lex.europa.eu/legal-content/EN/TXT/PDF/?uri=CELEX:52013SC0127&from=EN (last accessed 3 December 2017).

31 EU, *Council Directive 2014/95/EU*, op. cit., art. 1.

32 Ibid.

33 European Commission, *Non-financial Reporting Directive – Transposition Status*, (n.d.). https://ec.europa.eu/info/publications/non-financial-reporting-directive-transposition-status_en/ (last accessed 28 November 2017).

UK Modern Slavery Act

In March 2015, the UK Parliament passed the UK Modern Slavery Act, novel legislation seeking to increase transparency in supply chains in relation to slavery, forced labour and human trafficking.[34] The Act applies to certain large UK companies with an annual turnover of £36 million – an estimated 12,000 companies.[35] Unlike other due diligence or reporting legislation, the Act is not limited to companies conducting a threshold amount of business in the legislating jurisdiction, but rather applies to any company that carries on any amount of business in the UK.[36] It requires these companies to provide a 'slavery and human trafficking statement' for each financial year which either (1) provides information on the steps taken by the organization during that fiscal year to 'ensure that slavery and human trafficking is not taking place (i) in any of its supply chains, and (ii) in any part of its own business' or (2) states that the organization has taken no such steps to ensure non-occurrence of these events.[37]

According to the Act, a company's slavery and human trafficking report may include the following information: (1) the organization's structure, its business and its supply chains; (2) its policies in relation to slavery and human trafficking; (3) its due diligence processes in relation to slavery and human trafficking in its business and supply chains; (4) the parts of the business and supply chains where there is a risk of slavery and human trafficking taking place, and the steps it has taken to assess and manage that risk; (5) its effectiveness in ensuring that slavery and human trafficking is not taking place in its business or supply chains, measured against such performance indicators as it considers appropriate; (6) the training about slavery and human trafficking available to its staff.[38]

Slavery and human trafficking statements are to be made public. For failure to produce such a report, the Secretary of State can bring a civil claim for an injunction, or, in the case of Scotland, for specific performance.[39] While the government can take steps to enforce applicable companies to file a report, there are no legally binding requirements for these companies to conduct due diligence processes in relation to slavery and human trafficking in their supply chains – they may merely decide to file a report stating they have not taken any steps to identify, prevent, mitigate or remedy human trafficking and forced labour in their supply chains.[40]

34 UK, *Modern Slavery Act*, Eliz. 2, c. 30 (Eng.), 2015.

35 SHIFT, *Mapping the Provisions of the Modern Slavery Act Against the Expectations of the UN Guiding Principles on Business and Human Rights*, 2015. www.shiftproject.org/media/resources/docs/Shift_ModernSlaveryAct_UNGPs_July2015.pdf (last accessed 3 December 2017).

36 Ibid.

37 UK, *Modern Slavery Act*, op. cit., Part 6.

38 Ibid.

39 Ibid.

40 Ibid.

The UK Home Office has provided practical statutory guidance on fulfilling the requirements of the UK Modern Slavery Act, including in relation to applicability, content of the statement, etc.[41] It has also helped support the Transparency in Supply Chains Report Open Data Registry, an independent UK social enterprise which serves as a compendium of slavery and human trafficking statements in compliance with the publication requirements of the Modern Slavery Act.[42]

Normative Impacts and Likely Efficacy of Existing Mandatory Regulations

While the creation and implementation of regulation geared towards mandatory human rights due diligence and reporting are seen by many B&HR advocates as a step forward towards the implementation of the UNGPs and the realization of responsible global supply chains, the majority of the regulations discussed in this chapter are too nascent to evaluate for efficacy in terms of compliance and practical on-the-ground impacts. This section will therefore provide preliminary observations and commentary on the (1) normative impacts and (2) likely efficacy of mandatory due diligence and reporting obligations in the European context.

Normative Impacts

Due diligence is conceptualized as a sliding scale of state duties and business responsibilities by the UNGPs. As such, there are ongoing debates at the international level seeking to define and in some cases tip the balance of this scale. Developing state practice in the area of mandatory due diligence and reporting regulations is helping to build common interpretations and clarify conceptualizations of the state duty to protect human rights, specifically in the areas of (1) state obligations in relation to business entities with no state nexus and (2) extraterritorial obligations.

State Obligations in Relation to Business Entities with No State Nexus

According to the UNGPs, states may breach their duty to protect when human rights abuses committed by private actors can be attributed to them, or where they failed to take appropriate steps to prevent, investigate, punish and redress

41 UK Government Home Office, *Transparency in Supply Chains etc. A Practical Guide*, 2015. www.gov.uk/government/uploads/system/uploads/attachment_data/file/649906/Transparency_in_Supply_Chains_A_Practical_Guide_2017.pdf (last accessed 3 December 2017).

42 TISC, *What We're Doing: Report* (n.d.). https://tiscreport.org/what-were-doing (last accessed 15 May 2017).

such corporate abuse.[43] To avoid attribution, states are expected to require due diligence from companies with a strong state nexus and to encourage due diligence by actors without a strong link to the state. Increasingly, however, some have made the argument that states have an obligation to take affirmative steps to prevent human rights abuse through mandatory due diligence, regardless of any state nexus, given the authority and influence they hold over corporations domiciled in their territory.[44] The development of mandatory due diligence and reporting legislation outlined above, which are applicable to companies incorporated within a jurisdiction or which carry out business within the jurisdiction, regardless of state nexus, could demonstrate a shift towards a more expansive interpretation of the state duty to protect. As these types of regulations increase, a critical mass of similar state practice could shift the normative understanding and solidify this broader view of the scope of state obligations.

Extraterritorial Obligations

There is also ongoing debate as to the extent of a state's extraterritorial obligations to protect human rights from corporate-related abuses. Some international bodies, including the UNCESCR, argue that states have an obligation to protect against adverse human rights impacts outside their territories by any business over which it may exercise influence by regulatory or other means.[45] The existing mandatory due diligence bills support this definition of extraterritorial obligations in part. First, the French Duty of Vigilance Bill and the Dutch Child Labour Law both require companies to conduct due diligence for human rights risks posed not only by their own activities, but also the activities of companies they control or with whom they have commercial relationships. Because businesses can be held liable for abuses which they cause or contribute to, by requiring due diligence throughout supply chains, states are recognizing that they can leverage their influence over actors within their jurisdiction to seek to prevent human rights abuses outside of their territory through requiring companies to monitor their supply chains. Additionally, both laws apply to companies located outside of the state. By regulating the action of businesses not domiciled in the state, these provisions are another example of a state exercising extraterritorial jurisdiction to uphold its human rights obligations. Continued

43 UNGP 1.

44 For example, see UN, *General Comment on State Obligations under the International Covenant on Economic, Social and Cultural Rights in the Context of Business Activities, Committee on Economic, Social and Cultural Rights*, UN Doc. E/C.12/60/R.1, 17 October 2016; Chairmanship of the OEIGWG established by UNHRC, *Elements for the Draft Legally Binding Instrument on Transnational Corporations and other Business Enterprises with Respect to Human Rights*, Res. A/HRC/RES/26/9, 29 September 2017, www.ohchr.org/Documents/HRBodies/HRCouncil/WGTransCorp/Session3/LegallyBindingInstrumentTNCs_OBEs.pdf (last accessed 3 December 2017).

45 Ibid.

utilization of the long arm of the law to regulate, directly or by proxy, the actions of corporate actors extraterritorially can greatly impact the discourse on this subject.

Likely Efficacy

One way to evaluate the likely efficacy of existing mandatory regulations is through an analysis of the scope of due diligence requirements developed in these approaches; specifically: (1) whether they cover the full range of due diligence activities; (2) the limitations on applicable company size or sector; and (3) the frequency of obligations.

Full Range of Due Diligence Activities

According to the UNGPs, due diligence processes can be defined in three mains phases: 'assessing actual and potential human rights impacts; integrating and acting upon the findings; and tracking responses and communicating how impacts are addressed'.[46] The French Duty of Vigilance bill, the Swiss Responsible Business Initiative text, and the Dutch Child Labour Law all require that the full scope of due diligence processes be carried out, and provide for liability for human rights harms that occur in the absence of or failure to implement these processes. However, the EU Non-Financial Reporting Directive and UK Modern Slavery Act, by their very nature, only require the third phase of due diligence – reporting. They also importantly do not attach liability for failure to conduct due diligence processes, but failure to report on whether these processes were undertaken. While the scope of obligations is inherently limited in reporting requirements generally, it is important to highlight that these types of requirements in and of themselves are not sufficient to by proxy mandate due diligence. Reporting requirements must not be equated with due diligence obligations – and any conflation between the two could serve to cripple the efficacy of future regulations seeking to require these processes.

Limitations on Company Size or Sector

The UNGPs also make clear that the responsibility to respect, including by conducting due diligence, applies to all enterprises regardless of their size; and that small-and-medium enterprises (hereinafter 'SMEs') can still cause severe human rights impacts.[47] Nevertheless, in recognition of their perhaps more informal structures and capacity restrictions, business policies may be adapted for appropriateness to their size and circumstances.[48] All four of the already enacted

46 UNGP 17.
47 UNGP 14.
48 UNGP 15.

mandatory regulations on due diligence and reporting limit or will likely limit applicability to business entities of a certain size – based on the number of employees or annual turnover rate. Limitations such as these help to reinforce the distinction between large businesses and SMEs; however, by strictly delineating applicability of these regulations with hard-line definitions, these regulations can be seen to unjustifiably exempt SMEs. By not promulgating more flexible regulations that require SMEs to abide by size-appropriate due diligence and reporting, European actors are limiting the overall effectiveness of these mandatory requirements.

Frequency of Obligations

The majority of existing mandatory requirements underscore the importance of continued monitoring of human rights risks and recognize the fluidity of such situations by establishing that due diligence and reporting requirements are not one-off events. All of the existing and proposed regulations discussed require annual reporting except for the Dutch Child Labour Law. The limitation of the Dutch law to a one-time report with long-term validity will likely severely limit its effectiveness. The requirements as they are currently described do not require companies to re-evaluate the risks of child labour in their supply chains at periodic intervals, even following major changes in the composition of their supply chains. While third-party complaints can be brought against a company with concrete evidence of child labour in their supply chain at any time, it is unclear what steps will be taken if the company complied with the legal-binding instructions of the regulation at the time of initial reporting, but has since entered into a business relationship that had led it to contribute to or be linked to child labour. In order to avoid crippling the effectiveness of due diligence legislation from the outset, future binding regulations should ensure annual reporting.

Conclusion

As the need for more responsible business practices in the global economy draws into focus, states have begun taking steps to mandate sustainable global business practices. Leading this charge has been the EU and individual European countries.

The scope and content of these regulations, while too nascent to analyse their on-the-ground impacts, shed light on developing trends in mandating corporate respect for human rights. The shift towards requiring companies without a strong state nexus to conduct due diligence is arguably helping to establish and expand the current consensus of understanding of the scope of the state's duty to protect against human rights abuses committed by private actors. Additionally, by including an extraterritorial dimension, existing due diligence legislation could influence increased state action extraterritorially, and help bolster arguments supporting this interpretation of the UNGPs. Along the same lines, the efficacy of these regulations can be predicted based on the scope of due diligence processes that they mandate, the size limitations placed on applicability standards, and the frequency of due diligence and reporting requirements.

While the impacts of European leadership on mandating due diligence and transparency in global supply chains is yet to be seen, early ripple effects can be detected. For example, following French leadership on mandatory due diligence, other European states are considering similar legislation. Additionally, Australia is currently considering a Modern Slavery bill similar to that of the UK Modern Slavery Act. The European initiative to promote responsible supply chains through mandatory due diligence and reporting requirements represents a key first step in addressing the international challenges of fostering a sustainable global economy.

10 Due Diligence, Reporting and Transparency in Supply Chains

The United Kingdom Modern Slavery Act

Olga Martin-Ortega

Introduction

The UK Modern Slavery Act 2015 (hereinafter 'MSA') primarily aims to establish a comprehensive legal framework to combat slavery, servitude and forced or compulsory labour and human trafficking. It requires large businesses to disclose each year what actions they have taken to ensure there is no modern slavery in their business or supply chains. This is called the Transparency in Supply Chains (hereinafter 'TISC') provision (Section 54), which obliges commercial organizations to report on the efforts to assess the risks in their own supply chain and business practices, as well as prevent labour abuses from occurring, and remediating those that do.

Section 54 of the MSA appears in the context of international developments to address the human rights impact of corporate activity articulating the corporate responsibility to respect, as defined in the UNGPs. Through a series of domestic norms, corporations are obliged to disclose and report on their efforts to exercise due diligence in their supply chain of minerals (Section 1502 United States Dodd Frank Act); the risks of human trafficking in their supply chain (California Transparency in Supply Chains Act); their environmental, social and human rights impacts (EU Non-Financial Reporting Directive); and prepare a 'vigilance plan' regarding risks in their supply chain (French Duty of Vigilance Law).

The UK Modern Slavery Act Transparency in the Supply Chain Provision

Scope of the Act: What is Modern Slavery?

The term 'modern slavery' is used as an umbrella term to encapsulate a series of different violations that go beyond slavery-like abuses, but all share a common intention to exploit individuals for the purpose of work or services, through abuse that violates their human rights. However, 'modern slavery' is not an international legal term. The distinct terminology used is important, specifically as different abuses are covered by different international legal instruments and are therefore subject to different levels of protection and state juridical commitments.[1] The violations contemplated in the term modern slavery in the MSA are slavery, servitude, forced or compulsory labour, and human trafficking. The definitions of each offence are contained in Part I of the MSA and are based on internationally agreed definitions.[2]

More specifically in the context of the obligation imposed by Section 54, the statutory Guidance which has been developed by the government to help organizations in their reporting processes (hereinafter 'the Guidance') recognizes the blurred nature of the terms. The spectrum of abuses makes it difficult to determine at what point deplorable circumstances, such as poor working conditions and lack of health and safety awareness become violations of human trafficking, slavery or forced labour in a work environment. Despite this,

> businesses have a responsibility to ensure that workers are not being exploited, that they are safe and that relevant employment [...], health and safety and human rights laws and international standards are adhered to, including freedom of movement and communications.[3]

Reporting Requirements

Section 54 entered into effect several months after the MSA received royal assent, as it was not in the original Bill.[4] This provision was the result of intense campaigning and advocacy of a number of civil society organizations and business representatives and followed a government consultation. Whilst the insertion of the provision is understood by some as a victory of corporate accountability advocates, it is also true that it represents a triumph of industry over the imposition of more stringent forms of regulations.[5]

Section 54 obliges commercial organizations (as defined by the Act) to produce and publish a yearly 'slavery and human trafficking statement'.[6] The clause follows the rationale of other disclosure and reporting normative developments which portray transparency as a transformative tool for companies and an empowerment tool for consumers. The Guidance establishes this rationale,

1 J.A. Chuang, 'The challenges and perils of reframing trafficking as "modern-day slavery"'. *Anti-Trafficking Review*, 2015, 5, 146–149.

2 MSA, s.1–4.

3 Home Office, *Transparency in Supply Chains Etc. Guidance*, 2015, (Annex A), www.gov.uk/government/uploads/system/uploads/attachment_data/file/471996/Transparency_in_Supply_Chains_etc__A_practical_guide__final_.pdf (last accessed 12 February 2018).

4 The MSA received royal assent on 26 March 2015. Section 54 came into effect on 29 October 2015.

5 G. LeBaron and A. Rümkorf, 'Steering CSR through home state regulation: a comparison of the impact of the UK Bribery Act and Modern Slavery Act on global supply chain governance'. *Global Policy Journal*, 2017, 8, 15–28, 16.

6 Section 54: (1) A commercial organization within subsection (2) must prepare a slavery and human trafficking statement for each financial year of the organization.

clearly highlighting the aim 'to increase transparency by ensuring the public, consumers and employees and investors know the steps an organization is taking to tackle modern slavery'.[7] Therefore this provision seeks to use transparency as a tool to encourage informed business and procurement decision-making, and increase consumer choice by disclosing correct information. It also aims to drive organizations to better understand the risks and impacts of their supply chains. The Guidance also makes the business case for reporting, focusing on business benefits, including protecting and enhancing reputation and brand; protecting and growing customer base; improving investor confidence; staff retention and developing more trustworthy supply chains.[8] This approach, which relies on consumer and stakeholder action, rather than establishing sanctions for non-compliance or even poor compliance, deprives the MSA, and similar regulations of real teeth, as will be further discussed when analysing the consequences of non-compliance of this measure.

The MSA defines a slavery and human trafficking statement (hereinafter, statement) for a financial year as:

> (a) a statement of the steps the organization has taken during the financial year to ensure that slavery and human trafficking is not taking place (i) in any of its supply chains, and (ii) in any part of its own business, or (b) a statement that the organization has taken no such steps.[9]

Who Has to Report?

Section 54 establishes a commercial organization should report, i.e. produce a statement, if it: '(a) supplies goods or services, and (b) has a total turnover of not less than an amount prescribed by regulations made by the Secretary of State'. Determining the threshold was part of the government consultation on the provision.[10] The regulations were approved separately in October 2015 and establish that the total turnover prescribed for the purposes of the obligation to produce a statement is £36 million.[11]

The commercial organizations, which have to report, need to have a link to the UK, but there is no minimum level of UK business required to trigger the reporting obligation under the MSA, and no requirement for an organization to be physically located in the country. However, the Guidance notes that the government's intention is for a common sense approach to be applied so that organizations that do not have a demonstrable business presence in the UK will

7 Home Office, *Transparency*, op. cit., 3.

8 Ibid., 4.

9 MSA, s.54 art. 4.

10 Home Office, *Modern Slavery and Supply Chains Government Response*, 2015, www.gov.uk/government/uploads/system/uploads/attachment_data/file/448200/Consultation_Government_Response__final__2_pdf.pdf (last accessed 12 February 2018).

11 Modern Slavery Act 2015 (Transparency in Supply Chains) Regulations, October 2016, art. 2.

not be caught.[12] For the purpose of the obligation to report, they have to be a body corporate (wherever incorporated), which carries on a business, or part of a business, in any part of the UK, or a partnership (wherever formed), which carries on a business, or part of a business, in any part of the UK.[13] This has opened the reporting obligation to several entities that have not been covered by previous non-financial reporting experiences, such as to businesses that supply services (e.g. large law firms, consulting and accounting firms and insurance firms) and have not, until now, had to focus on their own supply chains. Interestingly it has brought within the remit of the reporting obligation a set of organizations, which could in principle be considered public entities, as they are regulated by the Public Sector Contracts Act 2015 (and their procurement considered public procurement).[14]

What Needs to be Included in the Statement?

There are only two prescriptive requirements: statements must be approved at the highest senior level in the company, by the board of directors (or equivalent) and signed by a director (or partner/member), ensuring those at the top of the organization take responsibility for the statement's content; and they must be published on the organization's website.

There is no prescribed content to the statement, only a set of minimum information that *may* include:

> (a) the organization's structure, its business and its supply chains; (b) its policies in relation to slavery and human trafficking; (c) its due diligence processes in relation to slavery and human trafficking in its business and supply chains; (d) the parts of its business and supply chains where there is a risk of slavery and human trafficking taking place, and the steps it has taken to assess and manage that risk; (e) its effectiveness in ensuring that slavery and human trafficking is not taking place in its business or supply chains, measured against such performance indicators as it considers appropriate; (f) the training about slavery and human trafficking available to its staff.[15]

Effective reporting can only be achieved if organizations have a good knowledge of their own supply chain and how their businesses are structured in terms of suppliers, contractors and subcontractors, as well as the origin of the products, materials and services that are used in their business activities. This allows

12 Home Office, *Transparency*, op. cit., 8.

13 MSA, s.54, art. 12.

14 See O. Martin-Ortega, 'Modern slavery and human rights risks in global supply chains: the role of public buyers'. *Global Policy*, 2017, 8(4), 512–552.

15 MSA, s.54, art. 5.

for a better understanding of the level of risks within the sector, business model and specific activity of an organization.[16]

With regard to organizational policies related to slavery and human trafficking, the Guidance further clarifies that commercial organizations need not have a standalone policy in place.[17] Instead, they may develop one or explain how current policies and practices are relevant to the cause. For policies to have the desired impact, they must be supported through effective communications.[18] Clear policy circulation is essential in any organization, but especially with regard to an issue such as modern slavery, which has only recently become a public policy and organizational priority. In order to become embedded as standard practice all staff needs to be aware of the responsibilities of the organization regarding its supply chain and incentivized to be part of the challenges the organization faces as a whole.[19]

Whilst Section 54 lists them separately, due diligence, risk assessment of the parts of the supply chain that are exposed to slavery and human trafficking, steps taken to assess and manage the risk, and the effectiveness to such responses, are inherently linked. Due diligence, in line with what is internationally understood as human rights due diligence, involves in itself a risk assessment process and the design of responses to the risks identified, including measuring the results of such responses and whether they are effective in the identification, prevention and mitigation of the human rights risks.[20]

The first step within a human rights due diligence process should be to identify potential risks within the supply chain, and prioritize action over them. This criterion is therefore linked to the first one in which organizations are asked to disclose their supply chain. It is not possible to map all supply chains and identify all risks at once, therefore the establishment of systems for prioritization of risk identification and response is essential.[21] In line with the underlying preoccupation for making the business case, the Guidance explains that modern slavery risk assessment should be part of an organization's wider approach to risk management and could form part of a more general risk assessment, which misses the specific nuances of the problem at hand. It suggests considering risks according to country risks, sector risks, transaction risks and business partnership risks.[22] A relevant addition is the reference to the need for

16 Martin-Ortega, op. cit., 516.

17 Home Office, *Transparency*, op. cit., 28.

18 Ibid.

19 Martin-Ortega, op. cit., 516.

20 See UNGP Principle 15(b); O. Martin-Ortega, 'Human rights due diligence for corporations: from voluntary standards to hard law at last?'. *Netherlands Quarterly of Human Rights*, 2014, 32(1), 44–74.

21 O. Martin-Ortega and A. Davies, *Protecting Human Rights in the Supply Chain. A Guide for Public Procurement Practitioners*, 2017, www.bhre.org/s/Knowledge-LUPC-Protecting-Human-Rights-in-the-Supply-Chain-2.pdf (last accessed 12 February 2018).

22 Home Office, *Transparency*, op. cit., 34.

appropriate resources to be deployed to ensure that risk assessment strategies can be effective.[23] An important element of due diligence processes is to engage suppliers and business partners. It is essential to inform suppliers of corporate policies and seek assurance from new suppliers that they are aware of the organization commitments. However, it is important to bear in mind that this does not necessarily guarantee that social commitments cascade down the chain, let alone that suppliers become more aware of their own responsibility to act for the prevention of violations in their own supply chain. Other mechanisms, such as effective auditing processes would allow institutions to be able to react to actual violations. Beyond engagement with their own suppliers, it is also important to collaborate with external actors, which brings added value to risk assessment, as well as responses to risks and remediation processes.[24] The Guidance encourages organizations to report on the effectiveness of their measures by providing information on existing or additional Key Performance Indicators related to anti-slavery actions.[25] As will be explained in more detail, effectiveness appears to be the least reported element. There is an inherent difficulty in establishing concrete measurement and benchmark criteria; however, without measurement organizations may be merely playing lip service to their responsibilities towards human rights and in the Act.

When to Report? The Report as a Live Instrument

Reports should be filed six months after the end of the financial year at the latest. Contrary to the mandatory reporting regulations that preceded the MSA in other countries, which required a one-off report, statements need to be published annually. This means that they are intended to be a live document, based on a process of discovery, commitment and acknowledgement of responsibility within each organization. As an organic document, it should reflect a process of due diligence which deepens every year.[26] The statement is not the outcome, the statement is the vehicle to commence, strengthen and own a sound due diligence process which allows organizations to know the risks their activities pose on human rights and to modify their practices to prevent such risks, establish procedures to react to such risks, mitigate their impact and when possible remediate them.[27]

What are the Consequences for Non-compliance?

In line with the spirit of the law, which is very much to encourage compliance and rely on the business case for due diligence and the capacity of stakeholders

23 Ibid.
24 Martin-Ortega, Davies, op. cit., 17.
25 Home Office, *Transparency*, op. cit., 36.
26 Martin-Ortega, 'Modern Slavery', op. cit., 519.
27 Ibid.

to react to information (or presumably a lack of it), the Act contains weak enforcement mechanisms. In fact, it is only concerned with the lack of publication of the statement but not the quality of the reporting and whether the exercise has any impact on the prevention, mitigation or remediation of human rights violations in supply chains. Legal sanctions for failing to comply with the obligation to publish the statements are limited to injunctive relief brought by the Secretary of State to compel the organization to report. If the organization fails to comply with the injunction it would be in contempt of court, which is punishable by an unlimited fine. It is important to remember that organizations will also comply with Section 54 if they declare that they have taken no steps toward MS in their supply chain.

This lack of proper enforcement is consistent with the concept of transparency, which the MSA represents. The risk is that a strong focus on the business case deprives the exercise of human rights due diligence of its material element, this is the substance to protecting human rights, beyond being a formal requirement, merely a compliance exercise. The fact that no agency or body has been given the competence or capacity to monitor the content of the statements nor whether such content reflects the reality of the organization's practice is an important deficiency of the Act. One that is common to all current non-financial reporting initiatives.[28] Relying on the action of external stakeholders is not enough to guarantee meaningful impact of these measures.

Current Practice on Reporting under the 'Transparency in Supply Chains' Obligation

There is no official central repository of statements; however, several organizations are compiling them.[29] At the beginning of the reporting process it was estimated that 12,000 commercial organizations would have to report; however, at the time of writing, close to the end of the second year of reporting, fewer than 3500 statements have been lodged in the Business and Human Rights Resource Centre (hereinafter 'BHRRC') repository. Collecting and systematizing statements has been left to civil society and the media, as has the monitoring of the quality and veracity of the statements.

The primary conclusion that can be drawn from the first two years of reporting is that the issue of corporate responsibility in supply chains has reached the agenda in the UK, at policy level, at corporate level and at media and public attention level. Whilst companies were slow to start reporting, especially the

28 M. Narine, 'Disclosing disclosure's defects: addressing corporate irresponsibility for human rights impacts'. *Columbia Human Rights Law Review*, 2016, 47(1), 134–137.

29 BHRRC Modern Slavery Registry, *Official Website*, www.modernslaveryregistry.org/, last accessed on: 12 February 2018; Unseen, *TISC Report*, https://tiscreport.org/ (last accessed 12 February 2018).

market leaders,[30] many organizations are putting in place modern slavery policies and there is certainly a discourse of awareness among large retailers. However, the reporting itself has been deficient in most cases and the lack of teeth of the legislation is apparent, both when it comes to the fact that significantly fewer companies than expected have reported and to the fact that no company has been compelled to report if they have not done so. As the BHRRC has put it in its analysis of the first 100 companies listed in the Financial Times Stock Exchange Index (hereinafter 'FTSE') the first year has shown 'patchy compliance'.[31] Only a small number of companies have produced rigorous statements describing robust action in some, not all, the criteria.[32]

The first months of implementation saw a disappointing lack of compliance with even the basic formal requirements of statements being signed by senior members of the organization or their publication on the company's website.[33] This has improved in subsequent reports but few companies fully comply with the requirements related to senior level involvement in the reporting process, and in the visibility and accessibility of the statement. Statements varied significantly in length and detail, albeit the second round of reporting has seen generally longer and more detailed statements than the first.[34]

Large corporations have started to devote significant attention to this issue, including significant resources. The most comprehensive statements have been made by large multinationals, 'which are usually consumer-facing, with complex international business models, and which are often exposed to investor scrutiny'.[35] Large retailers have seen intense media campaigns, and specific sectors have attracted particular attention, for example the textile sector, which came into the spotlight during the first year of reporting, due to migrant and child labour in the supply chain in Turkey.[36]

Reporting on the nature of the business and structure of the supply chain also varies. Most companies provided some description of their business structure, services, products and customers.[37] Many companies blame the difficulties of reporting on the structure of the supply chain, given the complexity of such

30 BHRRC, *FTSE 100 At the Starting Line. An Analysis of Company Statements under the UK Modern Slavery Act*. June 2017, https://business-humanrights.org/sites/default/files/documents/FTSE%20100%20Modern%20Slavery%20Act.pdf (last accessed 12 February 2018).

31 Ibid., 1.

32 Ibid.

33 Ergon, *Modern Slavery Statements, One Year On*, April 2017, http://ergonassociates.net/wp-content/uploads/2016/03/MSA_One_year_on_April_2017.pdf?x74739 (last accessed 12 February 2018).

34 Ibid.

35 Ibid.

36 See BHRRC, *Syrian Refuges in Turkish Garment Supply Chains. An Analysis of Company Action to Address Reports of Serious Exploitation and Abuse (Briefing Note)*, February 2016, https://business-humanrights.org/sites/default/files/160131%20Syrian%20Refugee%20Briefing%20FINAL.pdf (last accessed 12 February 2018).

37 BHRRC, *FTSE 100*, op. cit., 6.

chains. Equally, there is a significant gap in relation to identifying contractors, including labour providers, outsourced service providers and sub-contractors.[38] It is common that companies report only on suppliers of the first tier and no company reported substantially on suppliers in its second tier or beyond, where the risks of human rights abuses increase.[39]

Reporting organizations have focused mostly on showcasing policies, rather than explaining in detail what their due diligence procedures are. Most reports describe CSR statements and commitments and focus on the positive policies rather than go deeper into the identification of risks. This was true for the first year and it seems there has been little improvement in reporting on due diligence processes and outcomes in the second year.[40] Referring generally to CSR strategies and policies restricts to some extent the capacity of the reporting exercise to go beyond established processes primarily focused on corporate reputation rather than substantive addressing of corporate social impact.

Many companies state that modern slavery has been or will be included in aspects of companies' processes regarding mitigated risks.[41] For example, several companies report having revised or are in the process of revising, processes to engage with potential new suppliers prior to the beginning of the relationship. These include, for example, pre-qualification questionnaires. Another approach is to require their own suppliers to agree to modern slavery-related provisions in writing.[42] Interestingly, some companies report creating new positions, competences or even inter-departmental committees to deal specifically with issues of modern slavery.[43]

Most companies have focused on their own direct work force and have chosen to showcase policies and procedures such as whistle-blowing helplines, for their own employees to be able to voice concerns. In fact, companies have not reported having grievance mechanisms in place that specifically target abuses of workers' rights in their supply chain when these workers were employed by their suppliers, or even requiring suppliers to have grievance mechanisms themselves. Without diminishing the importance of measures that address workers directly employed, they do not necessarily have an impact on the remediation of abuses of those further down the supply chain.

Reporting on stakeholder engagement, particularly with non-governmental organizations and trade unions, is limited. There has to be specialized knowledge and understanding of the sectors and the rights at stake for monitoring and auditing to be effective, and these tend to come from these specialized organizations.

38 Ergon, *Modern Slavery*, op. cit., 3.
39 BHRRC, *FTSE 100*, op. cit., 6.
40 Ergon, *Modern Slavery*, op. cit., 4.
41 BHRRC, *FTSE 100*, op. cit., 9.
42 Ibid.
43 Ibid.

As could be expected, the introduction of Section 54, especially the suggestion of the training to staff as one of the categories to report on, has created intense activity of training and consultancy in the private sector, which has generally served as an awareness raising exercise but also, to some extent, an outsourcing of responsibility to consultants.

Whilst we need to continue to be highly critical of the processes, and be vigilant towards the significant number of organizations which still consider that the MSA does not add further responsibilities beyond existing regulations or voluntary codes,[44] it is important to highlight that, overall, the reporting process has had a positive impact. In terms of effectiveness and positive changing of behaviour, attention to the human rights conditions in the supply chain has become more prominent as part of companies' processes and priorities. Overall, a significant number of companies have increased efforts and policy change in response to the Act.[45]

Conclusions

The recent regulatory developments that impose mandatory corporate transparency are of great significance and have an impact on both the state obligation to protect and the corporate responsibility to respect. With regard to the corporate responsibility to respect, mandatory transparency has further consolidated the idea that corporations are responsible for the human rights impact of commercial activities and has brought corporate due diligence to the heart of corporate practice with regards to their human impact. Therefore, by leading companies to adopt human rights sensitive policies, including establishing due diligence procedures, reporting has the potential to shape corporate behaviour.[46] Reporting exercises raise stakeholder expectations with regard to corporate transparency on human rights issues.[47] They further empower civil society by making more information available, to expose corporate practices and advocate for change.

With regard to the state duty to protect, mandatory transparency has further strengthened the duty of states to develop law and policy to articulate the corporate responsibility to respect by supporting – and demanding – corporate due diligence.[48] Transparency requirements have also increased the extraterritorial reach of this obligation to protect, as they have a direct impact on the activities of companies abroad. Equally, states and corporate practice regarding transparency in supply chains has opened up a further accountability avenue: considering

44 Ergon, *Modern Slavery*, op. cit., 4.

45 BHRRC, *FTSE 100*, op. cit., 1.

46 A.P. Ewing, 'Mandatory human rights reporting'. In D. Baumann-Pauly and J. Nolan (eds), *Business and Human Rights: From Principles to Practice*, Oxford: Routledge, 2016, 129.

47 Ibid., 130.

48 As argued previously in Martin-Ortega, 'Human rights due diligence', op. cit., 62.

states' own commercial practices, especially through public procurement, and their impact on human rights.[49]

In the midst of this optimism, there are also some causes of concern and risks that should be considered as state duties and corporate responsibilities progress and these normative developments consolidate while others appear. This chapter has evidenced some through the analysis of the reporting practice under the MSA.

First, there is a risk that the MSA and other legislation imposing similar mandatory requirements contribute to the development of a concept of transparency which focuses on compliance with the act of reporting, rather than the procedure of due diligence as a substantive process to identify, prevent and mitigate human rights violations in supply chains. In this case, due diligence would be equated restrictively to reporting. Corporate compliance with the responsibility to respect would then be limited to publicly stating their values and commitment to do better, rather than a proper, substantive material, exercise of understanding, scrutinizing and remediating abuses in their supply chain. Already too many companies are using a tick-box approach, incorporating key words and generic language without providing meaningful information.[50] Reporting, per se, as a compliance exercise, does not address human rights impacts, let alone remediate them.

Second, the MSA represents a narrowly focused approach to human rights violations in supply chains, unlike other contemporary instruments, such as the French Duty of Vigilance or the EU Non-Financial Directive. Whilst those instruments focus more widely on human rights and social aspects, the narrow scope of the MSA leaves out many violations of labour rights, which are prevalent in most supply chains and equally deserve attention in order to transform supply chains into non-oppressive and abusive constructs. It can be argued that approaches such as the MSA and other reporting legislation, such as Section 1502 of US Dodd Frank Act, result in fragmentation of the attention towards the dynamics of human rights risk in the supply chain into very specific sectors (mining in the DRC and adjoining countries) and violations (forced labour, human trafficking). Whilst any advance in human rights protection should be welcome, we could be losing sight of the wider problem of how human rights abuses take place in supply chains. Providing targeted solutions to isolated problems leaves behind a wide range of abuses and does not encourage comprehensive structural change, by avoiding certain risky sectors, suppliers, countries, rather than by changing internal practices that perpetuate the vulnerability of individuals in supply chains.

Third, it is important to consider to what extent reporting and transparency are being used as tools to achieve what are (impossibly) wide goals: transparency as a tool to end conflicts, or eradicate modern slavery. Transparency legislation

49 See in general, Martin-Ortega, 'Modern slavery', op. cit.
50 BHRRC, *FTSE 100*, op. cit., 13.

was traditionally conceived as a means of addressing an information imbalance in the area of consumer protection and securities. Transparency focuses on stakeholders' reactions; the capacity of consumers and investors to assimilate information and take decisions that will prompt a change in corporate behaviour. However, there is no evidence that such stakeholder action has the capacity to motivate a change that will positively impact human rights.[51]

Finally, there is a practical risk that, at least initially, this kind of reporting exercise brings negative impacts to compliant companies. More transparency will necessarily attract more scrutiny towards certain companies, with the most compliant entities being at higher reputational risk. Directly related to this one, and to the more substantive issue is the risk of 'league tabling', the proliferation of companies' rankings based on their disclosure reports, therefore focusing on formal aspects rather than substance. This is not necessarily in accordance with the spirit of the corporate human rights due diligence standard, which requires material, substantive engagement, rather than formal tick-the-boxes (compliance) exercises.[52]

Bearing these risks in mind, the MSA is certainly a landmark development, and the way practice develops under its scope has the potential to influence future normative developments and shape responses to violations of human rights in supply chains. Hopefully these will promote substantive due diligence and verifiable transparency in order to make a real difference in the way we understand, monitor, and prevent the risks to human rights in the production of the goods and services that we consume, as well as and remedying violations when they occur.

51 Narine, op. cit., 137.
52 Martin-Ortega, 'Human rights due diligence', op. cit., 73–74.

11 Blending Together Human Rights Due Diligence with 'Criminal' Law

Opportunities and Pitfalls of the Italian Solution

Paola Cavanna

Setting the Stage[1]

There has been debate over whether and how companies can be held accountable for their impacts on society and those of their subcontractors and/or suppliers in a global context.[2] International instruments such as the UNGPs, the OECD Guidelines for Multinational Enterprises and the ILO Tripartite Declaration, among others, work as a point of reference for companies willing to respond to social expectations. They promote gradual persuasion, continuous improvement and combine 'carrots and sticks', thus contributing to a corporate culture respectful of human rights in global supply chains (hereinafter 'GSCs').[3] However, they lack sound monitoring and enforcement mechanisms.

As a response, in recent years several states have established mandatory requirements on businesses to disclose their potential impacts and mitigation measures with respect to particular human rights issues (mainly prevention of slavery and human trafficking). Initiatives such as the California Transparency in Supply Chains Act (2012),[4] the EU Directive on non-financial reporting (2014)[5] and the UK Modern Slavery Act (2015)[6] rely on market mechanisms, such as reputational risk, to steer compliance. Enforcement is typically taking

1 I wish to express my gratitude to Dr Irene Gasparini and Dr Marta Sosa Navarro for their valuable comments. The chapter has also been informed by fruitful discussions with Professor Angelica Bonfanti and Professor Marta Bordignon. However, any view expressed or conclusion drawn is the sole responsibility of the author.

2 International Federation for Human Rights, *Corporate Accountability for Human Rights Abuses – A Guide for Victims and NGOs on Recourse Mechanisms*, 2014, www.fidh.org/IMG/pdf/corporate_accountability_guide_version_web.pdf (last accessed 5 March 2018).

3 The concept of global supply chains refers to the cross-border organization of the activities required to produce goods or services and bring them to consumers through inputs and various phases of development, production and delivery: International Labour Conference, *Report IV – Decent Work in Global Supply Chains*, Geneva: ILO, 2016, 1.

4 Senate Bill No. 657.

5 OJ, L330, 15.11.2014.

6 Section 54.

the form of a further request to comply or to explain the reason for non-compliance. What these legislations have in common is the requirement to disclose, that is, companies' obligations to provide information on the broader implications of their activities on society.

No domestic legislation addressing the responsibility of businesses to monitor the entire supply chain currently exists, and wrongs at the bottom of the chain often remain without redress. Human rights advocates and several legal scholars argue that legally binding norms are necessary to ensure respect for human rights throughout GSCs.[7] Attempts to legalize human rights due diligence are under development both in Switzerland and in the Netherlands, while France has recently passed a law on corporate due diligence.

By means of illustration, in Switzerland a broad coalition of civil society organizations launched a popular initiative seeking to introduce a legal duty for Swiss-based companies to incorporate respect for human rights and the environment in all their business activities, both in Switzerland and abroad, through mandatory due diligence.[8] Crucially, a parent company would also be liable for damage caused by companies under its control where they have, in the course of business, committed violations of internationally recognized human rights or environmental standards, unless the parent company proves that it took all needed preventative actions to avoid the damage.[9]

Following the same line of reasoning, in February 2017, the Dutch Parliament adopted a law concerning a due diligence duty to prevent the delivery of goods and services that have come about with the help of child labour. If approved by the Dutch Senate, the law will require companies to examine whether child labour occurs in their supply chain. If that is the case, the company would have to develop a plan of action to combat child labour and draw up a declaration about their investigation and plan of action. Statements will be collected in a public register.[10]

Despite a general consensus on the need for corporate accountability, to date, France is the only country to have established a legally binding obligation for parent companies to identify and prevent adverse human rights and environmental impacts within its ***direct*** supply chain through a '***plan de vigilance***' to be

7 R. Blitt, 'Beyond Ruggie's guiding principles on business and human rights: charting an embracive approach to corporate human rights compliance'. *Texas International Law Journal*, 2012–13, 48(1), 33–62.

8 Swiss Coalition for Corporative Justice, *Official Website*, 2015, konzern-initiative.ch/?Lang=en (last accessed 5 March 2018).

9 The burden of proof is reverted from the victim to the corporation, which must prove that it took all needed preventative actions to avoid the damage. A rebuttable presumption is seen as a tool to ensure victims' effective access to remedy: EU Agency for Fundamental Rights, *FRA Opinion, 1/2017*, 10 April 2017, fra.europa.eu/en/opinion/2017/business-human-rights (last accessed 5 March 2018).

10 C. Van Dam, *Statutory Human Rights Due Diligence Duties in the Netherlands*, July 2016, www.rsm.nl/fileadmin/Images_NEW/Sites/Chair_IBHR/Publications/Van_Dam_-_Statutory_HRDD_duties_in_NL.pdf (last accessed 5 March 2018).

publicly disclosed. However, noncompliance (i.e. failure to implement a vigilance plan) is sanctioned through ordinary civil liability schemes following Articles 1240 and 1241 of the French Civil Code.[11]

These new initiatives have attracted great scholarly attention, while the full potential of the Italian law on corporate liability under Legislative Decree No. 231/2001 remains insufficiently explored.[12] This chapter intends to fill such a gap in the international literature by reviewing and assessing the Italian approach to ensure that companies act with due diligence in specific areas directly relevant to the protection of human rights (e.g. environmental protection, labour rights, etc.).

The structure of the remainder of the chapter is as follows: the next section provides for an overview of the Italian solution that blends together criminal law procedures with a due diligence defence. In particular, its compatibility with the UNGPs will be explored. By means of conclusion, the chapter considers the ability of the Italian system to provide redress for victims of business-related human rights abuses, also for preventive purposes.

The Italian Legislative Decree No. 231/2001

Since 2001, Italy has provided for a special form of corporate liability for certain offences committed 'in the interest or to the advantage' of the legal entity, by certain individuals who have specific position within the body (i.e. corporate officer or an employee subject to the supervision of a corporate officer).[13] Such a corporate liability, although formally defined as administrative, derives from the commission of a crime, and needs to be ascertained by a penal judge and according to criminal law procedures.[14] This adds to the liability of the natural person

11 The burden of proof falls on the claimants, who need to prove a fault by the company (resulting out of violations of the duty of vigilance) as well as a causal link between such a fault and the damage they have suffered.

12 Only a 2012 mapping pointed out the Italian law as an already existing due diligence regime: O. De Schutter, A. Ramasastry, M. Taylor and R. Thompson, *Human Rights Due Diligence: The Role of States*, 2012, corporatejustice.org/hrdd-role-of-states-3-dec-2012.pdf (last accessed 5 March 2018). The issue has been recently explored by the Human Rights International Corner, *Italian Legislative Decree N. 231/2001 on Administrative Liability of Legal Persons and B&HR Violations: A Brief Overview*, July 2017, docs.wixstatic.com/ugd/6c779a_ae42b0a57aad4620ba65b9708836f3ef.pdf (last accessed 5 March 2018).

13 Legislative Decree No. 231/2001, *Disciplina della responsabilità amministrativa delle persone giuridiche, delle società e delle associazioni anche prive di personalità giuridica, a norma dell'articolo 11 della legge 29 settembre 2000, n. 300*, issued on June 8, 2001 and entered into force on 4 July 2011. In the Italian literature, see G. Forti, 'Uno sguardo ai 'piani nobili' del d.lgs. N. 231/2001'. *Rivista Italiana di Diritto e Procedura Penale*, 4/2012, 1249–1298 and in light of a change in the legislation, F. Centonze and M. Mantovani (eds), *La responsabilità «penale» degli enti*. Bologna: Il Mulino, 2016.

14 V. Mongillo, 'The nature of corporate liability for criminal offences: theoretical models and EU member state laws'. In A. Fiorella (ed.), *Corporate Criminal Liability and Compliance Programs. Volume II – Towards A Common Model in the European Union*. Napoli: Jovene, 2012, 55–120.

who materially committed or attempted the offence and is independent of it, as it also exists where the offender has not been identified or cannot be charged, or where the offence is ruled out for a reason other than amnesty (Article 10).

Crimes entailing this special form of corporate liability are specifically listed under Articles 24 to 25 *duodecies* of Legislative Decree No. 231/2001, including extortion and corruption, money laundering, bribery and fraud; cybercrimes; manslaughter and breaches of health and safety legislation; environmental crimes; slavery, trafficking in human beings and labour exploitation.

Sanctions for legal entities include monetary fines up to €1,500,000 (€4,500,000 in case of a plurality of offences);[15] seizure of the profits resulting from the crime; publication of the judgment and disqualification measures (i.e. a ban on carrying out the business activity, suspension or withdrawal of licences and permits, prohibition to contract with the public administration, exclusion or revocation of financing and subsidies). The judge shall also order the confiscation of any proceeds resulting from the crime (Article 9).

In order to avoid incurring 'criminal' liability, the entity shall adopt and effectively implement an 'organization and management model' based on the analysis of the corporate context. Such a model should meet the requirements set by Articles 6 and 7 of Legislative Decree No. 231/2001.[16]

When the crime is committed by a senior manager, the company is not liable if it proves that (i) it had adopted and effectively implemented a compliance model suitable to prevent the kind of offence that occurred; (ii) a supervisory body had been appointed with the task of monitoring the functioning, updating and compliance with the model; (iii) the offence was committed by fraudulently overriding the compliance model; and (iv) the supervisory board had carried out its work properly (Article 6). Here, the burden of proof is on the company (*alter ego doctrine*).

Likewise, when the crime is committed by an employee subject to the control of the top management, the company is not responsible if (i) a compliance model suitable to prevent the kind of crime occurred had been adopted and effectively implemented; and (ii) the employee failed to comply with these rules (Article 7). Here, the burden shifts to the public prosecutor who must prove the compliance model was neither adequate nor effectively implemented.

15 Interestingly, pecuniary penalties are based on a quotas mechanism. Considering the economic and assets condition of the company, the judge defines the amount of each quota (which may range from a minimum of €258 to a maximum of €1,549) in order to ensure the efficacy of the penalty.

16 On the minimum requirements for an adequate compliance programme: A. Paludi and M. Zecca, 'Corporate responsibility and compliance programs in Italian Case Law'. In S. Manacorda, F. Centonze and G. Forti (eds), *Preventing Corporate Corruption. The Anti-Bribery Compliance Model*. Heidelberg: Springer, 2014, 397–416.

The adoption and the effective implementation of the compliance model before the commission of the crime can exclude liability.[17] Yet, the compliance model may also be adopted after a crime is committed. In such a case, the company is liable, but disqualification measures cannot be imposed (Article 17) and the economic sanctions can be reduced (Article 12). Similarly, precautionary measures can be suspended if the company is willing to adopt and effectively implement a compliance programme suitable to cover the organizational deficiencies, learning from the occurred crime (Article 49). This conveys the positive message that learning from failures and mistakes can help companies to improve. In these cases, however, the compliance programme must be more pragmatic, specifically providing for targeted measures to prevent the same offence being committed again, thus resolving the organization deficiency. This might be seen as weakening the presumption of innocence, making cooperation almost a default option for the corporation.[18] However, an affirmative due diligence defence is intended to assure that corporate liability will be imposed only in cases where the corporation itself had actually engaged in wrongful conduct, also providing an incentive for corporations to monitor their agents and employee's conduct.[19] Indeed, the company could avoid strict liability by providing that the criminal acts of agents or employees were directly contrary to corporate policies and that the corporation had undertaken substantial efforts to enforce those policies and prevent individual wrongdoing. It follows an analysis of the Italian Legislative Decree No. 231/2001 in light of the concept of due diligence as developed by the UNGPs. In addition, a focus will be placed on implications throughout supply chains.

Components of Due Diligence

Clearly, the Italian legislator did not intend to introduce the same concept of human rights due diligence as provided under the UNGPs since the Italian law

17 The mere adoption of the compliance model is not sufficient to preclude corporate liability. An effective compliance model should have some important characteristics: a deep analysis of the corporation; the ability to find the risky areas for the different types of crimes and ways to hinder illegal acts, keeping in mind the company's history and the characteristics of the other companies that operate in the same sector. The compliance model also has to determine what moments in the company's life are exposed to the risk of crimes, study specific procedures to use in those moments that allow for effective control, and use preventive controls and specific protocols to plan the company's decision making. It must follow the corporation's changes updating the model as soon as the risk structure evolves. See Tribunale di Milano, Uff. GIP, *IVRI holding-COGEFI*, Case No. 4728/2003, 20 September 2004.

18 M. Zanchetti, 'Italy'. In N. Bourtin (ed.), *The International Investigations Review*. London: Law Business Research Ltd, 2016, 170.

19 In general terms, E.S. Podgor, 'A new corporate world mandates a "good faith" affirmative defense'. *American Criminal Law Review*, 2007, 44(4), 1537–1543. See also R.A. Elias, 'The virtues of the due diligence defense for corporations in criminal cases: solving the problems of a corporation's vicarious liability for the crimes of its agents and employees'. *University of Puerto Rico Business Law Journal*, 2016, 7(1), 1–21.

came first. The piece of legislation has been modelled in part after the US Sentencing Guidelines for Organizations and was passed to meet the requirements of the OECD Convention on Combating Bribery of Foreign Public Officials in International Business Transactions (2011) as well as the UN Convention against corruption (2003). Nevertheless, Legislative Decree No. 231/2001 and the UNGPs resonate strongly together. It is also worth noting that the Italian Action Plan on B&HR, among other planned measures, expresses the commitment to conduct a comprehensive study of Legislative Decree No. 231/2001.[20] The remainder of this section will discuss each component of the human rights due diligence set forth in the UNGPs, highlighting both consistencies and divergences of the Italian law from the UNGPs perspective.

Identifying and Assessing

Legislative Decree No. 231/2001 suggests that companies conduct a specific analysis of the corporate structure and its operating context, in order to identify the activities in relation to which offences may be committed. The compliance model should be elaborated from a substantive point of view, avoiding merely recapitulating legal or very general rules. Rather it needs to be tailored to the specificities of the entity and to its previous history and it should be constantly updated, in order to adapt it to changes in an entity's structure and to the evolution of the legal framework.[21] In the same manner as the UNGPs, the specific context of operations is crucial to design a sound due diligence policy (UNGP 18). In particular, companies doing business abroad should be aware of the specific human rights challenges in their GSCs.[22]

As said, the Italian law also references the need to constantly update such an analysis, recognizing that an entity's structure and the relevant legal framework change over time. Likewise, under the UNGPs, companies should assess their human rights impact on a regular basis (UNGP 17, let. (c) and commentary to UNGP 18).

20 See the Italian NAP on B&HR 2016–2021, 14 December 2016, www.cidu.esteri.it/resource/2016/12/49117_f_NAPBHRENGFINALEDEC152017.pdf (last accessed 5 March 2018).

21 N. Selvaggi, 'Compliance programmes and "organisational faults" in Italian legislation: an overview of ten years of experience with Legislative Decree 231/2001'. *Eucrim, The European Criminal Law Associations' Forum*, 2012, 3, 127–130. In the Italian literature, C. Piergallini, 'Paradigmatica dell'autocontrollo penale (dalla funzione alla struttura del "modello organizzativo" ex d.lgs. 231/2001'. In M. Bertolino, L. Eusebi and G. Forti (eds), *Studi in onore di Mario Romano*. Napoli: Jovene, 2011, 2049–2107.

22 UNHRC, *Promotion and Protection of All Human Rights, Civil, Political, Economic, Social and Cultural Rights, including the Right to Development. Clarifying the Concepts of 'Sphere of Influence' and 'Complicity' – Report of the Special Representative of the Secretary-General on the Issue of Human Rights and Transnational Corporations and Other Business Enterprises, John Ruggie*, A/HRC/8/16), 2008, para. 20.

It is important to stress that while the UNGPs cover the full spectrum of human rights,[23] Legislative Decree No. 231/2001 targets only certain offences directly relevant to the protection of human rights (e.g. health and safety, environmental protection, labour rights).

Moreover, the Italian law lacks the requirement that the company's due diligence policy is developed in collaboration with its stakeholders.[24] The UNGPs, instead, call for stakeholder engagement both to gauge human rights risks as well as to track the effectiveness of the response and address misconduct in the supply chain.[25]

Preventing and Mitigating

The Italian law refers to identifying 'appropriate action' to prevent certain offences, including the management of financial resources. In order to avoid incurring in liability under Legislative Decree No. 231/2001, the company shall demonstrate that it has efficiently implemented a compliance model aimed at preventing the type of crime from occurring and that has established an internal body entrusted with monitoring and supervising the compliance with the paper model.[26] According to the UNGPs, the horizontal integration across the business enterprise of specific findings from assessing human rights impacts can only be effective if its human rights policy commitment is embedded into all relevant business functions.[27] UNGP 19 further elaborates on appropriate actions that companies are expected to take in response to identified impacts, depending both on the degree of the company's involvement (i.e. causing or contributing, or being directly linked) and the extent of its leverage.

23 Commentary to UNGP 18 specifies: 'The initial step in conducting human rights due diligence is to identify and assess the nature of the actual and potential adverse human rights impacts with which a business enterprise may be involved. The purpose is to understand the specific impacts on specific people, given a specific context of operations'.

24 On greater participation for sound compliance programs: A. Nieto Martín, 'Cosmetic use and lack of precision in compliance programs: any solution?'. *Eucrim, The European Criminal Law Associations' Forum*, 2012, 3, 124–127.

25 Commentary to UNGP 18 clarifies: 'To enable business enterprises to assess their human rights impacts accurately, they should seek to understand the concerns of potentially affected stakeholders by consulting them directly in a manner that takes into account language and other potential barriers to effective engagement. In situations where such consultation is not possible, business enterprises should consider reasonable alternatives such as consulting credible, independent expert resources, including human rights defenders and others from civil society'.

26 'A company needs to have established guidelines and control systems that take into account the risk of an offence being committed. If it has not, then it will be found to be "structurally negligent"': J.J. Gobert and M. Punch, *Rethinking Corporate Crime*. London: Butterworths, 2003, 111.

27 Commentary to UNGP 19.

Tracking Responses

Legislative Decree No. 231/2001 references the need for an autonomous supervisory body, which verifies the implementation and updating of the paper model, being provided with all pertinent information.[28] All its members must be independent and professional. A disciplinary system to punish non-compliance must be introduced. It might be argued that this goes beyond the (vague) requirement for companies to track their performance on preventing and mitigating their human rights risks under UNGP 20. Accordingly, tracking should: (a) be based on appropriate qualitative and quantitative indicators; (b) draw on feedback from both internal and external sources, including affected stakeholders. As said, the Italian law lacks the requirement for stakeholder engagement.

Communicating Externally

The Italian law does not call for the publication of the company's human rights due diligence plan in its annual report. However, since January 2017, large public-interest undertakings need to prepare, on an annual basis, a non-financial statement, including the compliance model adopted pursuant to Legislative Decree No. 231/2001.[29] As a result, the EU non-financial reporting directive and the Italian national decree end up complementing each other. Disclosure is, indeed, an important dimension of the UNGPs: companies should be prepared to communicate their commitment and actions externally, including to those groups likely to be affected by their operations. UNGP 21 provides that external communication should be of a form and frequency that reflects the enterprise's human rights impact and should be accessible to its intended audience. Information provided should be 'sufficient to evaluate the adequacy of an enterprise's response to the particular human rights impact involved'. Further guidance is given on how to ensure meaningful reporting, by stating that 'independent verification of human rights reporting can strengthen its content and credibility' and that 'sector-specific indicators can provide helpful additional detail'.[30]

28 V. Mongillo, 'The supervisory body ("Organismo Di Vigilanza") under Legislative Decree No. 231/2001'. In A. Fiorella (ed.), *Corporate Criminal Liability and Compliance Programs, Volume I, Liability 'ex Crimine' of Legal Entities in Member States.* Napoli: Jovene, 2012, 57–82.

29 See Legislative Decree No. 254/2016, concerning the implementation of Directive 2014/95/EU of the European Parliament and of the Council of 22 October 2014, and amending Directive 2013/34/EU as regard the communication of information to non-financial information and information on diversity by certain companies and certain large groups, art. 3.

30 Commentary to UNGP 21.

Remediation

Legislative Decree No. 231/2001 provides for a reasoned range of sanctions intended to incentivize remediation whenever possible. For instance, monetary penalties are based, *inter alia*, on the activities carried out to cancel or reduce the consequences of the fact and to inform the supervisory body about the offence. A temporary ban from engaging in business may be subjected to 'corporate probation', for the purpose of restoring lawfulness. Likewise, pursuant to Article 17, disqualification measures do not apply if (i) the company has fully compensated the occurred damages and it has eliminated the harmful or dangerous consequences of the crime; (ii) organizational deficiencies that determined the offence have been eliminated by means of adopting and implementing a compliance model suitable to prevent offences of the same sort as the one committed; and (iii) the profit obtained has been made available for purposes of confiscation. Similarly, the UNGPs expect that companies will remedy any harm that they have caused or contributed to, including through participation in judicial and non-judicial dispute resolution processes (UNGP 22). Remedy may take a number of forms including apology, compensation (financial or otherwise), cessation of a particular activity or relationship, arrangements to ensure the harm cannot recur, or another form agreed upon by the parties and which meets the effectiveness criteria set out in UNGP 31 (i.e. legitimacy, accessibility, predictability, equity, transparency, rights-compatibility, continuous learning, stakeholders engagement and dialogue).

Global Supply Chains

Under Legislative Decree No. 231/2001, Italian enterprises can also be held accountable for serious offences committed abroad, if the State in which the offense occurred has not yet proceeded against it.[31] This is an exception to the general principle of territoriality as a limit to the efficacy in space of Italian law. If the crime is, instead, committed in Italy by a manager or employee of a foreign company, both the perpetrator and the company may be prosecuted under Italian law despite the fact that the company is based abroad.[32] Coherently, under the UNGPs, human rights due diligence should cover adverse human rights impacts that the business enterprise may cause or contribute to cause through its own activities, or which may be directly linked to its operations, products or services by its business relationships, regardless of where they took place (UNGP 17). This means that the company's responsibility to conduct due diligence does not end at the legal boundary of the individual

31 See Legislative Decree No. 231/2001 and art. 7 Italian Criminal Code. Specific crimes, notably insider trading and market manipulation regarding securities traded on Italian markets but also slavery and trafficking in human beings may be punished even if entirely committed abroad, art. 4.

32 Pursuant to the Italian Criminal Code any offence may be deemed to have been committed in Italy even if a 'fragment' of the action occurred in Italy (art. 6).

enterprise, but it also covers business partners, entities in its value chain and any other non-state or state entity ***directly linked*** to its business operations, products or services. Discussion on the exact meaning of 'directly linked' is still ongoing.[33]

Final Remarks

By providing corporate 'criminal' liability for certain offences with a due diligence defence, Italy may seem to guarantee great access to judicial remedies for victims of human rights violations occurring in the context of business activities.[34] It may also represent a good example of the 'smart mix' approach, as called by Professor Ruggie.[35] Although the adoption and implementation of a compliance model pursuant to Legislative Decree No. 231/2001 is not mandatory by law, Italian companies and foreign companies doing business with or in Italy have programmes in place aimed at preventing relevant offences. Yet, proceedings against legal persons charged with 'administrative' offences covered by Legislative Decree No. 231/2001 have been very few.[36] The reason for this might be that even if in Italy criminal prosecution of natural persons who allegedly committed the crime is mandatory where, *prima facie*, an offence has been committed, proceedings under Legislative Decree No. 231/2001 are not. Moreover, it is important to stress that the Italian law does not expressly provide for the possibility of becoming a civil party in proceedings against the charged entity.[37] Despite no violation of EU law,[38] this may de facto limit the opportunity available to the victim to obtain full compensation for the harm suffered. Indeed, victims are obliged to bring a civil claim for damages against the entity

33 Professor Ruggie's open letter of 6 March 2017, business-humanrights.org/sites/default/files/documents/OECD%20Workshop%20Ruggie%20letter%20-%20Mar%202017%20v2.pdf (last accessed 5 March 2018).

34 Human Rights International Corner, *Remarks on the Italian Action Plan on Business and Human Rights 2016–2021*, May 2017, 4, https://docs.wixstatic.com/ugd/6c779a_7f3f54bdedab4632b8a79d7b6ad887d9.pdf (last accessed 5 March 2018).

35 See Commentary to UNGP 3: 'States should not assume that businesses invariably prefer, or benefit from, State inaction, and they should consider a smart mix of measures – national and international, mandatory and voluntary – to foster business respect for human rights'.

36 The *Thyssenkrupp* case represents the main one in which corporate liability has been established for not having ensured safe working conditions at the industrial plant in Turin, where – on 12 December 2007 – seven workers died in a fire accident and three others were seriously injured. A criminal proceeding is ongoing for the death of a migrant worker who was picking tomatoes in the field of Nardò (Apulia) in July 2015.

37 Under art. 185 of the Italian Criminal Code, the perpetrator of a criminal act and the persons who, in civil law, are liable for the perpetrator's acts are required to compensate the victim in respect of any offence which gives rise to pecuniary or non-material damage. Such a civil claim for restitution and damages may be brought in criminal proceedings by the person who suffered harm as a result of the criminal acts, or by his next of kin, against the person accused and the person liable in civil law (art. 74, Italian Criminal Code of Procedure).

38 ECJ, *Maurizio Giovanardi and Others*, C-79/11, 12 July 2012, para. 43.

outside the criminal proceedings; such a claim will be heard later, and this might undermine its effectiveness.[39]

Drawing upon the UNGPs, the paper has provided an overview of the Italian mode of liability that blends together criminal law procedures with a due diligence defence. By highlighting consistencies (e.g. preventive approach and transformative remedies) and divergences (e.g. scope; stakeholders' engagement; external communication) between the Italian law and the UNGPs, the objective has been to promote cross-fertilization of experiences and dialogue among legal practitioners, both domestically and between different countries. From the analysis, it is clear that the potential of Legislative Decree No. 231/2001 with regard to access to justice for victims of corporate crime should be more closely considered. Many scholars have welcomed the French law on corporate due diligence as the first one to legalize the concept of human rights due diligence and as a model in the area of B&HR.[40] The Italian Legislative Decree No. 231/2001 is not new, but its effect has been strengthened because of the updating of the list of relevant offences to be prevented, and the implementation of the EU Directive on non-financial reporting. Despite its shortcomings, it gives expression to the preventive approach behind the UNGPs, calling on companies to collaborate in the creation of preventive rules and, at the same time, defining the criteria for their liability. By being exonerated from liability, corporations are strongly encouraged to set up control mechanisms over their own activities and the supply chain, through the adoption of procedures aimed at preventing relevant offences. Reference to the UNGPs should help companies to adopt and implement preventive models tailored to their specific risks, avoiding window-dressing.

39 Italian Constitutional Court, Decision No. 218/2014.

40 European Coalition for Corporate Justice has defined the French law as 'a first historic step towards better human rights and environmental protection', calling for similar binding legislation at national, European and international level. European Coalition for Corporate Justice, *Press Release: France Adopts Corporate Duty of Vigilance Law: A First Historic Step towards better Human Rights and Environmental Protection*, February 2017, http://corporatejustice.org/news/393-france-adopts-corporate-duty-of-vigilance-law-a-first-historic-step-towards-better-human-rights-and-environmental-protection (last accessed 5 March 2018).

12 From Human Rights Due Diligence to Duty of Vigilance

Taking the French Example to the EU Level

Tiphaine Beau de Loménie, Sandra Cossart and Paige Morrow

Introduction

By going global, companies have outgrown the economic and political power of states. But there is a gap between the economic existence of multinational corporations and its legal recognition.[1]

Parent companies are shielded by legal principles such as the corporate veil and sovereign state jurisdiction, which prevent these companies from being held accountable when their business activities worldwide harm human rights or the environment. Yet it is precisely the parent company that directly or indirectly controls the business activities of the group, and furthermore may derive short-term profit from social and environmental dumping.

Although this business and human rights dilemma seems to be widely acknowledged, in recent years the debate has surreptitiously slipped into a systematic opposition between soft law and hard law. Behind an apparent desire to solve the B&HR issue, the same ideological debates are raging: on the one hand, the private sector advocates for preventive soft law and self-regulation mechanisms in order to maintain its ability to operate worldwide without facing legal consequences for its negative impacts. On the other hand, advocates of hard law recall the need to lift the corporate veil and ensure effective access to justice and remedy.

This chapter delves further into this ideological debate between soft law and hard law. It then explains how the *Loi relative au devoir de vigilance des sociétés mères et des entreprises donneuses d'ordre*, the pioneering French law on duty of vigilance, has reconciled these two visions by building on the soft legal concept of human rights due diligence (hereinafter 'HRDD') to create a binding legal duty to prevent, mitigate and, when needed, remedy human rights violations. Indeed, France is the first country to create a general obligation for certain large companies to implement HRDD. It is exceptional for holding companies liable

1 J.-P. Robé, A. Lyon-Caen and S. Vernac (eds), *Multinationals and the Constitutionalization of the World Power System*. Abingdon and New York: Routledge, 2016, 245.

for any harm that results from the failure to implement proper HRDD. The law was upheld by the French constitutional council (*Conseil constitutionnel*, hereinafter 'the Council') and passed into law on 27 March 2017,[2] although full compliance with the law was required only by the next fiscal year.[3] To conclude, the chapter reviews various options for taking this evolution to the European level.

Distinguishing Duty of Vigilance from Due Diligence

The private sector argues that soft law or self-regulation mechanisms are sufficient to mitigate the negative externalities of the globalized industry. These soft law instruments encourage parent companies to conduct environmental and HRDD throughout their value chains.[4]

HRDD may be defined as the internal measures and process by which a company identifies, prevents, mitigates and monitors the risks of human rights abuses, including environmental harm, throughout its value chain. The UNGPs provide that when a company performs HRDD, it 'should include assessing actual and potential human rights impacts, integrating and acting upon the findings, tracking responses, and communicating how impacts are addressed.'[5]

As HRDD has to date been voluntary, companies rarely face legal consequences for failing to properly carry it out. Financial and reputational consequences are marginal. Furthermore, the multiplication of soft law frameworks on B&HR has led companies to relax the scope and substance of their HRDD according to their needs.

There is a nascent international trend towards introducing legislative instruments to promote HRDD, but the few existing laws focus on reporting and fail to provide access to justice for victims of human rights abuses. They never sanction the lack of HRDD itself, but rather the lack of reporting on HRDD. As a consequence, the corporate veil remains in place and parent companies are still not held liable, even if the failure to properly carry out HRDD results in environmental harm or violations of human rights somewhere in the value

2 Conseil Constitutionnel, *Decision no. 2017-750 DC 23 Loi relative au devoir de vigilance des sociétés mères et des entreprises donneuses d'ordre*, March 2017, www.conseil-constitutionnel.fr/conseil-constitutionnel/root/bank/download/2017750DC2017750dc.pdf (last accessed 11 December 2017).

3 République française, *Loi no. 2017-399 du 27 mars 2017 relative au devoir de vigilance des sociétés mères et des entreprises donneuses d'ordre*, (hereinafter 'Loi relative au devoir de vigilance') Legifrance, JORF no. 0074, March 2017, art. 4, para. 3. www.legifrance.gouv.fr/affichTexte.do?cidTexte=JORFTEXT000034290626&dateTexte=&categorieLien=id (last accessed 11 December 2017).

4 OECD, *Guidelines for Multinational Enterprises*, Paris, 2011, http://dx.doi.org/10.1787/9789264115415-en (last accessed 11 December 2017). See also, OHCHR, *Guiding Principles on Business and Human rights*, 2011, www.ohchr.org/Documents/Publications/GuidingPrinciplesBusinessHR_EN.pdf (last accessed 11 December 2017). Unanimously adopted by the UNHRC as UN Doc A/HRC17/31, June 2011.

5 UNGP 17.

chain.[6] Moreover, existing requirements are often limited to specific sectors (e.g. conflict minerals)[7] or issues (e.g. forced and child labour).[8]

Hence, a number of companies have only superficially addressed human rights and environmental concerns through reporting or communication campaigns, rather than actual risk mitigation and prevention measures. 'Greenwashing' can be sued as a misleading commercial practice,[9] but such cases remain rare and only final consumers may be compensated while the direct victims of human rights abuses remain without remedy.

Soft law, HRDD and reporting may create a virtuous circle by providing prevention measures. But they leave many potential and actual victims without any access to either remedy or redress.

In this regard, the French law on duty of vigilance is a pioneering text, precisely because it builds on the upstream prevention measures of HRDD to create a specific legal duty to prevent human rights abuses and giving downstream access to justice on the basis of French tort law principles.

Analysis of the French Law on Duty of Vigilance

The law is inserted into French company law.[10] It imposes a duty of vigilance on any company that has, for two consecutive fiscal years, at least 5000 employees itself and throughout its French subsidiaries, or at least 10,000 employees itself and throughout its subsidiaries located in France and abroad.[11] It is estimated that the law will apply to approximately 150 companies; however, the French government has not disclosed the list of the affected companies.

The general duty of vigilance is threefold: it consists of the elaboration, the disclosure and the effective implementation of a Vigilance Plan (in French: *plan de vigilance*, hereinafter 'the Plan').

This Plan must include 'reasonable vigilance measures to adequately identify risks and prevent serious violations of human rights and fundamental freedoms, risks and serious harms to health and safety and the environment'.[12]

6 The Directive on Non-Financial Reporting leaves Member States to decide on the appropriate sanction for failure to properly report HRDD and does not create any liability for any harm that might be linked.

7 US Dodd–Frank Wall Street Reform and Consumer Protection Act, Pub.L. 111–203, H.R. 4173, sec. 1502.

8 See, for example, the UK Modern Slavery Act 2015, art. 30.

9 Sherpa, *Rana Plaza, already 2 years – Complaint against Auchan for Misleading Commercial Practices: The Associations take Civil Action* (Press Release), 8 June 2015, www.asso-sherpa.org/rana-plaza-already-2-years-complaint-auchan-misleading-commercial-practices-associations-take-civil-action (last accessed 11 December 2017).

10 Loi relative au devoir de vigilance, op. cit., art. 1. It appears in art. L. 225–102-4 of the Commercial Code.

11 Conseil Constitutionnel, *Decision no. 2017-750 DC 23*, op. cit., para. 3.

12 Loi relative au devoir de vigilance, op. cit., art. 1, para. 3.

These reasonable vigilance measures must cover risks and serious harms that derive from the parent company's activities, the activities of companies it controls directly or indirectly as defined under Article L.233–16, II of the French commercial code and further down the supply chain, and the activities of subcontractors and suppliers with which 'established commercial relations' are maintained.[13] The latter may be defined in the context of a specific jurisprudence as stable, regular commercial relationships, with or without a contract, with a certain volume of business and creating a reasonable expectation that such relations will last.[14]

The law indicates five types of measures that the Plans shall contain: (i) a risk mapping that identifies, analyses and ranks risks; (ii) procedures to assess the situation of subsidiaries, subcontractors or suppliers with whom 'established commercial relationships' are maintained; (iii) actions to prevent and mitigate risks and serious harms; (iv) an alert mechanism; and (v) a monitoring scheme to follow-up on the implementation and efficiency of measures.[15]

A decree of application issued by the State Council (*Décret en Conseil d'Etat*) might complement this list of measures and give further specifications on the content of the Plans at a future stage,[16] hinting that the list is indicative but not an exhaustive checklist, unlike certain reporting legislations. Each company should tailor its Plan to its business's specificities and it is left entirely to companies to determine what threats they pose to human rights, what indicators are relevant to the impacts analysis, what measures must be taken to prevent or mitigate the impacts, etc.

The Plan may also be drafted in association with stakeholders or within multilateral initiatives at the sectorial or territorial level. While this is not compulsory,[17] it is foreseen that many stakeholders will actually be involved in the drafting of Vigilance Plans as it seems unlikely that any company could map its impact without identifying its internal or external stakeholders. The law also explicitly requires consultation with trade unions for the establishment of the alert mechanism.[18] The precise timing and procedure for stakeholders' input is unspecified, leaving considerable discretion to the companies.

The duty of vigilance then requires effective implementation of the Plan. As a consequence, the measures in the Plan cannot be merely declaratory contrary to other reporting obligations. Compliance with the duty of vigilance entails a constantly renewed process of risk identification and remediation, where actual changes should be witnessed in terms of human rights impacts.

13 Ibid.

14 See French Commercial Code, art L. 442-6-I-5 and Cour de cassation, Chambre Commerciale, 18 December 2007, Décision no. 06-10.390.

15 Loi relative au devoir de vigilance, op. cit., paras. 4–9.

16 Ibid., art. 1, para. 11.

17 Ibid., art. 1, para. 4; Conseil Constitutionnel, *Decision no. 2017-750 DC 23*, op. cit., para. 22.

18 Loi relative au devoir de vigilance, op. cit., art. 1, para. 8 (4).

The third aspect of the duty of vigilance is a reporting requirement, increasing transparency and stakeholders' control over implementation. The Plan and a report on its effective implementation must be inserted into the company's annual report and made publicly available. It seems fair to expect that it will appear on the companies' website. The first Plans should be made available by 2018 and the first reports on implementation by the beginning of 2019.[19] Companies will also need to disclose their Plans to comply with the EU Non-Financial Reporting Directive.[20]

Through reliance on previous soft law instruments and HRDD concepts, the threefold duty of vigilance is thus clearly meant to ensure prevention of severe harms to human rights and the environment by companies. It also preserves the self-regulation capacity that business organizations were so keen to advocate for during the past decades.

Whenever this self-regulation proves flawed, the company might face judicial consequences and further be held liable in case of harm. Indeed, a two-step compliance mechanism is mandated in the event a company fails to perform its duty of vigilance. In the first instance, any person may give formal notice to the company of the violation. If the violation is not addressed within three months, any person with *locus standi* may apply to the court for an order compelling the company to comply.[21] The court may impose a periodic penalty payment as long as the company remains in violation of the law (*astreinte*).

The truly novel aspect of the French law is the fact that it links the mandatory HRDD of the Vigilance Plan to what could be construed as a duty of care (which does not generally apply under French law). Indeed, the duty of vigilance is linked to the general principles of the French law of tort, enshrined in Civil Code articles 1240 and 1241. In order to establish liability under these articles, claimants must prove a breach of a legal duty, harm and causation. Companies may thus incur civil liability and be required to remedy the damages, including under periodic penalty payment, whenever a breach of the duty of vigilance can be shown to have resulted in harm.[22]

The duty of vigilance has been defined as an obligation of means (*obligation de moyens*) and not as obligation of result (*obligation de résultat*),[23] meaning that companies must take all the steps in their power in order to reach a certain

19 Conseil Constitutionnel, *Decision no. 2017-750 DC 23*, op. cit., para. 31.

20 EU, Directive of the European Parliament and of the Council of 22 October 2014 amending Directive 2013/34/EU as regards disclosure of non-financial and diversity information by certain large undertakings and groups, 2014/95/EU, 22 October 2014, http://eur-lex.europa.eu/legal-content/EN/TXT/PDF/?uri=CELEX:32014L0095&from=EN (last accessed 14 February 2018) (hereinafter 'Non-Financial Reporting Directive').

21 Loi relative au devoir de vigilance, op. cit., art. 1, para. 12.

22 Loi relative au devoir de vigilance, op. cit., art. 2.

23 S. Cossart, J. Chaplier and T. Beau de Loménie. 'Developments in the field the French law on duty of care: a historic step towards making globalization work for all'. *Business and Human Rights Journal*, 2017, 2(2), 317–323.

result, but not that they imperatively have to reach this result. As a consequence, claimants may have the burden to prove the harm, but also the breach of the threefold duty of vigilance, because the latter will not be inferred merely from the occurrence of the damage and, last but not least, they may have to prove causation.[24]

However, disclosure of the Plan might help the claimants in building their cases and judicial interpretation of various elements of the law could slightly shift the burden of proof onto companies.[25] It can be expected that future cases will focus on whether or not companies 'effectively' implemented their Vigilance Plans, and whether the vigilance measures were 'reasonable'.

Finally, the judge may ask for the decision to be published and advertised, adding a reputational risk to the judicial one.[26]

While the French law is a significant achievement, the adopted version is a weakened version of the text first put forth by NGOs, trade unions and Members of Parliament (hereinafter 'MPs') in 2013. Proponents of the law initially tried to push for a criminal liability regime as well as a civil regime with a reversal of the burden of proof.[27] The weakening of the legislative proposal was due mainly to intensive business lobbying against the text, even before the Council.[28]

In addition, proponents of the law feared an ultimate setback when the text was referred to the Council. The latter is considered to be a political rather than a judicial body, and it has been thoroughly criticized for its lack of

24 S. Brabant and E. Savourey, *France's Corporate Duty of Vigilance Law, A Closer Look at the Penalties Faced by Companies, Revue Internationale de la Compliance et de l'Ethique des Affaires – Supplément à la Semaine Juridique Entreprise et Affaires,* No. 50, 14 December 2017, https://business-humanrights.org/sites/default/files/documents/French%20Corporate%20Duty%20of%20Vigilance%20Law%20-%20Penalties%20-%20Int%2527l%20Rev.Compl_.%20%26%20Bus.%20Ethics_.pdf (last accessed 11 December 2017).

25 As it is a civil statute and not a criminal one, French courts will not carry out any investigation but rather the appointed judge will adjudicate liability on the basis of the evidence adduced by the victim.

26 Loi relative au devoir de vigilance, op. cit., art. 2, para. 3.

27 See in French, Assemblée nationale, *Proposition de loi no. 1519, relative au devoir de vigilance des sociétés mères, déposée le 6 Novembre 2013,* No. 1519, 2013, www.assemblee-nationale.fr/14/propositions/pion1519.asp (last accessed 11 December 2017).

28 See in French, AFEP, *Proposition de loi sur la responsabilité des sociétés mères et entreprises donneuses d'ordre,* Press Release, March 2015, www.afep.com/uploads/medias/documents/Communique%20de%20presse%20PPL%20sur%20la%20responsabilite%20des%20soci%C3%A9tes%20meres%20et%20entreprises%20donneuses%20dordre.pdf (last accessed 11 December 2017); MEDEF, *Devoir de vigilance: une loi inefficace qui menace notre économie,* Press Release December 2016. www.medef.com/medef-tv/actualites/detail/article/devoir-de-vigilance-une-loi-inefficace-qui-menace-notre-economie.html (last accessed 11 December 2017). See also Conseil Constitutionnel, *Decision no. 2017-750 DC 2: Liste des contributions extérieures,* March 2017 www.conseil-constitutionnel.fr/conseil-constitutionnel/root/bank/download/2017750DC2017750dc_contributions.pdf (last accessed 11 December 2017). The referral before the Constitutional Council by 120 right-wing MPs benefited from the support of no less than five different briefs (*porte étroite*), from business organizations against only one for civil society.

independence vis-à-vis the executive branch, especially with regard to its structure, its proceedings and the nature of its decisions.[29] Several rulings enshrine freedom of enterprise within constitutional principles and show a clear bias in favour of a very liberal conception of company law.[30]

Nevertheless, the Council's decision over the text was guided by a political will for compromise and validated the core elements of the law. It deleted only the civil fine of maximum €30 million envisaged by the adopted text.[31] The Council otherwise reaffirmed the importance of fundamental principles of liability and stated that companies may be held liable under the statute, including for damages occurring in a foreign country.[32]

Given the inherently cross-border nature of B&HR issues, we can now expect increasing discussion about the introduction of similar requirements at the regional and international level. The next section reviews the options for introducing equivalent obligations across the EU.

Introduction of EU-level HRDD Obligations

There is currently no generalized EU requirement for companies to perform HRDD or to prevent or respond to adverse human rights impacts of their operations outside the EU – although there is increasing pressure to introduce such an obligation. Eight national Parliaments in 2016 used a procedure called the 'green card' initiative to call on the European Commission to propose a legal instrument to enhance corporate respect for the environment and human rights.[33] The Council of the EU also adopted Conclusions on B&HR that requested that the European Commission launch an EU Action Plan on Responsible Business Conduct that addressed HRDD, and called on all

29 J.-P. Chazal, 'Propriété et entreprise: le Conseil constitutionnel, le droit et la démocratie'. *Recueil Dalloz*, 2014, 19, 1101; V. Champeil-Desplats, 'La liberté d'entreprendre au pays des droits fondamentaux'. *Revue de droit du travail*, 2007, 1, 19.

30 Conseil Constitutionnel, *Decision no. 2016-741 DC 08 (Law Relating to Transparency, the Fight against Corruption and the Modernisation of Economic Life)*, December 2016, para. 103, www.conseil-constitutionnel.fr/conseil-constitutionnel/francais/les-decisions/acces-par-date/decisions-depuis-1959/2016/2016-741-dc/version-en-anglais.148584.html (last accessed 11 December 2017).

31 Conseil Constitutionnel, *Decision no. 2017-750 DC 23*, op. cit., paras. 8, 14 and 22, the civil fine is considered to be a sanction that is 'criminal in nature', and must therefore comply with the principles governing criminal legality. The Council stated that, while some terms of the law were too vague to comply with criminal legality principles, the text was otherwise intelligible. The periodic penalty payments may still act as a deterrent.

32 Conseil Constitutionnel, *Decision no. 2017-750 DC 23*, op. cit., paras. 22 and 27–29.

33 European Coalition for Corporate Justice, *Members of 8 European Parliaments Support Duty of Care Legislation for EU Corporations*, 31 May 2016, http://corporatejustice.org/news/132-members-of-8-european-parliaments-support-duty-of-care-legislation-for-eu-corporations (last accessed 11 December 2017).

companies whether transnational or domestic to integrate HRDD into their operations.[34]

To date, the EU has passed three relevant sector and issue-specific legal instruments that seek to address certain narrowly defined issues, such as environmental or social concerns, but are not specifically aimed at eliminating human rights violations. The first key example is the Timber Regulation, which requires environmental due diligence to prevent illegal logging, which threatens forest development and the commercial viability of operators acting legally.[35] The second example is the Conflict Minerals Regulation,[36] which establishes an EU-wide system of supply chain due diligence for importers of minerals from conflict-affected area.[37] From 1 January 2021, EU importers of tin, tantalum, tungsten and gold will be obligated to carry out due diligence on their supply chains, provided they import above a certain amount. The last relevant piece of legislation is the Non-Financial Reporting Directive,[38] which requires large public-interest entities (listed companies, banks, insurance undertakings and other companies that are so designated by Member States) with more than 500 employees to disclose in their management report relevant and useful information on certain policies, main risks and outcomes, including ones related to HRDD. Companies must disclose information regarding, at a minimum, environmental matters, social and employee aspects, respect for human rights, a description of due diligence processes implemented, anticorruption and bribery issues, and diversity in their board of directors. This obligation applies on a comply-or-explain basis, meaning that companies must either disclose their HRDD policies and measures if they have them, or explain why they consider that they are not required.[39]

The three options for the EU to introduce HRDD requirements would be to take a sector-specific approach (e.g. focused on the garment and footwear

34 Council of the EU, *Council Conclusions on Business and Human Rights*, Doc. 10254/16, 20 June 2016, paras. 6 and 8, https://ec.europa.eu/anti-trafficking/sites/antitrafficking/files/council_conclusions_on_business_and_human_rights_foreign_affairs_council.pdf (last accessed 11 December 2017).

35 EU, *Regulation of the European Parliament and of the Council Laying down the Obligations of Operators who Place Timber and Timber Products on the Market*, No. 995/2010 OJ 2010, L 295/23, 20 October 2010, http://eur-lex.europa.eu/legal-content/EN/TXT/PDF/?uri=CELEX:32010R0995&from=EN (last accessed 21 February 2018), (hereinafter 'Timber Regulation').

36 EU, *Regulation of the European Parliament and of the Council Setting Up a Union System for Supply Chain Due Diligence Self-certification of Responsible Importers of Tin, Tantalum and Tungsten, their Ores, and Gold Originating in Conflict-affected and High-risk Areas*, 2017/821 L 130/1, 17 May 2017, http://eur-lex.europa.eu/legal-content/EN/TXT/PDF/?uri=CELEX:32017R0821&from=EN (last accessed 21 February 2018) (hereinafter 'Conflict Minerals Regulation').

37 The due diligence requirements only apply to imports into the EU and do not impose obligations within the EU market.

38 Non-Financial Reporting Directive, op. cit.

39 Ibid., art. 1(1)(b), recital 6.

sector),[40] an issue-specific approach (e.g. targeted at eliminating child labour and/or forced labour), or a generalized, cross-sector approach. The third approach is most closely analogous to the French law and will therefore be focused on in this section – it is also an approach that has been favourably cited by the EU Fundamental Rights Agency (FRA) in an opinion solicited by the Council of the EU.[41]

Review of EU Competence to Legislate

A proposal for EU legislation to impose a HRDD requirement, as with any other EU instrument, must first establish that it falls within an area of EU competence as codified in the treaties.[42] The Timber Regulation relies on the EU's competence to legislate in the area of environmental law.[43] The Conflict Minerals Regulation's legal basis is the EU's Common Commercial Policy,[44] and applies only to goods that are entering the EU internal market. The Non-Financial Reporting Directive is based on the EU's competence to take measures to achieve freedom of establishment and the proper functioning of the Internal Market.[45] This legal basis may be invoked when laws in different Member States require companies to comply with divergent requirements in overlapping areas, which result in fragmentation of the common market.

Given the recent and anticipated legislation in Member States relating to HRDD, the EU is arguably competent to enact legislation that would harmonize their requirements. In addition to the French law, there is a draft law in the Netherlands to eliminate child labour.[46] Both the German[47] and the

40 For an example, see A. Dziedzic, C. Lelièvre, J. Povilonis, A. Alemanno and P. Morrow, 'Towards EU legislation on human rights due diligence: case study of the garment and textile sector'. *HEC Paris Research Paper*, 2017, No. LAW-2017–1207.

41 EU Fundamental Rights Agency, *Improving Access to Remedy in the Area of Business and Human Rights at the EU Level States*, Opinion 1/2017, 10 April 2017, p. 17: 'A recently adopted law in France could serve as a model for the EU'.

42 EU, *Consolidated Version of the Treaty on European Union*, OJ C 326, 26/10/2012, 13 December 2007, recital 3.

43 EU, *Consolidated Version of the Treaty on the Functioning of the European Union*, OJ C 326/47, 13 December 2007, art. 192(1) (hereinafter 'TFEU').

44 TFEU art. 207, which is an area of exclusive EU competence.

45 Proper functioning of the internal market (TFEU art. 114) and freedom of establishment (TFEU, arts. 49 and 50).

46 Government of the Netherlands, *Initiatiefvoorstel-Kuiken Wet zorgplicht kinderarbeid*, 19 December 2017, www.eerstekamer.nl/wetsvoorstel/34506_initiatiefvoorstel_kuiken (last accessed 21 February 2018).

47 Government of Germany, *National Action Plan: Implementation of the UN Guiding Principles on Business and Human Rights 2016–2020*, 16 December 2016, www.auswaertiges-amt.de/cae/servlet/contentblob/754770/publicationFile/230425/161221-NAP-DL.pdf (last accessed 11 December 2017).

Italian[48] NAPs on B&HR commit to evaluating the possibility of introducing mandatory HRDD in the future.

The argument for introducing EU-level HRDD would be that companies benefit from the legal certainty provided by uniform operating rules across the single market. An additional argument would be that it would facilitate transparency across the internal market by allowing relevant stakeholders to compare the relative CSR performance of companies.[49]

Determining the Scope of Obligation

The two clear options for determining to whom obligations should apply are (1) on the basis of size and (2) on the basis of activities. The first option is that taken by the Non-Financial Reporting Directive as well as the French law and the UK Modern Slavery Act.

The Timber Regulation and Conflict Minerals Regulation both employ the second option. Thus, the Timber Regulation applies to natural and legal persons solely on the basis of their activity in the EU timber market. The Conflict Minerals Regulation applies to all importers of conflict minerals above a *de minimis* threshold; it exempts small volume importers, as well as importers of recycled metals, by-products and pre-existing stocks. The Regulation also exempts companies further downstream from importers, such as manufacturers and retailers, although they will be encouraged to disclose their due diligence practices in a transparency database.

An activities-based approach is logical for targeting specific sectors, but for imposing generalized HRDD obligations it is more intuitive to follow the example of the Non-Financial Reporting Directive, which is principally limited to large companies with over 500 employees, including those traded on EU stock exchanges, insurers, banks and other companies deemed to be public interest entities by Member States. The downside is that foreign-based companies without the requisite presence in the EU would be exempt from the requirements.

Sanctions

A further challenge is the introduction of liability for harms that are linked to the failure to properly implement HRDD. EU legislation typically leaves the question of sanctions to Member States, with the exception of certain limited areas such as tax and competition law, where fines or sanctions may be

48 Government of Italy, *Italian National Action Plan on Business and Human Rights 2016–2021*, December 2016, www.cidu.esteri.it/resource/2016/12/49117_f_NAPBHRENGFINALEDEC152017.pdf (last accessed 11 December 2017).

49 Wouters, *Study: EU Competence to Legislate in the Areas of Company Duty of Care (Tort Liability) and Mandatory Human Rights Due Diligence*, 2016. Unpublished. On file with the authors.

imposed.[50] The Timber Regulation provides only that penalties should be 'effective, proportionate and dissuasive', and may include fines, the seizure of timber and timber products, and an immediate suspension of the authorization to trade.[51] Member States must determine the nature of the penalties without any limitations on their discretion or meaningful minimum standards.

The Conflict Minerals Regulation says only that Member States will establish the rules applicable to infringement of the Regulation, which must be communicated to the European Commission. In cases of violation, national authorities must issue a notice of remedial action to be taken by the importer.[52]

The Non-Financial Reporting Directive is even less specific, requiring only that Member States bring into force the 'laws, regulations and administrative provisions' necessary to transpose the Directive.[53] Thus, no EU-wide sanctions are in place for companies that fail to comply.

At a minimum, any legislative proposal should require Member States to ensure that penalties are effective, proportionate and dissuasive, as provided for by the Timber Regulation.[54]

That being said, the jurisdictional rules set out in Brussels I Regulation require a victim of human rights abuse by an EU-based company to be given access to justice in the EU Member State where the company is domiciled if certain requirements are met.[55] We could therefore expect future case law to explore the scope of civil liability across EU jurisdictions.[56]

Conclusion

The French law sets a new standard for corporate responsibility and raises the bar for other countries and the EU to follow. There is currently no equivalent of the French law at the EU level. A propitious moment to put forward such a

50 See, for example, EU, *Council Regulation (EC) No 1/2003 of 16 December 2002 on the Implementation of the Rules on Competition Laid Down in Arts. 81 and 82 of the Treaty*, January 2003, http://eur-lex.europa.eu/legal-content/EN/TXT/PDF/?uri=CELEX:32003R0001&from=NL (last accessed 21 February 2018), art. 23, authorizing the European Commission to impose fines directly on companies for violations of certain competition provisions.

51 Timber Regulation, op. cit., art. 19. By way of comparison, the US Lacey Act contains civil and criminal penalties including jail sentences of up to 5 years for trade in illegally harvested timber (Lacey Act § 3, 16 U.S.C. § 3371 (2008)).

52 Timber Regulation, op. cit., art. 16.

53 Ibid., art. 4.

54 Similar language is used in the EU Anti-Money Laundering Directive, art. 39.1–39.2.

55 EU, *Regulation 1215/2012 of the European Parliament and of the Council on Jurisdiction and the Recognition and Enforcement of Judgments in Civil and Commercial Matters*, OJ L 351/1, 20 December 2012, arts. 4(1), 5(3); ECJ, *Réunion Européenne SA and Others – Spliethoff's Bevrachtingskantoor BV – the Master of the vessel Alblasgracht V002*, C-51/97, 27 October 1998, para. 28.

56 See for example District Court of The Hague, *Dooh-Akpan-Oguru Efanga-Milieudefensie v.* Shell, *Interim Decision on Jurisdiction*, 30 December 2009, ECLI:NL:RBSGR:2009:BK8616 and *Yao Essaie Motto v. Trafigura Ltd and Trafigura Beheer BV*, HQ06X03370.

proposal for EU-wide HRDD could be in the report that the European Commission is required to submit to Parliament and Council by 6 December 2018 on the implementation of the Non-Financial Reporting Directive – which 'shall be accompanied, if appropriate, by legislative proposals'.[57] The use of the 'green card' initiative by eight national Parliaments, as well as the Council of the EU's Conclusions on B&HR, seem to indicate increasing (albeit still tentative) political support for introducing HRDD requirements across the EU.

57 Non-Financial Reporting Directive, op. cit., art. 3.

13 Corporate Human Rights Compliance and Disinvestment

Lessons from the Norwegian Sovereign Wealth Fund

Ludovica Chiussi

Setting the Scene: Human Rights and the Financial Sector

The B&HR discourse has reached well beyond the usual crowd of states and companies, as human rights violations and environmental concerns are gaining increasing relevance for financial actors.[1] In the words of John Ruggie, 'while attention in the business and human rights arena has thus far been on so-called front-line businesses [...], there is now growing interest in finance because the financial sector provides the means for front-line businesses to operate'.[2]

Financial services virtually affect the full range of human rights, both in contexts of conflict and peace.[3] The category of 'financial actors' covers a variety of different players, including intergovernmental financial institutions, private investment and commercial banks, trusts and sovereign wealth funds. Through their active shareholding, such actors represent an important drive in achieving sustainable development.[4] Yet despite the increasing recognition of their role in nurturing the realization of human rights and environmental protection – and in avoiding their infringement – we have only witnessed a marginal integration of the relevant international standards in their business model.[5]

1 See UN Environmental Programme and Institute for Human Rights and Business, *Human Rights and Sustainable Finance: Exploring their Relationship*, Inquiry Working Paper 16/01, February 2016, 25 ff; T. Hebb and others (eds), *The Routledge Handbook of Responsible Investment*. Abingdon: Routledge, 2016, 53 ff.

2 UNHRC, *Report of the UN High Commissioner on Human Rights on the Sectoral Consultation Entitled 'Human Rights and the Financial Sector'*, UN Doc. A/HRC4/99, 6 March 2007, para. 6.

3 See Danish Institute for Human Rights, *Values Added: The Challenge of Integrating Human Rights into the Financial Sector*. Copenhagen: Danish Institute for Human Rights, 2010, 6 ff.

4 UN Environmental Programme Finance Initiative, *Financing the UN Development System: Pathways to Reposition for Agenda 2030*, 8 September 2017, 70 ff; B.J. Richardson, 'Financial markets and socially responsible investing'. In B. Sjåfjell and B.J. Richardson (eds), *Company Law and Sustainability: Legal Barriers and Opportunities*. Cambridge: Cambridge University Press, 2015, 226 ff.

5 See M. Dowell-Jones, 'Financial institutions and human rights'. *Human Rights Law Review*, 2013, 13, 425.

Financial actors often formally operate several steps away from the violations perpetrated by the companies who benefit from their services. The question on whether and to what extent such actors can be held responsible for the conduct of companies within their portfolio is hotly debated, and one that falls beyond the scope of this chapter.[6] Be that as it may, there is no doubt that the financial sector falls under the scope of application of both the OECD Guidelines for Multinational Enterprises (hereinafter 'OECD Guidelines') and the UNGPs. The OECD Guidelines require TNCs to engage in due diligence in order to prevent and, eventually, address human rights impact that the they may cause, or contribute to, through their own activities, or through their business relationships.[7] With all due consideration for the nature and context of the services provided by the financial sector, its operations should be equally informed by international human rights standards.[8]

From a legal perspective, the issue of accountability (if not legal responsibility) of financial actors is being reshaped by a progressively tailored application of due diligence,[9] and by the adoption of ad-hoc instruments such as the Equator Principles,[10] the UN Principles on Responsible Investment[11] and the more recent G20/OECD Principles of Corporate Governance.[12]

From an economic standpoint, it has become clear that threats to the rule of law, violations of human rights and environmental harms may affect portfolio returns over time. As it has been recently put by the Governor of the Bank of England, 'the combination of the weight of scientific evidence and the dynamics

6 See L. Catà Backer, 'The corporate social responsibilities of financial institutions for the conduct of their borrowers: the view from international law and standards'. *Lewis & Clark Law Review*, 2017, 21, 26 ff; on the broader issue of international legal personality of corporations, the author shares the view according to which corporations are 'entities *sui generis*' whose legal capacity has to be assessed on a case by case basis; see V. Lowe, 'Corporations as international actors and international law makers'. *Italian Yearbook of International Law*, 2004, 14, 23 ff.

7 OECD, *Guidelines for Multinational Enterprises*. Paris: OECD Publishing, 2011, Chapter II.

8 The OECD Working Party on Responsible Business Conduct affirmed that 'as concerns the issue of financial institutions in their role as minority shareholders, including sovereign wealth funds and central banks, due regard must be paid to the sector specific characteristics and practical and legal concerns and restrictions'. In OECD, *Annual Report on the OECD Guidelines for Multinational Enterprises 2014: Responsible Business Conduct by Sector*. Paris: OECD Publishing, 2014, 118; OECD, *Due Diligence in the Financial Sector: Adverse Impacts Directly Linked to Financial Sector Operations, Products or Services by A Business Relationship*. Paris: OECD Publishing, 26–27 June 2014, 2.

9 See OECD, *Responsible Business Conduct for Institutional Investors: Key Considerations for Due Diligence under the OECD Guidelines for Multinational Enterprises*. Paris: OECD Publishing, 28 March 2017, 7 ff.

10 The Equator Principles Association, *Equator Principles*, 2011, www.equator-principles.com (last accessed 2 October 2017).

11 UN Principles on Responsible Investment, *Principles on Responsible Investment*, 2006, www.unpri.org (last accessed 2 October 2017).

12 OECD, *G20/OECD Principles of Corporate Governance*. Paris: OECD Publishing, 2015.

of the financial system suggest that, in the fullness of time, climate change will threaten financial resilience and longer-term prosperity'.[13]

Beyond their own responsibility to respect human rights, financial institutions can play a critical role in helping to set expectations for virtually every business sector. By imposing requirements on companies that the latter operates in compliance with basic rules and standards, financial actors can provide an important preventive tool to foster corporate accountability.

With regard to Sovereign Wealth Funds (hereinafter 'SWFs')[14] specifically, both their borrowing and lending can have human rights implications.[15] As institutional investors, SWFs have the fiduciary duty to act in the best long-term interests of their beneficiaries, which in their particular case is the country's present and future citizenry.[16] Given the long-term investment strategies of SWFs, and their usually active ownership, such investors are in a privileged position to bridge the gap between the normative dimension of human rights and its implementation in investor markets.[17]

13 M. Carney, *Breaking the Tragedy of the Horizon – Climate Change and Financial Stability*, 29 September 2015. www.bis.org/review/r151009a.pdf (last accessed 15 February 2018); see M. Bowman, *Banking on Climate Change: How Finance Actors and Transnational Regulatory Regimes are Responding*. Alphen aan den Rjin: Wolters Kluwer, 2014, 21.

14 The International Monetary Fund (IMF) defines SWFs as 'special investment funds created or owned by governments to hold foreign assets for long-term purposes', IMF, *Global Financial Stability Report: Financial Market Turbulence, Causes, Consequences, and Policies*. Washington: IMF, 2007, 45, www.imf.org/en/Publications/GFSR/Issues/2016/12/31/Financial-Market-Turbulence-Causes-Consequences-and-Policies (last accessed 15 February 2018); See F. Bassan, *The Law of Sovereign Wealth Funds*. Cheltenham and Northampton: Edward Elgar, 2011, 3 ff.

15 See S. Chesterman, 'The turn to ethics: disinvestment from multinational corporations for human rights violations – the case of Norway's sovereign wealth fund'. *American University International Law Review*, 2008, 23, 578 ff; P. Keenan and C. Ochoa, 'The human rights potential of sovereign wealth funds'. *Georgetown Journal of International Law*, 2009, 40, 1151 ff; B. Demeyere, 'Sovereign wealth funds and (un)ethical investment: using "due diligence" to avoid contributing to human rights violations committed by companies in the investment portfolio'. In G. Nystuen, A. Follesdal and O. Mestad (eds), *Human Rights, Corporate Complicity and Disinvestment*. Cambridge: Cambridge University Press, 2011, 183 ff; S. Ghahramani, 'Governments, financial markets, and international human rights: the state's role as shareholder'. *Yale Journal of International Affairs*, 2011, 6, 85–95; A. Cummine, 'Ethical sovereign investors: sovereign wealth funds and human rights'. In J.P. Bohoslavsky and J.C. Cernic (eds), *Making Sovereign Financing Human Rights Work*. Oxford: Hart, 2014, 163 ff.

16 The only international voluntary framework of investment and operational principles directed at SWFs are the Santiago Principles launched in 2008 by the International Working Group of Sovereign Wealth Funds and the International Monetary Fund. While they aim to guarantee transparency, clarity, and equivalent treatment to SWFs and private funds, they make no explicit reference to the issue of responsible investments.

17 See B.J. Richardson, 'Sovereign wealth funds and socially responsible investing: an emerging public fiduciary'. *Global Journal of Comparative Law*, 2012, 2, 127 ff; F. Bassan, 'Les fonds souverains et le normes éthiques pour l'investissement'. In L. Manderieux and M. Vellano, *Ethique globale, bonne gouvernance et droit international économique*. Torino: Giappichelli, 2017, 93–94.

With these premises in mind, this chapter is concerned with the divestment techniques as implemented by the Norwegian Government Pension Fund Global (hereinafter 'the Fund').[18] The Fund has been at the forefront of human rights issues for its divestment operations from foreign corporations.[19] The purpose of this contribution is to shed light on the Norwegian model and to assess its impact on the operationalization of international legal standards in the field.[20]

The Norwegian Government Pension Fund Global

With a current market value of about 1 trillion dollars, the Fund owns more than 2 per cent of all listed shares in Europe.[21] It invests the surplus income produced by Norway's oil profits in foreign financial instruments, such as bonds and equities.[22] Its largest equity asset includes, among others, Apple, Nestlé, Royal Dutch Shell, Microsoft Corp. and Novartis. Norges Bank, the Norwegian Central Bank, has been tasked by the Ministry of Finance with the management of the Fund, the operational management of which has been entrusted to Norges Bank Investment Management (hereinafter 'NBIM').

The purpose behind the creation of the Fund by the Norwegian Parliament was twofold. First, smoothing the impact of the fluctuating prices in the petroleum sector by investing a substantial portion of oil revenues abroad. Second, avoiding burning through the oil reserves in the course of one or two generations, leaving some of the benefits for future generations.[23] A feeling of déjà vu brings one back to the definition of sustainable development of the *Brundtland Report*, named after the very Norwegian Prime Minister who had a key role in the 1993 UN World Conference on Environment and Development.[24]

Sustainability and compliance with international human rights standards permeate the entire activity of the Fund. The Management Mandate to NBIM acknowledges that 'a good long-term return is considered dependent on

18 See A. Føllesdal, 'Engagement, divestment or both? Conflicts and interactions: the case of the Norwegian Pension Fund'. In J. Bohoslavsky and J. Letnar Černič, op. cit., 323 ff.

19 *The Economist*, 'Norway's Global Fund: how to not spend it', 24 September 2016, www.economist.com/news/business-and-finance/21707435-norways-global-fund-its-tough-small-democracy-run-worlds-biggest (last accessed 13 November 2017).

20 See L. Cata Backer, 'Sovereign wealth funds as regulatory chameleons: the Norwegian sovereign wealth funds and public global governance through private global investment'. *Georgetown Journal of International Law*, 2010, 41, 425 ff.

21 The Norwegian Government Pension Fund comprises the Government Pension Fund Global and the Government Pension Fund Norway.

22 As at September 2017, the Fund's asset allocation is 65.9 per cent equities, 31.6 per cent fixed income and 2.5 per cent unlisted real estate.

23 K. Halvorsen, *The Nordic Welfare Model*. Kristofer Lehmkuhl Forelesning, 2008, 10, brage.bibsys.no/xmlui/handle/11250/166974 (last accessed 15 February 2018).

24 UN World Commission on Environment and Development, *Our Common Future*, UN Doc A/42/427, 4 August, 1987, para. 84.

sustainable development in economic, environmental and social terms, as well as well-functioning, legitimate and efficient markets'.[25] The management of the Fund rests on three pillars: standard setting, active ownership and risk management. As to the first pillar, NBIM has indicated its expectations (based on internationally recognized standards such as the UN Global Compact, the UNGPs, the OECD Principles of Corporate Governance and the OECD Guidelines) in different areas ranging from climate change[26] to children's rights[27] and tax transparency.[28] In 2016, NBIM published its expectations towards companies with regard to human rights.[29] The document makes clear that companies are expected, in line with the UNGPs, to elaborate human rights policies and to adopt adequate measures to address the risk of adverse impacts from their operations. The importance of disclosure of information companies' practices is also emphasized. Regarding the third pillar, which focuses on risk management, the Fund put in place an integrated risk-monitoring that includes risk factors associated with environmental, social and corporate governance. The risk-based assessment is integrated in the Guidelines for Observation and Exclusion of Companies from the Fund.

The Guidelines for Observation and Exclusion of Companies from the Fund

The Guidelines for Observation and Exclusion of Companies from the Fund (hereinafter 'Guidelines') were adopted in 2004 by the Norwegian Ministry of Finance. After a major revision in 2010,[30] a new version was adopted in 2014, which was further amended in 2017.[31] The Guidelines reflect Norway's

25 Norges Bank, *Investment Mandate for CEO of Norges Bank Investment Management*, 13 December 2017, para. 2.1, www.nbim.no/contentassets/43615da4359c4a47a60ee55e03511589/nbim-ceo-investment-mandate---171213.pdf (last accessed 15 February 2018).

26 Norges Bank Investment Management, *Climate Change Strategy: Expectations towards Companies*, 2017, www.nbim.no/contentassets/e3f8e013de754cad905b686bdb50f76a/nbim_climatechange_2018_web.pdf (last accessed 15 February 2018). The document was first published in 2009 and last updated in 2017.

27 Norges Bank Investment Management, *Tax Transparency Expectations towards Companies*, 2017, www.nbim.no/contentassets/48b3ea4218e44caab5f2a1f56992f67e/expectations-document---tax-and-transparency---norges-bank-investment-management.pdf (last accessed 15 February 2018).

28 Norges Bank Investment Management, *Children's Rights Expectations towards Companies*, 2008, www.nbim.no/contentassets/d3bda851912f4bcc832520cd93700699/childrens-rights-expectations.pdf (last accessed 15 February 2018).

29 Norges Bank Investment Management, *Human Rights: Expectations towards Companies*, 2016, www.nbim.no/contentassets/3258fe10181544cc8e02566c7237fa5f/human-rights-expectations-document2.pdf (last accessed 15 February 2018).

30 The 2010 revision added key aspects linked to environmental law and climate change.

31 Norwegian Ministry of Finance, *Guidelines for Observation and Exclusion from the Government Pension Fund Global*, Oslo, 2017, www.regjeringen.no/globalassets/upload/fin/statens-pensjonsfond/formelt-grunnlag/guidelines-for-observation-and-exclusion-from-the-gpfg---17.2.2017.pdf (last accessed 15 February 2018).

obligations under international law and constitute the legal basis against which Norway sets its expectation towards companies benefitting from the financial services of its sovereign Fund. The purpose of the Guidelines is to make sure that the Fund, through its investments portfolio, does not contribute to serious violations of human rights and environmental standards, as well as to practices amounting to corruption.

At the time of the adoption of the Ethical Guidelines, an independent Council on Ethics was established to advise the Ministry of Finance on whether the investments of the Fund are consistent with the Guidelines.[32] The Council on Ethics is composed of five independent members nominated by Norges Bank and appointed by the Ministry. It provides recommendations to Norges Bank on the necessity to divest from certain companies, or to place such companies under observation. Since 2015, the final decision on exclusion or observation lies with the Executive Board of Norges Bank (while previously the final decision was made by the Ministry of Finance).

The Guidelines provide product-based and conduct-based criteria for observation and exclusion from the Fund. As to the product-based criteria, the Guidelines state that the Fund shall not invest in companies which themselves, or through entities control: (a) the production of weapons that violate fundamental humanitarian principles through their normal use; (b) the production of tobacco; and (c) the selling of weapons or military material to states that are subject to investment restrictions on government bonds as described in the management mandate for the Government Pension Fund Global, section 3–1(2)(c).[33]

With regard to the conduct-based criteria, companies may be put under observation or be excluded from the Fund if there is an unacceptable risk that the company contributes to, or is responsible for: (a) serious or systematic human rights violations, such as murder, torture, deprivation of liberty, forced labour and the worst forms of child labour; (b) serious violations of the rights of individuals in situations of war or conflict; (c) severe environmental damage; (d) acts or omissions that on an aggregate company level lead to unacceptable greenhouse gas emissions; (e) gross corruption; and (f) other particularly serious violations of fundamental ethical norms.[34]

A company that is being considered for observation or exclusion has the right to present information to the Council on Ethics, which will clarify the grounds for observation or exclusion. It may be noted that that the UN official reports

32 Ibid., Section 4.

33 Ibid., Section 2. A new product-based criterion was introduced in 2016. Observation or exclusion may be decided for mining companies which derive 30 per cent or more of their revenue from thermal coal or base 30 per cent or more of their operations on thermal coal.

34 Ibid., Section 3. In 2016, the Ministry of Finance added new conduct-based criteria related to unacceptable risk that the company acts or is responsible for omissions that lead to unacceptable greenhouse gas emissions.

can have a key role in the sources upon which the Council bases its investigation, as most recently seen in the *Atal* case.[35]

Should the Council on Ethics recommend observation or exclusion of the company, the latter will have the possibility to present its own comments.[36] The dialogue established between the company and the Council can be a powerful leverage tool, as throughout the process the company may be persuaded to take steps to address the issues that triggered observation or exclusion.

After receiving the recommendation from the Council on Ethics, the Executive Board of Norges Bank decides on the exclusion or observation of the company. The decision is also based on the likelihood of future norm violations, considering the human rights policies put in place by the company. In any case, the Bank will consider whether other measures, such as active ownership, may be more effective in reducing the risk of future violations.[37]

It is worth noting that abstract human rights policies do not suffice to avoid the exclusion of the company from the portfolio. As pointed out by the Council on Ethics in the case concerning Monsanto, 'it is unclear how the company intends to transform this policy into concrete acts, and the fact that such a policy exists will hardly in itself lead to substantial improvement'.[38] The same approach was followed towards Zuari Agro Chemicals Ltd, where the Council affirmed, that

> the fact that a company has a policy or code of conduct is not sufficient in itself to achieve reductions in the use of child labour. Nor it is sufficient that the company has established control mechanisms if these are not suited to detect instances of child labour.[39]

Finally, should Norges Bank decide to exclude the company from the Fund's portfolio, the Council on Ethics shall regularly assess whether the basis for exclusion still exists and, in case it does, shall recommend that the Bank revokes its decision.

35 Council on Ethics, *Recommendation to Exclude Atal SA from the Government Pension Fund*, 25 August 2017, 3, nettsteder.regjeringen.no/etikkradet-2017/files/2018/01/Recommendation-Atal-SA-20473.pdf (last accessed 15 February 2018).

36 *Guidelines for Observation and Exclusion from the Government Pension Fund Global*, op. cit., Section 5.

37 Ibid., Section 6.

38 Council on Ethics, *Recommendation to Exclude Monsanto Co. from the Government Pension Fund Global*, 20 November 2006, 20, nettsteder.regjeringen.no/etikkradet-2017/files/2017/02/Recommendation-Monsanto-ENG.pdf (last accessed 15 February 2018).

39 Council on Ethics, *Recommendation to Exclude Zuari Agro Chemicals Ltd. from the Government Pension Fund Global*, 18 April 2013, 10, nettsteder.regjeringen.no/etikkradet-2017/files/2017/02/Rec-Zuari-2013-eng.pdf (last accessed 15 February 2018).

A Closer Look at Divestment Cases: Serious Human Rights Violations, Severe Environmental Damage and Gross Corruption

Section 3(a) of the Ethical Guidelines includes 'serious or systematic human rights violations', such as murder, torture, deprivation of liberty and the worst forms of child labour as a basis of exclusion from the Fund's portfolio.

A pioneer case brought to the attention of the Council on Ethics has been *Wal-Mart Stores Inc.*[40] Wal-Mart was alleged to run its business operations in breach of internationally recognized human rights and labour rights, both through its suppliers across the globe, and in its own operations in North America. The Council on Ethics grounded its recommendation in four main points. First, the existence of a link between Wal-Mart's business operations and the reported violations. Second, the reasons behind such violations, identified as having the purpose to increase the company's profits. Third, the presence of direct and indirect responsibility in contributing to labour rights violations and failing to prevent such breaches within its supply chain. Fourth, the persistence of the breach or the likelihood of recurrence of the violation.[41] Following the recommendation of the Council on Ethics, in 2006 Norway's Ministry of Finance announced it would exclude Wal-Mart from its portfolio.

Assessing the threshold for what constitutes serious and systematic human rights violations according to the Guidelines can be a challenging task. The Council on Ethics often makes use of the interpretation given by international human rights courts and bodies, while also resorting to the threshold set by its own previous cases. In the *Wal-Mart* case, The Council stated that

> it appears to be a systematic and planned practice on the part of the company to operate on, or below, the threshold of what are accepted standards for the work environment. Many of the violations are serious, most appear to be systematic, and altogether they form a picture of a company whose overall activity displays a lack of willingness to countervail violations of standards in its business operations.[42]

The same approach was followed in the 2017 case concerning labour and human rights violations in the operations of Hansae Yes24 Holdings Co Ltd, where the Council recalled that the systemic nature of human rights violations requires an 'accumulation of violations that [...] constitute a pattern of

40 Council on Ethics, *Recommendation to Exclude Wal-Mart Stores Inc. from the Government Pension Fund Global*, 15 November 2005, nettsteder.regjeringen.no/etikkradet-2017/files/2017/02/Tilrådning-WM-ENG.pdf (last accessed 15 February 2018).

41 Ibid., 21–22.

42 Ibid., 22.

behaviour'.[43] However, in this case, Norges Bank opted for observation rather than exclusion, since the company had taken measures to progressively improve the working conditions of its employees.

Section 3(c) of the Guidelines states that 'companies may be put under observation or be excluded when if there is an unacceptable risk that the company contributes to or is responsible for severe environmental damage'. As it emerges from the very first environmental case brought before the Council on Ethics, the recommendation will take into account a number of factors, namely the entity and the irreversibility of the damage; the impact on human life and health; the relationship between the damage and violations of domestic or international law; the failure of the company in exercising due diligence; and the likeliness that the company's harmful practices will persist in the future.[44]

In assessing the risk of environmental damage, the Council on Ethics appears to be well aware of the work of specialized environmental agencies, as well as international organizations. In the recent case concerning the Indian company, Bharat Heavy Electricals Limited, the Council on Ethics assessed the impact of coal fired power plant on the world's largest mangrove forest, in Bangladesh. After a thorough analysis of the environmental impact assessment concerning the operations of the company, the Council has also given considerable weight to the report of the UN Educational Scientific and Cultural Organization on the risks associated with the project, as well as to the fact that the recommendations of the International Financial Corporation (World Bank Group) have not been followed. Against this backdrop, the Council recommended the exclusion of the Indian company from the Fund's portfolio.[45]

Cases concerning environmental standards often entail a joint assessment of human rights violations. This has been the case with the British metal and mining company Vedanta Resources Plc., the subsidiaries of which caused severe environmental damages and gross and systematic human rights in India.[46] When considering the environmental damages caused in India, the Council also assessed the violations perpetrated through the displacement and the deportation of indigenous peoples. It is interesting to note that in assessing the violations of the subsidiaries of the company, the Council was not caught in the

43 Council on Ethics, *Recommendation to Exclude Hansae Yes24 Holdings Co. Ltd from the Government Pension Fund Global*, 5 May 2017, nettsteder.regjeringen.no/etikkradet-2017/files/2017/06/Recommendation-Hansae-4.mai-2017-ENG-6.pdf (last accessed 15 February 2015).

44 Council on Ethics, *Recommendation to Exclude Freeport McMoRan Copper & Gold Inc. from the Government Pension Fund Global*, 15 February 2006, nettsteder.regjeringen.no/etikkradet-2017/files/2017/02/Freeport-2006.pdf (last accessed 15 February 2018).

45 Council on Ethics, *Recommendation to Exclude Bharat Heavy Electricals Limited from the Government Pension Fund Global*, 5 December 2016, nettsteder.regjeringen.no/etikkradet-2017/files/2017/05/BHEL-recommendation.pdf (last accessed on 15 February 2018).

46 Council on Ethics, *Recommendation to Exclude Vedanta Resources Plc. from the Government Pension Fund Global*, 15 May 2007, nettsteder.regjeringen.no/etikkradet-2017/files/2017/02/RecommendationVedanta.pdf (last accessed 15 February 2018).

thorny issue of corporate veil, but simply stated that 'Vedanta Resources, in its capacity as majority shareholder, exercises considerable influence over its subsidiaries'.[47]

An important point was also made on the disclosure of information of Vedanta. According to the latter's public statements, the company was conducting its operations 'in an environmentally and socially responsible manner', without however mentioning 'the approval of industrial plants or the conflict with indigenous people and local communities'.[48] When advising the divestment from the Fund, the Council on Ethics added that 'the company seems to lack interest in and willingness to do something about the serious and long-term damage that its operations inflict on people and the environment'.[49] The ongoing litigation before the UK Courts on the violations perpetrated by Vedanta's subsidiaries in India, might suggest that the Council on Ethics was right.[50]

According to Section 3 (e) of the Ethical Guidelines: '[c]ompanies may be put under observation or be excluded if there is an unacceptable risk that the company contributes to or is responsible for gross corruption'. The Fund's expectations regarding anti-corruption measures and policies have been recently clarified by Norges Bank Investment Management.[51]

In the case relating to the German company Siemens, which is also the first case related to corruption, the Council on Ethics clarified the definition of corruption, based on international conventions and Norwegian laws. According to the Council, corruption exists when a company gives or offers an advantage – or attempts to do so – in order to unduly influence a public official in the performance of public duties or in decisions that may confer an advantage on the company; or when the same behaviour is carried out towards a person in the private sector who makes decisions or exerts influence over decisions that may confer an advantage on the company. To qualify as 'gross', practices of corruption must be carried out in a systemic way, implying large sums.[52]

In cases related to corruption, the Council on Ethics will often rely on ongoing allegations before domestic courts, if any. In the case concerning the Chinese company ZTE Corp., the Council on Ethics pointed out that the

47 Ibid., 5.

48 Ibid., 32.

49 Ibid., 38.

50 On 13 October 2017, the UK Court of Appeal upheld a High Court ruling confirming the admissibility of a case brought against a subsidiary of Vedanta. At the time of writing, the case had not been heard on the merits.

51 Norges Bank Investment Management, *Anti-Corruption Expectations towards Companies*, 2018, www.nbim.no/contentassets/6ca89f09d9ec4af9b976c3dad755bd0c/expectations-document---anti-corruption.pdf (last accessed 15 February 2018).

52 Council on Ethics, *Recommendation to Exclude Siemens from the Government Pension Fund Global*, 15 November 2007, etikkradet.no/files/2017/05/Recommendation-on-Siemens-2007.pdf (last accessed 15 February 2018).

company and its representatives had been linked to corruption allegations in 18 countries and, therefore, it was likely that the company was responsible for practices amounting to gross corruption.[53]

The Council also assesses whether there is a risk that the gross corruption will continue, something that is crucial to whether the Council recommends excluding the company from the Fund. Key to this assessment is the company's anti-corruption programme, which may assist in assessing whether there is a risk that companies which have been involved in gross corruption will continue such practices in the future.

Finally, it is interesting to note that letter (f) of Section 3 of the Guidelines includes 'other particularly serious violations of fundamental ethical norms' for conduct-based exclusion. Letter (f) provides a sort of open clause that has been used in a number of cases concerning violations committed by onshore drilling and oil-exploration in the Western Sahara.[54]

Concluding Remarks: Divestment as a Leverage Tool

The practice of the Fund provides a good model of corporate governance, as well as an effective tool to operationalize expectations towards companies. As emphasized by the Council on Ethics, divestment from companies does not only avoid the Fund's complicity in serious violations, but may also influence companies to change their conduct, in line with the active ownership exercised by Norges Bank.

In assessing the effectiveness of the divestment procedure of the SWF, one cannot avoid addressing the consequence of the exclusion of the company in terms of future compliance with international standards. Divestment by selling equity shares does not necessarily have the same impact as the withdrawal of funding from, for example, a project, as is the case with The WB's Inspection Panel or the International Finance Corporation. Yet three elements make the Norwegian's divestment practice a useful tool for leverage.

First, the Ethical Guidelines provide a clear and quite comprehensive instrument on the basis of which companies should conduct their operations. Such an instrument does contain explicit reference to the regulatory framework on B&HR, although the latter is implicitly incorporated in the text of the Guidelines. Second, the Council on Ethics constitutes a forum where the UNGPs, the OECD Guidelines and the ILO instruments are interpreted and implemented, providing a concrete assessment of the expectations towards companies. Third,

53 Council on Ethics, *Recommendation to Exclude ZTE Corp. from the Government Pension Fund Global*, 24 June 2015, etikkradet.no/files/2017/05/ENG-Tilrådning-ZTE-24.-juni-2015-ENGELSK-amended-Nov.-2016.pdf (last accessed 15 February 2018).

54 Council on Ethics, *Recommendation to Exclude Kosmos Energy Ltd. and Cairn Energy Plc. from the Government Pension Fund Global*, 8 February 2016, https://nettsteder.regjeringen.no/etikkradet-2017/files/2017/02/ENG-Rec-Kosmos-and-Cairn-.pdf (last accessed 15 February 2018).

the transparency of the procedures of the Council on Ethics is an important asset, guaranteeing the legitimacy of the recommendations and allowing an instrumental role of civil society in putting pressure on the company.[55]

The practice of the Fund also offers interesting insights concerning the well-known challenges posed by corporations to international law. It shows that the strict division between the obligations of states and the obligations of economic actors is more blurred than theory may suggest. Although the recommendations of the Council on Ethics and the decisions of Norges Bank cannot be classified as state practice as such, the overall process of standard-setting by the Ministry and its constant dialogue with Norges Bank (which holds a management mandate from the Ministry) provides a form of *opinio juris* intertwined with elements of practice.

Interestingly, even though the Council on Ethics often emphasizes that international human rights law binds states and not companies, the latter can 'contribute to human rights violations'.[56] Such a contribution, which is framed in the concept of 'complicity', is assessed independently from state responsibility. The Council on Ethics affirmed that 'especially in countries where conditions are not conducive to the authorities' enforcement of all laws and regulations, companies have a particular ethical responsibility to ensure that minimum standards are complied with'.[57]

Sure enough, the Norwegian model is not immune to contradictions. The Fund holds shares in oil companies, Royal Dutch Shell being one of its major holdings. In November 2017, Norges Bank Investment Management advised the Ministry of Finance to remove oil and gas stocks from the benchmark index of the Fund.[58] According to the Executive Board, the 'vulnerability of government wealth to a permanent drop in oil and gas prices will be reduced if the fund is not invested in oil and gas stock'.[59] In the years ahead, we might assist in a progressive exclusion of oil companies from the Fund's portfolio. Although the purposes behind such divestment have little to do with human rights, financial and ethical reasons may, at times, point in the same direction.

55 Council on Ethics, *Annual Report*, 2008, 7, nettsteder.regjeringen.no/etikkradet-2017/files/2017/02/etikkradet_engelsk08-1.pdf (last accessed 15 February 2018).

56 Council on Ethics, *Recommendation to Exclude Wal-Mart Stores Inc.*, op. cit., 3.

57 Council on Ethics, *Recommendation to Exclude Monsanto*, op. cit., 20.

58 See Norges Bank, *Investment Strategy for the Government Pension Fund Global: Letter to the Ministry of Finance*, 16 November 2017, www.nbim.no/en/transparency/submissions-to-ministry/2017/investment-strategy-for-the-government-pension-fund-global/ (last accessed 25 November 2017).

59 Norges Bank Investment Management, *Petroleum Wealth and Oil Price Exposure of Equity Sectors: Discussion Note*, 28 November 2017, www.nbim.no/contentassets/029a50c7911948bb8523729f1e22199d/dn-4-17-petroleum-wealth-and-oil-price-exposure.pdf (last accessed 15 February 2018).

14 EU Approaches on 'Conflict Minerals'

Are They Consistent with the UN/OECD Supply Chain Due Diligence Standards?

Valentina Grado

Mineral Resources as a Fuelling Factor of Armed Conflicts and Human Rights Abuses

The link between mineral resources exploitation and armed conflicts is well documented. Mineral resources that drive conflicts have been fuelled by grievances on access to extraction rights, perceptions of unfair distributions of benefits, and pure economic reasons. Classic cases include the role played by diamonds to sustain conflicts in many African states.

Tin, tantalum, tungsten and gold (otherwise known as 3TG and labelled 'conflict minerals') have also played key roles in fuelling conflicts and extensive human rights violations, especially since the late 1990s in the Democratic Republic of the Congo (DRC). They are sourced from the DRC and the Great Lakes Region of Africa and mostly mined by artisanal and small-scale miners. The financing of the conflict in DRC through the mining and trading activities of 3TG takes two main forms. First, rebel groups and army units extort cash or minerals from miners who are often children or adults forced to work in the mines. Second, they extort money from traders and intermediaries at all stages of transportation between the mines and the point of export. Subsequently, those minerals are traded, and sometimes partially transformed in neighbouring countries where they are subsequently purchased by smelters/refiners located outside the Great Lakes Region. Smelters/refiners further process those minerals and others received from different parts of the world into metals. These metals are then used by component manufacturers before being incorporated into end products such as electronic devices.

NGOs and UN bodies have published detailed reports highlighting the role played by business enterprises that use 3TG or other minerals in fuelling armed activities and serious human rights abuses. Since the publication of those reports, the UN and the OECD have intensified their efforts to promote responsible business conduct and, in 2011 they developed a regulatory framework covering activities of corporate actors that impact negatively on human rights and conditions of conflict. More recently, the EU has adopted an integrated approach for responsible sourcing of minerals originating from conflict-areas that envisages, *inter alia*, a regulation setting up a Union system for supply chain due diligence.[1]

This chapter explores whether the EU institutions' proposals, and subsequent legislation, align with existing international standards measuring corporate behaviour affecting human rights in mineral-exploited conflict zones. Therefore, it will first briefly analyse the UNGPs, as they are widely considered to be an authoritative global point of reference for the topic of B&HR; in particular, it will focus attention on those Principles related to the corporate responsibility to respect human rights. Second, it will refer to the OECD Due Diligence Guidance for Responsible Supply Chains of Minerals from Conflict-Affected and High-Risk Areas, and similar principles contained in the OECD Guidelines for Multinational Enterprises, as amended in 2011. Third, it will briefly illustrate the proposals submitted, respectively, by the EU Commission and the European Parliament for a Union system to tackle a mineral trade linked to conflict and it will then highlight their conformity with the OECD Due Diligence Guidance. Lastly, it will conclude by explaining why the text agreed at the end of 'trilogue negotiations' and the subsequent EU Regulation 2017/821 are not totally consistent with this leading global standard for the mineral sector.

The Due Diligence and Supply Chain Provisions Envisaged in the UNGPs

On 16 June 2011 the UNHRC endorsed the UNGPs developed by the SRSGBHR, Professor Ruggie.[2] The UNGPs aim to operationalize the former UN 'Protect, Respect and Remedy' Framework developed in 2008.[3] As is well known, the Framework consists of three pillars: (a) the duty of states to protect human rights against abuses by third parties, including business enterprises; (b) the corporate responsibility to respect human rights; and (c) access to effective remedy for those who are harmed.

As far as the second pillar is concerned, the UNGPs (11–24) set out the responsibility of business enterprises to respect human rights. This means that they should avoid infringing on the human rights of others and should take measures to address adverse human rights impacts with which they are involved (UNGP 11). As the Interpretative Guide of the corporate responsibility to respect human rights specifies, adverse human rights impacts occur when an action removes or reduces the ability of the individual to enjoy his or her human

1 European Commission, High Representative of the EU for Foreign Affairs and Security Policy, *Joint Communication to the European Parliament and the Council, Responsible sourcing of minerals originating in conflict-affected and high-risk areas. Towards an integrated EU approach*, Join(2014) 8 final, 5 March 2014.

2 UNHRC, *Guiding Principles on Business and Human Rights: Implementing the United Nations 'Protect, Respect, Remedy' Framework*, UN Doc. A/HRC/17/31, 21 March 2011.

3 UNHRC, *Protect, Respect and Remedy: A Framework for Business and Human Rights*, UN Doc. A/HRC/8/5, 7 April 2008.

rights.[4] This responsibility, based on societal expectations according to Professor Ruggie, exists independently of states' abilities to meet their own human rights obligations and extends to all internationally recognized human rights (UNGP 12). It also applies to all enterprises regardless of their size, sector, operational context, and structure (UNGP 14).

The UNGPs identify several ways in which enterprises can be involved in human rights adverse impacts. Indeed, the responsibility to respect requires enterprises to: 'avoid causing or contributing to adverse human rights impacts through their own activities, and address such impacts when they occur' (UNGP 13(a)); and 'seek to prevent or mitigate adverse human rights impacts that are directly linked to their operations, products or services by their business relationships, even if they have not contributed to those impacts' (UNGP 13(b)). Most notably, the Commentary to UNGP 13 stipulates that the term 'business relationships' is intended to be understood widely, to include relationships with business partners, entities in their value chain, and any other state or non-state entity directly linked to their business operations, products, or services.

Under the UNGPs, in order to meet its 'responsibility' to respect human rights, an enterprise should have in place policies and processes, including: (a) a human rights policy commitment; (b) a human rights due diligence process to identify, prevent, mitigate, and account for how it addresses its human rights impacts; and (c) processes to enable the remediation of any adverse human rights impacts it has caused or contributed to be caused (UNGP 15).

In June 2010, Professor Ruggie published a discussion paper on the corporate responsibility to respect human rights in supply chains.[5] First, he distinguishes two scenarios: whether the enterprise is contributing to the abuse by its own actions or omissions (e.g. where the buyer demands significant last-minute changes in product specifications without adjusting price or delivery dates, thus pushing suppliers to breach international labour standards); or whether the enterprise is implicated in the abuse solely by the link to the goods or services it procures (e.g. without contribution from the enterprise, the product contains components that are manufactured by suppliers using child labour). In the first event, the responsibility to respect requires the enterprise to take appropriate steps to address those contributions (*inter alia*, termination and remediation). In the second event, the appropriate action – that we can label 'responsible sourcing' – depends on several factors, including: (a) what leverage the enterprise has in changing the behaviour of the entity causing the harm; and (b) how

4 OHCHR, *The Corporate Responsibility to Respect Human Rights: An Interpretative Guide*, UN Doc. HR/PUB/12/02, 2012, 5.

5 UNSRSG, *Corporate Responsibility to Respect Human Rights in Supply Chains*, paper presented at the 10th OECD Roundtable on Corporate Responsibility, Discussion Paper, 30 June 2010, OECD, Paris.

crucial the relationship is to the enterprise.[6] The combination of these variables will yield different conclusions as to what actions should be taken. Appropriate responses may include: mitigating the risk that the adverse impact continues/recurs (when the enterprise possesses the leverage); seeking ways to increase the leverage to enable mitigation (when the enterprise lacks the leverage); and considering ending the relationship either where the enterprise lacks the leverage or where it is unable to increase its leverage, or finally because of the severity of the adverse impact.

In addition, the discussion paper underlines that 'responsible sourcing' requires the enterprise to carry due diligence beyond the first tier of business relationships (all known to the company). Indeed, with regard to those additional tiers, not knowing about the human rights abuses linked to an enterprise's products or services is not a sufficient response by itself if the same enterprise should have reasonably known about them through due diligence. Therefore, the company, using due diligence, should first identify general areas of risk of serious human rights abuses in the supply chain (for example, because of the particular region or particular products or materials and their known sources) and prioritize these for human rights due diligence.[7] Second, the enterprise should mitigate such risks by seeking to ensure that intermediary entities in the supply chain are themselves practising due diligence and following appropriate standards. Finally, the enterprise should identify specific supply chain entities that are abusing human rights and take appropriate efforts to mitigate such abuse (directly or through intermediaries in the relationship chain); and, if mitigation is impossible, it should either take steps to end the relationship (whether directly or via intermediaries) or be able to demonstrate efforts made to mitigate the abuse.

The OECD Due Diligence Guidance for Responsible Mineral Sourcing

On 25 May 2011 the OECD Council meeting at the Ministerial level adopted the amendments to the Guidelines for Multinational Enterprises and a new Recommendation on Due Diligence Guidance for Responsible Supply Chains of Minerals from Conflict-Affected and High-Risk Areas (hereinafter, 'the OECD Guidance'). The latter can be regarded as the first example of how the due diligence and supply chain provisions contained in the UNGPs and the updated OECD Guidelines for Multinational Enterprises can be translated into operational terms in a specific context (conflict-affected and high-risk areas,

6 The Commentary to UNGP 19 states that appropriate action depends also on the severity of the abuse and whether terminating the relationship with the entity itself would have adverse human rights consequences.

7 UNGP 24 stipulates that where it is necessary to prioritize action to address adverse human rights impacts, the enterprise should first seek to prevent and mitigate those that are more severe.

hereinafter 'CAHRAs') and with regard to risks of adverse impacts associated with a particular sector (the mineral one).

Amended twice, the current OECD Guidance consists of: (1) an overarching five-step framework for risk-based due diligence in the mineral supply chain (Annex I); (2) a model supply chain policy for a responsible global supply chain of minerals from CAHRAs (Annex II); (3) suggested measures for risk mitigation and indicators for measuring improvement for upstream companies (Annex III); and (4) two Supplements on tin-tantalum-tungsten and gold (3TG) containing specific due diligence recommendations tailored to the challenges associated with the structure of the supply chain of those minerals.[8]

Before summarizing the detailed requirements set out in the Annexes and Supplements, it is important to highlight the key features of the OECD Guidance. In terms of its objective, the Guidance provides practical recommendations for companies to ensure they do not fuel conflict or abuses of human rights through their mineral and metal procurement practices ('responsible sourcing'). As far as the geographic and material scope are concerned, the recommendations apply to all companies that use whatever minerals are sourced from any CAHRA; therefore, the OECD Guidance does not focus either on any particular area, region, or country, or on 3TG only. The nature and extent of due diligence will depend on individual circumstances and will be affected by factors such as the size of the enterprise, the location of the activities, the situation in a particular country, and the nature of the products involved; therefore, this instrument adopts a flexible approach, allowing for a variety of options, operational schemes, and industry collaborative efforts. At the same time, the OECD Guidance points out the higher risks of significant adverse impacts, which may be associated with the exploitation of minerals from CAHRAs. Consequently, it requires all companies in the mineral supply chain – even those several steps removed from the layer providing the raw material inputs – to take reasonable steps and make good-faith efforts to prevent or mitigate any risks of those adverse impacts. Emphasizing progressive improvement over outcomes, the OECD Guidance confirms that 'responsible sourcing' requires the adoption of reasonable measures commensurate with the severity of the risk even where leverage is lacking.

As already mentioned, Annex I sets out a five-step framework for risk-based due diligence in the mineral supply chain. According to this framework, all companies in the mineral supply chain that use minerals sourced from CAHRAs should: establish strong company management systems (Step 1); identify and assess risks in the supply chain (Step 2); design and implement a strategy to respond to identified risks (Step 3); carry out independent third-party audit of supply chain due diligence at identified points in the supply chain (Step 4); and publicly report on supply chain due diligence (Step 5). This framework is very

8 OECD, *OECD Due Diligence Guidance for Responsible Supply Chains of Minerals from Conflict-Affected and High-Risk Areas*, Third Edition. Paris, OECD Publishing, 2016, 5.

similar to that set up in the UNGPs 15–21, except for the specific expectation concerning auditing. The OECD Guidance confirms therefore that: (i) where negative impacts can be directly linked to a company's product via a business relationship, even if it has neither caused nor contributed to them, the enterprise is not required to provide for remediation but it should design and implement a strategy to respond to identified risks; and (ii) companies should publicly report on their supply chain due diligence policies and practices when they are involved in severe human rights adverse impacts (or other significant adverse impacts, such as financing conflict).

With regard to Annex II of the OECD Guidance (concerning the model supply chain policy), first it highlights the different risks of significant adverse impacts that may be associated with extracting, trading, handling and exporting minerals from CAHRAs: serious abuses of human rights, labour rights and international humanitarian law; financing parties to the conflict (direct and indirect support to either non-state-armed groups or to public or private security forces); and non-conflict-specific high-risk areas' adverse impacts. Second, it provides instructions on how to mitigate the identified risks. This Annex calls on a company to immediately suspend or disengage with suppliers when it identifies a risk that they are sourcing minerals from any party committing serious human rights abuses, or any party providing direct or indirect support to non-state-armed groups. It allows trade to continue with supplies where a company identifies a risk that they are sourcing from any party providing direct or indirect support to public or private forces (not involved in serious human rights abuses), provided that a risk management plan is implemented.

As far as the two Supplements of the OECD Guidance are concerned, they provide specific guidelines on supply chain due diligence of 3T and gold. Both tools apply to companies potentially using 3TG from CAHRAs. Therefore, companies should preliminarily review their mineral and metal sourcing practices to determine the presence of 'red flag indicators' in their supply chain which trigger comprehensive due diligence as envisaged in the OECD Guidance. Most importantly, if a company in the supply chain is unable to determine whether the minerals in its possession come from 'red flag indicators', it should proceed to Step 1 of the Guidance and discontinue due diligence if the subsequent Step 2 can reasonably exclude 'red flag indicators' from its supply chain.

Both Supplements distinguish between the due diligence requirements of upstream and downstream companies in the supply chain. 'Upstream companies' refers to all the companies between the mine and the smelters/refiners (e.g. mining companies, local traders, or exporters from the country of mineral origin, international concentrate traders, mineral re-processors and smelters/refiners). 'Downstream companies' refers to all companies from smelters/refiners to retailers (e.g. metal traders, component manufacturers, product manufacturers, and retailers). In a nutshell, upstream companies should establish a system of control over the minerals in their possession (chain of custody or traceability) and establish on-the-ground assessment teams for generating verifiable, reliable, up-to-date information on the qualitative circumstances of mineral extraction, trade, handling, and export from CAHRAs. They should also provide the results of risk assessment to their downstream purchasers and have the smelters'/refiners' due diligence practices audited by independent third parties. Downstream companies should establish internal controls over their immediate suppliers and establish a system of transparency that will allow them to identify the smelters/refiners in their supply chains and assess whether they adhere to due diligence measures envisaged in the OECD Guidance. This distinction is based upon the fact that it is at the point of transformation – where minerals are smelted into metals – that the mixing of materials from different regions takes place. The smelters/refiners that handle raw minerals are, often in geographic terms, closer to the original source and they have therefore the primary responsibility to identify, assess and manage risks that the mining of minerals may have financed conflict (or human rights abuses); this is why the Supplements consider them the 'choke point' of the 3TG supply chains. By contrast, because after the stage of transformation it is impossible to trace back the origins of minerals, downstream actors' basic role is to find out which smelters their metals come from and assess those smelters' due diligence and outcomes based, *inter alia*, on independent audits.

In conclusion, the Supplements make clear that 'responsible sourcing' of 3TG is the responsibility of both downstream and upstream segments.

The European Proposals for a Union System for Mineral Supply Chains Due Diligence

On 5 March 2014 the EU Commission submitted a proposal for a Regulation of the European Parliament and of the Council setting up a Union system on responsible mineral sourcing.[9] This proposal focuses on 3TG minerals and metals from CAHRAs; in short, it envisages the creation of a voluntary self-certification system for importers seeking to import any of the four 3TG raw materials into the EU in a responsible manner (Article 3). Importers who opt in will need to: establish a management system to, *inter alia*, track the origin of the minerals purchased (Article 4); identify and assess the risks of adverse impacts in their mineral supply chain and implement a strategy to identify risks so as to prevent or mitigate adverse risks (Article 5); carry out audits via an independent third party (Article 6); and disclose relevant supply-chain-related information to their immediate downstream purchasers, the public and Member States' competent authorities (Article 7). Based on the information disclosed, the Commission is expected to publish and, in a timely fashion, update a list of

9 European Commission, *Proposal for a Regulation of the European Parliament and of the Council setting up a Union system for Supply Chain Due Diligence Self-certification of Responsible Importers of Tin, Tantalum and Tungsten, their Ores, and Gold Originating in Conflict-affected and High-risk Areas*, COM(2014) 111 final, 5 March 2014.

smelters/refiners in the supply chains of responsible importers that are considered responsible suppliers (Article 8).

The analysis in the following section will be limited to how this proposal fits (or does not fit) within the broader human rights due diligence context. The only positive feature that must be highlighted is its global geographic scope, covering 3TG raw materials coming from any CAHRA in the world. This may mitigate against potential stigmatization and disengagement by buyers from specific producing regions of 3TG that are conflict-affected (such as the DRC). With regard to the critical issues, the first is the material scope of the proposal because it is confined to 3TG and does not include a mechanism allowing other minerals to be added at a later date. In contrast, the OECD five-step framework for risk-based due diligence applies to all mineral supply chains. The second critical issue relates to the voluntary nature of its due diligence scheme. As outlined by the OECD Guidance, when risks of serious human rights violations may be part of a company's supply chain (such as, materials sourced from conflict areas through forced labour and child labour) formal due diligence requirements – in particular, due diligence reporting – should be mandatory, in order to prevent the less attentive companies from continuing their irresponsible sourcing business undeterred. The third critical issue is represented by its too-narrow due diligence scheme, it being limited to importers of 3TG raw materials (between 600 and 1000 importers, consisting of minerals/metals traders, smelters/refiners and component manufacturers). Therefore, it does not include end-user companies who place on the EU market semi-finished or finished products containing those materials. However, as the OECD Guidance very well points out, due diligence is not the responsibility of only some links in the supply chain but rather of the whole chain. In addition, if implemented only by those layers, it will be ineffective, leaving out an important part of the downstream segment and its significant leverage. The fourth issue concerns, instead, the due diligence obligations of (opted-in) importers of 3TG raw materials, consisting of 'management system obligations', 'risk management obligations', 'third-party audits obligations', and 'disclosure obligations'. Although they resembled the OECD Guidance five-step framework, Articles 4–7 impose requirements such as tracing minerals to the country of origin and carrying out audits on a middle group of importers of 3TG who also include downstream (post-smelting) companies (such as component manufactures) that according to the Supplements on 3TG should not be subject to those requirements. In particular, as mentioned before, both Supplements require downstream (post-smelting) companies to introduce a supply chain transparency system that allows the identification of smelters/refiners and the flow of specific information; in addition, they request independent third-party audits of smelters' or refiners' due diligence practices only. Lastly, with regard to the list of responsible smelters/refiners (the so-called 'white list'), those entities are not required to comply with any responsible sourcing criteria in order to be on the 'white list'. In contrast, the Supplements on 3TG consider the smelters/refiners responsible only if: (a) they establish a system of internal control over the minerals in their possession and on-the-ground assessment teams, and (b) have their due diligence practices audited by independent third parties.

On 20 May 2015 the European Parliament approved amendments reversing the regime proposed by the Commission.[10]

First, pointing out the need for due diligence along the entire supply chain (from the sourcing site to the final product), the European Parliament proposes that both upstream and downstream actors that first place 3TG, including finished products that contain those resources on the EU market, must conduct and publicly report on their supply chain due diligence in accordance with the OECD Guidance.

Second, in line with the nature of due diligence, the European Parliament highlights that the individual due diligence obligations should reflect the progressive and flexile nature of due diligence processes, and therefore the need for obligations to be tailored to a company's size, leverage, and position in its supply chain. Therefore, the Parliament makes a clear distinction between the standards established for companies at different points in the supply chain. With regard to downstream companies, as envisaged in the OECD Guidance, they must take all reasonable steps to identify and address any risk arising in their supply chains of minerals and metals sourced from CAHRAs. In this connection, they should be required to provide information on the due diligence practices they employ for responsible supply chains. As far as the smelters/refiners are concerned, they should undergo an independent third-party audit of their supply chain due diligence practices, with the view to also being included in the list of responsible smelters/refiners.

Lastly, importers of smelted and refined metals (such as component manufacturers) shall be exempted from carrying out independent third-party audits provided they submit substantive evidence that all smelters/refiners in their supply chain conform to the aforementioned requirement.

The third feature worth mentioning relates to the existing supply of due diligence industry systems aimed at breaking the link between conflict and the sourcing of 3TG. Because those schemes use independent third-party audits to certify smelters/refiners with systems in place to ensure responsible sourcing of minerals only, the European Parliament proposes that those industry schemes should be recognized in the Union system, provided that they meet high standards.

The last relevant feature is the exclusion of metal reasonably assumed to be recycled from the scope of the Regulation.

10 European Parliament, *Amendments Adopted by the European Parliament on 20 May 2015 on the Proposal for a Regulation of the European Parliament and of the Council Setting up a Union System for Supply Chain Due Diligence Self-certification of Responsible Importers of Tin, Tantalum and Tungsten, their ores, and Gold Originating in Conflict-affected and High-risk Areas*, P8 TA(2015)0204, 20 May 2015.

To summarize, the European Parliament's proposed amendments are much better aligned with the standards envisaged in the OECD Guidance. In terms of the first two sets of amendments, this conclusion is self-evident in the light of the provisions established in the Supplements on 3TG. As far as the last two sets of amendments are concerned, it is sufficient to highlight here that the OECD Guidance calls upon both upstream and downstream actors to participate in industry-wide schemes (recognizing the practical challenges posed by due diligence in CAHRAs), and it excludes recycled metals from its scope of application because it is difficult, if not impossible, to determine the origin of those materials. The only flaw is that the European Parliament's proposal is limited to 3TG.

The EU Regulation on 'Conflict Minerals'

Because the Regulation on 'conflict minerals' had to be adopted in co-decision by the European Parliament and the Council, in May 2015 the Parliament decided not to close the first reading position and to enter into informal negotiation with the Council and the Commission (in so-called 'trilogue'), to seek agreement on the final version of the Regulation. In November 2016, the EU Council, Commission, and Parliament reached an informal final agreement;[11] on this basis, Regulation (EU) 2017/821 (laying down supply chain due diligence obligations for Union importers of tin, tantalum and tungsten, their ores, and gold originating from conflict-affected and high-risk areas) was adopted on 17 May 2017.[12]

This Regulation requires Union importers of minerals or metals containing or consisting of 3TG into the EU to conduct mandatory due diligence if they are sourcing from CAHRAs anywhere in the world. Recycled minerals and importers of small volumes of 3TG (such as dentists and jewellers) will be exempted. The Commission will prepare a handbook that includes non-binding guidelines to help economic operators with the identification of CAHRAs; it will also provide, with help from external experts, an indicative, non-exhaustive list of CAHRAs. Importers of semi-finished or finished products are not required to carry out due diligence; however, big companies (i.e. those subject to EU law on 'non-financial reporting' – above 500 employees[13]) will be encouraged to make voluntary disclosures. The Commission intends to develop

11 European Council, *Proposal for a Regulation of the European Parliament and of the Council Laying Down Supply Chain Due Diligence Obligations for Union Importers of Tin, Tantalum and Tungsten, their ores, and Gold Originating from Conflict-affected and High-risk Areas*, Doc. 15115/16, 6 December 2016.

12 EU, *Regulation 2017/821 of the European Parliament and of the Council of 17 May 2017 Laying Down Supply Chain Due Diligence Obligations for Union Importers of Tin, Tantalum and Tungsten, their Ores, and Gold Originating from Conflict-affected and High-risk Areas*, OJ L 130, 19 May 2017, 1.

13 EU, *Directive 2014/95/EU of the European Parliament and of the Council of 22 October 2014 Amending Directive 2013/34/EU as regards Disclosure of Non-financial and Diversity Information by Certain Larger Undertakings and Groups*, OJ L 330, 15 November 2014, 1.

voluntary guidance for downstream companies and to create a voluntary transparency registry where companies can report on their due diligence practices.

As far as the due diligence obligations are concerned (Articles 4–7), even if they are better aligned with the OECD Guidance, there are still two main inconsistencies. First, with regard to the 'risk management obligations', metal importers (post-smelting companies) are required to operate a chain of custody or supply chain traceability system. Second, those companies will identify and assess the risks in their supply chain based primarily on available third-party audit reports from the smelters/refiners. As mentioned earlier, in accordance with the OECD Guidance they should instead be required to introduce a supply chain transparency system and assess smelters'/refiners' due diligence based not only on an independent audit but also on other sources of information (such as reports published by reputable consulting firms, NGOs, industry associations, or UN bodies).

The last two main features of this legislation are related to industry schemes and the list of responsible smelters/refiners. With regard to the former, the Regulation stipulates that, in order to avoid multiple burdens, existing and future industry schemes certifying smelters/refiners will be accredited 'as equivalent' by a delegated act adopted by the Commission, provided that they incorporate the overarching due diligence principles and the specific requirements of the OECD Guidance. As far as the latter is concerned (the 'white list'), it will include, first, the EU-based smelters/refiners of 3TG expected to implement the full range of measures envisaged in the law (included independent third-party audits) and, second, those smelters/refiners (mainly located outside the EU) covered by supply chain due diligence industry schemes recognized by the Commission.

In conclusion, the final text of the EU Regulation, when compared with the original framework proposed by the Commission, envisages due diligence standards that are slightly more aligned with those laid down in the OECD Guidance. Nevertheless, it still has four main shortcomings. First, it does not go beyond 3TG, while the OECD Guidance applies to all minerals sourced from CAHRAs. Second, the EU's mandatory provisions will apply only to companies that import minerals and metals in their raw forms. Enterprises that bring the very same minerals into the EU inside semi-finished or finished products are absolved from any mandatory due diligence public reporting, in contrast to the international standard that recommends all the segments of the supply chain to remain alert to risks and act accordingly. Third, companies whose annual imports fall below established thresholds are not required to demonstrate that they have sourced their minerals responsibly. Given, for example, that small quantities of gold are more likely linked to conflict, this exemption is totally in contrast with Professor Ruggie's indications. In the discussion paper mentioned earlier, he rejects merely numerical or threshold approaches to human rights responsibility and emphasizes that the riskiest procurement practices should be subject to basic checks and scrutiny. Finally, as stated above, the Regulation also contains inconsistencies in terms of the due diligence obligations imposed on metal importers (post-smelting companies).

15 ICT Companies' Responsibility to Respect Human Rights

Remarks in the Light of the EU General Data Protection Regulation

Angelica Bonfanti

Introduction

> Responsible ICT companies have become increasingly active in recent years in understanding and addressing the range of human rights issues linked to their products, services or technologies. They recognize that they can both positively and negatively impact their staff, workers in the supply chain, customers, users or the communities around their operations.[1]

The ability of information and communication technology (hereinafter 'ICT') corporations to negatively affect the enjoyment of human rights is worthy of consideration in light of the international legal framework on B&HR.

More specifically, this chapter focuses on the European ITC companies' responsibility to respect human rights. It explores the characteristics of the ICT sector and the connected risks on human rights. The author submits that, in order to grant effective personal data and human rights protection in this field, the recommendations enshrined in the UNGPs – including the second pillar on the corporate responsibility to respect human rights – should be coordinated with the EU General Data Protection Regulation[2] (hereinafter 'the GDPR') and the ECHR legal framework.

This chapter first focuses on the corporate responsibility to respect human rights and the suitability of corporate responsibility to include personal data protection issues. It then extends the developed reflections to two specific practices carried out by European ICT companies and their consistency with the aforementioned legal framework: the international transfer of personal data to

1 European Commission, *ICT Sector Guide on Implementing the UN Guiding Principles on Business and Human Rights*, 2012, www.ihrb.org/pdf/eu-sector-guidance/EC-Guides/ICT/EC-Guide_ICT.pdf (last accessed 3 March 2018), 8.

2 EU, *Regulation 2016/679 of the European Parliament and of the Council of 27 April 2016 on the Protection of Natural Persons with Regard to the Processing of Personal Data and on the Free Movement of such Data, and Repealing Directive 95/46/EC* (General Data Protection Regulation). On the GDPR see: M. Krzysztofek, *Post-Reform Personal Data Protection in the European Union: General Data Protection Regulation (EU) 2016/679*, Alphen aan den Rijn: Wolters Kluwer, 2017.

non-European countries and the handling by corporations of requests posed by governments to disclose stored personal data and conduct bulk data collections. Finally, it makes concluding observations.

Personal Data Protection as Part of the Corporate Responsibility to Respect Human Rights

Pursuant to the UNGPs, 'Business enterprises should respect human rights. This means that they should avoid infringing on the human rights of others and should address adverse human rights impacts with which they are involved'.[3] In order to implement their corporate responsibility to respect human rights, the UNGPs recommend companies adopt

> policies and processes appropriate to their size and circumstances, including: (a) A policy commitment to meet their responsibility to respect human rights; (b) A human rights due diligence process to identify, prevent, mitigate and account for how they address their impacts on human rights; (c) Processes to enable the remediation of any adverse human rights impacts they cause or to which they contribute.[4]

Pursuant to the *ICT Sector Guide on Implementing the UN Guiding Principles on Business and Human Rights* adopted by the European Commission (hereinafter 'the ICT Sector Guide'), the risks faced by ICT corporations affect mainly privacy and freedom of expression and include 'impacts on other rights arising from misuse of technology or customers and users' personal information by states – for example, impacts on individuals' right to life, liberty and security, and on the freedom from torture, cruel, inhuman and degrading treatment'.[5]

ICT companies include corporations that provide telecommunication services, services/platforms for search, social networking, cloud computing and other web services, as well as device and component manufacturers. Since their activities can negatively impact the enjoyment of several human rights, including the right to privacy, and affect the protection of personal data, their corporate responsibility to respect human rights should be implemented, taking into consideration the GDPR and the ECHR legal framework, especially its Article 8. This complies with UNGP 12, according to which,

> Because business enterprises can have an impact on virtually the entire spectrum of internationally recognized human rights, their responsibility to

3 UNGP, 11.

4 UNGP, 15.

5 European Commission, *ICT Sector Guide on Implementing the UN Guiding Principles on Business and Human Rights*, op. cit., 19.

> respect applies to all such rights. In practice, some human rights may be at greater risk than others in particular industries or contexts, and therefore will be the focus of heightened attention.[6]

The GDPR will be applied from 25 May 2018 to any processing of personal data in the context of the activities of ICT companies established in the EU,[7] being acknowledged that 'establishment implies the effective and real exercise of activity through stable arrangements'.[8] Moreover it will extend to the processing of data by corporations not established in the EU if the processing activities concern either the offering of goods or services or the monitoring of their behaviour within the EU.[9]

The Regulation provides that data processing is lawful only if certain conditions are met: where either the data subject has given consent to the processing, or the treatment is necessary in order to perform a contract to which the data subject is party, or in order to comply with a legal obligation held by the company responsible for the treatment, or to protect the vital interests of the data subject or of another natural person, or for the performance of a task carried out in the public interest, or for the purposes of the legitimate interests pursued by the processing company or by a third party, if such interests do not override the interests or fundamental rights and freedoms of the data subject.[10] Moreover, the GDPR establishes that the processing must satisfy the criteria of lawfulness, fairness and transparency, purpose limitation, data minimization, accuracy, storage limitation, integrity, confidentiality, and accountability.[11] The data subject must be granted the enjoyment of the rights to have the data treated transparently,[12] to be informed about the processing,[13] to rectify the data and 'be forgotten',[14] and to object to the data treatment.[15]

Pursuant to Article 40, corporations are encouraged to draw up 'codes of conduct intended to contribute to the proper application' of the GDPR, 'taking account of the specific features of the various processing sectors and the specific needs of micro, small and medium-sized enterprises'. Such codes should provide for fair and transparent processing, define the legitimate interests pursued by processing companies in specific contexts, and establish clear rules concerning the collection and pseudonymization of personal data, the information to be provided to the public and to data subjects, the exercise of the latter's rights, the notification

6 UNGP, 12, Commentary.
7 GDPR, recital 22.
8 GDPR, recital 22.
9 GDPR, art. 3.
10 Ibid., art. 6.
11 Ibid., art. 5.
12 Ibid., Chapter III, Section 1.
13 Ibid., Chapter III, Section 2.
14 Ibid., Chapter III, Section 3.
15 Ibid., Chapter III, Section 4.

of data breaches, and the transfer of data to third countries, and should specify the out-of-court proceedings and other dispute resolution procedures for resolving disputes between processing companies and data subjects.[16] The monitoring of compliance with a code of conduct may be carried out by an accredited body,[17] while the establishment of data protection certification mechanisms is encouraged.[18]

The adoption of codes of conduct and the provision for certification mechanisms pursuant to the GDPR is in line with the second pillar of the UNGPs. More specifically, the adoption of such codes should be coupled with the implementation of human rights due diligence (hereinafter 'HRDD') processes by ICT corporations, aimed at identifying, preventing, and mitigating the impacts of the data processing on the rights of the data subjects.

In this regard the ICT Sector Guide acknowledges that it can be helpful for ICT companies to identify the leading risks in the policy commitment.[19] More specifically, with reference to the protection of personal data and privacy, ICT companies should take into consideration a range of issues in determining whether their systems adequately protect individuals' personal data, including:

> how the company informs individuals about how their personal information will or may be used; whether the information [...] collected is necessary to the intended use(s); where information is stored (including location of servers and data centres); whether retention periods are appropriate to the intended use(s) [...]; whether security measures for retention and transfer of personal information are appropriate [...]; whether the company uses the highest level of privacy protection.[20]

Finally, risks might be addressed also within the terms of the contracts entered into with business partners, including suppliers, distributors, customers, and users. In this case, contracts should clearly indicate who has the responsibility to address human rights risks and how implementation will be monitored throughout the supply chain.[21]

The International Transfer of Data and the EU–US Privacy Shield

When implementing their corporate responsibility to respect human rights, European ICT companies should devote specific attention to the international transfer of data.

16 Ibid., art. 40.
17 Ibid., art. 41.
18 Ibid., art. 42.
19 European Commission, *ICT Sector Guide on Implementing the UN Guiding Principles on Business and Human Rights*, op. cit., 10.
20 Ibid., 43, 44.
21 Ibid., 24.

Article 44 GDPR provides that any transfer of personal data

> shall take place only if, subject to the other provisions of this Regulation, the conditions laid down in this Chapter are complied with by the controller and processor, including for onward transfers of personal data from the third country [...] to another third country [...]. All provisions in this Chapter shall be applied in order to ensure that the level of protection of natural persons guaranteed by this Regulation is not undermined.

The GDPR lists some alternative ways through which data transfers can be lawfully performed. The first is based on the decision of the European Commission assessing the adequacy of the third country system of law, through a positive evaluation of the rule of law, respect for human rights, relevant legislation concerning public security, national security and criminal law and the access of public authorities to personal data, the rules for the onward transfer of personal data to another third country, effective and enforceable data subject rights and effective administrative and judicial redress for data owners, the functioning of independent supervisory authorities, and the international obligations of the third country.[22]

As an alternative, Article 46 GDPR provides that data can be transferred if the company provides data subjects with appropriate safeguards, enforceable rights and effective legal remedies. This requirement is presumed to be satisfied, for instance, where the company follows binding corporate rules or standard data protection clauses adopted by a supervisory authority and approved by the European Commission, or adopts and respects an approved code of conduct or an approved certification mechanism, together with the binding and enforceable commitment of the receiving company in the third country to apply appropriate safeguards.

Thus, the GDPR leaves wide discretion to European ICT corporations to choose the most appropriate way for ruling international data transfers. An approach favourable to encourage the voluntary compliance with the standards on data protection is followed by the EU–US Privacy Shield, that is, the agreement ruling data transfer between the EU and the US, approved by the European Commission in July 2016.[23] The Privacy Shield was agreed upon only

22 General Data Protection Regulation, op. cit., art. 45.

23 European Commission, *Commission Implementing Decision Pursuant to Directive 95/46/EC of the European Parliament and of the Council on the Adequacy of the Protection Provided by the EU-U.S. Privacy Shield*, 12 July 2016; See: K. Daugirdas and J.D. Mortenson, 'European Union and the United States conclude agreement to regulate transatlantic personal data transfer'. *America Journal of International Law*, 2016, 110, 363; S.J. Deckelboim, 'Consumer privacy on an international scale: conflicting viewpoints underlying the EU-US privacy shield framework and how the framework will impact privacy advocates, national security, and businesses'. *Georgetown International Law Journal*, 2016, 48, 263; D. Jerker, B. Svantesson and D. Kloza (eds), *Trans-Atlantic Data Privacy Relations as A Challenge for Democracy*. Cambridge, Antwerp, Portland: Intersentia, 2017; F. Rossi Dal Pozzo, 'La tutela dei dati personali tra esigenze di sicurezza nazionale, interessi economici e diritti fondamentali della persona (dal "Safe Harbour" al "Privacy Shield")'. *Rivista di diritto internazionale*, 2016, 99(3), 690.

after that the ECJ in *Schrems* annulled the European Commission's decision 2000/50, approving the previous legal regime, the so-called Safe Harbour.[24]

In accordance with the ECJ in *Schrems*,

> recourse by a third country to a system of self-certification is not in itself contrary to the requirement laid down in Article 25(6) of Directive 95/46 that the third country concerned must ensure an adequate level of protection 'by reason of its domestic law or [...] international commitments'.[25]

However,

> the reliability of such a system [...] is founded essentially on the establishment of effective detection and supervision mechanisms enabling any infringements of the rules ensuring the protection of fundamental rights, in particular the right to respect for private life and the right to protection of personal data, to be identified and punished in practice.[26]

Thus, the provision for certification mechanisms and the respect of monitored codes of conduct – which, as anticipated, are tools strongly recommended also by the UNGPs – can be considered as a means through which a recipient country can ensure that data transfers from the EU comply with the European legal standards, and justify a positive assessment of adequacy by the European Commission. Against this backdrop, the EU–US Privacy Shield provides that only the US corporations that grant a level of protection equivalent to the European one through their voluntary acceptance of the Privacy Shield Principles can benefit from international data transfers from the EU.[27] These Principles, once accepted, become legally binding under US law.[28]

Nonetheless, the Privacy Shield can be criticized as far as onward transfers of data are concerned: in this regard it provides that they can be performed if third recipients contractually (and only contractually) commit themselves to

24 ECJ, *Maximillian Schrems v. Data Protection Commissioner*, C-362/14, 6 October 2015.

25 Ibid., para. 71. See: T. Bräutigam, 'The land of confusion: international data transfer between Schrems and the GDPR'. In *Legal Studies Research Paper Series*. University of Helsinki, Faculty of Law, no. 46; C. Kuner, 'Reality and illusion in EU data transfer regulation post Schrems'. *Legal Studies Research Paper Series*, 2016, 14.

26 ECJ, *Maximillian Schrems v. Data Protection Commissioner*, op. cit., para. 71.

27 International Trade Administration, *Privacy Shield Framework: Overview*, www.privacyshield.gov/article?id=OVERVIEW (last accessed 20 February 2018).

28 Ibid., 2: 'In order to rely on the Privacy Shield to effectuate transfers of personal data from the EU, an organization must self-certify its adherence to the Principles to the Department of Commerce (or its designee) ("the Department"). While decisions by organizations to thus enter the Privacy Shield are entirely voluntary, effective compliance is compulsory: organizations that self-certify to the Department and publicly declare their commitment to adhere to the Principles must comply fully with the Principles'.

respecting the aforementioned standards.[29] This would not necessarily lead to the effective enjoyment by European data subjects of an adequate level of protection. In the author's view, the EU–US Privacy Shield can also be criticized in terms of the provision for judicial remedies available to data subjects in the event that their rights are not respected. Pursuant thereto, the US recipient corporations must make alternative dispute resolution (ADR) mechanisms and arbitral proceedings available.[30] As concerns arbitration, it is explicitly established that

> the Privacy Shield Panel [...] has the authority to impose individual-specific, non-monetary equitable relief (such as access, correction, deletion, or return of the individual's data in question) necessary to remedy the violation of the Principles only with respect to the individual. These are the only powers of the arbitration panel with respect to remedies. [...] No damages, costs, fees, or other remedies are available.[31]

Given the limits concerning the mandate of such an arbitration panel, it is questionable whether these legal remedies are adequate to grant an effective and adequate level of protection to European data subjects, in line with what is required by Chapter VIII GDPR ('Remedies, liability and penalties') and the third pillar of the UNGPs.

Notwithstanding these criticisms, the EU General Court has dismissed the action for annulment brought by the NGO Digital Rights against the adequacy decision of the European Commission approving the Privacy Shield. The applicant had alleged that the decision is inconsistent with Articles 7, 8 and 47 of the Charter of Fundamental Rights of the European Union.[32] However, according to the General Court's order, should the use of electronic communication services result in the transfer to the US by a service provider of the data of which the applicant is controller, this transfer would be done in accordance with the applicable rules established by the Privacy Shield, approved by the European Commission, and would thus not constitute a breach of law by Digital Rights.

29 International Trade Administration, *Privacy Shield Framework: Obligatory Contracts for Onward Transfers*, www.privacyshield.gov/article?id=10-Obligatory-Contracts-for-Onward-Transfers (last accessed 20 February 2018): 'For transfers between controllers, the recipient controller need not be a Privacy Shield organization or have an independent recourse mechanism. The Privacy Shield organization must enter into a contract with the recipient third-party controller that provides for the same level of protection as is available under the Privacy Shield, not including the requirement that the third-party controller be a Privacy Shield organization or have an independent recourse mechanism, provided it makes available an equivalent mechanism'; K. Daugirdas and J.D. Mortenson, op. cit., 366.

30 K. Daugirdas and J.D. Mortenson, op. cit., 365.

31 International Trade Administration, *Privacy Shield Framework: Annex I*, www.privacyshield.gov/article?id=B-Available-Remedies (last accessed 20 February 2018).

32 General Court: *Digital Rights Ireland v. European Commission*, T-670/16, 16 September 2016; *Digital Rights Ireland v. Commission*, T-670-16, Order of the General Court (second Chamber), 22 November 2017.

The decision leaves several doubts; the same critical issues are the basis of another action for annulment, brought by the NGO La Quadrature du Net, currently pending before the Court.[33]

Thus, it is here submitted that when implementing their corporate responsibility to respect human rights, European ICT companies should take account of risks to human rights connected with the international transfer of data. The assumption of voluntary commitments in this field is in line with the international jurisprudence; however, in order to ensure an adequate level of protection clear standards and appropriate processes should be established so as to prevent the negative effects that might arise from the onward transfers and enable the remediation of incorrect treatments and the consequent adverse human rights impacts.

Bulk Data Collection, Generalized Disclosure of Data, and ICT Companies

According to the UN General Assembly, ICTs provide states surveillance-, interception-, and data-collection tools potentially inconsistent with the enjoyment and protection of the right to privacy, freedom of expression and information, and personal data protection.[34] Moreover the practice shows that

> Governments may make a range of requests that ICT companies provide information about customers and users for legitimate law enforcement purposes […]. These requests can be critical to a state's ability to meet its duty to protect human rights. However when such requests are illegal (in that they do not have a basis in national law) or are not in line with international human rights law […] this poses a direct challenge to an ICT company's ability to meet its responsibility to respect.[35]

Thus, understanding how the European ICT companies should handle these requests and whether and how they should be addressed and disciplined by the tools implementing the corporate responsibility to respect human rights are issues

33 General Court: *La Quadrature du Net e a. c. European Commission*, T-738/16: recours, 25 October 2016; Ordonnance du Tribunal (deuxième chambre), 26 October 2017.

34 UN General Assembly, *The Right to Privacy in the Digital Era*, UN Doc. A/RES/68/167, 18 December 2013; A/RES/69/166, 18 December 2014; UN Doc. A/C.3/71/L.39/Rev.1, 16 November 2016. On this topic see, among others: V. Mitsilegas, 'Surveillance and digital privacy in the transatlantic "war on terror": the case for a global privacy regime'. *Columbia Human Rights Law Review*, 2016, 47, 1; W.J. Schünemann, M.-O. Baumann (eds), *Privacy, Data Protection and Cybersecurity in Europe*. Cham, Switzerland: Springer, 2017; M. Tzanou, *The Fundamental Right to Data Protection: Normative Value in the Context of Counter-Terrorism Surveillance*. Oxford, Portland, Oregon: Hart Publishing, 2017.

35 European Commission, *ICT Sector Guide on Implementing the UN Guiding Principles on Business and Human Rights*, op. cit., 10.

worthy of consideration. A specific relevance in the context of this chapter should be devoted to bulk data collection and the generalized disclosure of stored data to governments. These practices are inconsistent with the GDPR and the ECHR legal framework and their negative impacts on human rights should be taken into account as part of the European ICT companies' responsibility to respect.

Under Article 23 GDPR, the EU and its Member States can restrict, by way of a legislative measure, the scope of the established obligations and rights 'when such a restriction respects the essence of the fundamental rights and freedoms and is a necessary and proportionate measure in a democratic society', in order to safeguard, among other objectives, national security, defence, public security, the prevention/investigation/detection or prosecution of criminal offenses or the execution of criminal penalties, general public interest, and the protection of judicial independence and judicial proceedings.

Likewise, pursuant to Article 8 ECHR, states can legitimately interfere with private communications only by way of legislative measures if and to the extent it is necessary

> in a democratic society in the interests of national security, public safety or the economic well-being of the country, for the prevention of disorder or crime, for the protection of health or morals, or for the protection of the rights and freedoms of others.[36]

More precisely, such domestic law must be 'accessible to the person concerned and foreseeable as to its effects'.[37] Given the specific character of state surveillance, 'the risks of arbitrariness are evident'.[38] Thus, domestic law must clearly identify the nature of offenses which may give rise to an interception order, provide a definition of the categories of people liable to have their telephones intercepted and a limit on the duration of interceptions, and establish the procedure for examining, using and storing the data obtained, the precautions to be taken when communicating the data to third parties, and the circumstances in which recordings must be destroyed.[39]

36 Art. 8.2 ECHR. On this topic see: M. Milanovic, 'Human rights treaties and foreign surveillance: privacy in the digital era'. *Harvard International Law Journal*, 2015, 56, 81; A. Terrasi, 'Il rapporto tra diritto alla privacy e protezione dei dati personali tra Corte di Giustizia dell'Unione Europea e Corte Europea dei Diritti dell'Uomo'. In M. Distefano (ed.), *La protezione dei dati personali ed informatici nell'era della sorveglianza globale. Temi scelti.* Napoli: Editoriale Scientifica, 2017, 127; E. Psychogiopoulou, 'The European Court of Human Rights, privacy and data protection in the digital era'. In M. Brkan and E. Psychogiopoulou (eds), *Courts, Privacy and Data Protection in the Digital Environment.* Cheltenham, Northampton: Edward Elgar, 2017, 32.

37 ECtHR, *Roman Zacharov v Russia*, App. No. 47143/06, Judgment of the Grand Chamber, 4 December 2015, para. 230; see M. Weiler, 'The right to privacy in the digital age: the commitment to human rights online'. *German Yearbook of International Law*, 2014, 57, 651.

38 ECtHR, *Roman Zacharov c. Russia*, op. cit., para. 230.

39 Ibid., para. 231; ECtHR, *Weber and Saravia v. Germany*, App. No. 54934/00, admissibility decision, 29 June 2006, para. 95.

According to a study developed in 2017 by the European Parliament on hacking by law enforcement agencies (hereinafter 'the 2017 EP Study'),[40] the French, German, Polish, English, Italian and Dutch domestic laws on hacking by law enforcement agencies are generally consistent with the recalled requirements.[41] In contrast, according to the ECJ in *Tele2 Sverige*, 'national legislation such as [the Swedish law providing for the bulk collection of data by service providers] [...] exceeds the limits of what is strictly necessary and cannot be considered to be justified, within a democratic society'.[42] Nonetheless EU law does not prevent

> a Member State from adopting legislation permitting, as a preventive measure, the targeted retention of traffic and location data, for the purpose of fighting serious crime, provided that the retention of data is limited, with respect to the categories of data to be retained, the means of communication affected, the persons concerned and the retention period adopted, to what is strictly necessary.[43]

To this aim the law must lay down

> clear and precise rules governing the scope and application of such a data retention measure and [impose] minimum safeguards, so that the persons whose data has been retained have sufficient guarantees of the effective protection of their personal data against the risk of misuse.[44]

The same approach is shared by the ECJ in *Digital Rights*, according to which pieces of legislation such as Directive 2006/24/CE on the retention of data generated or processed in connection with the provision of publicly available electronic communications services or of public communications networks[45]

40 European Parliament, *Legal Frameworks for Hacking by Law Enforcement: Identification, Evaluation and Comparison of Practices*, March 2017, www.europarl.europa.eu/RegData/etudes/STUD/2017/583137/IPOL_STU(2017)583137_EN.pdf (last accessed 20 February 2018).

41 A. Bonfanti, 'Intercettazione di comunicazioni telematiche e acquisizione di dati: sullo studio dell'Unione Europea su Legal Frameworks for Hacking by Law Enforcement'. *Diritti umani e diritto internazionale*, 2017, 11, 506; Id., 'La protezione dei dati personali nell'era digitale: considerazioni alla luce del quadro giuridico internazionale in materia di business e diritti umani'. *Ciberspazio e diritto*, 2017, 477; G. Ziccardi, 'Parlamento Europeo, captatore informatico e attività di hacking delle forze dell'Ordine: alcune riflessioni informatico giuridiche'. *Archivio Penale*, 5 April 2017, www.archiviopenale.it/parlamento-europeo-captatore-informatico-e-attivita-di-hacking-delle-forze-dellordine-alcune-riflessioni-informatico-giuridiche/articoli/15114 (last accessed 20 February 2018).

42 ECJ, *Tele2 Sverige AB v. Postoch telestyrelsen e Secretary of State for the Home Department vs. Tom Watson, Peter Brice, Geoffrey Lewis*, C-203/15 and C-698/15, Judgment of the Grand Chamber, 21 December 2016, para. 107.

43 Ibid., para. 109.

44 Ibid., para. 108.

45 *Directive 2006/24/EC of the European Parliament and of the Council of 15 March 2006 on the Retention of Data Generated or Processed in Connection with the Provision of Publicly Available Electronic Communications Services or of Public Communications Networks and Amending Directive 2002/58/EC*, 15 March 2006.

cause a 'wide-ranging' and 'particularly serious' interference with Articles 7 and 8 of the Charter of Fundamental Rights of the European Union.[46] This conclusion is based on the premise that not only does the Directive cover 'in a generalised manner, all persons and all means of electronic communication as well as all traffic data without any differentiation, limitation or exception being made in the light of the objective of fighting against serious crime',[47] but also it

> does not lay down any objective criterion by which the number of persons authorised to access and subsequently use the data retained is limited to what is strictly necessary in the light of the objective pursued. Above all, the access by the competent national authorities to the data retained is not made dependent on a prior review carried out by a court or by an independent administrative body [...].[48]

Thus, bulk interceptions and generalized data collection are condemned. In this regard the OHCHR is concerned 'about the increasing reliance of Governments on private sector actors to retain data "just in case" it is needed for government purposes', practice which is 'neither necessary nor proportionate'.[49] Therefore, in so doing, the OHCHR implicitly condemns the cooperation required by law enforcement agencies from ICT corporations consisting of bulk data collection and the generalized disclosure of stored personal data. In fact, as highlighted by the ICT Sector Guide,

> unless a company has robust processes in place for handling all requests, it can risk 'over complying', by agreeing either to requests that are illegal (because they do not have a basis in national law) or requests that are under domestic law but not in line with international human rights law – particularly, but not only, when operating in states with a poor human rights record.[50]

These latter hypotheses include also bulk data collection and the generalized disclosure of stored personal data, which the corporate responsibility to respect human rights should therefore properly address.

46 ECJ, *Digital Rights Ireland*, C-293/12, Judgment of the Grand Chamber, 8 April 2014, para. 37.
47 Ibid., para. 57.
48 Ibid., para. 62; see: F. Fabbrini, 'Human rights in the digital age: the European Court of Justice ruling in the data retention case and its lessons for privacy and surveillance in the United States'. *Harvard Human Rights Journal*, 2015, 28, 65; M. Nino, 'L'annullamento del regime della conservazione dei dati di traffico nell'Unione europea da parte della Corte di giustizia UE: prospettive ed evoluzioni future del sistema europeo di "data retention"'. *Il diritto dell'Unione Europea*, 2014, 19, 803; F. Di Matteo, 'La raccolta indiscriminata e generalizzata di dati personali: un vizio congenito nella Direttiva PNR'. *Diritti umani e diritto internazionale*, 2017, 11, 213.
49 OHCHR, *The Right to Privacy in the Digital Era*. UN Doc. A/HRC/27/37, 30 June 2014, para. 9; E. De Busser, 'Private companies and the transfer of data to law enforcement authorities. Challenges for data protection'. *Maastricht Journal of European and Comparative Law*, 2016, 478.
50 ITC Sector Guide, op. cit. 44.

Conclusion

Some conclusions can be drawn concerning the corporate responsibility to protect human rights in the ICT sector. Since European ICT companies must prevent the risks to the right to privacy and personal data protection, and remediate the related negative effects that their activities can cause, they must take the legal framework based on the ECHR and the GDPR into account. With specific regard to the international transfer of data and the handling of the requests posed by governments to disclose stored personal data, the tools implementing the ICT companies' responsibility to protect human rights should provide for commitments, mechanisms, and procedures appropriate to ensure that these activities comply with the international binding legal standards established by the ECHR and the GDPR.

However, the ICT corporations' responsibility to protect human rights should be coupled with the states adopting and implementing the legislative measures adequate to grant the enjoyment of an adequate level of personal data protection and the respect of the right to privacy. To this aim states shall strike a fair balance with the national security needs and avoid forcing ICT corporations to collect and disclose personal data if this is not necessary and proportionate with the public interests pursued.

Part III

Access to Remedy in Europe

16 Access to Remedy for the Victims of Corporate-Related Human Rights Abuse

Assessing the Contribution of the Fundamental Rights Agency

Carmen Márquez Carrasco

Introduction[1]

Every day around the world people are affected in their daily lives by the activities of companies. Some of these effects are beneficial in terms of wages, goods and services, and the contribution of wealth to the country. Other effects, however, may inhibit the exercise of individual human rights and in some cases violate them. The violation of human rights can occur in different places: in the workplace, in the community, or in the private sector. The impact of corporate human rights abuses around the world is enormous, with devastating effects on people and communities.

Over the past 30 years, globalization has increased the power and influence of TNCs significantly, particularly as a result of trade liberalization and international investment. However, the circumstances in which these companies may be held liable for human rights abuses and the ways in which victims can get justice have not kept pace with these developments.

The UN 'Protect, Respect and Remedy' framework adopted by the UNHRC in 2008[2] contains the three basic pillars that have served as a basis for the development of the UNGPs adopted in 2011:[3] the state duty to protect against human rights abuses committed by third parties, in particular by companies; the responsibility of businesses to respect human rights; and the need for more

1 The research leading to this publication has received funding from the research Project entitled 'La Implementación de los Principios Rectores de las Naciones Unidas sobre Empresas y Derechos Humanos por la Unión Europea y sus Estados Miembros' (DER2013-41956-P), and the Research Network "La Unión Europea y los actores no estatales" (DER2015-68728-REDT), funded by the Ministry of Economy and Competitiveness of the Government of Spain.

2 UNHRC, *Protect, Respect and Remedy: a Framework for Business and Human Rights*, UN Doc. A/HRC/8/5, 7 April 2008, paras. 10–26.

3 UNHRC, *UN Guiding Principles on Business and Human Rights: Implementing the United Nations 'Protect, Respect and Remedy' Framework*, UN Doc. A/HRC/17/31, 21 March 2011, www.ohchr.org/Documents/Publications/GuidingPrinciplesBusinessHR_EN.pdf (last accessed 14 December 2017).

effective access to remedies. These three pillars are complementary to each other and each supports the others to achieve sustainable progress.

The third pillar addresses the remedy dimension of the UNGPs, which is a key aspect of the Principles. It provides that the State's duty to protect includes ensuring access to an effective remedy for victims of corporate abuse, through judicial, administrative, legislative or other appropriate means, when such abuses take place within their territory and/or jurisdiction. The duty to remedy is also addressed by companies who are entrusted to develop operational-level grievance mechanisms. Among the judicial and non-judicial mechanisms, UNGP 26 recognizes the relevance of state-based judicial remedies as well as the state obligation to remove legal, practical and other relevant barriers to an effective remedy.[4] It has been highlighted that

> such barriers may include lack of jurisdiction by the courts of a particular state, questions of which law is to be applied, absence of duties of care on the parent company, availability of legal funding and representation, and many others. Overcoming these barriers requires of states that they develop a clear view of which barriers are problematic in their own legal systems, and develop coherent policies as to how they will address those barriers.[5]

The UNGPs further present an integrated set of redress methods that both states and business enterprises should apply to ensure that victims of human rights abuse have access to remedies. The state's obligation to provide an effective remedy where a human rights abuse has occurred is anchored in international human rights law. In cases where corporate-related human rights abuses have occurred within a state's territory and/or jurisdiction, the State must take appropriate steps 'to investigate, punish and redress' these abuses, through formal judicial mechanisms and complementary administrative, legislative and other State-based non-judicial grievance mechanisms. There is a complementary role for non-State-based grievance mechanisms to provide remedies through 'adjudicative, dialogue-based or other culturally appropriate and rights-compatible processes'.[6]

States have generally failed to comply with their obligation to protect human rights by ensuring that victims have access to effective remedies, including judicial remedies, especially when it comes to corporate human rights abuses occurring abroad. The EU is home to countless companies of all sizes and sectors, including TNCs, and is the world's largest trading bloc. Given that, increasingly victims of corporate human rights abuses attempt to seek remedies in the domestic European legal systems of the parent companies. According to Álvarez

4 UNGP, 26.

5 J.J. Alvarez Rubio and K. Yiannibas (ed), *Human Rights in Business. Removal of Barriers to Access to Justice in the European Union*. New York: Routledge, 2017, 3.

6 UNGP, 28, Commentary.

Rubio and Yiannibas, 'more and more litigants find their way into European courts concerning human rights abuses connected to European companies, either through civil litigation, or as injured parties in criminal cases'.[7]

The EU has contributed from the start to the UNGPs project and has supported its endorsement by the UNHRC and subsequent implementation in EU policies. As an international organization, the EU is one of the addressees of the UNGPs, particularly with regard to the first and third pillars, although the EU's action is conditioned by its competences in that respect. It has chosen to embrace the B&HR agenda and to focus most of its efforts in the field on promoting the UNGPs, as well as other instruments setting international standards in this area. The B&HR policy framework permeates the various EU competences it touches upon in several ways, as the B&HR debate is present in many legal and political areas.

Among the actions taken, the EU has recommended Member States to adopt NAPs to implement the UNGPs.[8] The NAPs launched initially did not adequately address the issue of access to remedy. While they all mentioned the third pillar of the UNGPs, little or no commitment could be found on how this issue could be addressed, in particular on access to legal remedies, either in the national or extraterritorial context. Nevertheless, some NAPs now make reference to access to remedy, including those of the UK (as revised in 2016), the Netherlands and Switzerland.

The recent study *Third Pillar*, carried out by the European Coalition for Corporate Justice, CORE and the International Corporate Accountability Roundtable (hereinafter 'ICAR'),[9] and the outcome of a very relevant research project[10] show that the existence of legal, institutional and procedural barriers prevent victims of corporate abuses from having access to effective remedies in the EU. The implementation of the third pillar on access to remedy by both the EU and its Member States is still pending. The issue is crucial and complex, as well as politically very sensitive.

7 Alvarez Rubio, Yiannibas (ed.), op. cit., 3.

8 C. Márquez Carrasco and K. Buhmann, 'Editorial introduction. The corporate responsibility to respect human rights: the emerging European Union regime'. *Human Rights & International Legal Discourse*, 2016, issue 1, 2–18; C. Márquez Carrasco, 'Los Planes Nacionales de Acción de los Estados miembros de la UE sobre empresas y derechos humanos. Especial referencia al Plan español'. In C. Márquez Carrasco and I. Vivas Tesón (eds), *La implementación de los Principios Rectores de las Naciones Unidas sobre empresas y derechos humanos por la Unión Europea y sus Estados miembros*. Madrid: Thomson-Aranzadi, 2017, 81–104.

9 G. Skinner, R. McCorquodale and O. De Schutter, *The Third Pillar. Access to Judicial Remedies for Human Rights Violations by Transnational Companies*. ICAR, CORE, ECCJ, 2013, http://corporatejustice.org/documents/publications/eccj/the_third_pillar_-access_to_judicial_remedies_for_human_rights_violation.-1-2.pdf (last accessed 14 December 2017).

10 J.J. Alvarez Rubio and K. Yiannibas (eds), op. cit., 3.

Against this background, the Council of the EU sought in its Conclusions adopted on 20 June 2016[11] an Opinion by the EU Agency for Fundamental Rights (FRA) on access to remedy. As stated officially,

> the FRA's Opinion aims to support the EU's work related to business and human rights, by offering advice on how to lower the barriers for access to remedies in cases of fundamental rights abuse by businesses in or linked to the EU.

On 10 April 2017 the FRA published the opinion on access to remedy in the field of business and human rights.[12]

Departing from the policy context, this chapter seeks to analyse the FRA Opinion, focusing on its contribution to foster EU and Member States' action to provide access to effective remedies and justice for victims of corporate-related human rights abuses. In order to test its significance and applicability, this chapter analyses its content and highlights perceived weaknesses or gaps.

Policy Context and Normative Guidance of the FRA Opinion on Access to Remedy in the Area of B&HR

At EU level, developments in the field of B&HR have happened in response to the UNGPs and to other instruments setting standards in this area.[13] The uptake of the UNGPs has been pursued through several initiatives in this regard, such as the promotion of NAPs, sectoral guides (employment, ICT, oil and gas), and the adoption of regulatory initiatives and policy.[14] Thirteen Member States have to date issued their own NAPs.[15]

11 See at www.consilium.europa.eu/en/press/press-releases/2016/06/20/fac-business-human-rights-conclusions/ (last accessed 15 December 2017).

12 FRA, *Improving Access to Remedy in the Area of Business and Human Rights at EU Level – Opinion 1/2017*, 10 April 2017, http://fra.europa.eu/en/opinion/2017/business-human-rights (last accessed 15 December 2017).

13 OECD Guidelines for Multinational Enterprises; ILO Tripartite Declaration on Multinational Enterprises and Social Policy + EU 2020 (2010), European Alliance for CSR (2006), EU Action Plan on Human Rights and Democracy in 2012 and 2015 (external dimension); UN Committee on the Rights of the Child, General Comment no. 16 (2013) on State obligations regarding the impact of the business sector on children's rights, www2.ohchr.org/english/bodies/crc/docs/CRC.C.GC.16.pdf (last accessed 13 December 2017).

14 See the survey included in the EU, *Commission's Staff Working Document on Implementing the UN Guiding Principles on Business and Human Rights – State of Play*, SWD 144 final, 2015, https://ec.europa.eu/anti-trafficking/sites/antitrafficking/files/swd_2015_144_f1_staff_working_paper_en_v2_p1_818385.pdf (last accessed 1 December 2017).

15 The NAPs launched are examined (although some of them are missing) in a report issued by the International Corporate Accountability Roundtable (ICAR) and the European Coalition for Corporate Justice (ECCJ) in August 2017. ICAR, *Assessments of Existing National Action Plans (Naps) on Business and Human Rights*, August 2017, https://static1.squarespace.com/static/583f3fca725e25fcd45aa446/t/599c543ae9bfdf40b5b6f055/1503417406364/NAP+Assessment+Aug+2017+FINAL.pdf (last accessed 1 December 2017).

Particularly in Europe, the EU and the CoE are the regional organizations that have been active in identifying ways that States may reduce barriers to access to remedy for corporate-related human rights abuse. The CoE's 2016 Recommendation to Member States[16] has been strengthened by the April 2017 FRA Opinion which provides options for lowering barriers within the EU consistently with the CoE's Recommendation and with the UNGPs. In its request, the Foreign Affairs Council asked FRA for an expert opinion on 'possible avenues to lower barriers for access to remedy [in the context of business-related human rights abuse] at the EU level, taking into account existing EU legal instruments and competences at EU and Member States' levels'.[17] The Council conclusions provide evidence of the need for action by the EU institutions and Member States to strengthen the remedy pillar of the UNGPs. It should be stressed that it is the first time that the Council has requested an opinion from FRA (usually the requests come from the European Parliament), which is very symbolic.

The FRA Opinion is based on three main pieces of normative guidance: the 2011 UNGPs as the leading global framework for B&HR, endorsed by the UN, the CoE and the EU; the 2016 CoE Recommendation on human rights and business, which adds detail and specificity in a European context with explicit reference to the UNGPs; and the 2016 UN guidance, composed of four documents that offer the most detailed advice on how to operationalize key aspects of the UNGPs.[18]

16 CoE, *Recommendation of the Committee of Ministers to member States on human rights and business*, CM/Rec 3, 2016, https://search.coe.int/cm/Pages/result_details.aspx?ObjectID=09000016805c1ad4 (last accessed 17 December 2017).

17 See at CoE, *Council Conclusions on Business and Human Rights – Press Release 359/16*, 20 June 2016. www.consilium.europa.eu/en/press/press-releases/2016/06/20/fac-business-human-rights-conclusions/ (last accessed 15 December 2017).

18 UN, HRC, *Business and Human Rights: Improving Accountability and Access to Remedy*, A/HRC/32/L.19, 29 June 2016. The *Accountability and Remedy Project* has been developed by the OHCHR. Part I of the Accountability and Remedy Project focussed on the use of judicial mechanisms concluded in June 2016 with the submission of a final report, together with an explanatory addendum, to the Human Rights Council. See http://ap.ohchr.org/documents/dpage_e.aspx?si=A/HRC/32/19 for the OHCHR's final report and www.un.org/en/ga/search/view_doc.asp?symbol=A/HRC/32/19/add.1 for the accompanying explanatory addendum (last accessed 18 December 2017). Part II of the *Accountability and Remedy Project* comprises an initial draft document (scoping paper) produced by OHCHR with the aim to provide a preliminary assessment of current practices and challenges with respect to the use of State-based non-judicial mechanisms as a way of enhancing access to remedy in cases of adverse human rights impacts that are business-related, and to identify areas where there may be a need for further research and/or legal development. Later, OHCHR undertook a sector study focused on the historical and potential responses of State-based NJMs to adverse human rights impacts occurring in four 'focus' business sectors: extractives, mining and natural resources; agribusiness and food production; infrastructure and construction; and textiles and manufacture of clothing. See at www.ohchr.org/EN/Issues/Business/Pages/ARP_II.aspx (last accessed 18 December 2017).

In the human rights context, the key aspects on which the FRA Opinion is grounded are: Article 8 of the Universal Declaration of Human Rights;[19] Article 2(3) of the ICCPR;[20] Principles 25–31 UNGPs;[21] the CoE Committee of Ministers Recommendation 2016 (3);[22] Article 47 of the Charter of Fundamental Rights of the EU;[23] and Article 13 of the ECHR.[24]

In terms of the EU action and mandate on this matter, the FRA Opinion is intended to be part of the upcoming EU Action Plan on Responsible Business Conduct. The EU mandate in this area is not very clear, although it does offer great potential in furthering the recommendations made in the FRA Opinion. The goal of the FRA Opinion to fit into the Action Plan is expected to be finalized soon. The request of the Council of the EU signals readiness (although the EU mandate is not very clear) and links competitive advantage through a strong B&HR framework into broad policy goals such as *Europe 2020*.[25]

19 UDHR, art. 8: 'Everyone has the right to an effective remedy by the competent national tribunals for acts violating the fundamental rights granted him by constitution or by law'.

20 ICCPR, art. 2(3): 'Each State Party to the present Covenant undertakes: (a) To ensure that any person whose rights or freedoms as herein recognized are violated shall have an effective remedy, notwithstanding that the violation has been committed by persons acting in an official capacity; (b) To ensure that any person claiming such a remedy shall have his right thereto determined by competent judicial, administrative or legislative authorities, or by any other competent authority provided for by the legal system of the State, and to develop the possibilities of judicial remedy; (c) To ensure that the competent authorities shall enforce such remedies when granted.'

21 UNGP 25: 'States must take appropriate steps to ensure, through judicial, administrative, legislative or other appropriate means, that when such abuses occur within their territory and/or jurisdiction those affected have access to effective remedy'.

22 CoE, *Recommendation of the Committee of Ministers to Member States on Human Rights and Business*, CM/Rec 3, 2016, op. cit., art. 3: 'Member States should ensure the effective implementation of their obligations under Articles 6 and 13 of the European Convention on Human Rights and other international and European human rights instruments, to grant to everyone access to a court in the determination of their civil rights, as well as to everyone whose rights have been violated under these instruments, an effective remedy before a national authority, including where such violation arises from business activity'.

23 Charter of Fundamental Rights of the EU, art. 47: 'Everyone whose rights and freedoms guaranteed by the law of the Union are violated has the right to an effective remedy before a tribunal in compliance with the conditions laid down in this Article. Everyone is entitled to a fair and public hearing within a reasonable time by an independent and impartial tribunal previously established by law. Everyone shall have the possibility of being advised, defended and represented. Legal aid shall be made available to those who lack sufficient resources in so far as such aid is necessary to ensure effective access to justice'. See: FRA, *EU Charter of Fundamental Rights – Article 47 (1 December 2009)*, http://fra.europa.eu/en/charterpedia/article/47-right-effective-remedy-and-fair-trial (last accessed 13 December 2017).

24 Art. 13 ECHR: 'Everyone whose rights and freedoms as set forth in this Convention are violated shall have an effective remedy before a national authority notwithstanding that the violation has been committed by persons acting in an official capacity'.

25 Europe 2020 Strategy, see at https://ec.europa.eu/info/business-economy-euro/economic-and-fiscal-policy-coordination/eu-economic-governance-monitoring-prevention-correction/european-semester/framework/europe-2020-strategy_en (last accessed 16 December 2017).

In particular, the Commission has stressed the role it has to play in the area of justice, by highlighting the 'establishment of a comprehensive EU Justice Policy to enforce the common values in particular concerning fundamental rights, equality and the rule of law upon which the EU is founded and in underpinning economic growth'.[26] The EU also stressed that this area should aim at building a consistent body of law which includes rules governing issues of jurisdiction and the recognition of enforcement of judicial decisions in civil and commercial matters. Outside of these areas, Member States remain competent to ensure effective remedies for victims of corporate-related human rights abuses. This illustrates how complex and problematic this area could be.

Content of the FRA Opinion

The FRA Opinion is based on the FRA's analysis of judicial and non-judicial remedies, together with implementation issues, organized in six main areas: lowering barriers to make judicial remedies more accessible; enhancing the effectiveness of judicial remedies – especially in extraterritorial situations; ensuring effective remedies through the criminal justice system; ensuring effective non-judicial remedies; improving transparency and data collection; and incentivizing action plans, coordination and due diligence.

The FRA Opinion contributes to raising awareness of the need for the EU to do more to improve access to effective remedies for victims of corporate abuse. In the Opinion, the FRA calls for more action to ensure access to remedies for victims of business-related human rights abuses. Too often, existing legal and practical barriers leave victims without access to an effective remedy. The EU and its Member States are therefore advised to take all appropriate steps to remove these obstacles and guarantee access to remedy for victims.

Existing legal and practical barriers to access to remedies by victims of corporate abuse have been examined by the aforementioned CORE and ICAR study, the research project *Human Rights in Business*[27] and the report by the United Nations Working Group on which the FRA's analysis has been built to a certain extent.[28] The FRA's analysis covers the areas of judicial and non-judicial remedies, as well as issues related to their effective implementation. Based on its findings, the FRA formulated 21 specific opinions on what actions the EU should undertake to increase access to remedies in the field of B&HR. From those opinions, and according to the six main areas, the actions recommended are set out below.

26 EU, *Commission's Staff Working Document on Implementing the UN Guiding Principles on Business and Human Rights – State of Play*, op. cit., 34.

27 Alvarez Rubio and Yiannibas (eds), op. cit., 3.

28 Report of the Working Group on the issue of human rights and transnational corporations and other business enterprises: 'National Action Plans on Business and Human Rights', A/69/263, 11 September 2014, https://documents-dds-ny.un.org/doc/UNDOC/GEN/N14/495/68/PDF/N1449568.pdf?OpenElement (last accessed 20 December 2017).

Regarding the first area – lowering barriers to make judicial remedies more accessible – recommendations include: ensuring minimum standards for needs-based legal aid, providing for broad legal standing and effect (collective redress and representative organizations); facilitating the burden of proof, bringing clarity on jurisdiction in the case of denial of justice (*forum necessitatis*) and accommodating persons in situations of vulnerability.[29] Among the specific recommendations, the following can be highlighted: ensuring sufficient legal aid, particularly for victims not residing in EU Member States; enhancing the possibilities of collective redress for business-related human rights abuse; facilitating access to evidence for victims of corporate human rights abuse; shifting the burden of proof (rebuttable presumption) from the victim to the corporate perpetrator of human rights violations; and clarifying the conditions of *forum necessitatis* jurisdiction to avoid denial of justice.

In the area of enhancing the effectiveness of judicial remedies (especially in extraterritorial situations), the FRA makes recommendations as to improving access to remedy in extraterritorial cases, leading on multilateral developments to facilitate access to remedy, guiding application of the 'Rome regime'[30] in order to ensure appropriate levels of damage awarded, and learning from the designation of applicable law in environmental cases.

The FRA Opinion comprises useful recommendations with respect to improving access to remedy in extraterritorial cases.[31] These include that the EU should mandate a platform for EU Member States to have a dedicated exchange on how best to address extraterritoriality through legislation and other measures, including subsidiary jurisdiction, to improve access to remedy for victims of business-related human rights abuse across the EU. In addition, the EU should encourage clarity on how and when *forum necessitatis* applies or equivalent systems are in place in the EU Member States to avoid denial of justice.[32] Another recommendation is that the EU and its Member States should lead on multilateral developments facilitating access to remedy through the Hague

29 FRA, *Improving Access to Remedy in the Area of Business and Human Rights at EU Level, Opinion 1/2017*, op. cit., 5–8.

30 Regulation (EC) No. 864/2007 of the European Parliament and of the Council of 11 July 2007 on the law applicable to non-contractual obligations (Rome II), L 199/40. *Official Journal of the European Union*, 31 July 2007, http://eur-lex.europa.eu/LexUriServ/LexUriServ.do?uri=OJ:L:2007:199:0040:0049:EN:PDF (last accessed 15 December 2017). See FRA, *Improving Access to Remedy in the Area of Business and Human Rights at EU Level, Opinion 1/2017*, op. cit., 9.

31 FRA, *Improving Access to Remedy in the Area of Business and Human Rights at EU Level, Opinion 1/2017*, op. cit., 9.

32 Obstacles to remedies may sometimes lead to situations where no effective access is possible within a given jurisdiction. In such cases, legal systems commonly allow for some form of exception to jurisdictional rules to avoid a denial of justice and ensure the required access to justice. This means that cases can be taken up provided that a reasonable link exists between the situation concerned and the forum (the court in question) even if the jurisdictional rules would prescribe another court (typically in another country in this context). The Latin term *forum necessitates* – jurisdiction by necessity – is the common label to refer to these exceptions.

Conference on Private International Law and guiding application and reform of Rome II Regulation.[33] More specifically the EU should provide guidance on when and how to make full use of the flexibility available under the public-policy clause of the Rome regime, particularly in extraterritorial settings. This should be done to ensure that appropriate levels of damages are awarded.[34] Finally, the EU could analyse the consequences of a revision of the Rome II Regulation, which would allow for exceptions, such as those already in place for environmental damages, in cases of corporate-related human rights abuse.

Concerning effective non-judicial remedies both state-based and non-state-based, the FRA Opinion stresses the need to strengthen the role of non-judicial mechanisms, and to ensure effective National Contact Points in all EU Member States, as well as incentivizing effective operational-level grievance mechanisms.[35]

Regarding action plans, coordination and due diligence, the FRA Opinion affirms that the EU should consider adopting an Action Plan, based on the same criteria as outlined in relation to NAPs, including indicators to measure achievement and through participatory dialogue with key stakeholders and civil society organizations. In this respect, the EU should support and facilitate the establishment of an open method of coordination in the area of B&HR.[36]

A particularly relevant recommendation is addressed to EU and Member States with regard to due diligence obligations. The FRA Opinion states that the EU could incentivize Member States to impose due diligence obligations, including for parent companies linked to human rights performance in subsidiaries or supply chains.[37] Implementing access to remedies in business-related human rights abuse would also benefit from stronger legislative incentives. It is highlighted that a recently adopted French law could serve as a model across the EU, adding to existing instruments such as the Non-Financial Disclosure Directive.[38] The French legislation (*devoir de vigilance* – 'duty of care')[39] obliges certain companies domiciled in France to conduct and document due diligence for their operations, including through their supply chains. Fines may be imposed for non-compliance. Due diligence is a key component of the UNGPs second pillar on corporate responsibility to respect human rights, which

33 FRA, *Improving Access to Remedy in the Area of Business and Human Rights at EU Level, Opinion 1/2017*, op. cit., 8–10.

34 Ibid., 30, 32–33.

35 Ibid., 48–61.

36 Ibid., 62–68.

37 Ibid., 17.

38 EU, 'Directive 2014/95/EU of the European Parliament and of the Council of 22 October 2014 amending Directive 2013/34/EU as regards disclosure of non-financial and diversity information by certain large undertakings and groups'. *Official Journal of the European Union* L 330/1, 15 November 2014, http://eur-lex.europa.eu/legal-content/EN/TXT/?uri=CELEX%3A32014L0095 (last accessed 16 December 2017).

39 *LOI no. 2017-399 du 27 mars 2017 relative au devoir de vigilance des sociétés mères et des entreprises donneuses d'ordre*, www.legifrance.gouv.fr/eli/loi/2017/3/27/2017-399/jo/texte (last accessed 17 December 2017).

complements the third pillar, since effective due diligence practices can also help to strengthen access to remedy.

In addition, regarding the responsibility of parent companies, the FRA's findings point out that national courts will need to set boundaries as to how far the responsibility of parent companies reaches and the conditions for attributing that responsibility, and rightly stresses that the EU can play an important role in enacting harmonizing measures and ensuring that national regulations do not create legal uncertainty, both for corporations and victims.

One of the areas that deserves special attention concerns criminal justice.[40] The FRA Opinion highlights several measures to ensure access to effective remedies through criminal justice in the area of B&HR, to encourage improved investigations of corporate crimes and to facilitate victims' claims in criminal procedures.[41] As noted by a commentator, 'even though a number of existing EU instruments require Member States to criminalize some forms of serious business-related human rights violations, these instruments are not used at their intended capacity'.[42] The Opinion makes reference to the Employers Sanctions Directive (2009/52/EC),[43] which obliges EU Member States to criminalize severe forms of labour exploitation, and the Anti-Trafficking Directive (2011/36/EU),[44] which sets out minimum rules concerning the definition of criminal offenses and sanctions in the area of trafficking in human beings.

According to those Directives, EU Member States are obliged to ensure that legal persons can be held accountable for offenses criminalized pursuant to these two instruments. Nevertheless, as noted,

> research conducted by FRA into the implementation of these instruments shows a lack of States' commitment to holding business companies to account for their involvement in severe forms of labor exploitation and trafficking in human beings. This failure to ensure full implementation of these instruments at national level is a serious issue that needs to be addressed by the EU institutions.[45]

40 FRA, *Improving Access to Remedy in the Area of Business and Human Rights at EU Level, Opinion 1/2017*, op. cit., 40–46.

41 Ibid., 11–12.

42 See N. Bernaz, *EU Fundamental Rights Agency Calls for Better Access to Remedies through Criminal Justice*, 27 April 2017, http://rightsasusual.com/?p=1152 (last accessed 16 December 2017).

43 See at EU, *Directive of the European Parliament and of the Council Providing for Minimum Standards on Sanctions and Measures against Employers of Illegally Staying Third-country Nationals*. 2009/52/EC OJ L 168/24, 18 June 2009, http://eur-lex.europa.eu/LexUriServ/LexUriServ.do?uri=OJ:L:2009:168:0024:0032:EN:PDF (last accessed 17 December 2017).

44 See at EU, *Directive of the European Parliament and of the Council on Preventing and Combating Trafficking in Human Beings and Protecting its Victims, and Replacing Council Framework Decision 2002/629/JHA*. 2011/36/EU OJ L 101/01, 5 April 2011, http://eur-lex.europa.eu/LexUriServ/LexUriServ.do?uri=OJ:L:2011:101:0001:0011:EN:PDF (last accessed 17 December 2017).

45 See commentary by N. Bernaz, *EU Fundamental Rights Agency Calls for Better Access to Remedies through Criminal Justice*, op. cit., paras. 4–5.

The EU is therefore strongly advised to make 'greater efforts to ensure proper implementation in the Member States of the existing EU criminal law instruments that are relevant to business and human rights.'[46]

Another aspect that needs further consideration at the EU level concerns cooperation among Member States in investigating corporate crimes. Due to the often transnational nature of business-related human rights abuses, effective and specific cross-border cooperation mechanisms are essential to ensure proper investigation of corporate crimes. In this regard, as indicated, 'the Opinion rightly underlines how the EU can play "a unique role" in facilitating cross-border investigations by making greater use of existing resources, such as Eurojust.'[47]

Conclusion

The FRA Opinion adds a meaningful contribution to the current debate on access to remedy for corporate-related human rights abuse. It can be considered as a useful tool to put pressure on Member States and on the EU institutions to encourage additional EU action, particularly from the European Commission.

The Opinion argues effectively in several passages that the EU internal market would be strengthened by establishing a more accessible and uniform system of judicial and non-judicial remedies for victims. For the first time, irrespective of whether a victim is located inside or outside the EU, a more uniform system of access to remedy is considered as a reinforcement of the European single market and not as a potential competitive disadvantage.

The Opinion does not limit its scope only to access to remedy, proposing individual legislative reforms, but also recommends that the EU considers the

46 Member States' obligation to avoid any impunity of severe human rights violations by legislating and enforcing criminal law provisions also extends to legal persons as perpetrators. Research conducted into areas of criminal victimization prominently relates to legal persons as criminal offenders, including criminal forms of exploitation of foreign workers and online hate crime, which relies on legal persons providing a platform. There is vast evidence that in these areas – as in others – legal provisions establishing responsibility and sanctions for legal persons are either missing at Member State level or not implemented. Interestingly, in both examples just mentioned there exist reports drafted by the Commission highlighting this lack of implementation of secondary EU law (see for the Employer Sanctions Directive: EU (European Commission), *Communication on the Application of Directive 2009/52/EC of 18 June 2009 Providing for Minimum Standards on Sanctions and Measures against Employers of Illegally Staying Third Country Nationals*, COM(2014) 286 final, 22 May 2014, http://ec.europa.eu/transparency/regdoc/rep/1/2014/EN/1-2014-286-EN-F1-1.pdf (last accessed 18 December 2017); for the Framework Decision on Racism: EU, European Commission), *Report on the Implementation of Council Framework Decision 2008/913/JHA on Combating Certain Forms and Expressions of Racism and Xenophobia by means of Criminal Law*, COM(2014) 27 final, 27 January 2014. http://ec.europa.eu/justice/fundamental-rights/files/com_2014_27_en.pdf (last accessed 18 December 2017). However, in neither case were infringement proceedings initiated.

47 See commentary by N. Bernaz, *EU Fundamental Rights Agency Calls for Better Access to Remedies through Criminal Justice*, op. cit., para. 4.

adoption of an Action Plan, based on the same criteria as outlined in relation to the NAPs, and establish an Open Method of Coordination in the area of B&HR. Another important contribution of this Opinion is that it suggests that the EU incentivize Member States to impose due diligence obligations on the model of the recently adopted French Law.

Overall, what is clear from the Opinion is that more needs to be done to improve victims' access to remedies in the field of B&HR, including through criminal justice.

The EU's approach seems to be becoming more proactive with regard to holding MNEs accountable for their actions abroad: this may serve as an indication of changing attitudes and perspectives about the exercise of extraterritorial jurisdiction over TNCs. Since national courts will need to decide how far the responsibility of parent companies reaches, on the basis of the relevant conditions for attributing responsibility, the EU can play an important role in enacting harmonizing measures and ensuring that national regulations do not create legal uncertainty, both for corporations and victims.

It is expected that this EU approach will translate into a more realistic political will and effective legal reform at Member States level since these are essential to give effect to the victim's human right to remedy.

17 Adjudicate This! Foreign Direct Liability and Civil Jurisdiction in Europe

Lucas Roorda

Introduction

Business and human rights litigation is on the rise in Europe. Increasingly, victims of corporate human rights abuses seek remedy for these abuses by bringing civil claims before the domestic courts of European States of TNCs: so-called 'foreign direct liability' (hereinafter: 'FDL') cases.[1] Some of these cases have gained attention in the mainstream media, specifically, the *Bodo Community v. Shell*,[2] *Trafigura*[3] and *Okpabi*[4] lawsuits in the United Kingdom, and the case *Akpan and Stichting Milieudefensie v. Shell*[5] in the Netherlands. Claimants in these cases often argue that it is impossible to find remedies in their own states because of dysfunctional legal systems and poor enforcement perspectives.

1 See H. Ward, '"Foreign Direct Liability": a new weapon in the performance armoury?', *AccountAbility Quarterly*, 2000, 14, 3. The terminology has been adopted in, amongst others: S. Joseph, *Corporations and Transnational Human Rights Litigation*. Oxford: Hart Publishing 2004 and L. Enneking, *Foreign Direct Liability and Beyond: Exploring the role of tort law in promoting international corporate social responsibility and accountability*. The Hague: Eleven International Publishing, 2012.

2 High Court of Justice, Queen's Bench Division, *The Bodo Community and Others v The Shell Petroleum Company of Nigeria Limited*, [2014] EWHC 1973 (TCC), June 20, 2014. See also J. Vidal, 'Shell accepts liability for two oil spills in Nigeria'. *The Guardian*, 3 August 2011, www.theguardian.com/environment/2011/aug/03/shell-liability-oil-spills-nigeria (last accessed 28 February 2018).

3 High Court of Justice, Queen's Bench Division, *Yao Essaie Motto & others v Trafigura Limited & Trafigura Beheer BV*, [2011] EWCA Civ 1150, date, and D. Leigh and A. Hirsch, 'The boat that reeked – toxic voyage of the Probo Koala'. *The Guardian*, 13 May 2009.

4 High Court of Justice, Queen's Bench Division, *HRH Emere Godwin Bebe Okpabi v Royal Dutch Shell plc & Shell Petroleum Development Company of Nigeria Ltd*, 26 January 2017, [2017] EWHC 89 (TCC), and Court of Appeals, *HRH Emere Godwin Bebe Okpabi and Others v. Royal Dutch Shell PLC & Shell Petroleum Development Company of Nigeria Ltd*, [2018] EWCA Civ 191, 14 February 2018, discussed in J. Vidal, 'Ogoni king: Shell oil is killing my people'. *The Guardian*, 3 December 2016, available at www.theguardian.com/world/2016/dec/03/ogoni-king-shell-oil-is-killing-my-people (last accessed 26 February 2018).

5 See Rechtbank Den Haag, *Akpan et al and Stichting Milieudefensie v. Royal Dutch Shell*, ECLI:NL:RBDHA:2013:BY9854, 30 January 2013 (hereafter: *Akpan* (2013)) and Gerechtshof Den Haag, *Akpan et al and Stichting Milieudefensie v. Royal Dutch Shell*, ECLI:NL:GHDA:2015:3586, 3587 and 3588, 18 December 2015 (hereafter *Akpan* (2015)).

However, they also face significant barriers when bringing their claims to foreign courts.

One of the most significant issues to be resolved when bringing FDL claims concerns jurisdiction: the competence of domestic courts to deal with such cases. More specifically, the jurisdiction *ratione personae*, i.e. jurisdiction over the parties to the dispute is often problematic. Claims concerning corporate human rights abuse are generally filed against both the parent company of a TNC and its local subsidiary, incorporated in the territory of another state. The latter is often accused of contributing directly to the harms, whereas the former is held liable for failing to prevent harm arising from the activities of its subsidiary. However, since TNCs are organized as groups of separate legal persons, foreign-domiciled subsidiaries are not evidently within the jurisdiction of the domestic courts of their parent company's home state.

As highlighted by the UNGPs and their underlying framework, jurisdiction is one of the barriers that states should address in order to improve access to remedy.[6] Additionally, it has received attention from the CoE and the European Parliament (hereinafter 'EP'), where the CoE's Committee of Ministers has specifically recommended European States to make their domestic courts more accessible for victims of corporate human rights abuses by extending their jurisdiction over foreign corporate defendants;[7] similar ideas were included in a draft report of the EP's Commission on Foreign Affairs,[8] although amended out of the final text.[9] The approaches followed by CoE and the EP are, however, indicative of the sort of proposals raised at European policy making level, so they are useful to guide the discussion here.

This chapter examines what possibilities exist within the EU for domestic courts to exercise jurisdiction *ratione personae* over corporate defendants in FDL cases. It does so from two angles. First, the chapter discusses the Brussels-I regime – formed by the Brussels-I Regulation (hereinafter 'the Regulation')[10]

6 See UNGP 26, Commentary; UNHRC, *Protect, Respect and Remedy: a Framework for Business and Human Rights Report of the Special Representative of the Secretary-General on the Issue of Human Rights and Transnational Corporations and other Business Enterprises, John Ruggie*, 7 April 2008, UN Doc. A/HRC/8/5, paras. 19 and 83.

7 See CoE, *Recommendation CM/Rec(2016)3 of the Committee of Ministers on Human Rights and Business*, 7 March 2016.

8 See EP, Committee on Foreign Affairs, *Draft Report on Corporate Liability for Serious Human Rights Abuses in Third Countries*, 2015/2315(INI)), 18 March 2016.

9 See EP, Committee on Foreign Affairs, *Amendments 1-257 on (2015/2315(INI))*, April 28, 2016, and *European Parliament resolution of 25 October 2016 on Corporate Liability for Serious Human Rights Abuses in Third Countries*, 2015/2315(INI).

10 *Regulation (EU) No. 1215/2012 of the European Parliament and of the Council of 12 December 2012 on Jurisdiction and the Recognition and Enforcement of Judgments in Civil and Commercial Matters (Recast)* (hereafter: Brussels-I Regulation).

and the Lugano Convention[11] – which partially harmonizes the rules on civil jurisdiction in European States. It discusses to what extent the regime applies to FDL cases against corporate defendants and how it has impacted such disputes. Second, the chapter explores some possibilities under residual grounds for jurisdiction in the EU Member States, examining three specific doctrines that have either already been used, or may hold promise for future claims. These two perspectives follow from the recommendations made by both the CoE and the EP's Committee on Foreign Affairs, concerning the extension of the Brussels-I Regulation, the extension of the possibility to join claims against corporate defendants, and the introduction of forum of necessity and asset jurisdiction. Finally, the chapter concludes with an evaluation of these proposals.

Jurisdiction under the Brussels-I Regime

The main instrument relevant to jurisdiction in transnational tort cases is the Brussels-I regime, constituted by the Brussels-I Regulation and the Lugano Convention. This regime lays down the rules for jurisdiction for contractual and non-contractual liability in Europe. The Regulation currently in force was preceded by the Brussels Convention of 1968[12] and by the previous Regulation 44/2001.[13] The current Regulation was adopted in 2012 after a recasting process and is sometimes referred to as Brussels-I *bis*. The Regulation is supplemented by the Lugano Convention of 2007, concluded between the EU, Denmark, and several States of the European Free Trade Association.[14] The Lugano Convention extends the Brussels-I regime to these non-EU States, and its provisions are the most similar to the Regulation. However, there are certain differences not pertaining to the discussion at hand.[15]

Scope and Purpose of the Regulation

The Regulation's purpose, stated in the Recitals[16] and clarified by the case law of the ECJ, culminates in four main objectives: (1) the free movement of

11 *Convention on Jurisdiction and the Recognition and Enforcement of Judgments in Civil and Commercial Matters of 30 October 2007* (hereafter Lugano Convention), entered into force on 1 January 2010, replacing the previous Lugano Convention of 1988.

12 *Convention on Jurisdiction and the Enforcement of Judgments in Civil and Commercial Matters Signed at Brussels, 27 September 1968.* Official Journal L 299, 31 December 1972.

13 Note that at the time of adoption not every Member State was covered by the Regulation; the UK and Ireland have since opted in, whereas Denmark is a party to the Lugano Convention.

14 Specifically, Iceland, Norway and Switzerland. As Denmark has the option to opt into certain EU laws and policies, it signed the Lugano Convention as a separate party.

15 See T. Hartley, *Civil Jurisdiction and Judgments in Europe*. Oxford: Oxford University Press, 2017, 6.

16 See A. Dickinson and E. Lein (eds), *The Brussels I Regulation Recast*. Oxford: Oxford University Press, 2015, 21.

judgments;[17] (2) the protection of EU-based defendants and weaker parties;[18] (3) legal certainty for litigating parties;[19] and (4) the promotion of mutual trust in each other's legal systems.[20] This has been further confirmed by the ECJ in *Handte v TMCS*,[21] where the Court emphasized the 'greatest possible degree of legal certainty' as the purpose of the 1968 Brussels Convention. Legal certainty, combined with the presumption that it is easiest to defend oneself in the courts of one's own state of domicile, reflects the Convention's general purpose of strengthening legal protection of EU citizens. This in turn benefits the internal market, as a higher level of legal certainty and predictability enables transnational interactions.

This purpose also follows the limited formal and territorial scope of the Regulation. Since it is intended to support the internal market, the Regulation is distributive in nature, rather than attributive, it divides jurisdictional competence between the Member States, but says little about how the Member States relate to third states. Thus, it does not fully harmonize the rules on jurisdiction of the Member States, but only applies to cases against defendants domiciled in an EU Member State.[22] In cases that fall outside of the scope of the Brussels-I regime, jurisdiction has to be assessed according to the domestic private international law of the particular Member State where the case is brought. There are certain exceptions to this rule, but domicile is the 'pivotal' criterion for applying the Brussels regime.[23] It is notable that the original European Commission's proposal for the recast Regulation currently in force would have extended its scope to all defendants, including those outside of the EU, but this was rejected by the Member States and the EP.[24]

The Regulation has a closed nature, meaning that it precludes the application of domestic rules or doctrines in cases that fall within the scope of the Regulation. In the landmark case *Owusu v Jackson*,[25] the ECJ discussed the nature of the Regulation and how it relates to other jurisdictional doctrines applied by the Member States. The case concerned the question of whether English courts could stay a case on the basis of *forum non conveniens*, when the defendant was domiciled in an EU Member State, but the facts were more connected to a non-Member State. The ECJ held that Article 2 of the Brussels Convention (now

17 See Brussels-I Regulation, Recitals 4, 6, 26 and 27.

18 Ibid., Recitals 14, 15 and 18.

19 Ibid., Recitals 15 and 16.

20 Ibid., Recital 26.

21 ECJ, *Handte v. TMCS*, C-26/91, 17 June 1992.

22 See Art. 4(1) Brussels-I Regulation: 'Subject to this Regulation, persons domiciled in a Member State shall, whatever their nationality, be sued in the courts of that Member State'.

23 Most notably in cases concerning employment, insurance or consumer contracts and where parties agree to submit their case before the courts of a Member State, see below.

24 See European Commission, *Proposal for a Regulation of the European Parliament and of the Council on Jurisdiction and the Recognition and Enforcement of Judgments in Civil and Commercial Matters (Recast)*, COM(2010) 748 final, 16 December 2010.

25 ECJ, *Owusu v. Jackson*, C-281/02, 1 March 2005, para. 8 (hereinafter '*Owusu*').

Article 4(1) of the Regulation) could only be derogated from in ways expressly provided for in the Brussels-I regime itself. As legal certainty through uniform application is the cornerstone of the regime, the ECJ concluded that doctrines such as *forum non conveniens* (hereinafter 'FNC') that only exist in some Member States, would undermine that uniform application.[26] Moreover, defendants can best conduct their defence in the courts of their domicile, rather than a foreign court that they are unable to reasonably foresee being sued in.[27]

Core Principles

The main rule of the Regulation is that claims should be brought where the defendant has his or her domicile.[28] Determination of domicile is different for natural persons and legal persons. For natural persons, domicile is determined by national law.[29] For legal persons, domicile under the Regulation is determined in accordance with Article 63(1), which defines domicile as the state where a company or other legal person has its statutory seat, central administration or principal place of business. These may be in different states, leaving the choice where to bring the claim up to the plaintiff in a particular case.

In order to ensure the highest degree of certainty, the interpretation of Article 63 is autonomous, meaning it is not contingent on the domestic law of the Member States.[30] Statutory seat refers to the place where the company is formally incorporated, according to its internal articles of incorporation.[31] Central administration and principal place of business require a more factual assessment of the company's operations.[32] The former refers to the place where the company takes its 'essential business decisions', whereas the latter is where the most important business dealings take place, most of the important

26 Ibid., para. 38: 'Respect for the principle of legal certainty, which is one of the objectives of the Brussels Convention (see, inter alia, Case C-440/97 *GIE Groupe Concorde and Others* [1999] ECR I-6307, paragraph 23, and Case C-256/00 *Besix* [2002] ECR I-1699, paragraph 24), would not be fully guaranteed if the court having jurisdiction under the Convention had to be allowed to apply the *forum non conveniens* doctrine', and para. 41, 'Application of the *forum non conveniens* doctrine, which allows the court seised [sic] a wide discretion as regards the question whether a foreign court would be a more appropriate forum for the trial of an action, is liable to undermine the predictability of the rules of jurisdiction laid down by the Brussels Convention, in particular that of Article 2, and consequently to undermine the principle of legal certainty, which is the basis of the Convention'.

27 See *Owusu*, op. cit., para. 42. See also ECJ, *Turner v Grovit*, C-159/02, 17 April 2004.

28 See Regulation, art. 4(1).

29 Ibid., art. 62 and Hartley, *Civil Jurisdiction and Judgments in Europe*, op. cit., 92–93.

30 Ibid., preamble, at (11).

31 Ibid., art. 63(1)(a).

32 Ibid., art. 63(1)(c). See P. Stone, *EU Private International Law*, 3rd ed. Cheltenham: Edward Elgar, 2014, p. 71, citing Court of Appeals, *The 'Revia'*, [1991] 2 Lloyds Rep 325, and Court of Appeals, *Young v Anglo American South Africa Ltd and others* [2014], EWCA Civ 1130, July 31, 2014.

personnel and assets are concentrated, and/or where most of its commercial activity takes place.

The Brussels-I Regime further provides for a number of special rules for jurisdiction for specific cases, such as tort cases, over which the court of the place where the harm occurred can exercise jurisdiction.[33] However, these rules are only applicable when cases fall within the scope of the Regulation and are not applicable to cases against non-EU domiciled defendants. Third-party state defendants can voluntarily submit to the jurisdiction of an EU domestic court, pursuant to a choice of a court agreement, bringing the claim within the scope of the Regulation. Such agreements are, however, rare in tort cases.[34] The Regulation does contain special *lis pendens* rules that also apply where related actions are pending in third states,[35] allowing EU courts to stay proceedings in a Member State, if similar proceedings are pending elsewhere. In contrast to the *lis pendens* rules concerning similar actions in Member States, EU courts have more discretion to continue the proceedings, for example when they are unlikely to be concluded within a reasonable time or to be enforced.[36] While these rules do not extend the jurisdiction of EU domestic courts, they do give the option to examine third-party state proceedings and decide whether or not to stay a case.

Relevance to FDL Cases

As may already be clear from the above description, the distributive nature of the Regulation means that the Brussels-I regime is not entirely applicable to FDL cases. Only claims against EU-domiciled parent companies fall within the scope of the Regulation and not those against foreign-domiciled subsidiaries. In the English case, *Vava v. AASA*[37] and its companion case *Young v. AASA*,[38] claimants tried to make the argument that the central administration of the South African subsidiary lay with its English parent company. This would have made the subsidiary 'domiciled' in the UK under Article 63(1) of the Regulation and allowed the court to exercise jurisdiction over it.

This argument was dismissed by the Court of Appeals in *Young*, arguing that 'central administration' should be assessed for each individual entity rather than

33 Regulation, arts. 7–8.

34 One exception is High Court of Justice, Queen's Bench Division, *The Bodo Community and Others v The Shell Petroleum Company of Nigeria Limited,* [2014] EWHC 1973 (TCC), 20 June 2014, where subsidiary SPDC accepted jurisdiction of an English court if the claimants dropped their claim against parent company Royal Dutch Shell.

35 See Regulation, art. 33.

36 Ibid., art. 33(1) and 33(2).

37 High Court of Justice, Queen's Bench Division, *Vava v Anglo American South Africa Ltd* [2013] EWHC 2131, 24 July 2013.

38 Court of Appeals, *Young v Anglo American South Africa Ltd and Others* [2014], EWCA Civ 1130, 31 July 2014.

for the entire corporate group and that the relevant decision-making took place at the subsidiary, not the parent.[39] While this case is only one domestic case, the Court made explicit reference to the rulings of other European domestic courts, an opinion issued by AG Darmon before the ECJ,[40] and several authoritative reports.[41] Consequently, it will likely be hard to raise similar arguments in future cases. Only when the parent company is said to have usurped the activities of its subsidiary and has taken substantial business decisions at the corporate headquarters, can it be said to have its central administration there.

Given that the Regulation in principle respects the separation of corporate legal personalities, it has a significant impact on FDL cases. This in particular concerns the rejection of FNC in cases within the scope of the Regulation, following the *Owusu* case cited above. Early B&HR cases featured protracted FNC litigation,[42] being a major bar even to claims against locally domiciled parent companies. While in these cases courts eventually sided with the plaintiffs and rejected the defendant companies' FNC arguments, this added years to the disputes' length and drained resources. Following *Owusu* however, English courts have structurally rejected motions to dismiss on the basis of FNC. Nonetheless, as recently as 2017, companies have tried to raise this defence even in cases against parent companies.[43]

Thus, the Regulation can be said to be the foundation of the current trend of B&HR claims in the EU.[44] It is also of indirect relevance because of its influence on Member State domestic law. Some Member States have extended the application of the Regulation to cases falling outside its scope,[45] whereas others have their courts interpreting domestic rules in conformity with the provisions of the Regulation on their own accord. For example, Dutch courts in the case *Akpan and Vereniging Milieudefensie v. Shell*[46] have, on request of the defendants, applied the ECJ case law to joined claims under domestic law, as discussed more extensively below. In this way, amendments to the Regulation or the

39 Ibid., paras. 38–43.

40 ECJ, *R v HM Treasury ex parte Daily Mail and General Trust PLC*, C-81/87, 27 September 1988, p. 453C, cited in *Young,* at paras. 41–42.

41 Ibid.

42 See in particular: House of Lord, *Connelly v RTZ Corporation plc* [1997] UKHL 30, [1999] CLC 533, 27 July 1997 (hereinafter 'Connelly'); House of Lords, *Lubbe & Ors. v. Cape plc.*, HoL [2000] 2 Lloyd's Rep., 20 July 2000, 383, No. 20 (hereinafter 'Lubbe').

43 See in particular High Court of Justice, Queen's Bench Division, *Dominic Liswaniso Lungowe & Others v Vedanta Resources Plc & Konkola Copper Mines Plc* [2016] EWHC 975 (TCC), 27 May 2016.

44 Wouters and Ryngaert have argued that even before *Owusu, forum non conveniens* was on the decline in the UK, at least in business and human rights cases, see J. Wouters and C. Ryngaert, 'Litigation for overseas corporate human rights abuses in the European Union: the challenge of jurisdiction'. *The George Washington International Law Review*, 2009, 40, 961–962.

45 See for instance Italian Law No. 218 of 31 May 1995, art. 3.

46 See Rechtbank Den Haag, *Akpan et al. and Stichting Milieudefensie v. Royal Dutch Shell,* ECLI:NL:RBDHA:2013:BY9854, 30 January 2013.

Lugano Convention and their interpretation by the ECJ can also affect claims filed under domestic law – including FDL cases.

The *lis pendens* rules of the Regulation have thus far not played a role in FDL cases, but may become relevant in the future. One can imagine situations where claims have been filed in the states where the impugned harms occurred, but that have been pending before local courts for an unreasonable amount of time. Alternatively, when harms concern entire communities, it is thinkable that some community members file lawsuits in local courts and others file in foreign – European – courts. Lastly, corporations have sometimes filed countersuits in local courts to frustrate European procedures.[47] In such situations, it will be interesting to see whether courts have the discretion under the Regulation's *lis pendens* rules to allow European proceedings to continue, or whether proceedings are stayed in favour of third state litigation.

Residual Jurisdiction in the Member States

As mentioned, the Brussels-I Regime only applies to cases that fall within its scope. Jurisdiction over claims against non-EU domiciled defendants has to be resolved according to the domestic law of the Member State where the claim is filed, the so-called 'residual' rules on jurisdiction.[48] Whereas the Regulation incorporates national doctrines of jurisdiction into the regime, individual domestic systems have also grown closer to the Brussels-I regime even when it does not formally apply. Nevertheless, a number of doctrines have persisted in Member States' law that may be of particular relevance to FDL cases. These are, in order of discussion, the possibility to join claims against defendants within and outside the court's jurisdiction, forum of necessity and jurisdiction based on the presence of assets in the forum.

Connecting Claims

In most EU Member States, it is possible to join claims with the same factual or legal basis together before the same court, in order to allow for expedient treatment of the case and prevent conflicting outcomes. Indeed, this is also possible under Article 8(1) Brussels-I Regulation,[49] if both claims are within its scope. Most domestic systems provide for similar requirements, i.e. that courts have ordinary jurisdiction over both defendants before the claims can be joined.

47 See High Court of Justice, Queens Bench Division, *Kesabo v African Barrick Gold Plc* [2013] EWHC 3198, 23 October 2013.

48 These rules have been categorized in a study by Professor Arnaud Nuyts, cited extensively below. See A. Nuyts, *Study on Residual Jurisdiction (Review of the Member States' Rules Concerning the 'Residual Jurisdiction' of their Courts in Civil and Commercial Matters Pursuant to the Brussels I and II Regulations)*, General Report, 3rd version, 6 July 2007.

49 See ECJ, *Roche Nederland v. Primus and Goldenberg*, C-539/03, 13 July 2006, and *Painer v. Standard VerlagsGmbH*, C-145/10, 7 March 2013, on copyright infringements.

In some systems however, claims against defendants normally outside of the court's jurisdiction can be joined with claims against defendants who are within the court's jurisdiction; specifically, claims against foreign-domiciled subsidiaries can be joined with claims against locally domiciled parent companies.

Two particular examples of this are English law and Dutch law. Under English law, courts can assume jurisdiction over foreign-domiciled defendants, if the court has jurisdiction over another defendant under the Brussels Regulation or common law, and the foreign defendant is a necessary and proper party to the claim.[50] No other connection with the forum is required, but the claimant must demonstrate that he/she has a 'good arguable case' against the foreign defendants to get permission to serve the claim against them. In the Netherlands, claims can be joined under Article 7(1) of the Code of Civil Procedure (*Rechtsvordering*, hereinafter 'Rv'), provided that the court has ordinary jurisdiction over at least one of the defendants. In principle, only a factual connection between the claims is required, and they need not necessarily be litigated on the same legal basis,[51] although the bases must on some level relate to merit joint discussion by the court.

Connecting claims has thus far been the primary way in which claimants have tried to get EU domestic courts to assert jurisdiction over foreign-domiciled subsidiaries, at least in the UK and the Netherlands.[52] The appeal of this construction is clear: pursuant to the Regulation, courts cannot refuse jurisdiction over parent companies, so a claim against a parent company can be used to 'anchor' a claim against the subsidiary. Its benefit is, however, more than just procedural: most European FDL cases have addressed the division of responsibilities between parents and subsidiaries, so it appears logical to assess the merits of these arguments together before the same court.

Forum of Necessity

Another concept common to several EU Member States and often cited in the context of jurisdiction as a condition for access to justice is forum of necessity, or *forum necessitatis*. Forum of necessity allows courts to assume jurisdiction over a claim even if there is no ordinary ground for jurisdiction, but declining to hear the case will lead to denial of justice for the claimant. Most states consider forum of necessity jurisdiction to follow from Article 6(1) of the ECHR, as a

50 Civil Procedure Rules (1998) S.I. 1998/3132, RSC Order 11, Rule 1(1)(c).

51 Art. 7(1) Rv.

52 Compare High Court of Justice, Queen's Bench Division, *Dominic Liswaniso Lungowe & Others v Vedanta Resources Plc & Konkola Copper Mines Plc*, [2016] EWHC 975 (TCC), 27 May 2016 (hereinafter 'Lungowe'); High Court of Justice, Queen's Bench Division, *HRH Emere Godwin Bebe Okpabi v Royal Dutch Shell plc & Shell Petroleum Development Company of Nigeria Ltd* [2017] EWHC 89 (TCC), 26 January 2017; and High Court of Justice, Queen's Bench Division, *AAA and Others v Unilever PLC and Unilever Tea Kenya Limited*, 27 February 2017 [2017] EWHC 371(QB), and the *Akpan* above.

corollary to the obligation to prevent a denial of justice,[53] although this has not been confirmed by the ECtHR.[54]

Necessity jurisdiction is provided for by different Member States, both in statutory law and case law,[55] and is theoretically possible in others. The most elaborate form arguably is established in the law of the Netherlands where a court can assume jurisdiction if there is no alternative forum available under Article 9(b) of the Code of Civil Procedure. Alternatively, a court can assume jurisdiction if there is an alternative forum, but it is unreasonable to require the plaintiff to turn to that forum, and there is some connection with the Netherlands under Article 9(c).[56] Most other states that recognize necessity jurisdiction also require a connection with the forum when it is absolutely impossible to bring proceedings elsewhere. Examples of these are Switzerland,[57] Belgium,[58] Portugal[59] and France.[60]

What factors lead to either impossibility or unreasonableness to bring proceedings can vary. Natural disasters or armed conflicts destroying the legal infrastructures are often mentioned as an example of impossibility.[61] Unreasonableness is often based on the particular circumstances of the claimant in relation to the case. An example of unreasonableness was given in a 2012 tort case concerning a Palestinian refugee against Libyan state agents accused of torture. According to the District Court of The Hague, even while some of the legal infrastructures still existed after the Libyan civil war, the plaintiff had reason to

53 See ECtHR, *Golder v. the United Kingdom*, App. No. 4451/70, 21 February 1975. L. Strikwerda, *Inleiding tot het Nederlandse Internationaal Privaatrecht*. Deventer: Kluwer, 2012, 234–235. See for example in the Dutch context Kamerstukken II 1999–2000, 26 855, No. 3, outlining the rationale behind introducing forum of necessity in the procedural law of the Netherlands.

54 See ECtHR, *Naït-Liman v Switzerland*, App. No. 2016, 21 June 2016 (hereinafter '*Naït-Liman*').

55 See for a more general discussion, L. Roorda and C. Ryngaert, 'Business and human rights litigation in Europe and Canada: the promises of *forum of necessity*-based Jurisdiction'. *Rabels Zeitschrift für ausländisches und internationales Privatrecht*, 2016. See also F. Ibili, *Gewogen rechtsmacht in het IPR*. The Hague: Kluwer, 2007, 108.

56 Ibili refers to these varieties as absolute and relative forum of necessity respectively. See Ibili, *Gewogen rechtsmacht in het IPR*, op. cit.

57 'If this Code does not provide for jurisdiction in Switzerland and if proceedings abroad are impossible or cannot reasonably be required to be brought, the Swiss judicial or administrative authorities at the place with which the facts of the case are sufficiently connected shall have jurisdiction', see art. 3 of Bundesgesetz über das Internationale Privatrecht (IPRG), 18 December 1987, SR 291; English translation by Andreas Bucher, available at www.andreasbucher-law.ch (last accessed 10 March 2018).

58 Art. 11 Wet houdende het Wetboek van Internationaal Privaatrecht (*Code of Private International Law*).

59 Civil Procedure Code, arts. 62, 65. CPC 1961.

60 French necessity jurisdiction has developed from case law, see S. Redfield, 'Searching for justice: the use of forum necessitatis'. *Georgetown Journal of International Law*, 2014, 45, 911.

61 See Gerechtshof (*Court of Appeals*) Den Haag, *Solvochem v Rasheed Bank*, ECLI:NL:GHSGR:2010:BO6529, 30 November 2010 regarding execution of a claim on the basis of breach of contract that could not be adjudicated in Iraq.

fear for his safety when returning to Libya to file his claim. Therefore, forum of necessity was granted under Article 9(c) Rv.[62] French courts have interpreted 'impossibility' quite widely, so that it more resembles Dutch 'unreasonableness'; for example, plaintiffs facing 'serious threats' back home may bring their case to France under necessity jurisdiction.[63] Belgian courts have accepted financial burdens as a possible ground for unreasonableness,[64] whereas this has been explicitly excluded in the Netherlands.[65]

A second requirement is that the case must have at least some connection with the forum state. The ECtHR has discussed the connection requirement in *Naït-Liman v. Switzerland*, thus far the only case dealing with necessity jurisdiction. The Court held that requiring connection is a legitimate and proportional restriction that is well accepted amongst the states that recognize necessity jurisdiction,[66] even when it is unreasonable to ask the plaintiff to avail him or herself of the more natural forum. Different connections may entail a 'sufficient connection', ranging from residence of the plaintiff in the forum state to the presence of assets of the defendant.[67] French courts have interpreted the necessary connection with France relatively widely, including residence and perhaps even financial connections.[68] However, not all cases require a connection with the forum: for instance the Dutch Code of Civil Procedure does not require a connection if it is wholly impossible to bring the dispute outside of the Netherlands.[69]

Interestingly, necessity jurisdiction has only been argued in one B&HR-related case in Europe. It was accepted by a French court in the *COMILOG* case, an employment case relating to the unfair dismissal of Congolese workers of a Gabonese logging company, later acquired by a French multinational.[70] The court considered that pursuant to a deal between the defendant and the governments of Gabon and Congo their case could not be heard there, and declining

62 See Rechtbank (*District Court*) Den Haag, *El-Hojouj v Unnamed Libyan Officials*, ECLI:NL:RBSGR:2012:BV9748, 21 March 2012.

63 Redfield, 'Searching for justice: the use of forum necessitatis', op. cit., 912, citing Cour d'Appel, Aix-en-Provence, 31 May 1923, *Journal du Droit International*, 1924, 204.

64 See Nuyts, *Study on Residual Jurisdiction*, op. cit., 85.

65 Ibid., *Gewogen rechtsmacht in het IPR*, op. cit., 133–134.

66 See *Naït-Liman* op. cit. Note that other than in *El-Houjouj* where the plaintiff had been granted asylum because of his persecution by the Libyan state, the presence of the plaintiff in *Naït-Liman* in the forum was unrelated to the facts underlying the case.

67 It should be noted that these factors need to be distinguished from *forum actoris* and asset jurisdiction per se; in fact, the plaintiff's presence in the forum state was 'blacklisted' as an exorbitant ground for jurisdiction under the Hague Conference Preliminary Draft Convention on Jurisdiction and Judgments, Summary of the Outcome of the Discussion in Commission II of the First Part of the Diplomatic Conference, 6–20 June 2001.

68 Cour d'Appel de Paris, 10 November 1960, *Journal du Droit International*, 1961, 426.

69 Art. 9(b) Rv.

70 See Cour d'Appel de Paris, Arrêt du 10 Septembre 2015, S11/05955 S11/05956 S/1105957 S11/05958 S11/05959 S11/05960.

jurisdiction would have resulted in denial of justice; the necessary link with France was found in the acquisition of COMILOG by the French multinational ERAMET.

It should however be noted that the FNC litigation in the early English cases did feature similar discussions where courts weighed the existence of a more 'natural' foreign forum against the factors linking the case to English jurisdiction, including the claimants' perspectives of achieving substantial justice in that foreign alternative forum.[71] While this is strictly not the same as necessity jurisdiction, such considerations may be informative for future litigation where the necessity argument is raised.

Jurisdiction over Assets

Another ground present in some Member States' domestic law is jurisdiction based on the location of assets of the defendant in the forum. Most states do recognize that courts can exercise jurisdiction over claims regarding such assets, and even have exclusive jurisdiction when such claims relate to immovable property. Pursuant to a few domestic laws however, plaintiffs can assert general jurisdiction over a defendant in a state where that defendant has assets, even when the claim is unrelated to those assets. The rationale behind this doctrine is that any damages that may be awarded are easily enforceable in the forum, instead of having to be recognized and enforced in another state. Asset jurisdiction has thus far not been raised as an argument in B&HR-related cases, nor have there been cases where foreign subsidiaries had assets supporting asset jurisdiction. Nevertheless, it was raised by the draft EP report as a recommendation for jurisdictional reform in EU Member States.[72]

Asset jurisdiction has been most closely associated with Swedish law,[73] under which, for a time, it was possible to litigate debt obligations in Sweden even if the value of the Swedish assets was small to negligible. This has become known to as the 'Swedish umbrella', referring to a situation where one would accidentally leave his umbrella in Sweden, and later find himself under the jurisdiction of a Swedish court for an unrelated claim.[74] Swedish courts have however later

71 See House of Lords, *Spiliada Maritime Corporation v. Cansulex Ltd* [1986] UKHL 10 [1987] AC 460, 19 November 1986, discussed in *Lubbe* and *Connelly*, op. cit.

72 See EP, Committee on Foreign Affairs, *Draft Report on Corporate Liability for Serious Human Rights Abuses in Third Countries*, 2015/2315(INI), 18 March 2016, 28.

73 See Swedish Code of Judicial Procedure (SFS 1942: 740), Ch. 10, Section 3, para. 1.

74 As observed in H. Smit, 'Common and civil law rules of in personam adjudicatory authority: an analysis of underlying policies'. *The International and Comparative Law Quarterly*, 1972, 21, No. 2. This problem has since then been repeatedly used as an example of exorbitant jurisdiction; see for example A. Cassese (ed.), *Realizing Utopia: The Future of International Law*. Oxford: Oxford University Press, 2012, 631, and C. Nwapi, 'Jurisdiction by necessity and the regulation of the transnational corporate actor'. *Utrecht Journal of International and European Law*, 2014, 30, 1, footnote 31.

limited the reach of this statute, holding that the value of the claim may not be disproportionate to the value of the asset.[75] Asset jurisdiction has also been recognized in Germany.[76] Here too, courts have later limited the extent of this ground: pursuant to a 1991 case of the German Supreme Court (*Bundesgerichthof*), cases now need a 'genuine connection' with Germany for the court to assert jurisdiction over the defendant through the location of assets.[77] Moreover, it has been suggested in the literature that the same limitation as in Sweden would apply here, namely that the value of the claim has to be proportional to the value of the assets.[78]

Discussion

If we accept that jurisdiction is a relevant barrier to judicial remedy, the question here is whether a broader adoption of the doctrines discussed above would improve access to remedy in EU FDL cases. The discussion here is based on recommendations made by the CoE's Committee of Ministers and the Draft Recommendations of the EP's Committee of Foreign Affairs.[79]

The first point of discussion is the Brussels-I Regulation. The CoE's Committee of Ministers has recommended non-EU states that are members of the CoE to accede to the Lugano Convention, whereas the Draft EP recommendations argued for extending the Brussels regime to cases against third state-domiciled defendants. Starting with the latter, this is unlikely in the near future; in the recent recasting process, a Commission proposal to that end was rejected by both the Member States and the EP. The main argument for this rejection was that the Regulation's distributive nature is based on the principle of mutual trust in each other's legal systems, a condition not fulfilled with regard to third states. Moreover, from the perspective of victims it is even questionable whether such an extension would be desirable; in fact it would imply that broader doctrines, such as those discussed above, would no longer be available in cases

75 See U. Maunsbach, 'Some reflexions concerning jurisdiction in cases on cross-border trademark infringements through the internet'. *Scandinavian Studies in Law*, 2004, 47, 510, referring to case NJA 1981, 386.

76 Code of Civil Procedure (*Zivilprozeßordnung*), section 23.

77 BGH 2.7.1991, Neue Juristische Wochenschrift (N.J.W.) 1991, 3092.

78 See also G. Dahnemann, 'Jurisdiction based on the presence of assets in Germany: a case note'. *The International and Comparative Law Quarterly*, 1992, 41.

79 It should be noted that the UNCESCR recently adopted General Comment No. 24 on state obligations under the ICESCR in the context of business activities, which also recommended restraint in the application of *forum non conveniens*; for the purposes here, it is assumed that accession to the Lugano Convention and adoption of the Brussels-I regime answers to that call. See UNCESCR, *General comment No. 24 (2017) on State Obligations under the International Covenant on Economic, Social and Cultural Rights in the Context of Business Activities*, 10 August 2017, UN Doc. E/C.12/GC/24, paras. 43–44.

against non-EU domiciled defendants, who would thus have to be sued in their countries of origin.[80]

Broader accession to the Brussels regime via the Lugano Convention would in that respect be more interesting. First, it would create a more uniform jurisdictional regime across Europe – not just within the EU. While the regime is designed primarily to improve legal certainty for defendants, clear and unequivocal rules also benefit claimants.[81] Second, insofar as newly acceding states would have domestic doctrines allowing courts to decline jurisdiction, these would be precluded by the Brussels Regime, possibly increasing access to court. Nevertheless, these benefits are somewhat speculative; it is unknown whether there have been cases filed in non-EU CoE Member States that were rejected on this basis.

On a separate note, at the time of writing, the negotiations on the departure of the UK from the EU ('Brexit') are still ongoing. The conditions, under which this departure will take place, or even whether the departure will be finalized at all, are still unclear. This has some consequences for the discussion above. As the majority of cases in the EU have taken place in the UK, and the Brussels regime has had a significant impact on the rules related to jurisdiction in the UK – in particular, on the rejection of *forum non conveniens* – the departure of the UK from the Brussels regime could have a major effect on the viability of FDL cases in Europe. This could be remedied by the UK acceding to the Lugano Convention, but it remains to be seen whether this will happen and under what conditions.[82]

Concerning the residual grounds under domestic law discussed here, a couple of remarks can be added concerning the extent to which they are relevant to FDL cases. Jurisdiction over assets has been raised as a hypothetical possibility, but there has been no case so far where the subsidiary had assets in the state of its parent company, let alone assets that would satisfy the requirements to assert jurisdiction. Given the foreign direct investment-structure by which corporate groups are generally organized,[83] it is more often the case that the parent has assets in the place of the subsidiary's domicile, not the other way around.

Joining claims seems to offer better prospects, it having been the primary way in which courts have asserted jurisdiction over corporate defendants domiciled outside of the EU, as discussed above. What this would require is for

80 The Commission proposal did include a *forum necessitatis* provision, which is also mentioned in the Draft EP Recommendation, but, as discussed here as well, it is questionable whether this uniform application of necessity would be the appropriate counterbalance.

81 This would include benefiting from uniform interpretation by the ECJ. See ECJ, *The Lugano Convention*, Opinion 1–03, 7 February 2006.

82 The UK has lobbied to reinstate *forum non conveniens* as a possibility under the Brussels-I Regulation in the Regulation's recasting process, in contravention of *Owusu*.

83 See for example P. Muchlinski, *Multinational Enterprises and the Law*, 2nd edn. Oxford: Oxford University Press, 2007, for a general reflection on the organizational structure of transnational corporate groups.

domestic courts to be able to join cases between defendants ordinarily within the court's jurisdiction and defendants ordinarily outside of it. This was indeed recommended by the CoE's Committee of Ministers.

However, recent cases before the English courts cast some doubt on the utility of the connected claims doctrine.[84] In particular, defendants have argued that the 'anchor' claims against the parent companies are without merit, and are merely empty vessels to persuade the courts to exercise jurisdiction over the subsidiary – the actual object of the claimant's complaints. The result of this defence has been mixed: the Court of Appeals in *Lungowe v Vedanta* rejected a motion to dismiss on these grounds, whereas the Court of Appeals in *Okpabi* did allow a similar motion and rejected the case. Much seems to depend on the degree of involvement of the parent with its subsidiary,[85] meaning that the strength of the 'necessary and proper party' argument is highly dependent on the substantive merits of the primary claim against the parent.

The Dutch Court of Appeals in the *Akpan* case did allow a very similar claim to proceed on the same grounds, applying the same substantive law as the *Okpabi* court.[86] The Dutch court, however, approached the issue from a more procedural perspective; its primary concern was whether the use of the connected claims doctrine under Article 7(1) Rv would amount to 'abuse of process'. The court then found that while the claim against the parent company only had a small chance of success, this was more than merely hypothetical and did not amount to abuse of process. Nevertheless, this is, thus far, the only decision by a Dutch court on this point, so it remains to be seen whether connected claims remain a viable ground for jurisdiction under Dutch law.

A couple of conclusions can be drawn from this comparison. First, the utility of the connected claims doctrine depends in a large part on the strength of the underlying claim against the parent company, which is a questionable development in and of itself.[87] Second, these recent cases have shown a divergence in how courts assess that strength, both between domestic English courts, as well as between English and Dutch courts. English courts do disagree on the type of evidence required to make a case against the parent company arguable, whereas English and Dutch courts disagree on taking a more substantive or procedural approach respectively. Third, the lawsuits filed under this doctrine all concern

84 See *Lungowe*, *Okpabi* and *AAA*, op. cit.

85 As required by *Caparo v. Dickman*, as interpreted in *Chandler v. Cape*. Compare E. Aristova, 'Suing TNCs in the English Courts: the challenge of jurisdiction', *Conflict Of Laws.net*, 1 February 2017, http://conflictoflaws.net/2017/suing-tncs-in-the-english-courts-the-challenge-of-jurisdiction/ (last accessed 27 February 2018) and L. Roorda, 'Okpabi v. Shell: a setback for business and human rights?'. *UCALL Blog*, 13 February 2017, http://blog.ucall.nl/index.php/2017/02/okpabi-v-shell-a-setback-for-business-and-human-rights/ (last accessed 5 March 2018).

86 See *Apkan* (Appeals), op. cit. Both cases concern facts occurred in Nigeria, and Nigerian substantive law has to be applied to both claims.

87 See L. Roorda, 'Okpabi v. Shell on appeal: foreign direct liability in troubled waters'. *Rights as Usual*, 23 February 2018, http://rightsasusual.com/?p=1194 (last accessed 27 February 2018).

cases from common law systems, where claims against parent companies were based on common law negligence. This may not be possible in cases coming from civil law systems, which may not have written or unwritten duties of care for parent companies pursuant to their domestic law.[88]

That leaves forum of necessity, which may be informative for future FDL cases. As forum of necessity has only been raised in one B&HR-related claim, it remains somewhat speculative as to whether this would be a viable way to litigate against foreign corporate defendants in EU courts. Much will depend on how courts will look at the consecutive requirements of impossibility or unreasonableness and connection to the forum. Factual impossibility is rare, and arguably does not apply to the above cases but is more than hypothetical: one can imagine litigation against private military or security companies for actions taken in conflict areas, where the legal infrastructure has entirely broken down,[89] or such companies have gotten immunity from local litigation.

With the current trend of EU FDL cases, arguing unreasonableness is more likely, while the basis for this could be that local courts are not able to process the type of complicated litigation these cases entail, moreover that there is no practical possibility to litigate for lack of legal assistance or legal aid, or that litigation is impossible because of local government corruption. The connection requirement would, as in the *COMILOG* case above, be found in the subsidiary's partial or whole ownership by the EU-domiciled parent company. On the other hand, as noted above, EU domestic courts have applied different standards to necessity litigation, so whether these arguments would be accepted is up for discussion. It is likely that most cases currently going on in EU domestic courts would not fall within the definition, as the doctrine has mostly been applied restrictively and only as a matter of last resort.[90]

Conclusion

The interaction between two parallel frameworks, the Brussels regime and the domestic law of the individual Member States, has created a somewhat confusing landscape for claimants looking for remedies regarding transnational corporate human rights abuses. From this landscape, opportunities have arisen that could benefit claimants, some of which have already been explored, some may still need to be tried, and some provide false perspectives. This chapter has given

88 Note that in such cases, the applicable law is the law of the state where the harm occurred, pursuant to the Rome II Regulation.

89 Such litigation has taken place in US courts under the Alien Tort Stature. See Court of Appeals for the 4th Circuit, *Al Shimari v. CACI Premier Technology, Inc.*, No. 15-1831 (4th Cir. 2016), 21 October 2016; District Court of Columbia, *Saleh v. Titan Corp.*, 436 F. Supp. 2d 55, 29 June 2006.

90 See Roorda and Ryngaert, 'Business and human rights litigation in Europe and Canada', op. cit.: Nwapi, 'Jurisdiction by necessity and the regulation of the transnational corporate actor', op. cit.; Redfield, 'Searching for justice: the use of forum necessitatis', op. cit.

a bird's eye view of this landscape, and examined those opportunities and their merits.

What has thus far been absent and may need more discussion is a more systematic approach of European states to this problem. Attention to jurisdiction as an issue to be addressed in domestic legal and policy reform has been lacking, let alone initiatives to actually start a reform. The NAPs currently published in the EU barely mention access to judicial remedies or jurisdiction, and it is indicative that all recommendations on jurisdiction in the EP Committee's draft report were amended out of the final version. Nevertheless, the continuing inflow of cases may eventually force states' hands, as their courts keep grappling with procedural litigation on jurisdiction over foreign corporate defendants in FDL disputes.

18 The Civil Liability of the Parent Company for the Acts or Omissions of Its Subsidiary

The Example of the *Shell* Cases in the UK and the Netherlands

Claire Bright

Introduction

In corporate law, under the principle of separate corporate personality, each legal entity forming the MNC has a distinct and autonomous legal personality and is normally liable separately. This principle prevents the automatic imposition of liability upon parent companies for the activities of their subsidiaries.[1] MNCs can therefore hide behind their corporate structure to ensure the immunity of parent companies – which generally hold most of the funds – for the acts or omissions of their subsidiaries. This largely contributes to the creation of the regulatory gap in which MNCs operate.[2] However, such artificial partitioning of legal personalities fails to take into consideration the fact that very often the parent company is the 'mind' of the entire MNC and the decisions it takes can have important consequences in the countries where its subsidiaries operate.[3]

Various litigation strategies have been elaborated with the aim of circumventing the corporate veil. In particular, a number of cases have focused on the direct liability of parent companies on the basis of an act (generally a decision at the origin of the damage) or an omission (a failure to act and take positive steps

1 P.I. Blumberg, 'Accountability of multinational corporations: the barriers presented by concepts of the corporate juridical entity'. *Hastings International and Comparative Law Review*, 2004, 24, 297–304.

2 M. Anderson, 'Transnational corporations and environmental damage: is tort law the answer?'. *Washburn Law Journal*, 2001, 401: 'The distinctive regulatory problem posed by MNCs is their ability to operate an integrated command and control system through two disaggregated institutional structures. The first of these structures is the collection of discrete corporate units – parent, subsidiary, sister, and cousin companies – that make up the MNC group. The second disaggregated structure housing the MNC is the global system of separate nation-states in which those corporations are registered and do business.'

3 C. Bright-Staath and B. Wray, 'Corporations and social environmental justice: the role of private international law'. In A. Duval and M.A. Moreau (eds), *Towards Social Environmental Justice?* EUI Working Papers, 2012, 75.

in order to prevent or remedy the damage).[4] The proceedings brought both in the Netherlands and in the UK against Shell in relation to the environmental damage caused by oil spills in the Niger Delta are particularly interesting in this respect.

Background of the Cases

The disputes arose out of oil spills that resulted in environmental damage which affected wide areas of land and water as well as the health and livelihood of various local communities in the Niger Delta.

In the Dutch case (the '*Milieudefensie* case'),[5] several separate proceedings were brought in the Netherlands by four Nigerian fishermen and farmers from the villages of Goi, Oruma and Ikot Ada Udo together with a Dutch NGO (Milieudefensie) against Shell and, more specifically, the parent company (Royal Dutch Shell, hereafter 'RDS', and former parent company Shell Petroleum) and its Nigerian subsidiary (Shell Petroleum Development Company of Nigeria, hereafter 'SPDC', and former subsidiary Shell Transport and Trading Company). The claimants were asking compensation for the environmental damage caused by oil spillages which affected their livelihoods. They were claiming that the damage was due to wrongful acts and negligence of both the subsidiary and the parent company. The claimants were also asking the defendant to remedy the soil and water pollution and make provisions for the prevention of new leakages and environmental damage.[6] This case is particularly important as it was the first time that a Dutch multinational corporation was sued in the Netherlands for environmental damage allegedly caused abroad by its foreign subsidiary.

In the English case (the '*Okpabi* case'),[7] proceedings were brought in the UK by approximately 42,500 Nigerian citizens against Shell – both the parent company (RDS) and the Nigerian subsidiary (SPDC) – seeking compensation for the oil pollution on similar grounds. This case followed the *Bodo* litigation,[8] which concerned a group of 15,000 Nigerian residents who brought proceedings in the UK against Shell, seeking compensation for oil spills in the areas of

4 FIDH, 'Corporate Accountability for human rights abuses: a guide for victims and NGOs on recourse mechanisms', 2016, www.fidh.org/IMG/pdf/corporate_accountability_guide_version_web.pdf (last accessed 5 March 2017).

5 Court of Appeal of The Hague, *Eric Barizaa Dooh of Goi and others v. Royal Dutch Shell Plc and Others*, 200.126.843 (case c) + 200.126.848 (case d), 18 December 2015, https://uitspraken.rechtspraak.nl/inziendocument?id=ECLI:NL:GHDHA:2015:3586 (last accessed 5 March 2018).

6 C. Bright, 'Quelques réflexions à propos de l'affaire Shell aux Pays-Bas'. In SFDI, *L'entreprise multinationale et le droit international*. Paris: A. Pédone, 2016, 127.

7 Court of Appeal, *His Royal Highness Emere Godwin Bebe Okpabi and Others v. Royal Dutch Shell Plc and Shell Petroleum Development Company of Nigeria Ltd*, [2018] EWCA Civ 191, 14 February 2018.

8 High Court, *The Bodo Community and others v Shell Petroleum Development Company of Nigeria Ltd*, [2014] EWHC 1973, 20 June 2014.

Bodo and Gokona. That case was settled for a total of £55 million plus costs prior to the substantive trial and SPDC admitted liability.

In both the *Milieudefensie* case and the *Okpabi* case, Shell disputed the international jurisdiction of the European courts.

The Issue of Jurisdiction

In the Dutch case, the court asserted its international jurisdiction regarding the claims against the parent company on the basis that it has its headquarters in the Netherlands. In application of EU Regulation 44/2001,[9] where a MNC has its statutory seat, central administration or principal place of business on the territory of a Member State, the forum of that State has jurisdiction to hear the case. With regard to the claims against the Nigerian subsidiary on the other hand, the Dutch court asserted its international jurisdiction on the ground of Dutch national law, and more specifically Article 7(1) of the Dutch Code of Civil Procedure which allows connected claims – here the claims against the parent company and the one against the subsidiary – to be heard by the same forum when 'the claims against the various defendants are connected to the extent that reasons of efficiency justify a joint hearing'.[10]

In the *Okpabi* case, the English court's jurisdiction in relation to RDS was based on Article 4 of the Recast Brussels Regulation, as Shell has its registered office in England.[11] The claimants had relied on English law to establish jurisdiction to try the claim against SPDC, and more particularly Paragraph 3.1(3) of Practice Direction 6B which provides that a claimant may serve a claim form out of the jurisdiction with the permission of the court where a claim is also made against another defendant and (a) there is between the claimant and the defendant a real issue which it is reasonable for the court to try; and (b) the claimant wishes to serve the claim form on another person who is a necessary or proper party to that claim.

9 *Council Regulation (EC) No. 44/2001 of 22 December 2000 on Jurisdiction and the Recognition and Enforcement of Judgments in Civil and Commercial Matters*. Article 2.1 of the Regulation 44/2001 provides that: 'Subject to this Regulation, persons domiciled in a Member State shall, whatever their nationality, be sued in the courts of that Member State.' Article 60(1) of the Regulation adds that: 'For the purposes of this Regulation, a company or other legal person or association of natural or legal persons is domiciled at the place where it has its: (a) statutory seat, or (b) central administration, or (c) principal place of business.'

10 Article 7(1) of the Dutch Code of Civil Procedure provides that: 'If legal proceedings are to be initiated by a writ of summons and a Dutch court has jurisdiction with respect to one of the defendants, then it has jurisdiction as well with respect to the other defendants who are called to the same proceedings, provided that the rights of action against the different defendants are connected with each other in such a way that a joint consideration is justified for reasons of efficiency.'

11 Art. 4 of the Recast Brussels Regulation is the successor of the art. 2 of the Regulation 44/2001 and has the same wording. Regulation (EU) No. 1215/2012 of the European Parliament and of the Council of 12 December 2012 on jurisdiction and the recognition and enforcement of judgments in civil and commercial matters (recast).

On appeal in the *Milieudefensie* case, Shell submitted that the initiating claims against the parent company on an evidently inadequate basis constituted an abuse of procedural law on the part of the claimants, merely designed as a means of bringing the action against the Nigerian subsidiary before the Dutch forum.[12] Similarly, in the *Okpabi* case, Shell argued that the claims had nothing to do with the English jurisdiction and should proceed in Nigeria. In particular, the defendants sustained that the claimants' strategy of bringing a claim against the parent company was 'a device being used cynically by the claimants' to bring claims, that would otherwise have no connection whatsoever with the English territory, to trial in the English courts.[13]

In both cases, Shell contended that the claims against the parent company were bound to fail.[14] As a result, both the English and the Dutch courts were called upon to decide on the likelihood that the claim against the parent company could be awarded.

The Duty of Care on the Part of a Parent Company Arising Out of Operations of a Subsidiary

The Okpabi *Case*

In the *Okpabi* case, the claimants argued that the parent company exercised a high degree of control and direction over the Nigerian subsidiary and that it owed them a duty of care in respect of the oil pollution that allegedly caused them damage. In particular, they alleged that the parent company breached that duty of care by failing to ensure that repeated oil leaks were expeditiously and effectively cleaned up in order to minimize the risk to their health, land and livelihoods, and by failing to take appropriate measures to address the well-known systemic problems of its operations in Nigeria – which included inadequate maintenance of the equipment and failure to protect pipelines from third party interference and to implement adequate systems for detecting leaks and shutting down pipelines – all failures which led to repeated oil spills.[15]

The first instance judge, Fraser J sitting as a judge in the Technology and Construction court in this case, gave a ruling upon preliminary issues of law,

12 https://milieudefensie.nl/publicaties/bezwaren-uitspraken/s-the-response-of-milieudefensie-and-the-nigerian-plaintiffs-to-shell2019s-argument-for-non-jurisdiction (last accessed 5 March 2018).

13 High Court, *His Royal Highness Emere Godwin Bebe Okpabi and Others v Royal Dutch Shell PLC and Shell Petroleum Development Company of Nigeria Ltd*, [2017] EWHC 89 (TCC), 26 January 2017, para. 16.

14 Ibid., para. 71; Court of Appeal of The Hague, *Eric Barizaa Dooh of Goi and others v. Royal Dutch Shell Plc and Others*, op. cit., para. 3.2. The test that should be applied is 'whether the claims against the parent company could possibly be awarded, which SPDC did not believe is possible.'

15 High Court, *His Royal Highness Emere Godwin Bebe Okpabi and Others v Royal Dutch Shell PLC and Shell Petroleum Development Company of Nigeria Ltd*, op. cit., para. 98.

after having considered a number of well-known cases on these issues. English case law has recognized that parent companies may owe a duty of care to the workers of their subsidiaries and the local communities directly affected by their operations.[16] As a result, a claim in negligence against a parent company arising out of the operations of its subsidiary might give rise to liability.[17] The court had formulated the question in these terms in the *Lubbe* case:[18]

> [w]hether a parent company which is proved to exercise de facto control over the operations of a (foreign) subsidiary and which knows, through its directors, that those operations involve risks to the health of workers employed by the subsidiary and/or persons in the vicinity of its factory or other business premises, owes a duty of care to those workers and/or other persons in relation to the control which it exercises over and the advice it gives to the subsidiary company?

In the case *Caparo v Dickman*,[19] the court set out a threefold test to decide whether a duty of care may arise in a particular case: the foreseeability of the harm, the proximity of the relationship between the parties and whether it would be fair, just and reasonable for such duty of care to be imposed.[20] A number of cases have since been rejected on the basis that they did not satisfy these criteria.[21]

The Court of Appeal recently reaffirmed the existence, in certain circumstances, of such duty of care in the case *Chandler v Cape*.[22] The court found that a parent company may, in certain circumstances, owe a duty of care for the health and safety of its subsidiary's employees. Arden LJ identified four factors which indicate the existence of a duty of care on the part of the parent company

16 C. Bright, 'Le devoir de diligence de la société mère dans la jurisprudence anglaise'. *Droit Social*, 2017, 828.

17 Court of Appeal, *Ngcobo and others v Thor Chemicals Holdings Ltd and others*, 9 October 1995 (unreported) in which Maurice Kay J stated that: 'the fact that the law does not impose liabilities upon companies in respect of the acts or omissions of other companies in the same group simply by reason of their common membership of the same group does not mean that circumstances cannot arise where in more than one company in the same group each incurs liabilities in respect of damage caused to a particular plaintiff.'

18 House of Lords, *Lubbe and others v Cape Plc*, [2000] 1WLR 1545, 20 July 2000.

19 House of Lords, *Caparo Industries Plc v Dickman*, [1990] 2 AC 605, 8 February 1990.

20 'What emerges is that, in addition to the foreseeability of damage, necessary ingredients in any situation giving rise to a duty of care are that there should exist between the party owing the duty and the party to whom it is owed a relationship characterised by the law as one of "proximity" or "neighbourhood" and that the situation should be one in which the court considers it fair, just and reasonable that the law should impose a duty of a given scope upon the one party for the benefit of the other.' Ibid., per Lord Bridge.

21 Court of Appeal, *Thompson v The Renwick Group Plc*, [2014] EWCA Civ 635, 13 May 2014; High Court, *AAA and others v Unilever Plc and Unilever Tea Kenya Limited*, [2017] EWHC 89 (TCC), 27 February 2017.

22 Court of Appeal, *Chandler v Cape*, [2012] EWCA Civ 525, 25 April 2012.

arising out of the operations of its subsidiary: (1) the businesses of the parent and subsidiary are in a relevant respect the same; (2) the parent has, or ought to have, superior knowledge on some relevant aspect of health and safety in the particular industry; (3) the subsidiary's system of work is unsafe as the parent company knew, or ought to have known; and (4) the parent knew or ought to have foreseen that the subsidiary or its employees would rely on its using that superior knowledge for employees' protection.[23]

Fraser J noted other factors were added to the list by Tomlinson LJ in the case *Thompson v The Renwick Group Plc*: the fact that the parent company is better placed, because of its superior knowledge or expertise than the subsidiary in respect of the harm; and that because of that feature, it is fair to infer that the subsidiary will rely upon the parent deploying its superior knowledge in order to avoid the harm.[24] Although the English courts have recognized that a duty of care is more likely to be found in respect of employees or former employees of the subsidiary,[25] in appropriate circumstances, claims arising out of the local communities adversely affected by the operations of the subsidiary might also give rise to liability.[26]

Relying on these well-established principles, Fraser J found that the second and third limbs (proximity and reasonableness) of the *Caparo* test were not satisfied. Fraser J considered that the relationship between the ultimate holding company of the Shell Group and the claimants in the Niger Delta was not a close one.[27] In addition, the judge found that RDS was not better placed than SPDC in respect of the harm and therefore that it was not fair to infer that, because of that feature, the subsidiary would rely upon the parent deploying its superior knowledge, in application of the principle described by Tomlison LJ in *Thompson v Renwick Group*.[28] The judge noted that (1) RDS did not hold shares directly in SPDC; (2) RDS did not conduct any operations in Nigeria; (3) only a minority (two) of officers of RDS sat on the Executive Committee of the Shell Group; (4) RDS was in fact not permitted to conduct operations in Nigeria due to licensing requirements; (5) there was a joint venture in existence engaged in such activity in Nigeria of which RDS was not a member; and (6) imposing a duty of care upon RDS would potentially impose 'liability in an indeterminate amount, for an indeterminate time, to an indeterminate class'.[29]

23 Ibid., para. 80.

24 High Court, *His Royal Highness Emere Godwin Bebe Okpabi and Others v Royal Dutch Shell PLC and Shell Petroleum Development Company of Nigeria Ltd*, op. cit., para. 79.

25 Court of Appeal, *Ngcobo and others v Thor Chemicals Holdings Ltd*, op. cit.; Court of Appeal, *Chandler v Cape*, op. cit.

26 House of Lords, *Lubbe and others v Cape Plc*, [2000] 1WLR 1545, 20 July 2000.

27 High Court, *His Royal Highness Emere Godwin Bebe Okpabi and Others v Royal Dutch Shell PLC and Shell Petroleum Development Company of Nigeria Ltd*, op. cit., para. 114.

28 Ibid., para. 117.

29 Ibid., para. 114.

With regard to the third limb of the *Caparo* test of reasonableness, the judge noted that (1) SPDC had statutory liability under the law of Nigeria for oil spills (which was one of strict liability) and that concepts of fairness, justice and reasonableness did not therefore require (or argue in favour of) the imposition of a duty of care upon RDS; (2) it was difficult to see how the test of fairness, justice and reasonableness could justify the claimants in seeking further and far wider damages from RDS than those to which they are entitled from SPDC; (3) RDS was prohibited, by the law of Nigeria, from performing operations in Nigeria; (4) RDS merely held shares in its subsidiaries as if it were an investment holding company; and (5) the relevant activities were carried out by SPDC as part of the joint venture with the Nigerian state.

In considering the factors listed by Arden LJ in *Chander v Cape*, the judge noted that (1) RDS was not operating the same business as SPDC and that, as the ultimate holding company, it limited itself to holding shares, and dealing with the financial matters that affected it; (2) RDS did not have superior or specialist knowledge compared to the subsidiary and in fact SPDC was the one with all the specialist knowledge relevant to a licensed operating company;[30] (3) RDS could have only a superficial knowledge or overview of the systems of work of SPDC and, given the scale of the activities of the many companies in the Shell Group, the degree of knowledge held by RDS could never sensibly be considered as comprehensive, or anything other than knowledge at a very high or superficial level; and (4) RDS could not be said to know that SPDC was relying upon it to protect the claimants as SPDC was a wholly autonomous subsidiary with considerable income and sizeable assets of its own and there was simply no evidence that SPDC ever did rely upon RDS.[31] The court affirmed that 'RDS simply has no experience whatsoever of oil operations in Nigeria, which is an extraordinarily difficult place to carry on such activities'.[32] And the court hence concluded:

> Absent the existence of proceedings on foot in England against RDS, there is simply no connection whatsoever between this jurisdiction and the claims brought by the claimants, who are Nigerian citizens, for breaches of statutory duty and/or in common law for acts and omissions in Nigeria, by a Nigeria company.[33]

On 14 February 2018, the Court of Appeal affirmed this decision on the basis (in the majority opinion) that that claimants could not demonstrate a properly arguable case that RDS owed them a duty of care. Such a decision can be ques-

30 Ibid., para. 116. Fraser J added: 'Indeed, rather to the contrary, SPDC has all the specialist knowledge relevant to an operating company licensed by the relevant Minister in the Nigerian Government under the relevant legislation. Its state of knowledge is far more specialist than, and wholly superior to, that of RDS so far as Nigeria is concerned.'

31 Ibid., para. 116.

32 Ibid., para. 117.

33 Ibid., para. 119.

tioned on various levels. First of all, the strict adherence to the principle of separate legal personality denies the economic reality of the unity of the various entities and the fact that the different components of the same group of companies are all connected. In addition, this decision negates the regulatory function that can and should be played by European courts as home states' forum in their duty to respect human rights.[34] Amnesty International warned that this ruling 'sets an especially dangerous precedent. If it stands, then the UK Courts have given free rein to multinational companies based in the UK to abuse human rights overseas. Poor communities and developing countries will pay the price.'[35]

This decision is in sharp contrast with the position adopted by the Court of Appeal of The Hague in the Dutch case.

The Milieudefensie *Case*

The District Court of The Hague had dismissed the claims from the villages of Goi and Oruma on the basis that the oils spills were the result of sabotage rather than poor maintenance of the materials and that the Nigerian subsidiary could not have prevented the leaks. The District Court found, however, that the Nigerian subsidiary was liable for the oil spills near the village of Ikot Ada Udo because it could easily have prevented this sabotage, and ordered the defendant to pay compensation. However the court rejected the claims against the parent company, finding that under Nigerian law there was no general duty of care on parent companies to prevent their subsidiaries from inflicting damage on others through their business operations.[36]

The Court of Appeal of The Hague reversed that ruling in its decision of 18 December 2015 and affirmed that: 'it cannot be ruled out in advance that a parent company may, in certain circumstances, be liable for damages resulting from acts or omissions of a (sub)subsidiary'.[37]

The claimants were arguing that the parent company knew or ought to have known about the systematic failure of the Nigerian subsidiary in terms of maintenance of the pipelines and that the resulting environmental damage was a foreseeable consequence of such failure. The claimants added that the parent company had the knowledge, possibilities and means to prevent it. In other words, the parent company was negligent and failed to adequately control and

34 C. Bright, 'L'accès à la justice civile en cas de violations des droits de l'homme par des entreprises multinationales [The Access to Civil Justice for Victims of Corporate Human Rights Violations]'. European University Institute, 2013, http://hdl.handle.net/1814/29602 (last accessed 5 March 2018).

35 www.amnesty.org/en/latest/news/2017/01/uk-shell-ruling-gives-green-light-for-corporations-to-profit-from-abuses-overseas/ (last accessed 4 March 2018).

36 District Court of The Hague, *Akpan v. Royal Dutch Shell Plc et al.*, C/09/337050/HA ZA 09-1580, 30 January 2013, para. 4.26.

37 Court of Appeal of the Hague, *Eric Barizaa Dooh of Goi and others v. Royal Dutch Shell Plc and Others*, op. cit., para. 3.2.

supervise the maintenance of the pipelines and the clean-up of oil spills in Nigeria. By failing to utilize its knowledge and control of its Nigerian subsidiary in such a way as to prevent the oil spill and its consequences, the parent company breached the duty of care that it owed to the Nigerian farmers and fishermen.[38]

The Court of Appeal of The Hague stated that:

> considering the foreseeable serious consequences of oil spills to the local environment from a potential spill source, it cannot be ruled out from the outset that the parent company may be expected in such a case to take an interest in preventing spills.[39]

The court added that the parent company may indeed owe a duty of care in accordance with the criteria set out in *Caparo v Dickman*. The Court of Appeal went on to add that

> the more so if it has made the prevention of environmental damage by the activities of group companies a spearhead and is, to a certain degree, actively involved in and managing the business operations of such companies (which is not to say that without this attention and involvement a violation of the duty of care is unthinkable and that culpable negligence with regard to the said interests can never result in liability).[40]

Here the Court made a reference to the voluntary CSR commitments undertaken by Shell as a group, and found that the parent company's duty of due diligence was somewhat enhanced by Shell's CSR commitments, in particular with regard to the adverse impacts that its activities can have on the environment. In contrast to the conclusion reached by Fraser J in the *Okpabi case*, the Court of Appeal of The Hague suggests that the company does have superior knowledge to that of the subsidiary in relation to environmental damage and uses the code of conduct adopted by the company not only as proof of that knowledge but also as the standard of overview and monitoring expected from the parent company.

The Court of Appeal of the Hague added that the parent company should monitor compliance with the standards established by the company with regard to environmental protection, and the group policy defined to achieve these goals and ambitions in a coordinated and uniform way. The Court then set out a test by asking a series of questions relevant to decide on the merits of the case, including: (a) which (maintenance) standards applied to an old pipeline whose

38 https://milieudefensie.nl/publicaties/bezwaren-uitspraken/s-the-response-of-milieudefensie-and-the-nigerian-plaintiffs-to-shell2019s-argument-for-non-jurisdiction (last accessed 10 March 2018).

39 Court of Appeal of the Hague, *Eric Barizaa Dooh of Goi and others v. Royal Dutch Shell Plc and Others*, op. cit., para. 3.2.

40 Ibid., para. 3.2.

insides were no longer monitored like the one in question; (b) were these maintenance standards complied with; (c) if so, what is this evidenced by, and if not, shouldn't this have been noted within the context of the supervision performed by the parent company (the audits); (d) shouldn't it have been noted with an adequate reporting system in place and (e) why was it not. Another question is (f) whether the parent company – considering the autonomy and individual responsibility of (the management of) the subsidiary – was sufficiently equipped (as far as knowledge, possibilities and means are concerned) to intervene adequately in case of evident negligence by the subsidiary.[41] As the decision of the Court of Appeal of the Hague was limited to preliminary issues of procedural law, the court did not apply this test to the facts of the case. However, this test suggests that quite a high threshold is expected of the parent company which must properly monitor compliance with the human rights and environmental standards within the group.

The Court of Appeal pointed out that the assertion by Shell that the parent company did not know about the spillage and the condition and maintenance of the pipeline locally was not an adequate defence.[42] Parent companies can therefore no longer hide behind their own ignorance since a key factor is whether the company knows or ought to have known the foreseeable adverse human rights impacts that the operations of its subsidiaries may have on the environment or the local communities.

The court rejected Shell's argument as to the fact that there are no decisions by Nigerian courts in which group liability is accepted on these grounds, and considered that this does not mean that Nigerian law by definition provides no basis for assuming a duty of care owed by the parent company in the context of cleaning up pollution and preventing repeated spills arising out of the operations of its subsidiary. The court found that since Nigerian law as a *common law* system is based on English law, and common law, especially English case law, are important sources of Nigerian law, a basis for assuming such duty of care could be found in decisions such as *Chandler v Cape*.[43]

The Court of Appeal concluded that it could not be ruled out that the parent company could be liable for damages resulting from the conduct of its subsidiary and considered that the claims against the parent company and the Nigerian subsidiary are so closely connected that it is essential to hear and determine them together in order to avoid the risk of irreconcilable judgments resulting from separate proceedings. The court also ordered Shell to give the claimants access to a number of internal documents in order to support their case.[44]

This case is a very interesting one as, although the Dutch courts are yet to give a decision on the substantive issues involved, it made a number of rather

41 Ibid., para. 6.9.
42 Ibid., para. 6.8.
43 Ibid., para. 3.2.
44 Ibid., para. 7.3.

powerful assertions on the potential liability of the parent company for the conduct of its subsidiaries and also on the threshold of the duty of care expected from the parent company.

In addition, it is in line with the more recent English case *Lungowe v Vedanta*,[45] which concerned proceedings brought in England by Zambian citizens against an English corporation (Vedanta Resources Plc, hereafter 'Vedanta') and its Zambian subsidiary (Konkola Copper Mines Plc, hereafter 'KCM') for the damage they had allegedly suffered as a result of the environmental pollution caused by discharges from a copper mine owned and operated by KCM. The court was called upon to decide whether the claimants' claim against KCM had a real prospect of success. Relying on the well-established principles to prove the existence under English law of a duty of care owed by the parent company arising out of the operations of its subsidiary, Simon LJ found that the claim against the parent company was arguable and therefore could not be dismissed and that there was 'a serious question to be tried which should not be disposed of summarily'.[46]

Conclusion

Civil litigation has a key role to play in the struggle for an enhanced accountability of MNCs. The UNGPs reaffirmed that states have a duty to respect human rights, which entails that they must ensure that their companies respect human rights wherever they operate and provide access to remedy for the victims when adverse human rights impacts occur. The European states, home states of many MNCs, have an important regulatory role to play in this respect.[47] This regulatory role can only be played if victims of human rights abuses committed overseas by European-based corporations are allowed access to European tribunals. Through the recognition that, in appropriate circumstances, parent companies may owe a duty of care to the employees and local communities directly affected by the operations of their subsidiaries abroad, the gates to the European tribunals are open. The first hurdle to access to justice can be overcome. There remain, however, many more obstacles before European-based companies and their subsidiaries can be held accountable for the adverse human rights impacts of their operations abroad.

45 Court of Appeal, *Lungowe v Vedanta Resources plc*, [2017] EWCA Civ 1528, 13 October 2017.

46 Ibid., para. 90.

47 C. Bright, 'L'accès à la justice civile en cas de violations des droits de l'homme par des entreprises multinationales [The Access to Civil Justice for Victims of Corporate Human Rights Violations]. European University Institute, 2013, http://hdl.handle.net/1814/29602 (last accessed 5 March 2018).

19 Corporate Liability and Human Rights

Access to Criminal Judicial Remedies in Europe

Adriana Espinosa González and Marta Sosa Navarro

Introduction

At present, access to criminal judicial remedy within Europe for human rights violations perpetrated by corporations can be said to be fundamentally circumscribed to domestic courts.

At an international level, the International Criminal Court (ICC)[1] cannot exercise its exceptional jurisdiction over corporations.[2] Moreover, as some authors have put it, 'international criminal law is not the panacea that solves all the theoretical and practical obstacles surrounding the debate on corporate human rights obligations'.[3] Thus, other potentially game-changer initiatives currently discussed at the international level, such as the UN Treaty on B&HR or the creation of a World Court of Human Rights, should be monitored.[4]

At the domestic level, European civil courts' competence to hear cases involving subsidiaries' activities in third countries is very limited, although some States accept certain grounds for extraterritorial jurisdiction. One of these grounds is provided by the civil procedure rules on joint hearings. Its development has been encouraged by the 2016 CoE Recommendation on Human Rights and

1 Most European States have ratified the Statute of Rome, which regulates the ICC. UN General Assembly, *Rome Statute of the International Criminal Court (last amended 2010)*, 17 July 1998.

2 First, the court can only investigate crimes committed after 2002. Furthermore, core international crimes do not cover the bulk of human rights violations committed by corporations, which lay more within the scope of labour rights or access to resources by affected communities.

3 An interesting exception is found in the *News TV S.A.L.* and *Akbar* cases before the Special Tribunal for Lebanon. See also N. Bernaz, 'Corporate criminal liability under international law. The News S.A.L. and Akhbar Beirut S.A.L. cases at the Special Tribunal for Lebanon'. *Journal of International Criminal Justice*, 2015, 13, 313–330.

4 On the current debates on the UN Treaty on B&HR see A. Espinosa, 'El control de las empresas transnacionales mediante instrumentos vinculantes'. In L. Ghiotti and A. Guamán, *América Latina bajo el signo del Libre Comercio: análisis y alternativas*, forthcoming; and N. Bernaz, *Including Corporate Criminal Liability for International Crimes in the Business and Human Rights Treaty: Necessary but Insufficient*. Business and Human Rights Resource Centre, Debate blog series, https://business-humanrights.org/en/including-corporate-criminal-liability-for-international-crimes-in-the-business-and-human-rights-treaty-necessary-but-insufficient (last accessed 29 November 2017).

Business (hereinafter 'CoE Recommendation').[5] In this sense, the Dutch Civil Code allowed a court to assert its competence over claims against Shell parent corporation (the Dutch-based Royal Dutch Shell; hereinafter 'RDS') and its Nigerian-based subsidiary in *Friday Alfred Akpan et al. c. Shell* (2013).[6]

Another commonly mentioned tool is the *forum necessitatis* doctrine, which is recognized in some European states[7] as an exceptional ground for jurisdiction. It was also recalled in the CoE Recommendation.[8] The doctrine has also been considered as born out of the ECHR, in particular of the right to access to justice as established at Article 6(1). The ECtHR has taken Article 6 to imply a right to access to court, in civil and criminal cases alike, which is both effective and practical.[9]

However, the cited ruling in *Akpan v. Shell* illustrates that these procedural rules do nothing by themselves to lift the corporate veil, nor do they directly elucidate the role of the parent entity in the impacts caused by its foreign subsidiary. The tribunal only held the subsidiary responsible for the oil spills that severely damaged the Nigerian claimants' lands, while dismissing claims of negligence against the parent RDS. The decision was based on Nigerian law, which the Dutch Court considered applicable to the case pursuant to the *lex loci damni* rule.[10]

Other obstacles faced by civil law include the overwhelming tendency of judges involved in private law cases to refrain from acting against the separate legal personality principle, and the fact that victims bear the burden to prove that the company exercised control over the subsidiary and that it breached duty of care standards.

Hence, as barriers to access remedy through civil litigation remain in general terms not addressed, criminal law presents a complementary avenue for victims of corporate human rights violations, which is so far largely unexplored. This chapter will discuss the challenges, which have already become patent in pursuing the criminal path, and the proposals that are emerging to address them.

5 CoE, *Recommendation of the Committee of Ministers to Member States on human rights and business*, CM/Rec (2016)3, 2 March 2016, para. 35.

6 District Court of the Hague, *Friday Alfred Akpan et al v Shell*, case C/09/337050/HA ZA 09-1580, 30 January 2013, paras. 4.5, 4.6.

7 States having a *forum necessitatis* based on statute include the Netherlands, Switzerland, Belgium and Spain. Other countries have developed the doctrine on case law (such as France or Germany). See L. Roorda and C. Ryngaert, 'Business and human rights litigation in Europe: the promises held by forum of necessity-based jurisdiction'. *The Rabel Journal of Comparative and International Private Law*, 80(784), 2016, 8; D. Augenstein and N. Jägers, 'Judicial remedies-the issue of jurisdiction'. In J.J. Álvarez Rubio and K. Yiannibas (eds), *Human Rights in Business: Removal of Barriers to Access Justice in the European Union*. London: Routledge, 2017, chapter 1.4.2.

8 To this respect, see Roorda, Ryngaert, op. cit., 5.

9 ECtHR, *Golder v. United Kingdom*, App. No. 4451/70, Judgment, 21 February 1975, paras. 31–32; ECtHR, *Markovic and Others v. Italy*, App. No. 1398/03, Judgment, 14 December 2006, para. 92. See in this regard, Roorda, Ryngaert, op. cit., 7.

10 District Court of the Hague, *Akpan v. Shell*, op. cit., paras. 4.27–4.32.

Access to Criminal Judicial Remedy in Europe

Foundations of Criminal Law to Obtain Remedy: Regional versus International

From a material perspective, given the cross-border nature of the acts generally under scrutiny in cases of human rights violations by corporations, treaty law should be examined in the first place. The OHCHR has recently noted that the 'implementation of international treaties has led to the creation of new criminal offenses which may be extended to corporate entities as well as individual offenders'.[11] In this sense, European institutions call in fact for adequate domestic legal systems to guarantee the effective applicability of international law obligations in this context. In words of the CoE,

> Member States should [...] ensure that business enterprises can be held liable under their criminal law or other equivalent law for the commission of: (i) crimes under international law caused by business enterprises; (ii) offences established in accordance with treaties [...]; (iii) other offences constituting serious human rights abuses involving business enterprises.[12]

Strictly under international law there is a vast number of instruments to which a victim of a violation could resort to claim justice. Starting from international criminal law, the Rome Statute, which defines core international crimes, may be invoked to prosecute grave violations of human rights perpetrated by corporations in those domestic legal systems that recognize liability of legal persons. In the scope of international labour law, the 'eight ILO core Conventions'[13] apply to all ILO Members, irrespective of whether they have ratified them or not, as the standards they set have been reproduced in the 1998 ILO

11 OHCHR, *The OHCHR Accountability and Remedy Project, Illustrative Examples for Guidance to Improve Corporate Accountability and Access to Judicial Remedy for Business-related Human Rights Abuse,* Companion Document to A/HRC/32/19 and A/32/19/Add.1, 5 July 2016 (hereinafter 'OHCHR Illustrative Examples'). Illustrative example No. 1.2 includes treaties related to rights of children, worst forms of child labour, forced labour and human trafficking. See the Opinion of the European Union Agency for Fundamental Rights, 'Improving access to remedy in the area of business and human rights at the EU level', 1/2917, 41.

12 CoE, *Recommendation of the Committee of Ministers to Member States on human rights and business*, op. cit., Appendix 4, item 4.3.

13 ILO. *Freedom of Association and Protection of the Right to Organise Convention*, 1948 (No. 87); *Right to Organise and Collective Bargaining Convention*, 1949 (No. 98); *Forced Labour Convention, 1930* (No. 29); *Abolition of Forced Labour Convention*, 1957 (No. 105); *Minimum Age Convention*, 1973 (No. 138); *Worst Forms of Child Labour Convention*, 1999 (No. 182); *Equal Remuneration Convention*, 1951 (No. 100); *Discrimination (Employment and Occupation) Convention*, 1958 (No. 111).

Declaration on Fundamental Principles and Rights at Work.[14] There are also some relevant crime-specific instruments such as the Optional Protocol to the Convention on the Rights of the Child on the Sale of Children, and Child Pornography (hereinafter 'OPSC'),[15] which has been singled out as the only human rights treaty that provides expressly for legal accountability (criminal, civil or administrative) of legal entities, including business corporations,[16] or the UN Convention for Transnational Organized Crime, whose Article 10 specifically addresses liability of legal persons.[17]

As regards the CoE, examples of instruments that recognize liability of legal persons include the Criminal Law Convention on Corruption,[18] the Convention on Cybercrime,[19] the Convention on Action against Human Trafficking,[20] the Convention on the Protection of Children against Sexual Exploitation and Sexual Abuse,[21] and the Convention on Preventing and Combating Violence against Women and Domestic Violence.[22]

Civil versus Criminal Jurisdiction

Global figures still show a clear preference for civil jurisdiction. According to the latest Corporate Legal Accountability Annual Briefing published by the Business and Human Rights Resource Centre, from the 227 lawsuits against companies over alleged human rights violations in the last decade, only 37 have involved

14 *ILO Declaration on Fundamental Principles and Rights at Work*, June 1988; UNGP, Commentary on Principle 12. For a discussion on the flaws that impede the effective enforcement of the standards here contained see P. Alston, 'Core labour standards and the transformation of the international labour rights regime'. *European Journal of International Law*, 2004, 5, 457–521.

15 UN General Assembly, *Optional Protocol to the Convention on the Rights of the Child on the Sale of Children, Child Prostitution and Child Pornography*, 16 March 2001, A/RES/54/263.

16 International Commission of Jurists, *Proposals for Elements of a Legally Binding Instrument on Transnational Corporations and Other Business Enterprises*, October 2016. www.icj.org/wp-content/uploads/2016/10/Universal-OEWG-session-2-ICJ-submission-Advocacy-Analysis-brief-2016-ENG.pdf (last accessed 30 November 2017). See Article 3.4 of the OPSC. All EU Member States have signed the OPSC and, except for Ireland, are also Contracting Parties.

17 UN General Assembly, *United Nations Convention against Transnational Organized Crime: Resolution Adopted by the General Assembly*, 8 January 2001, A/RES/55/25. See S. Rodríguez López, 'Criminal liability of legal persons for human trafficking offences in international and European law'. *Journal of Trafficking and Human Exploitation*, February 2017, 1, section 3.1, para. 1, www.uitgeverijparis.nl/reader/199279/1001296456 (last accessed 30 November 2017).

18 CoE, *Criminal Law Convention on Corruption*, 27 January 1999.

19 CoE, *Convention on Cybercrime*, 23 November 2001.

20 CoE, *Council of Europe Convention on Action against Trafficking in Human Beings*, 16 May 2005, CETS No. 197.

21 CoE, *Council of Europe Convention on the Protection of Children against Sexual Exploitation and Sexual Abuse*, CETS No. 201, 12 July 2007.

22 CoE, *Council of Europe Convention on Preventing and Combating Violence against Women and Domestic Violence*, 11 May 2011.

criminal charges. Of this 37, only 13 have resulted in verdicts against companies or their managers or employees.[23]

Nevertheless, some authors still push for the criminal avenue by holding that if the spirit of civil law systems is to be respected, the role of criminal judicial mechanisms to tackle human rights violations perpetrated by corporations should be enhanced.[24] This approach does not imply the abandonment of civil law as an avenue for victims of corporate human rights abuses to seek justice and remedies. Moreover, in the past few years we are witnessing a number of legislative processes towards the establishment of corporate legally binding obligations to respect human rights in civil law. The recent French 'duty of vigilance' law[25] stands as the clearest example, but there are also promising ongoing processes taking place in Switzerland[26] and the Netherlands.[27] Moreover, some recent decisions adopted by courts in civil law and common law countries also present positive signals for victims of human rights abuses resulting from companies' subsidiaries or business relations abroad.[28]

The aforementioned examples show that the civil law pathway is by no means lost. This being said, it is obvious that strong emphasis needs to be put on the need for urgent action to lift pressing barriers that victims face to access justice.[29] At the same time, one cannot be blind to the advantages that criminal jurisdiction offers at some stages. For instance, civil settlements are often confidential and do

23 Business and Human Rights Resource Centre, *Corporate Legal Accountability Annual Briefing: Corporate Impunity is Common and Remedy for Victims is Rare*, April 2017, https://business-humanrights.org/sites/default/files/documents/CLA_AB_Final_Apr2017.pdf (last accessed 29 November 2017).

24 See in this sense, C. Kaeb and D. Scheffer, 'The paradox of Kiobel in Europe'. *American Journal of International Law*, 2013, 107, 855.

25 *Loi no. 2017-399 du 27 mars 2017 relative au devoir de vigilance des sociétés mères et des entreprises donneuses d'ordre*, www.legifrance.gouv.fr/eli/loi/2017/3/27/ECFX1509096L/jo/texte (last accessed 29 November 2017).

26 The country is in the process of holding a referendum on a Responsible Business Initiative promoted by citizens. The Bill, which has the support of 120,000 valid signatures, would amend the Swiss constitution to introduce a duty of care on Swiss companies based on human rights due diligence obligations. See Swiss Coalition for Corporate Justice, *The Responsible Business Initiative: Protecting Human Rights and the Environment*, 2015, http://konzern-initiative.ch/?lang=en, last accessed on 29 November 2017.

27 The Child Labour Due Diligence Bill is, at the time of writing, pending approval by the Dutch Senate. For more information on the content of the law, see MVO Platform, *Frequently Asked Questions about the new Dutch Child Labour Due Diligence Law*, 2017, www.mvoplatform.nl/bestanden/FAQChildLabourDueDiligenceLaw.pdf (last accessed 29 November 2017).

28 See in this respect www.bhrinlaw.org, joint project by ECCJ, CORE, ICAR, *Above Ground* and *Public Eye* (last accessed 29 November 2017).

29 See for example, F. Gregor, *The EU's Business: Recommended Actions for the EU and its Member States to Ensure Access to Judicial Remedy for Business-related Human Rights Impacts*, December 2014. www.bhrinlaw.org/documents/eu_business.pdf (last accessed 30 November 2017); Amnesty International, B&HR Resource Centre, *Creating a Paradigm Shift: Legal Solutions to Improve Access to Remedy for Corporate Human Rights Abuse*, POL 30/7037/2017, September 2017, 2–3.

not require an admission of guilt or wrongdoing. This approach, as the Sixth Corporate Crime Principle puts it, 'can entrench corporate impunity because it does little to deter future harm or provide justice for victims'.[30] Second, criminal prosecution places the burden of investigation on the Prosecution, in contrast to civil litigation where the victims of corporate abuse have to bare the high costs of investigation, evidence collection and legal advice.[31] This problem has been addressed by the OHCHR *Accountability and Remedy Project. Illustrative Examples for Guidance to Improve Corporate Accountability and Access to Judicial Remedy for Business-related Human Rights Abuse* (hereinafter 'OHCHR Illustrative Examples').[32] In respect to this specific issue, Policy Objectives 15 and 16 are designed to overcome financial obstacles to private claims.

European Criminal Law Responses to Human Rights Violations Committed by Corporations. Obstacles and Challenges

The European regional system of human rights protection is well-developed,[33] but corporate criminal accountability for human rights violations is not fully addressed by it, despite calls from the ECtHR case law which specifically recognizes the duty of states to protect individuals from other individuals' human rights-threatening actions, even through the establishment of criminal offenses.[34]

So what are the obstacles and challenges faced by a victim of corporate related human rights violations when seeking judicial remedy through criminal law before European domestic courts?

Legal and Practical Issues

In Europe, despite existing variations and differences among the enforcement mechanisms implemented from state to state, the trend points towards a recognition of corporate criminal liability (saving the well-known German exception, most jurisdictions have enacted some form of corporate criminal liability).[35]

30 IAR and Amnesty International, *10 Corporate Crimes Principles*, Principle 6. www.commercecrimehumanrights.org/principles/principle-six/ (last accessed 30 November 2017).

31 A. Clapham, 'The question of jurisdiction under international criminal law over legal persons: lessons from the Rome Conference on an International Criminal Court'. In M.T. Kamminga and S. Zia-Zarifi (eds), *Liability of Multinational Corporations*. Leiden: Brill-Nijhoff, 2000, 140.

32 OHCHR, *Illustrative Examples*, op. cit., 29–33.

33 For an overview of the European System of Protections see C. Fernández Liesa, *El Derecho internacional de los derechos humanos en perspectiva histórica*. Madrid, Civitas, 2013, chapter 10, 323–336.

34 ECtHR, *M.C. v. Bulgaria*, App. No. 39272/798, Judgment, 4 December 2003, para. 150.

35 For a country-by-country detailed review of corporate criminal liability in Europe see Clifford Chance, Corporate Criminal Liability Report, www.cliffordchance.com/briefings/2016/04/corporate_criminalliability.html, 2016. See also M.J. Kelly, *Prosecuting Corporations for Genocide*. Oxford: Oxford University Press, 2016, 193–203.

Hence, despite the lack of homogeneity, there are some relevant examples within the EU legislation regulating corporate criminal liability for human rights violations. These include the Framework Decision on Racism and Xenophobia, which the ECtHR has referred to in *Delfi A.S. v. Estonia*, where it defined the legal obligations of internet news portals in respect of content that may amount to hate crime,[36] the Employer Sanctions Directive[37] and the Anti-Trafficking Directive.[38]

In respect of the Employer Sanctions Directive, relevant dispositions are Article 9, which obliges EU Member States to criminalize particularly severe forms of labour exploitation, and Article 11, which obliges Member States to ensure that legal persons can be held liable for offenses criminalized according to Article 9. This liability does not however exclude liability of natural persons as perpetrators, inciters or accessories in the offense. Under Article 5 of the Anti-Trafficking Directive, 'Member States shall take the necessary measures to ensure that legal persons can be held liable for the offenses referred to in Arts. 2 and 3'.[39]

Another interesting instrument is the 2012 Victim's Rights Directive, which, in the context of criminal proceedings against legal persons, establishes the right of victims under Article 16 to obtain within reasonable time a decision of the criminal court on compensation by the offender.[40]

Legal Challenges

The European Parliament has specifically called on states to 'legislate in a coherent, holistic, effective and binding manner in order to meet their duty to prevent, investigate, punish and redress human rights violations, including those perpetrated in third countries, directly or indirectly, by corporations acting under their jurisdiction'.[41] Within the more specific area of corporate criminal liability, the Parliament demands a coherent and common response from Member States to tackle corporate abuse with extraterritorial implications.[42]

36 *Council Framework Decision 2008/913/JHA of 28 November 2008 on Combating Certain Forms and Expressions of Racism and Xenophobia by Means of Criminal Law*; ECtHR, *Delfi AS v. Estonia*, App. No. 64569/09, Judgment, Grand Chamber, 16 June 2016 (cited in the FRA Opinion).

37 EU, *Directive 2009/52/EC on Providing Minimum Standards on Sanctions and Measures against Employers of Illegally Staying Third-country Nationals*, OJ L 168/24, June 2009, paras. 22–25, arts. 9–10.

38 EU, *Directive 2011/36/EU on Preventing and Combating Trafficking in Human Beings and Protecting its Victims, and Replacing Council Framework Decision 2022/629/JHA*, OJ L 101, 5 April 2011, arts. 5–6.

39 Ibid., art. 5.1.

40 EU, *Directive 2012/29/EU of the European Parliament and of the Council of 25 October 2012 Establishing Minimum Standards on the Rights, Support and Protection of Victims of Crime, and Replacing Council Framework Decision 2001/220/JHA*, OJ L 315/57, 14 November 2012, art. 16.1.

41 European Parliament, Committee on Foreign Affairs, *Resolution on Corporate Liability for Serious Human Rights Abuses in Third Countries*, 2015/2315 (INI), 25 October 2016, para. 17.

42 Ibid., para. 26.

The *Lahmeyer* case, which was attempted to be brought before German courts, illustrates the consequences of this lack of common standards for corporate accountability.[43] After some investigation, the prosecution closed the case claiming that the German company and its employees had no legal duty to check if the affected population in Sudan had been resettled before the flooding commenced, an assertion which, in words of the European Centre for Constitutional and Human Rights, 'highlights the inadequacy of the current definition of managers' human rights obligations when operating abroad and the urgent need for a reform of the applicable laws'.[44]

Prosecutors' discretionary powers may occasionally get in the way of access to justice. Even when presented with evidence, prosecutors may decline to open investigations. These attributions pose independence and impartiality problems, especially in those countries in which the public prosecutor is named by the Government, when this may affect the decision to follow up or not allegations of corporate abuse.

A possible example of corporate or political influence over criminal prosecution can be found in the context of the *Galdikas* case in the UK. After six of the 30 Lithuanian victims of human trafficking received £1 million civil settlement from the company, the Crown Prosecution Service decided not to pursue a criminal investigation without a proper justification.[45]

In a heterogeneous jurisdictional reality such as Europe, where the prosecutors' functions vary from state to state, it is difficult to identify a proposal that is able to tackle systematically the described 'bias' risk. However, Policy Objective 4.3 of the OHCHR Illustrative Examples suggests the implementation of a comprehensive enforcement policy as a way of counterbalancing the use of discretion on the part of enforcement agencies as to whether to investigate and/or take enforcement action.[46]

Protection of the 'sacrosanct' independence and impartiality of investigators and prosecutors may also be guaranteed, according to the Corporate Crimes Principles, through

> legal measures (e.g. statutory requirements that ensure transparency about how and when ministers have oversight of the prosecutor's office) and

43 For more information on the *Lahmeyer* case see ECCHR, *Reckless Development: Forced Displacement due to Lahmeyer Dam Construction*, see www.ecchr.eu/en/our_work/business-and-human-rights/lahmeyer-case.html (last accessed 29 November 2017).

44 Ibid.

45 This is a landmark case, as it has triggered the first judgment in favour of modern slavery victims of a British company. High Court of London, *Galdikas & Ors v DJ Houghton Catching Services Ltd & Ors*, [2016] EWHC 1376 (QB), 10 June 2016.

46 This enforcement policy should '(a) clearly set out how decisions are made regarding whether to investigate or commence enforcement action and the factors that will be taken into account; (b) have been developed wherever possible following appropriate public consultation', OHCHR, *Illustrative examples*, op. cit., Add. 1, Policy Objective 4.3.

> sanctions to protect the independence and impartiality of law enforcement, as well as practical measures to ensure their personal security and that of their families.[47]

Another remarkable problem is the higher standard of proof required in criminal proceedings, in comparison with civil claims. In corporate crimes, this adds to the complexities that derive from corporate structure, corporate liability tests and extraterritorial elements, which require specialized knowledge and additional resources. These demands often fall within underfunded and undertrained enforcement agencies.

The famous *Trafigura* case illustrates the difficulties that may appear as a result of this higher evidentiary threshold, together with insufficient resources and inadequate training.[48] Claims from victims were settled in the UK after Trafigura agreed to pay $100 million dollars for damages. However, the UK's enforcement authorities decided to decline investigating possible criminal charges alleging the 'limited experience in complex investigations' and 'lack of appropriately skilled and experienced staff'.[49]

In this regard, Policy Objective 6 of the OHCHR Illustrative Examples establishes that enforcement agencies should 'have access to the necessary resources, training and expertise', and gives specific examples on how to improve access to the necessary financial, technical and specialized resources needed.[50] Other organizations suggest the designation of specialized prosecutors for human rights violations committed by corporations.[51] The FRA proposes resort to EU resources, such as facilitation of cross-border justice provided by Eurojust, peer review by Member States and sharing of best practices as means to optimize the EU resources when investigating corporate abuse.[52]

Practical Challenges

From a more practical perspective, victims may encounter some specific obstacles in criminal proceedings. In the context of labour exploitation, the FRA detected a lack of authorities that could be easily addressed and be responsive to workers' rights.[53] In the same line, in its 2016 Report on progress made in the fight

47 ICAR and Amnesty International, *10 Corporate Crimes Principles*, op. cit., Commentary to Principle 1. The commentary to this principle also includes a list of factors to consider when prioritising corporate crime cases for investigation or prosecution.

48 *Trafigura* lawsuits (re: Côte d'Ivoire). See https://business-humanrights.org/en/trafigura-lawsuits-re-c%C3%B4te-d%E2%80%99ivoire#c9344 (last accessed 11 February 2018).

49 *The Guardian*, 'UK authorities "lack resources" to investigate Trafigura over toxic waste', 23 July 2015, www.theguardian.com/world/2015/jul/23/uk-authorities-lack-resources-to-investigate-trafigura-over-toxic-waste (last accessed 28 November 2017).

50 OHCHR, *Illustrative examples*, op. cit., Policy Objective 6.

51 Proposal presented by ECCHR at the Conference 'Business and Human Rights: International Law Challenges, European Responses' (University of Milan, May 2017).

52 FRA Opinion 1/2917, op. cit., 46.

53 Ibid., 44.

against trafficking, the European Commission reported that 'victims are frequently refused assistance at police stations or misidentified as offenders, and subsequently prosecuted and convicted'.[54]

Increasing awareness on this problem has led the OHCHR to refer to the protection of victims within its Policy Objective 7, which calls for enforcement agencies to be 'sensitive to the particular needs of individuals and groups at heightened risk of vulnerability or marginalization'.[55] Concerns about the implications of this obstacle for victims' access to justice has also received practical responses, as some trade unions (Italy, Cyprus, Netherlands and Slovenia) have established systems for handling complaints and for monitoring abusive behaviour in high-risk sectors.[56]

Finally, it is essential to overcome the obstacles posed by the cross-border cooperation required in certain cases involving human rights violations in non-EU countries, as the *Lima Holding BV* case in the Netherlands illustrates.[57] Lima Holding BV was the parent company of Riwal, a company involved in the construction of the separation wall in occupied Palestinian territory, considered unlawful by the ICJ in 2004.[58] After the case had been brought before the prosecution by *parties civiles* for complicity with war crimes and crimes against humanity, the prosecution dismissed the case because of its complexity and on the basis of a probable lack of cooperation of the Israeli authorities.[59]

The OHCHR recommends in this regard the creation of joint investigation teams and active involvement with the relevant bilateral and multilateral initiatives, so that '(a) requests for mutual legal assistance can be made and responded to; and (b) information can be exchanged between enforcement agencies and/or judicial bodies in cross-border cases'.[60]

Conclusion

Concerns about the inadequacy of the legal framework to guarantee harmonized access to judicial remedy in Europe for victims of corporate abuse have

54 European Commission, *Report on the Progress Made in the Fight against Trafficking in Human Beings*, COM (2016) 267 final, 19 May 2016, 10.

55 OHCHR, *Illustrative Examples*, op. cit., Policy Objective 7.

56 Eurofund, *Regulation of Labour Market Intermediaries and the Role of Social Partners in Preventing Trafficking of Labour*, 2016, 37.

57 *No Further Investigation into Crane Rental Company*, 14 May 2013, Press Release available online www.om.nl/vaste-onderdelen/zoeken/@31796/no-further/ (last accessed 12 February 2018).

58 ICJ, *Advisory Opinion Concerning Legal Consequences of the Construction of a Wall in the Occupied Palestinian Territory*, 9 July 2004.

59 For a detailed analysis of the case, see V. Azarov, 'Investigative or Political Barriers? Dutch Prosecutor Dismisses Criminal Complicity Case against Riwal', *Rights As Usual*, 29 May 2013 rightsasusual.appspot.com/?p=543, last accessed on 28 November 2017.

60 OHCHR, *Illustrative examples*, op. cit., Policy Objective 9.

been raised by European institutions,[61] legal and human rights organizations,[62] academics and international lawyers.[63] Regarding the former, the CoE Parliamentary Assembly specifically acknowledged the problem by calling for a series of measures directed to enforce business respect of human rights.[64]

Although suggested and discussed reforms in civil law remedies are undoubtedly important, it is also necessary to question whether civil law is always the best route to litigate human rights-related cases. One may ask to what extent can civil litigation be used to vindicate values and interests protected by human rights, including human rights violations for which the word 'tort' is too timid.[65] Moreover, is the award of pecuniary damages the best remedy a victim of human rights abuses can expect? And what about the financial costs, expertise and other resources needed that in civil law remedies are carried by the victims? These and other questions have put the focus on criminal law as a potential complementary avenue to guarantee access to justice for victims of human rights violations.

Through the examination of the main challenges in criminal procedures to access judicial remedy, this chapter is an attempt to map out the general and specific aspects conditioning criminal prosecution of human rights violations committed by corporations.

The research has specifically aimed at shedding some light on what is becoming an increasingly demanded path to fight corporate impunity in cases involving European companies and victims from non-European countries. Although at the European level there is currently no legally binding instrument serving as a basis for criminal prosecution of corporations by domestic or regional courts, by analysing the legal and practical obstacles inherent to the prosecution of corporations before European criminal courts, this chapter's ultimate goal has been to highlight this path's main challenges. The findings have ultimately evidenced that, in order to guarantee access to justice to victims of corporate abuses through criminal law, policy and legal amendments, both at a regional and domestic level, are urgently needed.

61 See, for instance FRA Opinion 1/2017, op. cit., p. 21, para. 3.

62 International Commission of Jurists, *Proposals for Elements of a Legally Binding Instrument on Transnational Corporations and Other Business Enterprises*, op. cit., 30–31; European Centre for Corporate Justice, *Access to Justice*, http://corporatejustice.org/priorities/14-access-to-justice, last accessed on 29 November 2017.

63 Leigh Day, Leigh Day submission to the Joint Committee on Human Rights Inquiry on Business and Human Rights, 31 August 2016, 8–10, available at www.leighday.co.uk/LeighDay/media/LeighDay/documents/Corporate%20accountability/2016_08_31-LEIGH-DAY-SUBMISSION-TO-THE-JCHR1.pdf, last accessed on 12 February 2018.

64 CoE Parliamentary Assembly, *Recommendation*, 1936 (2010), *Human Rights and Business*, 6 October 2010, para. 2.

65 International Commission of Jurists, *Proposals for Elements of a Legally Binding Instrument on Transnational Corporations and Other Business Enterprises*, op. cit., chapter 10.

20 European Trends in Tort Law Remedies to Address Corporate Human Rights Abuses

Florentine Vos

Introduction

This chapter identifies and establishes how civil law remedies suitable to effectively address corporate human rights abuses can be developed. After determining a yardstick by which to measure whether a remedy is effective, this chapter will identify developments in the remedies provided for by the tort laws of European countries and analyse their relevance for human rights violations perpetrated by corporations. Subsequently, this chapter will consider the root of these developments and finally it will seek to establish how tort laws of European countries can offer more effective remedies for corporate human rights abuses.

This chapter shows that European jurisdictions, in principle, continue to hold strictly to the compensatory purpose of tort law. European states have been remiss in adopting appropriate remedies to corporate human rights abuses such as those proposed by the UNGPs. Nevertheless, limited developments in tort law in European jurisdictions show that other purposes of tort law are gaining ground, thus making a wider range of remedies available.

The Importance of Civil Law Remedies

Tort law remedies (in the sense of reparations) are often overlooked in academic discourse on B&HR. However, they are of exceeding importance because tort law is one of the few, if not the only, direct avenues for victims of human rights abuses by corporations. Tort law allows victims themselves to bring a direct claim, without interposition of a public body such as a criminal prosecutor. The appeal of tort law can be seen in the increase of lawsuits for corporate human rights violations brought before national civil courts.[1] Tort law remedies are further of importance because liability rules can only be effective if the law also

1 See N. Jägers and M. van der Heijden, 'Corporate human rights violations: the feasibility of civil recourse in the Netherlands'. *Brooklyn Journal of International Law*, 2008, 33(3), 835; C. van Dam, *European Tort Law*. Oxford: Oxford University Press, 2013, 347.

provides an effective remedy in reaction to a violation:[2] if no equitable outcome can be obtained through the courts, a claimant will have no incentive to bring a (costly and time-consuming) claim.

Due to the tendency to extra-judicially settle cases on corporate human rights abuses, uncertainty has persisted over what the available remedies are. However, there now appears to be a trend in which cases against corporations for serious wrongdoing, involving mainly environmental damage and consequential harm to health, are not settled but rather are brought to a (more or less successful) conclusion in court and result in the award of remedies.[3] This brings remedies further to the forefront of B&HR cases.

For example, a 2006 decision (though later overturned on jurisdictional grounds) of the Administrative Courts of Toulouse awarded three French holocaust survivors €20,000 in damages against Société nationale des chemins de fer français (SNCF), the French national railway company, and the French Government for their involvement in the forced transportation to concentration camps in the Second World War.[4] A second significant decision is the 2013 ruling of the District Court of the Hague in which it ordered a Nigerian subsidiary of Shell to pay compensation for losses resulting from the violation of its duty of care, to those farmers neighbouring an abandoned wellhead, by negligently leaving behind the wellhead without adequately securing it, thus making it easy for saboteurs to unscrew its valves and cause oil spills.[5]

What is an Effective Remedy?

Determining what qualifies as an effective remedy for corporate human rights abuses requires a yardstick. The effectiveness of a legal remedy can be ascertained by the degree to which it meets the aim for which it is issued. According to the Commentary to the UNGPs, the aim of remedies for corporate human rights violations should be 'to counteract or make good any human rights harms that have occurred'.[6] To fulfil this purpose, the UNGPs suggest the following remedies: apologies, restitution, rehabilitation, financial or non-financial

2 Van Dam, op. cit., 346–347.

3 L. Enneking, *Foreign Direct Liability and Beyond: Exploring The Role of Tort in Promoting International Corporate Social Responsibility and Accountability*. The Hague: Eleven International Publishing, 2012, 120.

4 Administrative Tribunal for Toulouse, Second Chamber, *Lipietz et al v. Prefect of Haute-Garonne and the Sociètè Nationale des Chemins de Fer Français*, No. 0104248, 6 June 2006.

5 District Court of The Hague, *Final Judgment of the District Court of The Hague concerning the Alleged but Disputed Liability in Tort on Shell Companies for Damage Caused by an Oil Leakage in 2004 at the Village of Goi in Nigeria*, ECLI:NL:RBDHA:2013:BY9854; BY9845-BY9850, 30 January 2013. Due to the complexity of calculating such damages, the court agreed to the claimant's request to refer the case to special follow-up proceedings for the further pleading on, and determination of, the damages.

6 UNGP 25, Commentary.

compensation, and punitive sanctions, as well as the prevention of harm through, for example, injunctions or guarantees of non-repetition.[7]

This chapter considers to what extent the tort laws of European states have developed to promote these remedies. It is noteworthy that the UNGP 25 leaves states the option to offer an effective remedy for corporate human rights abuses 'through judicial, administrative, legislative or other appropriate means'. Thus, states could also meet the goals of the UNGPs regarding effective remedies through other legal systems next to, or instead of, tort law, such as through administrative or criminal law.

Developments in the Law of Remedies

This section analyses the developments within the tort laws of European states in monetary and non-monetary remedies, insofar as they may be relevant to cases of human rights violations perpetrated by corporations.

However, it should preliminarily be noted that, in the case of transnational violations of human rights allegedly committed on the territory of a non-European state by a European MNC, the available remedies and the amount of damages recoverable are likely to be determined in accordance with the law of the state where the damage occurred. More specifically, as far as the European Union Member States are concerned, pursuant to Article 4 of the 2007 *Rome II Regulation*[8] the applicable law to non-contractual obligations is the law of the state where the damages occurred, unless the tort is manifestly more closely connected with another country. According to its Article 3, these general rules also apply in case they result in the application of substantive law of a non-European state. In the event of B&HR extraterritorial wrongdoing it is likely that the applicable law would, therefore, be the law of the host state of the corporation.[9] Under Article 7, claimants for environmental damage may also unilaterally elect to have the claim governed by the law of the country where the event giving rise to the damage occurred. Article 15 of *Rome II Regulation* provides that the applicable law to extra-contractual obligations shall govern also

> (c) the existence, the nature and the assessment of damage or the remedy claimed; (d) within the limits of powers conferred on the court by its procedural law, the measures which a court may take to prevent or terminate injury or damage or to ensure the provision of compensation

7 J. Zerk, 'Corporate liability for gross human rights abuses: towards a fairer and more effective system of domestic law remedies'. A report prepared for the Office of the UN High Commissioner for Human Rights, 2014, 62, www.ohchr.org/Documents/Issues/Business/DomesticLawRemedies/StudyDomesticeLawRemedies.pdf (last accessed 17 February 2018).

8 *Regulation (EC) No 864/2007 of the European Parliament and of the Council of 11 July 2007 on the Law Applicable to Non-contractual Obligations (Rome II)*, OJ L 199, pp. 40–49 (2007).

9 R. Meeran, 'Tort litigation against multinational corporations for violation of human rights: an overview of the position outside the United States'. *City University of Hong Kong Law Review*, 2011, 1–41.

and '(f) persons entitled to compensation for damage sustained personally'. The award of damages according to that law can give rise to situations in which the remedies available to the claimant are not appropriate, and where the maximum amount of compensation is too low to cover the costs of the litigation,[10] for example due to different fee arrangement structures and recoverability of legal costs. Therefore, according to some authors, the calculation of damages as set out under the law of the host state where the harm occurred could have considerable detrimental impact on the ability of victims of extraterritorial corporate wrongdoing in developing countries to obtain justice.[11] In this context it is noteworthy that preamble 19 to the *Rome II Regulation* provides that 'specific rules should be laid down for special torts/delicts where the general rule does not allow a reasonable balance to be struck between the interests at stake'.

Developments in Monetary Remedies

There have been three trends in the area of monetary remedies in Europe relevant to corporate human rights abuses: (i) the 'covert' award of non-compensatory damages; (ii) the rise of remedies offered for non-pecuniary loss; and (iii) the growing protection for the loss of a (mere) infringement of a right or interest.

Non-compensatory Damages

The first trend concerns the much-debated potential development of non-compensatory or even punitive damages. Non-compensatory damages are relevant to B&HR because the increase in the amount payable can have an important deterrent function on corporate tortfeasors. It corrects the risk-benefit economic analysis that might tempt corporations to commit human rights abuses. Moreover, it signals to society the disapproval of such misconduct. The victim might, further, find recognition for the severity of the suffered harm.[12]

A number of European jurisdictions are progressively permitting the award of non-compensatory damages in tort law. England and Wales have allowed the award of exemplary damages since the case of *Rook v. Barnard* in 1964.[13] More recently, a comparable trend has been followed by France, Germany, Spain, Switzerland, Greece, Slovakia and the Scandinavian countries.

10 G. Skinner, R. McCorquodale and O. De Schutter, *The Third Pillar: Access to Judicial Remedies for Human Rights Violations by Transnational Business*, ICAR, CORE and ECCJ, 85.

11 Meeran, op. cit., 19.

12 Van Dam, op. cit., 350–351.

13 House of Lords, *Rooks v. Barnard*, [1964] A.C. 1129 (per Lord Devlin), 21 January 1964.

In France, there has long been a suspicion in the literature that the courts show their displeasure with a defendant's conduct by the level of compensation they award.[14] However, as no heads of damages had to be distinguished by the French courts, this does not appear in the reasoning of the decisions.[15] Punitive damages could, however, soon step out of the shadows in France. The 2016 preliminary Bill reforming French tort law allows for a civil fine in cases of 'lucrative wrongdoing' of up to 10 per cent of the highest gross amount of worldwide turnover, to be paid into a special compensation fund or, if non-existent, to the French Treasury.[16] Further, in 2010, the French Court of Cassation rendered a decision that appears to step away from the view that punitive damages are intrinsically contrary to French public policy.[17] In Germany, tortious damages consist of a compensatory factor and a penalization factor.[18] Likewise, in Sweden, the amount awarded in personal injury cases is set to reflect the degree of culpability of the tortfeasor and the severity of the committed tort.[19] Spanish and Swiss laws also have similar aggravating elements in the awarding of damages – for example, in relation to industrial and road traffic accidents or wrongful termination of employment.[20] In addition, Swiss and Spanish courts have to some extent recognized punitive damage awards.[21] In Slovakia, a recent case has drawn attention for its departure from the compensatory principle of tortious damages. The Slovakian court held that the grave fault of the respondent justified the high amount of damages awarded because the

14 Van Dam, op. cit., 350–354; The Law Commission, *Aggravated, Exemplary and Restitutionary Damages* (*Consultation Paper No. 132*), 2014 https://s3-eu-west-2.amazonaws.com/lawcom-prod-storage-11jsxou24uy7q/uploads/2016/08/No.132-Aggravated-Exemplary-and-Restitutionary-Damages-A-Consultation-Paper.pdf (last accessed 17 February 2017). R. Youngs, *English, French & German Comparative Law*. London: Routledge, 2007, 487.

15 Ibid.

16 French Consumer Code, L.622-1 ff.

17 Cour de Cassation, *Schlenzka & Langhorne v. Fountaine Pajot*, 02-C-01-074942, 1 December 2010. See also the suggestions regarding punitive damages in two legislative proposals: P. Catala, 'Avant-projet de réforme du droit des obligations et de la prescription (Articles 1101 à 1386 du Code civil) Et Du Droit De La Prescription (Articles 2234 à 2281 du Code civil)', 2005, Article 1371; and Terré Draft: F. Terré Pour Une Réforme Du Droit De La Responsabilité Civile, 2011, Article 54 and Article 69).

18 Youngs, op. cit., 491. Van Dam, op. cit., 349, 351. See for example *Caroline of Monaco v. WAZ Media*, Bundesgerichtshof VI ZR 332/94. See German Civil Code paras. 252, 842, 845.

19 B. Askeland, 'Punitive damages in Scandinavia'. In H. Koziol and V. Wilcox (eds), *Punitive Damages: Common Law and Civil Law Perspectives*. Vienna: Springer, 120.

20 Spain: General Law on Social Security, art. 123 (re. industrial accidents). See also: art. 20, Insurance Contract Act and Act 35/2015, Act 30/1995. P. del Olmo, 'Punitive damages in Spain'. In H. Koziol and V. Wilcox (eds), op. cit., 137–154. Switzerland: Labour Law, arts. 336a and 337c; Gender law, art. 5; Intellectual Property Law, art. 423.

21 Swiss Court of Appeal, *S.F. Inc. v. T.C.S. AG Swiss*, Basler Juristische Mitteilungen 1991, 31. Spanish Supreme Court, *Miller Import Corp. v. Alabastres Alfredo*, S.L., 13 November 2001. C. Nagy, 'Recognition and enforcement of US judgments involving punitive damages in continental Europe'. *Nederlands Internationaal Privaatrecht*, 2012, 7–10.

purpose of Slovakian tort law is not only compensation but also prevention and sanction.[22]

Non-pecuniary Loss

The second trend in the area of monetary remedies is the rise of remedies offered for non-pecuniary loss.[23] Such remedies are important to victims of corporate human rights abuses because the latter often give rise to intangible harm, such as outrage, humiliation, degradation and insult. Remedies for non-pecuniary loss aim to address these forms of harm.[24] Furthermore, they can also somewhat restore the claimant's loss of self-confidence, or offer some solace.[25] Moreover, damages for non-pecuniary loss can take the gravity or seriousness of the infringement into account by considering the emotional impact on the victim. This can serve to punish gross misconduct.[26]

Pursuant to several European states' tort laws, compensable harm generally covers both material and non-material damages for losses such as pain and suffering, the loss of amenity in personal injury cases, and injuries to human dignity, liberty or other personal rights in other types of tort cases, and also loss of profits.[27]

In particular, Italy and Germany have taken steps in this direction. In 2008, Italy abandoned the differentiation between moral and material damages – a distinction also not known in France or (explicitly) in the Dutch Civil Code.[28] Earlier, 2002 reforms in Germany established formally that non-pecuniary loss can be compensated in case of injury to body, health, freedom, or sexual self-determination.[29] Such compensation for pain and loss of amenity and enjoyment of life takes into account not only the claimant's vulnerability but also the degree of fault on the part of both parties, thus reflecting the tortfeasor's

22 A. Bell and T. Thiede, '13th Annual Conference on European Tort Law'. *European Review of Private Law*, 2014, 5, 800–801. See also R. Heard (ed.), 'Punitive damages in Europe: concern, threat or non-issue?', 2012, www.swissre.com/library/archive/Punitive_damages_in_Europe_Concern_threat_or_nonissue.html (last accessed 17 February 2018).

23 B. Koch, 'Mainstream in the development of European tort law'. *Geneva Papers*, 2006, 31, 270; Andrew Bell 'Conference Report: 15th Annual Conference on European, Tort Law'. *European Review of Private Law,* 2016, 6, 800.

24 The Law Commission, 'Aggravated, exemplary and restitutionary damages', op. cit., 8.

25 S. Lindenbergh and T. Wallinga, 'Compensation of non-pecuniary loss in the Netherlands: past, present, predictions'. *Chinese Journal of Comparative Law*, 2015, 308.

26 V. Janecek, 'Exemplary damages: a genuine concept?'. *European Journal of Legal Studies*, 2013, 6, 198.

27 Enneking, op. cit., 2, 566.

28 Corte di Cassazione, Sezioni Unite, 11 November 2008, No. 26974, in *Rivista diritto civile*, 2009, II, 97. Youngs, op. cit., 491. See French Code Civil, arts. 1146–1152. See Dutch Civil Code, arts. 6:95 and 6:106.

29 U. Magnus, 'Reform of German tort law'. Working Paper No. 127, 2003, 4–5; German Civil Code, para. 253(2).

mischief plus a penalizing factor in order to prevent recurrence. German law considers such remedy as compensatory because it is the satisfaction of a right.

Furthermore, alongside the growing acceptance of awards for non-pecuniary damage, the increase of the amounts, and the wider class of (secondary) victims who can claim them, merit consideration.[30]

Protection of an Infringement of a Right or Interest

The third trend in the area of monetary remedies goes hand in hand with the growing acceptance of recovery for non-pecuniary damage. It is the increasing protection for the loss resulting from a (mere) infringement of a right or interest, such as life, liberty, dignity, physical and mental integrity, and privacy.[31] To this effect, legislation has been introduced in Austria and Croatia, and jurisprudence has been rendered in Greece, Portugal, Norway and Finland.

The 2003 amendment to the Austrian Civil Code, for example, allows for compensation for the infringement of the right to privacy.[32] In Croatia, the Civil Obligations Act of 2006 introduced an objective approach to awarding immaterial damages for the infringement of personality rights.[33] In 2015, a Greek court awarded damages for the infringement of religious identity and feelings.[34] That same year, the Norwegian Supreme Court awarded damages for injury to a (pure ideal) interest, namely for loss of enjoyment of trees that had been illegally felled.[35] In Portugal, the Supreme Court awarded (considerable) damages for the violation of a claimant's right to self-determination and development of her personality.[36] Another remarkable judgment was given in 2015 by the Supreme Court of Finland, which held that the aim of compensating mental suffering, through damages for non-pecuniary loss, is to compensate the violation of the claimant's human dignity and self-esteem.[37]

Recognition of the right to damages strengthens the protection of human rights in tort law. Such damages will increase the amounts recoverable for infringement of human rights, thus bolstering the function of monetary damages. Moreover, it sends a strong warning about the social undesirability of such conduct and offers the victim recognition of the harm done to him/her by virtue of the infringement of his/her right in itself.

30 Koch, op. cit., 273–275; Bell, op. cit., 1224.
31 Enneking, op. cit., 2, 130; Koch, op. cit., 272.
32 Koch, op. cit., 272. Austrian Civil Code Section 1328a.
33 Bell, op. cit., 1220. Civil Obligations Act and Act on Amendments and Supplements to the Civil Obligations Act (promulgated by Decisions Nos. 01-081-05-768/2, 4 March 2005.
34 Bell, op. cit., 1225. Areios Pagos, 9 June 2015, 1156/2015.
35 Bell, op. cit., 1228. Supreme Court, 6 May 2015, HR-2015-00989-A, 2014/2121; Rt 2015, 216.
36 Bell, op. cit., 1228. Supreme Court, 2 June 2015, Proc no 1263/06.3TVPRT.P1.S1.
37 Bell, op. cit., 1223. Supreme Court, 29 June 2015, KKO 2015:50.

Developments in Non-monetary Remedies

This section now turns to the second category of remedies in tort law: non-monetary remedies. There has been limited development in this area. Although non-monetary remedies, in the form of court-specific performance orders and injunctions, are generally available pursuant to most European states' tort laws, the courts appear to maintain a reserve in making such awards.[38] There has also been little movement to adopt new and creative types of orders suitable to the B&HR context.

The ECtHR adopts the position that reparations in kind are preferred to monetary compensation.[39] Domestic European civil courts, however, usually conceive of specific performance only as a secondary remedy.[40] Also, preventative remedies are – in principle – readily available in European jurisdictions, such as (preliminary) mandatory or prohibitory injunctions, guarantees of non-repetition, and declaratory relief.[41] Nonetheless, the courts are hesitant to grant such measures.[42]

Notwithstanding this continued reserve, it is not uncommon that victims seek such forms of relief. For example, as summarized by Enneking, in the Shell Nigerian oil spills case before the Dutch courts, in addition to damages, the claimants sought a declaratory judgment that Shell and Shell Petroleum Development Company of Nigeria (hereinafter 'SPDC') had acted unlawfully, as well as injunctions ordering: the repair and future maintenance of the oil pipelines and wellheads involved; the clean-up of the contaminated areas; the exercise of diligence and adherence to best practice in future operations in the affected areas; and the adoption of effective contingency plans in order to limit the risks and consequences of future oil spills.[43]

A second example is the relief sought in the apartheid litigation in the US courts against several multinationals. The claimants sought a broad spectrum of remedies, including many innovative measures. As again summarized by Enneking, these remedies included: monetary relief (compensatory and punitive damages); the set-up of a trust fund; restitution and disgorgement of all funds

38 Enneking, op. cit., 565.

39 Van Dam, op. cit., 25–26; P. de Tavernier, J. van der Weide, 'Harmonising tort law – exploring the concept of fault', *BW Krant Jaarboek*, 2016, 30, 11, 117.

40 A. Zwart-Hink, A. Akkermans and K. van Wees, 'Compelled apologies as a legal remedy'. *University of Western Australia Law Review*, 2014, 38(1), 107–108; Youngs, op. cit., 479; Dutch Civil Code art. 6:103.

41 Youngs, op. cit., 479.

42 See for examples: Court of Appeal, *Sithole v. Thor Chemicals*, 1999 AL ER (D) 102 (CA); High Court, *Guerrero v. Monterrico Metals plc*, 2009, EWHC 2475; 2010 EWHC 3228; G. Skinner, R. McCorquodale and O. De Schutter, *The Third Pillar: Access to Judicial Remedies for Human Rights Violations by Transnational Business*, 2013, 86. https://business-humanrights.org/en/pdf-the-third-pillar-access-to-judicial-remedies-for-human-rights-violations-by-transnational-business (last accessed 17 February 2018).

43 District Court of the Hague, op. cit.; Enneking, op. cit., 564.

linked to aiding, conspiring with, or benefiting from apartheid; the appointment of an independent international historical commission; the creation of affirmative action and educational programmes; production by the respondents of documents related to their activities in apartheid South Africa; and injunctive relief preventing the respondents from destroying, transferring, or modifying such documents.[44]

The last remedy to consider is the specific court order that the respondent apologizes to the claimant. The ECtHR seems to encourage states to order apologies. In *Ozturk v. Turkey*, the ECtHR actively considered that national courts, instead of awarding financial compensation for non-pecuniary damage, might consider other sanctions 'such as the issuance of an apology'.[45] The ECtHR has held that apologies form a restriction on the right to freedom of expression that can be permitted, provided that the interference is prescribed by law and necessary in a democratic society.[46] In addition, jurisdictions which do not distinguish between material and non-material damage seemingly hold potential to accept the argument that apologies form a remedy that offers reparation to the victim and are therefore partially suitable. Nevertheless, there is a very limited number of cases in European jurisdictions in which an apology was ordered as a remedy.[47]

Intrinsically Unsuited?

The above remarks show that European states have been slow to provide remedies suited to address corporate human rights abuses. European courts, generally speaking, do not award most remedies considered effective by the UNGPs.[48] Declaration of right and recitation only serve as additional consideration. Apologies, restitution, rehabilitation, and non-financial compensation, although generally available among civil law jurisdictions, continue to fall significantly behind the award of financial compensation. This leads to the obvious question: why have European countries not further developed such remedies?

No Remedy without Cause

The tort laws of European countries have not developed such effective remedies for violations of human rights perpetrated by corporations such as those suggested by the UNGPs because they go beyond the purpose for which tort law in most European states generally provides remedies.

44 Enneking, op. cit., 108.

45 ECtHR, *Cihan Ozturk v. Turkey*, App. No. 17095/03, 9 June 2009.

46 ECtHR, *Ovchinnikov v. Russia*, App. No. 24061/04, 16 December 2010; ECtHR, *Kania v Poland*, App. No. 35105/04, 21 June 2011.

47 Zwart-Hink *et al.*, op. cit., 59. Apologies have been ordered in Slovakia, Russia, Turkey, Ukraine, and Poland.

48 Zerk, op. cit., 62.

The legal remedies correspond to the aim for which such remedies are awarded. Various purposes have been suggested for tort law, such as compensation, deterrence, vindication or punishment.[49] The predominant goal of tort law in most European jurisdictions is that of compensation. Such European jurisdictions offer mainly compensatory remedies, and not a wider range of non-compensatory remedies inclusive of the remedies suggested by the UNGPs.

According to the UNGPs, an effective remedy against corporate human rights abuses could, and often does, require more than just the (monetary) compensation offered by tort law in European states.[50] In this respect, it is noteworthy the UNGPs at first instance appear to suggest a compensatory approach to remedies for human right abuses in that they should 'counteract or make good any human rights harms that have occurred'.[51] As shown above, however, the remedies subsequently suggested, such as apologies, restitution, rehabilitation, and punitive sanctions, indicate that deterrence, recognition, and punishment are aims that an effective system of remedies must also fulfil.

Compensatory Damages Are not Enough

Remedies for corporate abuses of human rights cannot be effective if, alongside compensation, the other aims of deterrence, punishment and restitution are not met. Human rights are inalienable fundamental rights, and as such they warrant a high degree of protection.[52] This includes preventive protection through deterrence. The need for deterrence in order to protect human rights effectively is supported by the ECHR, pursuant to which states are obliged to take positive measures to prevent inter-private violations of human rights, such as corporations harming individuals.[53]

Moreover, abuses of human rights justify a resort to non-compensatory measures, because they reflect values and interests of such importance that they should be protected over and above the concern to avoid loss if they are infringed.[54] The gravity of the human rights abuses is not conveyed by compensatory damages alone. Further, non-compensatory damages may function to correct a misbalance of power between the corporate violations and the individual victim. Human rights are of such fundamental nature that corporations should not be in a position to weigh the economic risk and come down on the side of human rights abuse, or at least not without condemnation.

49 Van Dam, op. cit., 347–353. See also K. Abraham, *The Forms and Functions of Tort Law*. St. Paul: Foundation Press, 2017, 16–24.

50 Zerk, op. cit., 93; UNGP 25, Commentary.

51 UNGP 25, C.

52 The Law Commission, *Aggravated, Exemplary and Restitutionary Damages*, op. cit., 119.

53 Van Dam, op. cit., 223.

54 The Law Commission, *Aggravated, Exemplary and Restitutionary Damages*, op. cit., 120.

To convey both these messages, non-compensatory damages can be justified. In addition, a compensatory model, which attempts to measure the loss to the victim may result in a less appropriate remedy than a non-compensatory model that can take account of the respondent's actions and the societal context.

Remedies Are a-Changin'

The compensatory aim of tort law entails that primary regard is given to the position of the claimant in determining the damages. This leaves little room to take account of the corporate identity of the tortfeasor, the wider effects on society, or to specifically award certain (levels of) damages for corporate wrongdoings. Thus, as a result of the disparity between the purpose of remedies in human rights and in tort law, the latter falls short in providing an effective remedy for corporate human rights abuses.

Notwithstanding the limitation imposed by the compensatory framework of tort law, the developments identified in European domestic systems appear to show growing allowance of a wider notion of compensation or even a slowly developing acceptance of non-compensatory remedies. This indicates a developing acceptance of the other functions of tort law, such as deterrence, punishment, condemnation, recognition and vindication.

Some remedies are developed in plain sight. For example, the growing allowance of damages for non-pecuniary losses for an increasing number of rights serves a number of different purposes.[55] Such remedies are symbolic to a degree, since remedy for a pure infringement of a right cannot compensate the damage done to, for example, a claimant's privacy, right to life or dignity.[56] Thus, in offering such a remedy, tort law provides recognition of, but not necessarily compensation for, a wrong. Furthermore, the damages awarded serve to vindicate the claimant's legally protected rights.[57] In addition, remedies for non-pecuniary losses can also function as deterrence for conduct that otherwise would be economically profitable, if only the pecuniary losses were compensated.[58]

Other remedies are developed more covertly. Many European jurisdictions already award remedies that, strictly speaking, do not conform to the compensatory principle. These include: statutory fixed damages (e.g. payable even beyond the real loss suffered), aggravated damages, financial penalties for violation of injunctions, restitutionary damages, correlative gain and the

55 Van Dam, op. cit., 348.

56 Ibid.

57 Ibid., 349.

58 S. Sugarman 'Tort damages for non-economic losses'. In M. Bussani and A. Sebok (eds), *Comparative Tort Law*. Cheltenham: Edward Elgar, 2013, 205.

disgorgement of profit, and moral damages.[59] At present, however, most European jurisdictions, rather artificially, frame such non-compensatory measures in the wording of the compensatory principle. In addition, a regulatory function of tort law is already practised in certain specific areas such as in competition law and environmental law.[60]

In light of the above, it could be said that, by holding on in principle to compensation as the aim of remedies in tort law (and marginalizing as anomalies elements that do not conform to this picture) the true picture has become distorted.[61] In order to gain access to a wider range of remedies than currently awarded in tort laws of European states, victims of corporate human rights abuse could either appeal to this distortion directly or seek to frame their claim within this wider notion of compensation. The latter is more advisable, as the civil courts of European countries, in principle, strongly cling to the notion that only compensatory damages can be awarded in the law of tort. For example, in practice an argument under this approach could advance that non-pecuniary losses should be awarded for infringement of human rights as this infringement harms the victim's human dignity, which requires satisfaction.

Conclusion

According to the UNGPs, the aim of remedies provided for human rights abuses perpetrated by corporations is to counteract or make good any human rights harms that have occurred. The UNGPs suggest the following remedies: apologies, restitution, rehabilitation, financial or non-financial compensation, and punitive sanctions.

Measured against the UNGPs, tort laws in Europe have currently not developed to offer a full range of effective remedies for corporate human rights abuses. Over the past years the types and use of private law remedies available in civil jurisdictions for corporate wrongdoings have remained largely the same. The focus of the tort system is still on monetary compensation. Punitive damages remain out of bounds, although aspects of fault and gravity do transpire in the amount of damages awarded in certain jurisdictions. Non-monetary remedies are sufficiently available, but they are not often awarded. In some cases, claims for declaratory judgments and injunctions have been made. Despite the ECtHR's support for civil courts to issue more non-monetary remedies and more compelled apologies, domestic courts in European jurisdictions remain hesitant to award such remedies.

59 A. Verheij, 'Should private lawyers reconsider the compensatory principle in an age of administrative enforcement?'. *European Review of Private Law*, 2015, 23/4, 563; Janecek, op. cit., 198.

60 M. Green and O. Moréteau, 'Restating tort law: the American and European styles'. *Journal of European Tort Law*, 2012, 3, 307.

61 The Law Commission, *Aggravated, Exemplary and Restitutionary Damages*, op. cit., 123.

The purpose for which remedies are awarded steers which remedies are available. The compensatory aim of tort law in European countries limits tort law from developing an effective system of remedies to address corporate human rights abuses. Nevertheless, even though European jurisdictions in principle hold tight to the compensatory aim of tort law, in practice there is some movement away from this (sole) purpose of tort law. In the future, this will hopefully create additional room for more diverse types of remedies.

Concluding Remarks

Angelica Bonfanti

According to the European Commission,

> One of the aims of the EU is to ensure that economic growth goes hand in hand with social justice, respect for human rights, high labour and environmental standards, and health and safety protection. This applies to external as well as internal policies, and so also includes trade and investment policy.[1]

To this end 'corporate respect for human rights and its embedding in corporate operations and value and supply chains is indispensable to sustainable development and achieving the SDGs'.[2] Indeed as demonstrated by Paolo Farah in his chapter to this book '[t]he necessary precondition for the realization of SDGs is the inclusive governance framework',[3] involving all stakeholders, including governments, civil society and private sector.

Starting from these assumptions, this book carries out a legal analysis of the developments in the field of B&HR at European level, in order to assess whether they are effective in granting the protection of human rights from the negative impacts that business activities can unfortunately cause. Some conclusions can be drawn on the basis of the reflections developed by the contributors. As a general remark it should be noted that the B&HR challenges posed by international law receive specific response at European level. Indeed the EU, the CoE, and their Member States have been adopting policies, legislations, measures and case law specifically addressing the main B&HR concerns, such as the

1 European Commission, *Trade for All. Towards a more Responsible Trade and Investment Policy.* October 2015, available at: http://trade.ec.europa.eu/doclib/docs/2015/october/tradoc_153846.pdf (last accessed 20 February 2018), 20. See A. Bonfanti, 'La tutela dei diritti umani nella politica commerciale e sugli investimenti dell'Unione europea: la comunicazione "Commercio per tutti", tra regionalismo e multilateralismo economico', *Diritti umani e diritto internazionale*, 2016, 10, 233.

2 Council of the EU, *Council Conclusions on Business and Human Rights*, Doc. 10254/16, 20 June 2016, paras. 6, 8.

3 See the chapter by Paolo Farah.

states' obligations and responsibility to protect human rights, the status and content of the corporate accountability to respect human rights, the human rights due diligence, the duty of vigilance over the supply chain, the connected extraterritorial application of human rights treaties, and victims' access to remedies. However, the approaches developed by the EU, the CoE, and the European domestic legal systems not only differ from each other as regards their content but often diverge as regards their effectiveness.

Following the UNGPs' structure, in the Editor's view the state duty to protect human rights has received a significant, but in some regards still not decisive, interpretation at European level, at least pursuant to the CoE approach. On the one hand, the case law developed by the ECtHR has certainly evolved as concerns the application of the ECHR procedural and substantive standards to cases of corporate abuse. As demonstrated by Marco Fasciglione, the ECtHR case law in this area '

> is built around [...] substantive obligations to regulate and control corporate activities including the licensing, setting up, and control of dangerous activities and the provision of information about them to the general public; [...] procedural obligations to ensure an informed decision-making process encompassing public participation, public investigations, scientific studies, and environmental impact assessments; and [...] obligations related to law enforcement and the judicial process, including access to justice and the provision of effective remedies.[4]

However, on the other hand, the ECtHR approach is not fully satisfactory in terms of the extraterritorial application of the ECHR, when MNCs' activities abroad are concerned. As Claire Methven O'Brien concludes:

> there is no basis in the ECHR for a general state duty to control the conduct abroad of business enterprises incorporated under states parties' laws or having their headquarters in their territories, even when such conduct leads to human rights abuses.[5]

This is also due to the fact that

> violations occur in no jurisdictional 'black hole' but in 'host' states, with laws, courts, regulators, civil society watchdogs and human rights obligations of their own, even if these are or appear to be imperfect from the point of view of advocates of extraterritoriality, or indeed victims.[6]

4 See the chapter by Marco Fasciglione.
5 See the chapter by Claire Methven O'Brien.
6 Ibid.

Moreover, in cases where a state nexus occurs, the introduction of sectoral legislation establishing socially responsible procedures in fields such as public procurement regulation would be welcomed. However, as emphasized by Deborah Russo, regardless of the concern about human rights violations that may occur throughout the supply chain and 'the need to strengthen state accountability, compliance with the UNGPs is still limited. Particularly in the field of public procurement, the practice of states falls short of the mark'.[7]

More optimistic conclusions are drawn by Leonardo Borlini about the protection of human rights through the EU PTAs. According to him, 'the practice of making the effect of economic and trade agreements mainly dependent upon the respect for human rights, democratic principles and, more recently, sustainable development standards is clearly the standard *modus operandi* of the EU'.[8] The inclusion of human rights clauses, development chapters and CSR norms 'serve[s] to promote a synchrony between "development" and "progress" in third countries' and leaves the parties 'with adequate domestic policy space to meet their human rights obligations when pursuing business-related policy objectives'.[9]

In recent years, European domestic and EU legislation has been adopted in order to regulate the corporate responsibility to respect human rights. At the domestic level, for instance, in February 2017 the Dutch Parliament adopted a law concerning a due diligence duty to prevent the delivery of goods and services produced with child labour.[10] In addition, in 2017 France established a legally binding obligation for parent companies to identify and prevent adverse human rights and environmental impacts within their supply chain through a *plan de vigilance* to be publicly disclosed.[11] Italy has had in place since 2001 Legislative Decree No. 231/2001, which establishes the administrative liability of corporations for any of the crimes specifically listed in the Decree.[12] Moreover, a broad coalition of civil society organizations in Switzerland has launched a popular initiative seeking to introduce a legal duty for Swiss-based companies to incorporate respect for human rights and the environment in all their business

7 See the chapter by Deborah Russo.

8 See the chapter by Leonardo Borlini.

9 Ibid.

10 MVO Platform, *Frequently Asked Questions about the New Dutch Child Labour Due Diligence Law*, 14 April 2017, www.mvoplatform.nl/news-en/frequently-asked-questions-about-the-new-dutch-child-labour-due-diligence-law (last accessed 9 March 2018). See the chapter by Cindy S. Woods.

11 République française, *Loi n° 2017-399 du 27 mars 2017 relative au devoir de vigilance des sociétés mères et des entreprises donneuses d'ordre*, Legifrance, JORF no. 0074, March 2017, www.legifrance.gouv.fr/affichTexte.do?cidTexte=JORFTEXT000034290626&dateTexte=&categorieLien=id (last accessed 9 March 2018). See the Chapter by Tiphaine Beau de Loménie, Sandra Cossart and Paige Morrow.

12 Legislative Decree No. 231/2001, *Disciplina della responsabilità amministrativa delle persone giuridiche, delle società e delle associazioni anche prive di personalità giuridica, a norma dell'articolo 11 della legge 29 settembre 2000, n. 300*. See the chapter by Paola Cavanna.

activities through mandatory due diligence.[13] For its part, the 2015 UK Modern Slavery Act aims to establish a comprehensive legal framework to combat slavery, servitude and forced or compulsory labour and human trafficking, by requiring large corporations to disclose each year the actions they have taken to ensure there is no modern slavery in their business or supply chains.[14] The regulation of the Norwegian Government Pension Fund is also noteworthy in this context.[15]

At the EU level, at least two legislative initiatives have been enacted: the Conflict Minerals Regulation,[16] and the Non-Financial Reporting Directive.[17] These have paved the way to EU Member States' domestic reforms. However, they are weak as concerns the imposition of sanctions for lack of compliance, generally left to the discretion of the Member States.[18]

As a general overview, it can be noted that some of the aforementioned legal instruments have a broad scope of application, as concerns the abuses they aim to prevent, such as the Non-Financial Reporting Directive[19] and, at domestic level, the French law establishing the corporate *devoir de vigilance*[20] and the regulation of the Norwegian Government Pension Fund.[21] Others aim at preventing specific abuses, such as the UK Modern Slavery Act,[22] or at regulating specific sectors, such as the EU Conflict Minerals Regulation.[23] And others, such as Italian Decree No. 231/2001,[24] have strong deterrent effects but would need to be improved through an updated revision. Finally, a regulation that does not directly address B&HR, such as the GDPR, should be taken into

13 Swiss Coalition for Corporative Justice, konzern-initiative.ch/?Lang=en (last accessed 9 March 2018).

14 UK Modern Slavery Act, www.legislation.gov.uk/ukpga/2015/30/contents/enacted (last accessed 9 March 2018). See the chapter by Olga Martin-Ortega.

15 See the chapter by Ludovica Chiussi.

16 EU, *Regulation of the European Parliament and of the Council Setting up a Union System for Supply Chain Due Diligence Self-certification of Responsible Importers of Tin, Tantalum and Tungsten, their Ores, and Gold Originating in Conflict-affected and High-risk Areas*, 2017/821 L 130/1, 17 May 2017, http://eur-lex.europa.eu/legal-content/EN/TXT/PDF/?uri=CELEX:32017R0821&from=EN (last accessed 9 March 2018) (hereinafter 'Conflict Minerals Regulation'). See the chapter by Valentina Grado.

17 EU, *Directive 2014/95/EU of the European Parliament and of the Council of 22 October 2014 Amending Directive 2013/34/EU as Regards Disclosure of Non-financial and Diversity Information by Certain Large Undertakings and Groups*, 2014/95/EU 2014 O.J. (L 330), 15 November 2014. See the chapter by Cindy S. Woods.

18 See the chapter by Tiphaine Beau de Loménie, Sandra Cossart and Paige Morrow.

19 See the chapter by Cindy S. Woods.

20 See the chapter by Tiphaine Beau de Loménie, Sandra Cossart and Paige Morrow.

21 See the chapter by Ludovica Chiussi.

22 See the chapter by Olga Martin-Ortega.

23 See the chapter by Valentina Grado.

24 See the chapter by Paola Cavanna.

account within the context of the ITC companies' accountability to respect human rights.[25]

The aforementioned legal instruments all establish processes and mechanisms that have the effect of implementing the human rights due diligence (HRDD). In so doing they attribute to the corporate responsibility to respect human rights a binding status, either at EU or domestic level. This outcome can be certainly considered as one of the main European legal responses to the international challenges posed by the UNGPs.

Among the shortcomings of the aforementioned legal instruments, Tiphaine Beau de Loménie, Sandra Cossart and Paige Morrow emphasize that some mainly focus on reporting and fail to provide access to justice for victims of human rights abuses. Indeed,

> they never sanction the lack of HRDD itself, but rather the lack of reporting on HRDD. As a consequence, the corporate veil remains in place and parent companies are still not held liable, even if the failure to properly carry out HRDD results in environmental harm or violations of human rights somewhere in the value chain.[26]

Thus, these instruments can be criticized as regards their effectiveness. As stated for instance by Olga Martin-Ortega, there is the risk that they

> contribute to the development of a concept of transparency which focuses on compliance with the act of reporting rather than the procedure of due diligence as a substantive process to identify, prevent and mitigate human rights violations in supply chains.[27]

Other instruments, such as the French law on the duty of vigilance, originally established a mechanism in the event that a company failed to comply. However, the proposed civil penalties were struck down by the Constitutional Council.[28] On the other hand, Italian Decree No. 231/2001 provides for the administrative liability of corporations that have committed any of the listed crimes.[29] Sanctions include monetary fines, seizure of the profits resulting from the crime, publication of the judgment and disqualification measures.

25 EU, *Regulation 2016/679 of the European Parliament and of the Council of 27 April 2016 on the Protection of Natural Persons With Regard to the Processing of Personal Data and on the Free Movement of Such Data, and Repealing Directive 95/46/EC* (General Data Protection Regulation). See the chapter by Angelica Bonfanti.

26 See the chapter by Tiphaine Beau de Loménie, Sandra Cossart and Paige Morrow.

27 See the chapter by Olga Martin-Ortega.

28 See the chapter by Tiphaine Beau de Loménie, Sandra Cossart and Paige Morrow and Conseil Constitutionnel, Décision no. 2017-750 DC du 23 mars 2017.

29 See the chapter by Paola Cavanna.

As a positive remark it is noteworthy that most of these instruments are suitable to cover the MNC's supply chain, regardless of where it is localized. Indeed, they generally provide for extraterritorial application and standards to be fulfilled by MNCs operating abroad. In the words of Cindy S. Woods:

> Because businesses can be held liable for abuses which they cause or contribute to, by requiring due diligence throughout supply chains, states are recognizing that they can leverage their influence over actors within their jurisdiction to seek to prevent human rights abuses outside of their territory through requiring companies to monitor their supply chains.[30]

Thus, pursuant to the European approach, the corporate responsibility to respect human rights is likely to extend extraterritorially, so as to include the activities performed abroad by the subsidiaries of the European MNCs.

Lastly, access to remedies in Europe is a very critical issue. In this regard the UNGPs have not received a strong implementation either at EU or at domestic level. At EU level, the recasting process of EU Regulation Brussels-I has not led to the introduction of criteria for the attribution of civil jurisdiction specifically responding to the needs of B&HR; at domestic level, courts often base their jurisdiction on residual grounds, but piercing the corporate veil is still very complex and its demonstration burdensome for victims. As stated by Lucas Roorda '[t]he interaction between [...] the Brussels regime and the domestic law of the individual Member States has created a somewhat confusing landscape for claimants looking for remedies regarding transnational corporate human rights abuses'.[31] Notwithstanding this, Claire Bright highlights that 'through the recognition that, in appropriate circumstances, parent companies may owe a duty of care to the employees and local communities directly affected by the operations of their subsidiaries abroad, the gates to the European tribunals are open'[32] and 'the first hurdle to access to justice can be overcome'.[33] Likewise, Carmen Márquez Carrasco concludes that 'the EU's approach seems to be becoming more proactive with regard to holding MNEs accountable for their actions abroad: this may serve as an indication of changing attitudes and perspectives about the exercise of extraterritorial jurisdiction over TNCs'.[34]

According to the FRA Opinion on Access to Remedies,[35] some legal reforms should be enacted: the EU should consider publishing a European Action Plan and establishing an Open Method of Coordination in the area of B&HR, while

30 See the chapter by Cindy S. Woods.

31 See the chapter by Lucas Roorda.

32 See the chapter by Claire Bright.

33 Ibid.

34 See the chapter by Carmen Márquez Carrasco.

35 FRA, *Improving Access to Remedy in the Area of Business and Human Rights at EU Level – Opinion 1/2017*, 10 April 2017, http://fra.europa.eu/en/opinion/2017/business-human-rights (last accessed 15 March 2018).

legal reforms should be adopted in order to make MNCs accountable for their torts abroad and to facilitate victims' access to civil and criminal remedies.

In terms of victims' access to remedies, according to Adriana Espinosa González and Marta Sosa Navarro, even though '[g]lobal figures still show a clear preference for civil jurisdiction, the role of criminal judicial mechanisms to tackle human rights violations perpetrated by corporations should be enhanced'.[36] In fact, according to them, '[o]ne may ask to what extent can civil litigation be used to vindicate values and interests protected by human rights, including human rights violations for which the word "tort" is too timid'.[37] Finally, tort law remedies different from the merely compensatory ones should be introduced within the European domestic tort laws, in order to better meet the UNGPs recommendations.[38]

Given this complex scenario, the evolution *de lege ferenda* of the European responses to the B&HR international law challenges deserves specific attention. The domestic implementation of the UNGPs as foreseen in the already adopted 14 EU Member States' NAPs might lead to a more homogeneous framework,[39] especially if we consider that 'dismissing the UNGPs as too "soft" or "voluntary" an approach to corporate human rights accountability fails to acknowledge the crucial role that states' domestic law plays in their effective implementation'.[40] However as observed by the European Network of National Human Rights Institutions, Member States' NAPs 'mostly describe historical actions, and lack specific commitments capable of demonstrably improving UNGPs implementation at national level'.[41] Thus, in order to implement the UNGPs, Member States should necessarily adopt a 'smart mix' of planned mandatory and voluntary measures and actions to be effectively implemented in order to prevent and redress corporate-related human rights violations.[42]

The EU could also consider introducing HRDD requirements – either through a sector-specific approach, an issue-specific approach or a generalized, cross-sector approach[43] – establishing a comprehensive EU Justice Policy to enforce its common values and build a consistent body of law, and revising the rules on attribution of jurisdiction and the recognition of enforcement of judicial decisions in civil and commercial matters.[44] Moreover, in line with the Conclusions of the Council of the EU in June 2016,[45] the EU could adopt an EU

36 See the chapter by Adriana Espinosa González and Marta Sosa Navarro.

37 Ibid.

38 See the chapter by Florentine Vos.

39 See the chapter by Marta Bordignon.

40 See the chapter by Daniel Augenstein.

41 European Network of National Human Rights Institutions, *Recommendations for the Next EU Strategy on CSR*, April 2015, para. 2.

42 See the chapter by Daniel Augenstein.

43 See the chapter by Tiphaine Beau de Loménie, Sandra Cossart and Paige Morrow.

44 See the chapter by Carmen Márquez Carrasco.

45 Council of the EU, *Council Conclusions on Business and Human Rights*, op. cit., para. 6.

Action Plan on Responsible Business Conduct, addressing the implementation of the UNGPS, including with regard to due diligence and access to remedy.

As a concluding remark, the Editor highlights that a specific role might be played by the negotiation of the B&HR treaty, which hopefully could tackle some of the most complex and currently unsettled issues. As correctly stated by Daniel Augenstein, within this context, the EU should 'assume a more proactive position in exploring complementarities between [the B&HR treaty] and the UNGPs', eventually overcoming the criticism that the negotiation could 'erode the consensus built around the UNGPs and undermine efforts directed at their further implementation'.[46] It is the view of the contributors to this book that the B&HR treaty might provide answers to crucial matters, such as, for instance, the definition of an appropriate scope of extraterritorial human rights protection in the B&HR domain[47] and the inclusion of human rights clauses within public procurement regimes.[48] Should the treaty on B&HR be adopted and be ratified by a large number of home and host states, and should it provide for solutions suitable to strengthen the state and corporate commitments to protect and respect human rights,[49] it would certainly contribute to improve the already significant outcomes achieved at European level, through the development of more effective and less fragmented responses to the B&HR international challenges.

46 J. Ruggie, *A UN Business and Human Rights Treaty?*, 28 January 2014; *A UN Business and Human Rights Treaty Update*, May 2014, www.business-humanrights.org/ (last accessed 8 February 2018), quoted by Daniel Augenstein in his chapter.

47 See the chapters by Daniel Augenstein and Claire Methven O'Brien.

48 See the chapter by Deborah Russo.

49 See S. Leader, 'Coherence, mutual assurance and the rationale for a treaty'. In S. Deva and D. Bilchitz (eds), *Building a Treaty on Business and Human Rights*. Cambridge: Cambridge University Press, 2017, 79.

Index